THE
CHARLTON HUNT

A History

THE CHARLTON HUNT

A History

Simon Rees

Phillimore

1998

Published by
PHILLIMORE & CO. LTD.
Shopwyke Manor Barn, Chichester, West Sussex

© Dr. Simon Rees, 1998

ISBN 1 86077 076 2

Printed and bound in Great Britain by
BOOKCRAFT
Midsomer Norton, Avon

Contents

List of Illustrations vi
Foreword by His Grace the Duke of Richmond and Gordon xi
Preface xiii
Acknowledgements xiv
Author's Note xv
List of Subscribers xvii

I	The Regular Society	1
II	Monmouth and Grey	5
III	Roper	13
IV	Bolton	31
V	Richmond and Tankerville	45
VI	Delawarr	63
VII	Tom Johnson	83
VIII	A Memorable Season	99
IX	The Grand Chase	111
X	The Hunting Diaries	127
XI	Ringwood '41	137
XII	Roper's Chair	149
XIII	Death of old Tom	163
XIV	The Sun Begins to Set	181
XV	Goodwood and After	199

Appendices

1	Fox Hall, Charlton	223
2	Members of the Charlton Hunt	226
3	Pedigree of Charlton Hounds	235

Notes and References 275
Bibliography 279
Index 281

List of Illustrations

Colour Plates (between pages 128/9)
   I   'Diana' by Jean Antoine Houdon, 1780. Marble 210 cm high.
        By permission of the Calouste Gulbenkian Museum, Lisbon.
        This masterpiece of 18th-century European sculpture is unusual in two ways; the goddess is naked and she is running. Diana the huntress was traditionally clothed while the nude Diana was represented as a reclining figure. The marble startled contemporaries and the physiological precision of her body shocked them. The sensous carving evokes the smoothness of her flesh, emphasised by contrast with her soft hair crowned by a crescent moon, the quiver of arrows and the tall reeds next to her legs.
        The sculpture was commissioned by the Duke of Saxe-Gotha and completed in 1780. However it could not be safely delivered because of war and was resold to Catherine the Great of Russia. In 1928, Calouste Gulbenkian, the Armenian banker, purchased it from the Soviet government. At the time they were in need of foreign currency and were tentatively willing to sacrifice their national art treasures. Naturally they did not want to make the sale of works from the Hermitage public, and Gulbenkian understood the delicacy of their position. However after long patient negotiations, he eventually succeeded in acquiring a number of paintings, pieces of furniture and other objets d'art, including the Diana sculpture, which are now in the Gulbenkian museum in Lisbon.
   II   Fox Hall, Charlton.
   III   Charles Lennox, 2nd Duke of Richmond, by Thomas Phillips.
        By permission of the Trustees of the Goodwood collections.
   IV   The Grand Chase. Laishley MS. Private collection.
   V   Uppark from the south west, by Pieter Tillemans.
        Uppark (The National Trust), Photographic Library/John Hammond.
   VI   Bay Bolton, a hunter, by John Wootton. By permission of the Trustees of the Goodwood collections.
   VII   Tapster, a hound, by John Wootton. By permission of the Trustees of the Goodwood collections.
   VIII   Grey Carey, son of Grey Ramsden. a hunter, by John Wootton.
        By permission of the Trustees of the Goodwood collections.
   IX   Grey Cardigan, a hunter, by John Wootton. By permission of the Trustees of the Goodwood collections.
   X   Sultan, a hunter, by John Wootton. By permission of the Trustees of the Goodwood collections.
   XI   Red Robin, a hunter, by John Wootton. By permission of the Trustees of the Goodwood collections.
   XII   Sheldon, a hunter, by John Wootton. By permission of the Trustees of the Goodwood collections.
   XIII   3rd Duke of Richmond and Lord George Lennox with the Charlton Hunt, by George Stubbs.
        By permission of the Trustees of the Goodwood collections.
   XIV   Mary, Duchess of Richmond and Lady Louisa Conolly (née Lennox) watching racehorses exercising,
        by George Stubbs (detail). By permission of the Trustees of the Goodwood collections.

Monochrome Illustrations
   1   Minutes of the Charlton Hunt, 29 January 1738 3
        Goodwood MS 2003, p.79. West Sussex Record Office.
   2   James, Duke of Monmouth, by Sir Godfrey Kneller 7
        By permission of the Trustees of the Goodwood collections.
   3   Ford Grey, 1st Earl of Tankerville, by Sir Peter Lely 8
        By kind permission of Lord Braybrooke, photograph English Heritage.
   4   Mr. Roper, called Edward, attributed to Sir Godfrey Kneller 10
        By kind permission of the Viscount Cowdray, photograph Courtauld Institute of Art.
   5   Charles Seymour, 6th Duke of Somerset, by J.B. Closterman 15
        Petworth (The National Trust), Photographic Library/Derrick E. Witty.

List of Illustrations

6 Richard Boyle, 3rd Earl of Burlington, by Sir Godfrey Kneller 19
   Devonshire Collection, Chatsworth. Reproduced by permission of the Chatsworth Settlement
   Trustees, photograph Courtauld Institute of Art.
7 Lieutenant General Sir Charles Wills, by an unknown artist 19
   Private collection, photograph by courtesy of the National Portrait Gallery, London.
8 Charles Lennox, 1st Duke of Richmond, by Sir Godfrey Kneller 20
   By permission of the Trustees of the Goodwood collections.
9 George Brudenell, 3rd Earl of Cardigan, by Charles Jervas 20
   By kind permission of the Honourable Mrs. Brudenell.
10 George Henry Lee, 2nd Earl of Lichfield, by Jan Vanderbank. Private collection. 21
11 Anne, Duchess of Richmond, by Sir Godfrey Kneller 21
   By permission of the Trustees of the Goodwood collections.
12 James, 3rd Earl of Berkeley, by Sir Godfrey Kneller 22
   Photograph by courtesy of the National Portrait Gallery, London.
13 Louise, Countess of Berkeley, by Sir Godfrey Kneller 22
   By permission of the Trustees of the Goodwood collections.
14 Anne, Countess of Albemarle, by Jan Vanderbank, 1732. Christie's Images. 23
15 Charles Lennox, 2nd Duke of Richmond, as Earl of March, by Sir Godfrey Kneller 23
   By permission of the Trustees of the Goodwood collections.
16 Louise, Duchess of Portsmouth, by Sir Godfrey Kneller 24
   By permission of the Trustees of the Goodwood collections.
17 Charles Lennox, 2nd Duke of Richmond with Sarah, his wife, by Jonathan Richardson 25
   By permission of the Trustees of the Goodwood collections.
18 Henrietta, Duchess of Bolton, by James Maubert. Photograph courtesy of Sotheby's 27
19 Charles Howard, 3rd Earl of Carlisle, by Michael Dahl. Private Scottish collection 28
20 Lord William Beauclerk, miniature by Christian Friedrich Zincke. Christie's Images 29
21 Henry Lowther, 3rd Viscount Lonsdale, by Enoch Seeman 29
   Reproduced by kind permission of the Pennington family from the Muncaster collection,
   photograph Courtauld Institute of Art
22 William Greville, 7th Baron Brooke, attributed to Michael Dahl 30
   Warwick Castle, photograph Courtauld Institute of Art.
23 Charles Powlett, 3rd Duke of Bolton, by Sir Godfrey Kneller 32
   Photograph courtesy of Sotheby's.
24 Anne, Duchess of Bolton by Sir Godfrey Kneller 33
   Golden Grove Collection, photograph Carmarthen Museum.
25 List of hounds 1721. Goodwood MS 2003, p.10. West Sussex Record Office. 34
26 Mr. Roper, called Charles, by Jonathan Richardson 36
   Reproduced by kind permission of the Pennington family from the Muncaster collection,
   photograph Courtauld Institute of Art.
27 Henry Herbert, 9th Earl of Pembroke, attributed to Jonathan Richardson. Wilton House Trust. ... 37
28 James Graham, 1st Duke of Montrose, by JB de Medina. Private Scottish collection. 37
29 George, 5th Baron Forrester, British School 38
   Gorhambury collection by kind permission of the Earl of Verulam,
   photograph Courtauld Institute of Art.
30 Charlotte, Lady Forrester, miniature by an unknown artist 38
   Gorhambury collection by kind permission of the Earl of Verulam,
   photograph Courtauld Institute of Art.
31 Lieutenant General Sir Phillip Honywood, mezzotint by J. McArdell after Bartholomew Dandridge.
   Photograph by courtesy of the National Portrait Gallery, London. 39
32 Francis, 2nd Earl of Godolphin, by Sir Godfrey Kneller. Photograph courtesy of Sotheby's. 42
33 Lieutenant General Charles Churchill, by Jonathan Richardson 42
   Photograph courtesy of Sotheby's.

34	Lavinia, Duchess of Bolton, by Francis Wheatley	43
	Private collection, photograph by courtesy of the National Portrait Gallery, London.	
35	Lavinia (Fenton), Duchess of Bolton as Polly Peachum in *The Beggar's Opera*, William Hogarth	44
	Christie's Images.	
36	The Honourable Charles Howard, attributed to John Wootton	48
	Photograph by courtesy of the National Portrait Gallery, London.	
37	Stephen Fox, 1st Earl of Ilchester, by an unknown artist	48
	Photograph by courtesy of the National Portrait Gallery, London.	
38	Richard, 1st Baron Edgecumbe, by Sir Joshua Reynolds	49
	Private collection, photograph by courtesy of the National Portrait Gallery, London.	
39	The Right Honourable William Conolly, by Rosalba Carriera	49
	Private collection, photograph Paul Mellon Centre for studies in British Art.	
40	Philip Meadows, Esq., by J.A. Adolph. Norfolk Museums Service (Norwich Castle Museum).	49
41	Garton Orme, Esq., by Jonathan Richardson	54
	Holburne Museum and Crafts Study Centre, Bath.	
	Mrs. Charlotte Orme, by an unknown artist	
	Photograph by courtesy of the National Portrait Gallery, London.	
42	The old kennels at Charlton	58
43	List of hounds 1731. Goodwood MS 2003, pp.22, 23. West Sussex Record Office	58
44	Sir Conyers Darcy at Newmarket, by John Wootton	60
	Photograph by courtesy of the National Portrait Gallery, London.	
45	Henry Arthur Herbert, 1st Earl of Powis, manner of Thomas Hudson	61
	Powis Castle, The Powis Collection (The National Trust), photograph Courtauld Institute of Art.	
46	Thomas Villiers, 1st Earl of Clarendon, attributed to Thomas Hudson	61
	Private collection, photograph by courtesy of the National Portrait Gallery, London.	
47	The Honourable George Shirley, by Charles Jervas	61
	Private collection, photograph Courtauld Institute of Art.	
48	Augustus, 4th Earl of Berkeley, ascribed to G. Hamilton	62
	By permission of R.J.G. Berkeley Esq., Berkeley Castle, photograph Courtauld Institute of Art.	
49	John West, 1st Earl Delawarr, engraving by Lord Byron 1719	65
	By courtesy of the National Portrait Gallery, London.	
50	William Cavendish, 3rd Duke of Devonshire, by William Hoare	74
	Photograph courtesy of Sotheby's.	
51	George Montague, 1st Earl of Halifax, by Sir Godfrey Kneller	74
	Photograph by courtesy of the National Portrait Gallery, London.	
52	Robert Walpole, 2nd Earl of Orford, by John Wootton	74
	Photograph by courtesy of the National Portrait Gallery, London.	
53	Charles Calvert, 5th Baron Baltimore, attributed to Herman van der Mijn, c.1730	75
	By permission of the Peale Museum, Baltimore City Life Museums.	
54	Pedigree of Luther. Goodwood MS 2003, p.124. West Sussex Record Office	80
55	William, 2nd Earl Cowper, attributed to Bartholomew Dandridge	84
	Private collection, photograph Paul Mellon Centre for studies in British Art.	
56	The Honourable John Spencer, by Jan Vanderbank	85
	Private collection, photograph by courtesy of the National Portrait Gallery, London.	
57	Charles Spencer, 3rd Duke of Marlborough, by Isaac Wood	85
	Photograph by courtesy of the National Portrait Gallery, London.	
58	Emily, Duchess of Leinster. Crayon drawing	87
	By permission of the Trustees of the Goodwood collections.	
59	George Brudenell, 1st Duke of Montagu, by Thomas Hudson	88
	Private collection, photograph by courtesy of the National Portrait Gallery, London.	
60	Charles Newby, Esq., attributed to Thomas Phillips	88
	Photograph by courtesy of the National Portrait Gallery, London.	

List of Illustrations

61 The Honourable Edward Legge, by William Hoare 88
    By permission of Leeds Museums and Galleries (Temple Newsam House), photograph
    Courtauld Institute of Art.
62 The Honourable Henry Pelham, by William Hoare 92
    Rockingham Castle collection, photograph Courtauld Institute of Art.
63 List of hounds 1737. Goodwood MS 2003, pp.41/2/3. West Sussex Record Office 94-6
64 Elizabeth (Chudleigh), Countess of Bristol. Engraving 100
    Photograph by courtesy of the National Portrait Gallery, London.
65 Thomas Watson, 3rd Earl of Rockingham, by Enoch Seeman 101
    Rockingham Castle collection, photograph Courtauld Institute of Art.
66 Thomas Pelham-Holles, 1st Duke of Newcastle, by William Hoare 104
    Photograph courtesy of Sotheby's.
67 Henry Clinton, 2nd Duke of Newcastle, by William Hoare 104
    Photograph by courtesy of the National Portrait Gallery, London.
68 Richard Lumley, 2nd Earl of Scarbrough, by Sir Godfrey Kneller 105
    Photograph by courtesy of the National Portrait Gallery, London.
69 Mary, Viscountess Molyneux, by Michael Dahl, 1695 107
    In the collection of the Duke of Buccleuch, Boughton House, Northamptonshire.
70 Anthony Browne, 6th Viscount Montagu, by Vandiest. Christie's Images. 110
71 The Grand Chase. Goodwood MS 152. West Sussex Record Office 112/3
72 Charles Beauclerk, 2nd Duke of Saint Albans, by Michael Dahl 117
    Photograph by courtesy of the National Portrait Gallery, London.
73 Charles Bennet, 3rd Earl of Tankerville, by an unknown artist 118
    Private collection, photograph by courtesy of the National Portrait Gallery, London.
74 General Henry Hawley by David Morier. Photograph courtesy of Sotheby's. 119
75 William Fauquier Esq., by George Knapton 120
    By permission of the Dilettante Society, photograph Courtauld Institute of Art.
76 Lieutenant General Philip Honywood, by Thomas Gainsborough, 1765 121
    John and Mabel Ringling Museum of Art, Florida.
77 Map of Sussex, by Philip Overton and Thomas Bowles, 1740 .... 122/3
78 Charles Fitzroy, 2nd Duke of Grafton, by J.B. Van Loo. Photograph courtesy of Sotheby's. 128
79 Francis Seymour-Conway, 1st Marquess of Hertford by George Morland 131
    By kind permission of the Marquess of Hertford, photograph Paul Mellon Centre for studies
    in British Art
80 Sir Robert Smyth, Bt. and his family, attributed to Andrea Soldi. Yale Center for British Art. 133
81 Simon, 1st Earl Harcourt, by Robert Hunter 138
    Private collection, photograph Courtauld Institute of Art.
82 Charles Pelham Esq., by an unknown artist 143
    Brocklesby Park collection, by kind permission of the Earl of Yarborough.
83 George Keppel, 3rd Earl of Albemarle, by Jean Etienne Liotard, 1768 151
    Photograph courtesy of Sotheby's.
84 William Battine, Esq., Jr., by Thomas Phillips 152
    By kind permission of Lord Egremont, photograph Courtauld Institute of Art.
85 Robert Darcy, 6th Earl of Holdernesse, by George Knapton 154
    By permission of the Dilettante Society, photograph Courtauld Institute of Art.
86 Sir William Middleton, Bt., attributed to Thomas Hudson 159
    Laing Art Gallery, Newcastle-upon-Tyne, photograph Courtauld Institute of Art.
87 John, 2nd Duke of Montagu, by Thomas Hudson 160
    In the collection of the Duke of Buccleuch, Boughton House, Northamptonshire.
88 Lord George Lennox, by George Romney 161
    By permission of the Trustees of the Goodwood collections.
89 Thomas Coke, 1st Earl of Leicester, attributed to Jonathan Richardson 165

90 Monumental inscription in Singleton Church to the memory of Tom Johnson 168
91 William Cavendish, 4th Duke of Devonshire, attributed to George Knapton 170
      Devonshire Collection, Chatsworth. Reproduced by permission of the Chatsworth Settlement Trustees, photograph Courtauld Institute of Art.
      By kind permission of the Earl of Leicester and the Trustees of the Holkham Estate, photograph Courtauld Institute of Art.
92 Brice Fisher Esq, by Thomas Hudson. Photograph courtesy of Sotheby's. 171
93 Admiral Isaac Townshend, by Jeremiah Davison. National Maritime Museum, London. 172
94 Francis Scott, Earl of Dalkeith, attributed to Thomas Bardwell 173
      In the collection of the Duke of Buccleuch and Queensberry KT.
95 John Lindsay, 20th Earl of Crawford, attributed to Allan Ramsay 174
      Photograph by courtesy of the National Portrait Gallery, London.
96 John Campbell, 4th Earl of Loudoun, by Allan Ramsay. National Galleries of Scotland. 179
97 William Anne Van Keppel, 2nd Earl of Albemarle, by Sir Godfrey Kneller 179
      By permission of the Trustees of the Goodwood collections.
98 John Leslie, 10th Earl of Rothes, by Sir Joshua Reynolds 180
      In a private collection, photograph Paul Mellon Centre for studies in British Art.
99 John Manners, Marquess of Granby, by Sir Joshua Reynolds 182
      Belvoir Castle collection. Photograph by courtesy of the National Portrait Gallery, London.
100 John, 2nd Earl of Ashburnham, by William Hoare 182
      Photograph by courtesy of the National Portrait Gallery, London.
101 James Peachey, 1st Baron Selsey, attributed to Sir William Beechey 183
      Present location unknown, photograph Courtauld Institute of Art.
102 James Fitzgerald, 1st Duke of Leinster, by Francis Cotes 183
      By permission of the Trustees of the Goodwood collections.
103 Percy Wyndham O'Brien, Earl of Thomond, attributed to Thomas Phillips after William Hoare .. 185
      By kind permission of Lord Egremont, photograph Courtauld Institute of Art.
104 Sir Matthew Fetherstonhaugh, Bt., by Pompeo Batoni 189
      Uppark (The National Trust), Photographic Library/John Hammond.
105 Henry Pleydell Dawnay, 3rd Viscount Downe, attributed to Jean Etienne Liotard 189
      Private collection.
106 George Augustus, 3rd Viscount Howe, by Francis Wheatley 193
      By permission of the Pennington-Mellor-Munthe Trust, photograph Courtauld Institute of Art.
107 Augustus, Viscount Keppel, by Sir Joshua Reynolds. National Maritime Museum, London. 194
108 The Honourable William Keppel by Sir Joshua Reynolds 197
      Museu Nacional de Arte Antiga, photograph Jose Pessoa, Arquivo Nacional de Fotografia, Instituto Português de Museus.
109 Sir Thomas Saunders Sebright, Bt., by Pompeo Batoni. Christie's Images. 198
110 Charles Lennox, 3rd Duke of Richmond, by an unknown artist 200
      By permission of the Trustees of the Goodwood collections.
111 The stable block at Goodwood 202
      Photograph by permission of the Trustees of the Goodwood collections.
112 The old kennels at Goodwood 203
      Photograph by permission of the Trustees of the Goodwood collections.
113 List of hounds 1757. Goodwood MS 2015, p.1. West Sussex Record Office. 204
114 George Wyndham, 3rd Earl of Egremont. Crayon drawing 205
      By permission of the Trustees of the Goodwood collections.
115 Map of Sussex, The Great Survey, by Thomas Yeakell and William Gardner, 1778 206-13
116 Charles Lennox, 4th Duke of Richmond, by an unknown artist 214
      By permission of the Trustees of the Goodwood collections
117 Tom Grant, pencil sketch by R.B. Davis 215
118 Estate map of 1731. West Sussex Record Office. 224
119 Estate maps of 1765 and c.1767, by Yeakall and Gardner. West Sussex Record Office. 224

Foreword

by His Grace the Duke of Richmond and Gordon

The Charlton Hunt is extremely important in the history of my family.

The 1st Duke of Richmond and Lennox, son of Charles II, bought a Jacobean house at Goodwood in 1697 in order to hunt in Charlton forest. As this book explains, this was the first properly organised fox hunt in the country and became extremely illustrious with all sorts of ennobled people taking part.

The history of hunting at Goodwood has been one of ups and downs over the last three centuries. My great-grandfather (7th Duke) as the Earl of March finally re-established the Goodwood Hunt in 1883 but it lasted only 12 seasons, packing up in April 1895. That was the end of a hunt at Goodwood, though the local hunt (Chiddingfold, Leconfield and Cowdray) has continued to meet occasionally at Goodwood House and Molecomb up to quite recent times. Unfortunately my grandfather contracted polio in the First World War and never rode again. My father was much more interested in cars than horses as is my son, the present Earl of March. My brother and I rode a little when we were young, but then in the War we went to the USA, and that was that. However, my granddaughter aged 12 is riding and my grandson aged three (the 12th Duke!) has just started, so who knows?

However, horses have continued to be an important part of Goodwood's life in the present. The Racecourse is still thriving after nearly two hundred years, and the race horses still use the Goodwood House stables which were first built for the 3rd Duke's hunters which participated in the Charlton Hunt. So the stables can't yet be turned into a motor museum! The very same stables also accommodated the dressage horses which took part in the International Dressage events put on by my wife and myself at Goodwood Park over the 21 years from 1973 to 1993.

The top foreign dressage riders used to say that the first reason why they enjoyed coming to Goodwood was because their horses slept at night!

We have discovered that it is perfectly possible to run both horse and car racing: indeed there are many similar problems in doing so, provided of course you don't try and do them at the same time in the same place! Is it not surprising that car engines are still measured in horse power?!

I am deeply grateful to Dr. Simon Rees for writing this book which is a significant addition to the history of Goodwood and of our Family.

Author's Note

There are records in the Duke of Richmond's diaries, and in various letters, of almost three hundred days when hounds went out from the kennels at Charlton, Findon and Bolderwood in the New Forest. On over three quarters of these days there is a record of the draw, the find, the run and the outcome. To include them all in the text verbatim would have been tedious and repetitive and some seventy days have been selected for inclusion. They can be followed more or less on the contemporary maps reproduced in the book, but the names of many of the smaller coverts are not shown. However for those who would wish to discover exactly where and how far foxes and hounds ran 250 years ago, they can be found, with only a few exceptions, on a modern 1:25,000 Ordnance Survey map.

Spelling in the 18th century, except on official and legal documents, was phonetic and very inconsistent, especially in informal writing, such as letters or diaries. Whilst this may be interesting and amusing, it undoubtedly distracts the reader, so, braving the fierce criticism of the purists, all spelling has been modernised.

Some of the events took place before and some after the introduction of the Gregorian calendar in 1752, so the difficulties of sorting out Old Style and New Style have been avoided by quoting all dates in their modern equivalent.

Preface

'In a deed box at Goodwood', wrote the Earl of March in 1910, 'there has lain, undisturbed for many years, a bundle of old papers and letters, tattered and discoloured with age, and in some cases almost illegible, but possessing for myself a most absorbing interest, for they represent all that remains to chronicle the forgotten glories of the old Charlton Hunt.' These papers, now preserved in the West Sussex Record Office, contain a remarkably complete record of the hunt at Charlton, which began in the 1670s, flourished until the death of the 2nd Duke of Richmond in 1750, was revived by the 3rd Duke in 1757 and was finally wound up by the 4th Duke in 1813. They consist of hunting diaries, letters, minutes of hunt meetings, legal documents, bills and accounts, lists of hounds, hunting songs and a long piece of allegorical blank verse outlining the early history.

Charlton is unique in several ways. Although hunting with hounds is as old as man, the Charlton hunt appears to be the first documented pack of hounds to be entered to fox alone and it attained a popularity amongst the nobility and gentry which has not since been equalled. It grew up in the turbulent closing years of the reign of Charles II, whose illegitimate sons and their heirs were prominent in the hunt annals. Almost every noble family in the land had a representative at Charlton; for a period of many years, it could count amongst its subscribers almost half the Knights of the Garter. It was also the first hunt to establish a club, election to which was necessary before one was allowed to follow the hounds, although guests were permitted, provided they did not stay too long. Perhaps uniquely too, the members built themselves a dining hall, where they could meet together after hunting, and many of them also built hunting boxes, in which they would stay for days or weeks at a time during the season. In the closing years, the hounds were moved to Goodwood, and from being a buzzing centre of feverish activity, the little village of Charlton quietly lapsed back into the sleepy Sussex hamlet which it is today.

My fascination with Charlton began 40 years ago, when an old manuscript account of the grand chase of 1739 used to hang in the *Fox Inn* at Charlton. Next door were the former hunting boxes of the Duke of Devonshire and Lord Harcourt and, just down the road, the old kennels, now converted into cottages. The curious tall building known as Fox Hall was then leased to the manager of the saw mills nearby, but walking past, the echoes of those old hunting songs became unmistakable and it seemed a great shame that Charlton's glorious history should become more and more of a distant memory.

The Charlton Hunt is now a dining club for foxhunters in the old Charlton country under the patronage of the Duke of Richmond and Gordon, Viscount Cowdray and Lord Egremont. The tradition of the blue and gold livery lives on and, by kind permission of the Landmark Trust, our annual dinner is still held at Fox Hall, the Great Room of the old Charlton Hunt.

Simon Rees

Treyford, October 1997

Acknowledgements

I am exceedingly grateful to His Grace the Duke of Richmond and Gordon who kindly lent me the leather-bound volume *Pedigree of Charlton Hounds* from the library at Goodwood and thereby, unwittingly, gave me the idea of writing this history. It has truly been a labour of love. I wish to thank him also for allowing me free access to the pictures in the Goodwood collection and for kindly consenting to write a foreword. Mr. Timothy McCann and the staff at the West Sussex Record Office have been most helpful and cooperative in making available all the records relating to the Charlton Hunt and providing me with photocopies. I am also indebted to the staff of the National Portrait Gallery Archive in London whose courteous help enabled me to locate so many pictures of the people who frequented Charlton in the 18th century.

I would like to thank all those who have kindly given permission to reproduce images. They are acknowledged in the List of Illustrations, unless it was their wish to remain anonymous. I am indebted to many people who have enabled me to acquire illustrations and reproduce them in the book. They include Mrs. Rosemary Baird and Mrs. Valerie Lambirth at Goodwood, Mr. James Kilvington at the National Portrait Gallery, Sarah Wimbush at the Courtauld Institute of Art, Miss Véronique Gunner at Sotheby's, Miss Emma Strouts at Christie's, Dr. Rosalind Marshall at the Scottish National Portrait Gallery, Mrs. Elizabeth Grant at the Bath Preservation Trust, Maria Rosa Figueiredo at the Calouste Gulbenkian Museum in Lisbon, Mr. Ed Gibbons at the National Trust Photographic Library, Mr. G.E. Hughes of English Heritage, Mr. Peter Day at Chatsworth, Mr. St John Gore of the Dilettanti Society, Julia Naismith at the Holburne Museum and Craft Study Centre at Bath, Mr. Gareth Fitzpatrick of the Living Landscape Trust at Boughton House, Vitoria Mesquita at the Museum of Ancient Art in Lisbon, Mr. Colin Starkey at the National Maritime Museum, Mr. Stephen Drew at the Norwich Castle Museum, Emma Lauze at the Paul Mellon Centre for studies in British Art, Mrs. Nora Laishley, Mr. Dean Krimmel at the Peale Museum in Baltimore, Mr. Glen Gentele at the Ringling Museum in Sarasota, Florida, Mr. R.W. Stedman at the Wilton Estate, Mr. Timothy Goodhew at the Yale Center for British Art in Connecticut and the staff of the Carmarthen Museum.

I have exchanged much interesting correspondence about Fox Hall with the late Mrs. Charlotte Haslam, who was historian to the Landmark Trust, with Mrs. Rosemary Baird, Mr. Christopher Pringle and Mr. Richard Pailthorpe. I have not always agreed with their views, but I am grateful to them for their stimulating comments which have contributed greatly to the conclusions I have set out in Appendix 1. I would also like to acknowledge the help and advice given to me by Mr. Gordon Fergusson, the secretary of the Tarporley Hunt and finally, I would like to thank Mr. Noel Osborne and Nicola Willmot at Phillimore for their expert professional help in producing the book.

List of Subscribers

Dr. and Mrs. John Aldridge
Terence Allan
Y.M. Allen
D.M. Allerton
Mrs. Peter Andreae
Ian Anstruther, Susan Anstruther
Rosamund Audley
Colin Baillieu
Anthony Bamford
M.J. Barclay
Alison Barlow
Mrs. Richard Barlow
Virginia Beard
Mr. David Benson, Lady Elizabeth Benson
Mrs. Lavinia Black
Jenny Bland
Miss J. Blois (Hon. Sec., Albany Bassets)
Mrs. P.A. Blunt
Jimbo Bolton
Russell Bowes
J.S. Brice, Esq. (Master, Rangitiki Hunt, New Zealand)
Dr. D.H. Brooks
Sir Rupert Buchanan-Jardine
N.B. Buckland, MFH
Mark Burrell
Michael Camps
Carbery Hunt, County Cork
Mr. and Mrs. Robin C. Chaventré
Christie's (British Picture Department)
Mr. and Mrs. D.J. Church
Derek Clarke
Kath Clegg (MDH, Saddleworth)
The Viscount Cowdray
Jane Craddock
Christopher R. Cradock
John Cripps
Caroline Crossman
Judy Newsom Davis
Dr. Anthony Douglas-Hamilton
N.G.H. Draffan, MA, FRICS
Nicholas Dugdale

C.E. Durrell, MH
Jennifer (Gladwin) Edmonds
E.F. Edwards
Clare and Olly Ellwood
Rosemary Elstone
Bruce and Elizabeth English
D.R.L. Evans
Dr. Margaret Evans
James P. Farber, Jr.
Alys Ferguson
Capt. J.G. Fergusson (Hon. Secretary, Tarporley
   Hunt Club)
Maj. M.W.S. Fleming
C.H.R. Fookes
C.T. de Montalt Fraser
Suzanne Garner and Charlotte Garner
Nita P. Garry
Richard Gilchrist
Hardy Gillingham
Mr. and Mrs. Neville Girardot
T.L. Gosling
Tracey L. Gower, Nick L. Fawcett
Ted Green
Vivienne Grellis
David Hadley
James Haigh, MBE
Mrs. Peter Hamilton
Dr. David M. Hansell
Dr. P.L.S. Hard
Bryan Harper
Jeremy Dering Harris
Mrs. B.Y. Harrison, MH
Jean Heaver
John Hedges and Mark Hedges
Anthony Heller
Jonathan Henty
J.C. Hett
John and Catherine Hickman
Hamish Hiddleston
Miss Sophie Hill
Colin A. Hislop

The Charlton Hunt

Mrs. Paddy Hollington
Alan Holmes
Charles Spencer Homan, Charlotte Amelia Homan, Henry William James Homan
Noel Horgan
D.E.J. Hunt, DSC*
Major D. Ide-Smith
Jean and Robin Illius
Eve and Colin Jeffries
Marjorie Jennings
James S. Jones, ex-MH
Jim Keble-White
Robin C. Kelton
Claire Kemp
Thomas S. Kenan
Anthony Langdale
Oliver Langdale, MFH
Philip Langdale
Geoffrey Lawson
Shaun Lawson
Mrs. E.N. Layton (née Diana Charlton)
Jeremy W.S. Lewis
Mr. T.C. Lilburn
John Limbocker, Jr., MFH
The Squire de Lisle
J.B. Lowthian (MFH, Ullswater)
Timothy J. McCann
Mr. and Mrs. S. McCarthy
Alison and Corbett McDonald
Lawson McDonald and Patricia Mavroleon
Mr. and Mrs. McGovern
The Earl and Countess of March
Christopher Marks
Margaret Marlow
Colin R. Marsh
Brian Matthews
Stanley M. Mayes, Joy R. Mayes
Clare Minto
Richard Mitton
David Moore-Gwyn
John Edward Maxwell Morris
Timothy and Arlene Morris
A.M. Murphy
Denis J. Murphy, MFH
Lance and Andra Neeley
Douglas Newman
Rona S. Owen
Ian N. Ozanne, Esq.
Richard Pailthorpe
John W. Parker
Mr. C.W. Parrett
Timothy Parsons

Peter Payan
William Sulby Payne
Nigel and Sophia Peel
Mrs. Anthea Philip
Miranda Phillimore
Maurice E. Pinto
Michael Poland
Geoff Potter
David Potterton
Caroline Poulmenti
Brian Powell, MDH
James Provan
Gordon D. Rees
Howard Rees
Michael Rees
David Reynolds, MFH
A.D. Richardson, MFH
The Duke and Duchess of Richmond
Mrs. Susan Roberts
G.A. Robinson
Raymond Rowlands
Berris Russ (Hunter Valley Hunt, Australia)
James Sankey
D.D. Scott
M. Doreen Shaxson
Patricia Sherlock
V.M. Shields, MFH
Jacqueline Shore
Giles Sim
A. Skillman
M.L.H. Stent
Paul Stern
Robert J.E. Strudwick
Steven Swan
Jean Symons
Mick Tarrant (Vine & Craven Terrier Man)
A.J. Taylor
Hugh Taylor
Maurice J. Thomas, MFH
Peter Thomas
John Tucker
John Tylor
Desmond Walsh (Ormond Hunt)
David W. Wates
Hamish Watson
Michael Weld
Stan Whale
Sir Richard Baker Wilbraham
Kenneth and Jean Williams
Peter Winkworth
William Young and Robert Young
Marita Zonabend

xvi

— I —
THE REGULAR SOCIETY

> We have all heard of Goodwood but where is Charlton, and what of it? A little more than a hundred years ago these questions would have been exactly reversed; then all the world had heard of Charlton, while the glories of Goodwood slumbered in the womb of time.[1]
>
> T.J. Bennett (1863)

On Sunday 29 January 1738, 20 gentlemen met in London for their annual dinner. Their tradition was a proud one, going back over sixty years, famous the length and breadth of our islands and well known in many countries of continental Europe. Everyone had heard of Charlton, the centre of the fox-hunting world. Nearly all the noble families of England had a representative and during the season Charlton was the most important centre of society outside London. It was popular for the hunting and the good fellowship, and frequented by people of quality and fashion, many prominent at court and in politics. In fact it had become so popular that some way of restricting entry had now become a necessity.

The chairman, Lord Delawarr, called the assembled company to order to hear the master and proprietor of the hunt, the Duke of Richmond, make an important proposal. The duke rose to his feet, and expressing a view that the prosperity of Charlton was paramount to them all, 'proposed to form the Members of this Hunt into a regular society, which was agreed to Nemine Contradicente and the following articles were resolved on and subscribed by the members then present and afterwards by the absent members'. The rules of the society were read out. The clear intention was that only members would be permitted to hunt at Charlton, election would be by ballot, visitors would be strictly limited and one black ball would be sufficient to exclude! And the duke reserved the right to bring whoever he liked from Goodwood to dinner!

At the general meeting of the members of the Charlton Hunt held at the *Bedford Head Tavern* in London on Sunday 29 January 1738:

> It is this Day agreed by Us whose Names are hereunto subscribed, that no Person shall be of the Charlton Hunt, who was not an Original Subscriber to the Building of the Great Room at Charlton or a Subscriber to this Agreement unless admitted under the following Rules.
>
> 1st. No person to be admitted but by Ballot.
>
> 2nd. Any person that is desirous to be admitted a Member of the Hunt must be proposed at Charlton, by one of the Society, and his name affixed up in the Great Room at Charlton, in the Form and manner following viz.
>
> I recommend.. to be a Member of the Charlton Hunt.
>
> As Witness my hand...

3rd. The person proposed is not to be Balloted for, in less than seven Days after his name is affixed up in the Great Room at Charlton; Nor is such Ballot to be by less than nine persons of the Society, and the Ballot to be betwixt the hours of Four & Eight in the Afternoon.

4th. One black Ball is an Exclusion.

5th. No person so excluded to be put in Nomination again that year.

6th. If any Member of the Hunt is desirous that a Friend may come to Charlton, he must first ask the Consent of Such Members as are at that time at Charlton, which Leave must be obtained by Ballot of the Members then present, if they are not less than three in number Provided such person so admitted, does not Stay more than the Space of 8 days; and the person so brought down, is to have his Expenses defrayed by the member that recommends him.

7th. If any Stranger is seen in the Field a hunting, he may be invited that day by any of the Company and his Reckoning to be paid by the persons then present.

8th. The Duke of Richmond to bring whoever he pleases from Goodwood to Dinner at Charlton.

9th. Any Additional Article may be made by a Ballot of nine persons, such Ballot to be in the Great Room at Charlton to be determined by the Majority.

10th. If any Dispute arise about the meaning of any of the above written Articles, it shall be decided by the Majority of the Members present at the General Annual Meeting in London.

These articles were agreed by those present: Lord Delawarr (in the chair), the Dukes of Grafton, Richmond and St Albans, the Earls of Godolphin and Lifford, Viscount Harcourt, Lord Henry Beauclerk, Lord Nassau Powlett, Hon. John West, Count Maurice of Nassau, Rt. Hon. William Conolly, Sir Henry Liddell, General Kirke, Colonel Huske, Richard Honywood, Ralph Jenison, Edward Pauncefort, William Fauquier and M. de Marpon.

A list was subsequently drawn up of the absent members, which included 12 of the original subscribers to the building of the Great Room (the banqueting hall) and 50 other members of the hunt.[2]

Thus was formed, 60 years after hounds were first kennelled at Charlton, the earliest hunt club. Everyone knew of the events which had filled those years, starting in the political turmoils of the 1670s with the Duke of Monmouth and Lord Grey, followed by Mr. Roper's long and prosperous tenure of office, by the Duke of Bolton and finally by the Duke of Richmond, after a long and bitter struggle for supremacy with Lord Tankerville. Now in his ninth season, the duke was enjoying his role as master and proprietor at Charlton, where he owned a comfortable hunting box.

Returning to Goodwood a few days later in early February, he was surprised when a porter brought him a thick envelope inside which was a document entitled

THE HISTORICAL ACCOUNT OF THE RISE AND PROGRESS OF THE CHARLTON CONGRESS[3]

To his grace the Duke of Richmond, Lennox and Aubigny &c

My Lord,

The fine chases I have seen at Charlton, the kind and generous reception I have received from your Grace and the rest of the agreeable company there, though an unworthy stranger

---

[1] The Formation of the Charlton Hunt Club, 'The Regular Society'.

Annual Meeting Present

Lord Delawarr in the Chair
Duke of Grafton
Duke of Richmond
Duke of St Albans
Earl of Godolphin
Earl of Lifford
Visco. Harcourt
Lord Hen: Beauclerk
Lord Nassau Paulet
Hon.ble Jn. Wett
Count Mau.e of Nassau
Rt. Hon.ble W.m Conolly Esq
S.r Hen: Liddal Bar.t
Major Gen.l Huske
Colonel Huske
Rich.d Heywood Esq.
Ralph Jennyson Esq.
Edw.d Pauncford Esq.
W.m Fauquiere Esq.
Monsr. de Marpon

(20)

(79)

At the General Meeting of the Members of the Charlton Hunt held at the Bedford head Tavern in London. On Sunday January 29.th 1737/8.

The Duke of Richmond proposed to form the Members of this Hunt into a regular Society, which was agreed to Nemine Contradicente, & the following Articles were Resolved on and Subscribed by the Members then present and afterwards by the absent Members. Viz.t

It is this Day agreed by us whose names are hereunto Subscribed, that no Person shall bee of the Charlton Hunt, who was not an Original Subscriber to the Building of the Great Room at Charlton or a Subscriber to this agreement unless admitted under the following Rules.

1.st No person to be admitted but by Ballot.

2.d Any person that is desirous to be admitted a Member of the Hunt, must be proposed at Charlton, by one of the Society, and his name affixed up in the Great Room at Charlton, in the Form and manner following (viz.t) I recommend .... to be a Member of the Charlton Hunt. As witness my hand ....

3.d One person proposed is not to be Balotted for, in less than Seven Days after his name is affixed up in the Great Room at Charlton, nor is such Ballot to be by less than nine persons of the Society, and the Ballot to be betwixt the hours of Four & Eight in the Afternoon.

4.th One black Ball is an Exclusion.

5.th No person so excluded to be put in Nomination again that Year.

6.th If any Member of the Hunt is desirous that a Friend may come to Charlton, he must first ask the Consent of such Members as are at that time at Charlton, which Leave must be obtained by Ballot of the Members then present, if they are not less than three in number, Provided such person so admitted, does not stay more than the space of 8 Days; and the person so brought down, is to have his Expences defrayed by the Member that recomends him.

7.th If any Stranger is seen in the Field a hunting, he may be invited that day by any of the Company and his Reckoning to be paid by the persons then present.

8.th The Duke of Richmond to bring whoever he pleases from Goodwood to Dinner at Charlton.

who can never have it in his power to make the grateful acknowledgement which nevertheless glows in his plebeian breast, as it has been my nightly dream so it has been my daily talk and my study to learn as much as I could of the first rise and long continuance of the most agreeable society of the kind that ever was, here it is my Lord, rough and unhewn I send it to you, omissions you will excuse, the whole you must despise but I have eased my mind and have the satisfaction of taking this occasion to assure your Grace with all respect that nobody can be more your Grace's

most Obedient and most Humble serv^t

Enclosed were 30 pages of blank verse running to 737 lines. Who the anonymous scribe was is entirely speculative, but the author thinks it may have been one Andrew Charlton, who is briefly referred to in the poem as having been about at Charlton in Roper's time and subsequently is found writing letters in the same deferential manner to the Duke of Richmond. His name does not appear amongst the members, yet his letters seem very well informed about matters connected with the hunt. An alternative guess, found by the author on a scrap of paper and written by an unknown hand, is General Honywood, one of the original subscribers to the Great Room. As a historical document, the poem is invaluable, being the only written record of the events at Charlton up to 1737, other than the hound book, which dates from 1721. The story that follows relies heavily on these two sources.

— II —

Monmouth and Grey

The hamlet of Charlton, a tything of the parish of Singleton in West Sussex, lies a mile north of Goodwood racecourse and a mile east of the road from Chichester to Midhurst. Our poet describes the valley, which takes its name from the river Lavant, with its four villages, small and pretty then, as mercifully they still are, surrounded by the Sussex downs.

>*Amidst the south Saxonian hills, there runs*
>*a verdant fruitful vale, in which at once*
>*four small and pretty villages are seen.*
>*East Dean, the one does first supply the spring,*
>*whence milky Lavant takes his future course.*
>*Charlton the next, the beauty of the four;*
>*from twenty chalky rills fresh vigour adds.*
>*Then swiftly on, his force redoubled, he*
>*through all the meads to Singleton does glide;*
>*more strength he there receives. At West Dean next,*
>*his last recruit he makes; then boldly runs,*
>*till less confined, he wider spreads his fame;*
>*and passing Lavant, there he takes his name.*

The poet goes on to describe the local landmarks, familiar to all who know the area today; St Roche's Hill, now known as the Trundle, Levin Down, Bow Hill and the ancient yew forest of Kingley Vale.

>*A vast high mountain to the south does bear*
>*the name of one Saint Roke, unknown elsewhere.*
>*Northward and rising close above the town,*
>*another mountain's known by Levin down.*
>*But lo! the next great pointe de vue;*
>*the great conspicuous Bow, his bulk so vast,*
>*his length and height, his head so near the clouds;*
>*from Gallias [French] shore he's plainly seen and known,*
>*the boldest landmark of our British coast.*
>*With yews and black thorn his great crest is crown'd,*
>*green all the winter, long and white in spring.*
>*'Tis here wise nature, scorning all low arts,*

> *her various beauties on each side imparts;*
> *from Kingly bottom, here the wand'ring eye*
> *with southern prospect all the ocean views;*
> *sees all the trade that passes to enrich*
> *our British isle, or please luxurious tastes.*

On the downs to the north of the village lies Charlton Forest, a large wood extending to over 800 acres, in former times the property of the Fitzalans, Earls of Arundel, where this great family enjoyed the pleasures of the chase, having a hunting seat at Downley, near Singleton on the verge of the forest. It thus seems likely that the pleasant woods and downs of Charlton were appropriated to the enjoyment of hunting and the chase and of later years, as we shall see, it was exclusively to fox hunting. From this circumstance only, Charlton derives its celebrity.

And so the poet tells us in allegory how Diana, the virgin huntress herself, selected Charlton as the ideal place to establish the first headquarters of the fox-hunting world; but apparently for gentlemen only!

> *In this sweet vale by hills and downs enclos'd,*
> *an age ago Diana fix't her court.*
> *The British fierceness to Diana known,*
> *the inbred goodness of their coursers to,*
> *like all her sex, she everywhere would be*
> *ador'd, but how to suit it with her chastity?*
> *The country's beauty and the British hounds*
> *tempted the goddess here to raise her fame.*
> *At last, in private, weighing well her scheme,*
> *she thus resolves! 'I'll be ador'd by men,*
> *by Britons bold, where nymphs shall ne're resort;*
> *rough is their nature and they love all sports.*
> *A new one I'll invent to fit their taste;*
> *their hounds, their horses and their daring youth,*
> *at once I'll suit them and they'll still do good;*
> *the wily fox their furious chace shall be.*
> *A small but well chose band I'll then select*
> *from all the huntsmen Britain can produce,*
> *and Charlton is the place where I will fix*
> *my temple, where my votaries shall hunt.*

This is a challenging resolve, but as a result the Charlton Hunt Club of today is still for gentlemen only! Like the modern hunt chairman, the goddess then goes on to appoint her joint masters, in the event perhaps not too wisely! Who, then, were to be the 'votaries' of this noble pastime, she now reveals.

> *And then her thoughts were where to choose her band,*
> *and such who would her laws and rights maintain.*
> *A grosveneur [huntsman], a name the Norman brought,*

Monmouth and Grey

2   James, Duke of Monmouth, proprietor of Charlton hounds from about 1675 to 1683.

*she thought was requisite to rule the whole,
since she in decency could not appear.
The first firm maxim she laid down was this:
that blood in ev'ry vein should be the best.
To answer this, the first brave youth she chose
had graceful mien with waving locks adorn'd,
but empty head, tho' sprung from royal loins;
vigorous he was and Monmouth was his name.*

The son of King Charles II, James, Duke of Monmouth and Buccleuch was born in 1649 during the king's exile in Holland. His mother was the ravishing Lucy, daughter of William Walter, lord of Roche Castle in Pembrokeshire. In 1648, she had travelled to the Hague as a royalist spy known as 'Mrs. Barlow' under the protection of her cousin John Barlow of Barlow Hall, Colchester. Evelyn described her as 'bold, brown and beautiful' and Baronne d'Aulnoy in his memoirs recalled that 'her beauty was so perfect that when the king saw her he was so charmed and ravished and enamoured that he knew no other sweetness or joy than to love her and be loved by her'.[4] They were reputed to have been married in 1648 at Liège by Dr Cosin, the Bishop of Durham. Did Charles really marry Lucy? Was Monmouth really illegitimate? He certainly believed, or was persuaded to believe he was born in wedlock, but these are questions which remain unresolved, cloaked as they are in political intrigue which even today goes to the heart of the succession of the monarchy.[5]

*With him came Tankerville, associate he
in all his follies and his infamy.
How could a goddess be so much deceiv'd?*

3 Ford Grey, 3rd Baron Grey of Warke, who kept a pack of hounds at Charlton with the Duke of Monmouth under the management of Mr. Roper from about 1675 to 1683. He was later created Earl of Tankerville and rebuilt the house at Uppark.

Tankerville refers to Ford, Lord Grey, later Earl of Tankerville, who was born at Uppark in West Sussex in 1655. He was christened after his maternal grandfather Sir Edward Ford, whose family had owned Uppark and the manor of East Harting for two centuries. Sir Edward was the inventor of the first effective pump for raising water to a considerable height. He was 'a most ingenious mechanist and being encouraged by Oliver Cromwell and invited by the citizens of London in 1656 he raised the Thames water into all the highest streets in the city ninety three feet high in four eight inch pipes to the wonder of all men and the honour of the nation with a rare engine of his own invention done at his own charge and in one year's time'.[6] Ford Grey's paternal grandfather, the first Lord Grey, had been Speaker of the House of Lords. His family estates were at Warke and Chillingham in Northumberland, but his son Ralph, having married Sir Edward Ford's only child Catherine, elected to live at Uppark. Ralph survived his father but a year, dying in 1675 when Ford inherited the title and estates at the age of twenty.

These were the days of the Popish plot and the Exclusion bill. James, Duke of York, the king's brother and heir, was a catholic. The king himself was a clandestine catholic. Popular sentiment decreed that the successor to the throne should be a protestant. The Country party was formed, headed by the Lord Chancellor, the Earl of Shaftesbury, who had decided that the Duke of York, who had just taken a catholic bride as his second wife, must not, indeed would not, succeed. In 1675, he formed and presided over a private society to promulgate the Duke of Monmouth's rightful claim to the throne. They called themselves the Green Ribbon Club and Monmouth, their patron, was a regular visitor. Grey was also a member and became Monmouth's close friend and associate, and it was certainly this relationship which led to their setting up a hunting establishment in Charlton near Grey's home at Uppark.

During the growing agitation against the papists, Monmouth became the champion of the protestants, setting off on a series of tours, ostensibly sporting and social, but actually political and revolutionary. In 1679, he visited the flagrantly anti-papist town of Chichester, where Grey held the office of Elector-General. The events of the previous months explain the highly excited feelings then prevalent at Chichester as elsewhere. On 20 November 1678, the Lords had passed an Act to disable papists from sitting in parliament, in spite of the protest of the Duke of York and seven other peers. On 2 December, the Commons had voted an address to the king upon the growth of popery, and the king had in consequence on 30 December prorogued, and on 24 January 1679 dissolved the parliament, summoning a new one to meet on 6 March. It was in this interval of political struggle that the Duke of Monmouth put himself forward to influence the elections and direct public suspicion against the court of the king, his father. As the king had already pledged himself to the King of France to declare himself a catholic and as the Duke of York had also done so, Monmouth had little difficulty in becoming the hero of protestant excitement.

'Of the old cavaliers,' wrote Lord Macaulay,

> many participated in the prevailing fear of popery, and many bitterly resenting the ingratitude of the king for whom they had sacrificed so much, looked on his distress as carelessly as he had on theirs. Even the anglican clergy, mortified and alarmed at the apostacy of the Duke of York, so far countenanced the opposition as to join cordially in the outcry against the Roman Catholics. When the Duke of Monmouth travelled, he was everywhere received with not less pomp and with far more enthusiasm than had been displayed when the king had made progresses through the realm. He was escorted from mansion to mansion by long cavalcades of armed gentlemen and yeomen. Cities poured forth their whole population to receive him.[7]

His reception in Chichester is described in a letter written by the bishop, Guy Carlton, who had been recently translated from the see of Bristol. Owing to the disturbed state of public feeling, he found himself immediately involved in the political tumults of the time, so as to become liable to reproach and suspicion in his own cathedral city. He wrote an account of the Duke of Monmouth having visited Chichester as the popular representative of the strong protestant distrust of the king's policy. Archbishop Sancroft was the prelate addressed. These extracts from the letter contain the only known contemporary reference to Monmouth in the hunting field in Sussex and refer to Mr. Roper, the huntsman, of whom more anon in the following chapter.

Chichester, Tuesday 17th February 1679

Most Reverend Father and My Most Honoured Lord

By the several relations even in this town and the country adjacent, and both very false and various, I beg leave to give your Grace a true account of the Duke of Monmouth's arrival and reception into the city of Chichester on Saturday February 7th inst. The Elector-general Grey (for so is his title in this country) being here in Chichester, went out to bring him into the city attended with broken shopkeepers, butchers, carpenters, smiths and such like people, all dissenters and petitioners, to the number of fifty or threescore. The duke was in a scarlet suit and cloak, which the great men for petitioning for a parliament called the Red Flag to let see beforehand what our doom would be ere long; and had the reception rested there, no other could be expected from such a rabble of brutes. But the great men of our cathedral welcomed him with bells and

4   Mr. Roper, huntsman of the Charlton hounds from 1675 to 1723, as a younger man. In this portrait he is called Edward.

bonfires made by wood had from their houses to flare before his lodgings, personal visits made to him, complemented at the lighting from his horse with all that was in their houses proffered to his service, and to be at his disposal...

In these bell and bonfire solemnities I would not join, nor go to give him personal visits. I thought it did ill become clergymen, of all others, to open our arms so wide with acclamations of joy to embrace a man that lay under the Duke of Monmouth's circumstances at this time, a person that was highly under the king's displeasure for its obstinate perseverance in disobedience to his sovereign, and that kept no company here but known enemies to the king and his government. I was mightily blamed, cried out upon and condemned for not doing all homage imaginable to so excellent a person as the Duke of Monmouth was. I told them if he deserted that rascal company that flocked to him, and would return to that obedience and loyalty he owed his father and his sovereign, then no man should honour him more than I should do; but till this were done, I would never think him worthy of honour from any good man or loyal subject. Whether in doing this I cannot tell whether I failed in the point of manners, but I think I did not, and I am sure I did not in mine affection and loyalty to the king my master ...

Neither the mayor of this city nor any gentlemen (and there are diverse of them and persons of good quality that live in it) went out to meet the duke, nor hath ever since come to visit him, or any gentleman in the country about us hath so much met him in the field to hunt with him since he came, save Mr Butler of Amberley, a burgess with Mr Garroway for Arundel, and his brother-in-law Roper ...[8]

This raises the question of when the fox hounds at Charlton were established. Bearing in mind that Grey inherited the title in 1675 around the time he met Monmouth in the Green Ribbon Club, it must have been about this date. It also raises another question of where the hounds came from. Most probably Lord Grey's family would have kept some hounds at Uppark and they were moved to Charlton, perhaps supplemented by a draft brought by Roper from Kent. In those days, many people were breeding hounds of one sort or another, so more could have come from other hound owners in Sussex and elsewhere.

But to continue with our allegorical history. Not everyone was pleased about the goddess Diana's new hunting establishment at Charlton. An important objector was Venus, the goddess of love, who felt she had lost two of her men to the chase!

> *These two had both been Venus votaries,*
> *and still obey'd her soft enticing laws.*
> *When first the queen of love of this was told,*
> *she vow'd revenge and thus to Mars complain'd.*
> *'Shall thus my subjects be seduc'd away*
> *to hunt and sport Diana's foolish way?'*

Oh dear! How many other ladies have complained that their paramours are more interested in hunting than the lures of the fair sex! But 'Venus votaries' they undoubtedly were, as we shall hear. Monmouth had been married at 13 to Anna, Countess of Buccleuch, then only 12 herself. They exchanged respect rather than love and, although she bore him three children, Anna was too cold, strait-laced, too seriously intellectual to hold Monmouth's interest. At this time, Monmouth and his uncle, the Duke of York, together with Lord Mulgrave were all courting the same mistress, who managed for some weeks to hide the fact from each of them; this was the artful Moll Kirke, maid of honour to the Duchess of York. But she was only a passing fancy, and he soon took the lovely Eleanor Needham as his mistress. She bore him four children in less than four years, one of whom, Henrietta, became Duchess of Bolton and was a notable frequenter of Charlton years after Monmouth's death. But the love of his life was undoubtedly Henrietta Wentworth, the young mistress of the palace of Toddington in Bedfordshire, with whom he spent an idyllic five months in hiding before his flight to the continent in 1683. Branded as an outlaw after the death of his father and sought in Holland by numerous English agents of the new king James II, he found refuge with his mistress in the remote village of Gouda, near Rotterdam, where the plans of his ill-starred invasion were hatched.

Of Grey, a different story emerges. He had married in 1680 Mary, daughter of George, Earl of Berkeley, but this did not prevent him from seducing her 18-year-old younger sister Henrietta. The family were outraged and sued Grey in the High Court. Grey calmly stated that 'I married her elder sister and expected to find a maiden's head; but not finding it, I resolved to find one in the family if any be left!'.[9] At the trial he was found guilty 'of the most odious abuse of confidence, the meanest duplicity, the basest falsehood, the most ungenerous, the most ungrateful and most unfeeling selfishness', but while the judge was preparing to sentence, a Mr. Turner inexplicably appeared in the court room. Henrietta refused to go with her father as she claimed to be married to Mr. Turner (planted there by Grey) and was therefore under his protection.[10]

So Grey was released, but soon afterwards became implicated in the notorious Rye House Plot, a scheme to murder the king and the Duke of York at the Rye House on the way from Newmarket to London. It failed and, although Monmouth managed to avoid being directly implicated, he certainly knew of it. Grey was less fortunate and was arrested, brought before the council and committed to the Tower. Arriving there, the 'gates were shut so he stayed in the messenger's hands all night, whom he furnished so liberally with wine, that he was dead drunk'.[11] Next morning he escaped, leaving the drunken messenger fast asleep and rode to Uppark where he was united with Henrietta and sailed with her to exile in Holland to join Monmouth and begin to plan their fatal invasion of England.

> *But now alas! confusion seiz'd the land,*
> *and Mars with malice calls his sons to arms.*
> *First Monmouth's breast he with ambition fir'd*
> *to head his army; soon away he flew*
> *and took the then thought faithful Tankerville*
> *along with him, to share his fortunes all.*
> *But oh! how far unfit was Monmouth's skill*
> *to lead on British troops or seize the throne.*
> *He went, he came, he fought, betray'd, was ta'en;*
> *he lost his head and Cupid lost a dart.*

At the death of the king and the accession of James II in 1685, Monmouth landed at Lyme Regis on the Dorset coast and proclaimed himself king at Taunton on 20 June. However he was overtaken and defeated by Royalist forces at Sedgemoor on 6 July. He escaped but was captured in the early hours of 7 July by Lord Lumley, taken to London and beheaded on Tower Green on 15 July. Grey, who was in command of Monmouth's cavalry at Sedgemoor, was taken prisoner and condemned for high treason. However he had no scruples about disclosing the complicity and hiding-places of many of his fellow rebels and, helped by a bribe to the Treasury of £40,000, he obtained a pardon and by the autumn of the same year was back in royal favour. Later when William and Mary ascended the throne after the Glorious Revolution of 1688, Grey's political acumen was recognised and he was appointed First Lord of the Admiralty, created Earl of Tankerville and was later First Lord of the Treasury and Lord Privy Seal. He returned to his estates at Uppark and by 1690 was building the beautiful house which still stands today. It seems likely he would have continued to hunt at Charlton, but of that there is no evidence. He died in 1701, and by this time the hunt was in the capable hands of Mr. Roper.

How much time Monmouth and Grey actually spent at Charlton is not known but their last visit before going into exile would have been before the discovery of the Rye House Plot in 1683. The evidence that Monmouth liked his hunting at Charlton is contained in an old manuscript written in about 1810,[12] in which it states 'Harry Budd, who had been gamekeeper to the Dukes of Richmond, died at Charlton in the year 1806 aged about 94 having always lived there. He remembered many of the old Charlton hunt and said his grandfather had heard the Duke of Monmouth talk that if he got the crown he would keep his court at Charlton'.[13] Alas, that was not to be!

— III —

ROPER

Mr. Roper[14] was a Kentish gentleman of Wellhall, Eltham, an experienced hunting man in his middle thirties, whose connection with Sussex was through his wife, the second daughter of Mr. James Butler of Amberley, a member of parliament for Arundel. Our poet describes how Diana gave him free rein to organise the pack and notes that daily wants were not forgotten!

> *Ropero then she brought and gave to him*
> *the care and management of all her mente;[15]*
> *he deep in knowledge by experience taught,*
> *could talk upon her darling subject well.*
> *Pleas'd with the sage, she gave him ample power*
> *to cast, to cull, to breed, to do his best.*
> *With pleasure great, the goddess saw her court;*
> *each day gave joy, each day increas'd their sport.*
> *Bacchus and Ceres did their board supply;*
> *and Martha made their beds and made their pie.*

Unfortunately, Roper's tenure of office at Charlton was abruptly cut short by the Monmouth rebellion and in order to avoid the fearful retribution of Judge Jeffrey's Bloody Assize which followed, all of Monmouth's associates who were able to immediately fled abroad.

> *Guiltless Ropero too was forc'd to fly*
> *in those bad days when honesty was crime;*
> *enough for Jeffrys to pronounce his doom,*

Roper went to France to hunt with St Victor, a celebrated French huntsman, who kept a pack of hounds at Chantilly, returning after the accession of William and Mary in 1688, when he resumed the management of the hounds at Charlton.

> *To France then went the ablest huntsman here*
> *and made acquaintance with Saint Victor there,*
> *'till William came and settl'd peace at home.*
> *Diana calls, Ropero soon returns;*
> *his queen as soon declares him grosveneur.*

By all accounts Roper was an expert huntsman and showed excellent sport. He 'had the reputation of keeping the best pack of fox-hounds in the kingdom'.[16] The Charlton hounds became the most famous in England, attracting the nobility and gentry in increasing numbers to enjoy the sport of fox hunting. Among the earliest names mentioned was William Cavendish, Marquess of Hartington, 'great Devon's first born heir'.

He was a keen Charlton man and continued to support the hunt for many years. His daring exploit of riding down Levin Down, one of the steepest hills near Charlton, and leaping a five-barred gate at the bottom, was long remembered; jumping fences out hunting on the downs at that time was practically unknown.

> *A Pyrenean path is still there seen,*
> *where Devon's duke, full speed, did drive his well*
> *bred courser down, and flying leap't five bars;*
> *incredible the act! but still 'twas fact.*

Many others are mentioned as visiting Charlton in the early years of the 18th century. General Charles Compton, a younger son of the Earl of Northampton 'droll and good but not concise', Sir Robert Guldeford, one of Roper's Kentish friends, who was a 'papist … of Norman race', Andrew Charlton 'be his name rever'd' (for what reason, it does not reveal), could he be the author of the poem? The poet goes on to regret the passing of three young Charlton hunters who went to Spain and were punished by Diana for deserting her! A younger son of Lord Dormer 'not military then, but quitting her train, was kill'd in Spain'; 'Goring the young, the beauty of mankind, inglorious of a fever died in Spain' (probably a son of Sir William Goring of Burton); and worst of all, Roper's son was killed fighting at the battle of Almanza on 25 April 1707.

> *Young Ropero, brave and like his size*
> *tall, on Almanza's fatal plains did fall.*
> *These three unhappy youths thus taken off,*
> *the goddess thought was warning full enough*
> *to stop that crime desertion in the rest,*
> *and they all vow'd allegiance once again.*
> *But old Ropero most of all was hurt,*
> *the loss of such a son few fathers know.*
> *Diana, conscious of the old man's grief,*
> *resolv'd some reparation she would make;*
> *she soon found means and doubled his estate;*
> *he thankful bow'd, to her devoting all.*

It was during this period of popularity when

> *fame now had loudly sung of Charlton sports;*
> *from France Saint Victor came to see his friend;*
> *the great Tuscanian duke too had been there;*
> *William the third, the great, once saw a chace,*

5 Charles Seymour, 6th Duke of Somerset, 'The Proud Duke'.

that the famous quarrel erupted between Roper and the Duke of Somerset, who objected, perhaps with some justification, to the Charlton hounds hunting on his estate, presumably without permission.

Hence jealousy that gnawing fiend began
to rouse the spleen of a much prouder man;
the second duke of Britain and his name
was Seymour, Somerset his title was,
his castle Petworth, distant three small leagues.

Born in 1662 the sixth son of Lord Seymour of Trowbridge, Charles Seymour's succession to the dukedom of Somerset and his acquisition of the Percy estates, including the manor of Petworth, were the result of an extraordinary series of events. His grandfather was the younger brother of William, Duke of Somerset, a close confidante of Charles I, whose title went into abeyance during the commonwealth, but who was restored to his dignities by Charles II at the restoration, only to die a month later. After the early death of his next two successors, the title devolved on his cousin Francis, Charles' elder brother, whose own life was cut short at 20 by a Genoese nobleman, who shot him dead at the door of an inn. Apparently his wife had been insulted by the duke's companions.

Through his brother's misfortune, Charles succeeded to the dukedom in 1678 and it was then through his marriage to Elizabeth, sole heir of Joscelyn Percy, 11th and last Earl of Northumberland, that he came to acquire the manor of Petworth. This little red haired girl, whose father died when she was three years old, was born in 1667 and inherited estates which were truly vast. She was the last of the Percys. It was said that a journey could be made from Sussex to Northumberland without leaving Percy land.

Sacrificed to the ambition of her grandmother, the dowager Countess of Northumberland, the unhappy child was given in marriage three times in three years, all before her 16th birthday. Her first husband was Henry Cavendish, Earl of Ogle, of whom the bride's kinswoman Dorothy, Countess of Sutherland, wrote, 'My Lord Ogle does prove the saddest creature of all kinds that could have been found fit to be named for my Lady Percy; as ugly as anything young can be'.[17] Perhaps fortunately he died a few months later, but not long afterwards she was married again, this time certainly against her will.

Her new husband was Thomas Thynne of Longleat. Popular rumour was rife at the time. 'It is reported that Mr Thomas Thynne is privately married to the Countess of Ogle and that a Mr Brett at Richmond, who was instrumental in it, hath a reward of £10,000.'[18] Thynne sent for a parson to Longleat and the marriage took place in the presence of 'Mr Brett who gave her, the Lady K. Brett and her daughter the Lady Orory and two or three more'.[19] Thynne or 'Tom of the Ten Thousand' as he was called was a man of great wealth, but of bad character and an ally of the Duke of Monmouth. He was described in 1681 as 'a dissolute rake who was personally repulsive to Lady Ogle, then only fourteen'.[20] But by bribery and with the help of the child's grandmother, he managed to carry through the marriage rite.[21] Three months later, Elizabeth contrived to escape to Holland accompanied by Lady Temple and Henry Sidney. Hearing this, Thynne sent a challenge to Sidney, but later thought better of it.[22] However the greed which attracts suitors to a rich heiress soon caught up with Thynne, as he was murdered in Pall Mall a few months later at the instigation of his rival Count Konigsmarck, a Swedish nobleman, who was said to be Lady Elizabeth's lover. Although Konigsmarck was acquitted by the personal intervention of the king, his accomplices were hanged in Pall Mall at the scene of the crime.

Widowed twice by the age of 15, Lady Elizabeth was married thirdly to the Duke of Somerset in 1682. Mercifully this marriage seems to have been a happier one. At her coming of age in 1688, work was started on the complete remodelling of Petworth House, including the building of the magnificent west façade. Queen Anne appointed the duke Master of the Horse in 1702 and he is credited with having been the instigator of Ascot Races. Despite his rather tortuous inheritance of the premier protestant dukedom (the Norfolks being catholics) and the vast Percy estates, which included two quite unexpected murders, the Duke of Somerset, generally known as 'The Proud Duke', was 'a man in whom the pride of birth and rank amounted almost to a disease'.[23] He is said to have insisted on his children always standing in his presence, and to have cut the inheritance of one of his daughters when he fell asleep and woke to find her seated.

Little wonder then that he objected to Roper and his Charlton hounds hunting near his house. The duke protested to Sir William Goring who lived nearby at Burton.

> 'Sir William, who's this man that daily boldly dares thus in my sight to scour along those azure hills we see, nay even up to Petworth walls he comes?'
> 'My Lord, Diana's hounds they are; I know Ropero, good old man, her grosveneur.'
> 'Diana's grosveneur! that place I'll have.'
> 'My Lord, a temple she at Charlton has, at Compton too another still she has, at Findon likewise does a temple stand.'

With ire stamm'ring, his slaves he loudly call'd. 'I'll have hounds, I'll have horses, see't be done. Sir Knight, Diana's huntsman we will be. What land pray has Ropero here, good Sir? Where do his manors lie? What right has he?'
'My Lord, I'm told his land in Kent does lie; his right I doubt the goddess will maintain.'
'Nor gods nor goddesses I heed, but straight a temple I will raise with speed. Diana then may like it if she please.'
He gave the word, 'twas done, he call'd it Twines,[24] a pretty spot and just upon the downs.

The duke set about establishing his hunt and attempted to lure the gentlemen of Charlton away by offering them sumptuous hospitality.

>*In stalls magnificent his coursers lay,*
>*in spacious kennels all his hounds did play;*
>*thrice times a week he sent his cooks o'er night*
>*and made a feast the goddess to appease.*
>*For she to see his pride was angry grown*
>*and bid her old Ropero keep his ground.*

But war had been declared and the packs began to interfere with each other in the field.

>*A civil war of course was now began;*
>*she [Diana] knew her power and stood by her old man.*
>*In Andrew's form[25] was spy, to tell*
>*e'er dawn of day appear'd, which way he went;*
>*then after them under the wind he drew*
>*and often took their fox and swore 'twas his;*
>*had found in such a wood and ran two hours.*

Eventually Sir William Goring, acting as mediator, managed to settle the quarrel.

>*This discord lasted for some months or more,*
>*till one day, when the knight, the duke not out,*
>*in friendly manner to Ropero spoke:*
>*'Brother, I think we spoil each other's sport.'*
>*'I think so too, but who is most to blame.'*
>*Strong were the arguments on both sides held,*
>*the two old champions, both were loath to yield.*
>*At last preliminaries strong were drawn,*
>*all war and future discord should desist.*

But it was too much for the proud duke to swallow and, accepting defeat with an ill grace, he abandoned his hounds and new kennels, and gave up.

>*But soon the haughty sovereign's pride rebell'd;*
>*he gave away his hounds and left the field.*
>*Now peace return'd, Sir William joins the court,*

all lucky days now bless their rural sport.
Neglected stands the stately temple Twine,
a nest for vermin or a sty for swine.

Although the hounds spent most of the season at Charlton, it was often necessary to take them further afield to coverts which were too far to hack there and back in a day. For this reason, as mentioned above, Roper used kennels at Findon, near Worthing to the east and at Uppark, near Compton in the west, moving the whole establishment for a week or more at a time, so that they could have several days sport in different surroundings. The kennels at Uppark were those which formerly belonged to the previous proprietor Lord Grey, who, as Earl of Tankerville, had died in 1701. The house and estate had passed to Mary, his daughter and heir who was married to Lord Ossulstone, later also created Earl of Tankerville. Of their son, the second earl, we shall hear more in the next chapter.

The remoteness of Charlton and the slow means of travel of those times meant that members of the hunt would have to stay in Charlton for several days or more. Many built their own hunting boxes to avoid having to find lodgings, but the most pressing requirement was a place to meet for dinner in the evening. In about 1720, the Duke of Grafton and Lord Burlington suggested they should raise a subscription to build a banqueting room. Lord Burlington offered to design it.

Till now in homely manner they had liv'd,
a small dark cell and one poor light had serv'd
to tell the chase and sing the goddess praise,
till Grafton's duke and Burlington came down
to see their sport, so far beyond their own;
then Boyle, by instinct all divine, began:
'Is this an edifice for such a band?
I'll have the honour to erect a room,
shall cost Diana's train but such a sum.'
They all agreed and quickly paid it down,
and now there stands a sacred dome, confes't
the finest in the country, most admir'd.

Richard Boyle, Earl of Burlington, became well known as an amateur architect, a great collector of pictures and as the patron of Gay and Pope, and of Kent the architect. The portico at Burlington House, Piccadilly is not his design, he being only 23 in 1718 when it was erected, but the building at Charlton may well have been one of his earliest works. It was finished around 1722 and was called The Great Room. Our poet referred to it as the Dome and it was popularly known as Fox Hall.

From the evidence available the list of people who subscribed in 1720 would have looked like this. The names are given as they were styled at the time and are taken from the list drawn up in 1738 and recorded in the minutes.

Duke of Grafton (2nd)
Duke of Newcastle (1st)
Marquess of Winchester (3rd Duke of Bolton)

6 Richard Boyle, 3rd Earl of Burlington, the famous architect, who designed the Great Room at Charlton, later known as Fox Hall.

7 General Sir Charles Wills, a subscriber to the Great Room.

> Marquess of Hartington (3rd Duke of Devonshire)
> Earl of Burlington (3rd)
> Earl of Carlisle (3rd)
> Earl of Godolphin (2nd)
> Earl of Halifax (1st)
> Earl of Lichfield (2nd)
> Viscount Lonsdale (3rd)
> Count Maurice of Nassau
> Hon Charles Compton
> Hon Anthony Lowther
> Hon Henry Pelham
> Hon John West
> Sir William Gage
> Sir Phillip Honywood
> Sir Charles Wills
> Charles Churchill
> Thomas Coke
> Robert Colvile

There were certainly other subscribers who were not in the list because they were dead in 1738 by the time it was drawn up. Their names can only be a matter of conjecture. However,

8   Charles Lennox, son of Charles II and Louise de Keroualle, Duchess of Portsmouth, was created Duke of Richmond at the age of three and was Master of the Horse when he was nine!

9   George Brudenell, 3rd Earl of Cardigan, a likely subscriber to the Great Room at Charlton. He was Master of the Royal Buckhounds and became an important avuncular figure to the Earl of March, later 2nd Duke of Richmond.

circumstantial evidence suggests that the following had sufficient contact with Charlton, as will be apparent, to make it likely that they were also subscribers:

>   Duke of Bolton (2nd)
>   Duke of Richmond (1st)
>   Earl of Berkeley (3rd)
>   Earl of Cardigan (3rd)
>   Lord Brooke (7th)
>   Lord Forrester (5th)
>   Lord William Beauclerk

Charles Fitzroy, Duke of Grafton, was a passionate fox hunter, whose devotion to Charlton lasted to the end of his long life. His father the first duke, a natural son of Charles II by Barbara, Duchess of Cleveland, had been killed at the siege of Cork in 1690. In 1722 he founded a pack of his own hounds at Euston in Suffolk and hunted much of East Anglia, which he shared with Sir Robert Walpole; he also had kennels at Croydon, whence he would take the hounds to hunt in Surrey, Sussex and Kent.

The Earl of Lichfield was another descendant of Charles II. He was son and heir of Sir Edward Lee, created Earl of Lichfield in anticipation of his marriage to Lady Charlotte Fitzroy (then aged 10), daughter of the king by Barbara, Duchess of Cleveland. The earldom of Lichfield had formerly been held by Charles Stuart, 11th Seigneur of Aubigny, who succeeded as Duke

10   George Henry Lee, 2nd Earl of Lichfield, a subscriber to the Great Room, was a grandson of Charles II and Barbara, Duchess of Cleveland.

11   Anne, Duchess of Richmond, wife of the 1st Duke.

of Richmond and Lennox in 1660. After his death in 1672, these dukedoms were conferred on the three-year-old son of the king and the French beauty Louise de Keroualle, who was later made 12th Seigneur of Aubigny by Louis XIV. She must have been a very insistent woman as at the age of nine the young Duke of Richmond was appointed Master of the Horse! But he was a ne'er-do-well and a turn-coat both in religion and politics. 'Good looking if good for nothing else,' it was later said. He was so devoted to Charlton and hunting that he acquired a house at Goodwood in 1697 so that he could be within easy reach of the village. One of his saddler's bills from 1705 survives, and included in the 43 items is 'a Larg Tand hoggs Leather hunting sadle & flapps stiched with gould with sterrips and Leathers & guirths' for '£01 10s 00d'![26] That seems quite a bargain these days!

His duchess was Anne, the widow of Lord Belasyse, whom he married in 1692. On a hunting day, he would ride from Goodwood over the hill to the meet at Charlton with his wife's brother George Brudenell, Earl of Cardigan, who was a frequent visitor. Their father Francis, Lord Brudenell was a Jacobite and had spent four years in the Tower for high treason. George Brudenell was in Rome with his younger brother James when his grandfather died and he inherited the title. As well as acquiring an appreciation of art and architecture the two boys were enjoying a life of dissipation and only returned to England very reluctantly nearly three years later, bringing with them George's old and very ugly Italian mistress, a woman of the worst repute.[27] A year later he married and became a reformed character and was appointed Master of the Royal Buckhounds to Queen Anne and George I. He became an important avuncular figure to the Richmond children, Lady Anne, Lady Louisa and Charles, Earl of

12 James, 3rd Earl of Berkeley, whose aunt Lady Henrietta, sister of Lady Grey, had been so shamefully seduced by Lord Grey in the early days of Charlton. He would very likely have been a subscriber to the Great Room.

13 Louisa, Countess of Berkeley, elder daughter of Charles, 1st Duke of Richmond. She died of smallpox aged twenty-three.

March. Lady Louisa married James, Earl of Berkeley, in 1710, but sadly, she survived but six years and died of smallpox at the tender age of twenty-three. Lady Anne became Countess of Albemarle and had 15 children, her husband William Keppel being the son of the first Earl, a Dutchman who came over as page boy to King William in 1688.

Their son Charles, Earl of March, was born in 1701. He was by all accounts a precocious boy and from the earliest age mad keen on riding and hunting, which was greatly encouraged by his father and uncle Cardigan, but caused his mother much concern. At the age of 12, he had a serious riding accident, one which caused even greater concern to his mother because it followed close upon a riding mishap which befell his father. His mother revealed her anxieties in a letter to her mother-in-law, Louise, Duchess of Portsmouth, whom her husband was visiting at Aubigny at the time.

Goodwood, Friday 24th July 1713

After the Duke of Richmond has given you an account of the danger Lord March has lately escaped, your grace will easily forgive my begging the continuance of your usual compassion towards me in joining with me to prevail with Lord Duke to promise his son shall not this year or two venture any more riding what you sportsmen call fine hunters; for indeed Madam, as he is very young, weak and extremely rattle-headed, his life upon those horses will be in the greatest of danger; and since he has so lately escaped with life and limbs, through God's great mercy, 'twould be presumption to run him in the like danger again. Hunting being a qualification not necessary to make a fine gentleman, I think a fond mother may reasonably ask this favour,

14 Lady Anne Lennox, younger daughter of the Duke of Richmond, who married William, 2nd Earl of Albemarle.

15 Charles Lennox, Earl of March who succeeded as 2nd Duke of Richmond in 1723.

especially for an only son, which your grace by experience knows to be a dear creature. Besides the danger of it when a youth gives himself up to these kind of sports, it certainly makes them neglect their books and learning, which is of much greater use and consequence than any diversions can prove. All these considerations (with that of his being an only heir to so great titles and estate) will I hope prevail with your grace to interest yourself in this affair, and if your grace can get Lord Duke's firm promise, 'twill allay a thousand dreadful fears attends me constantly. I know Lord Duke's having been a very young horseman himself makes him incline to humour his son in trying to be the same, but Lord March's being one of the tallest youths that ever was seen of his age, makes him most excessively weak in his limbs, a fault I hope will mend when he has done growing and begun to spread. I had hardly overcome my fears for Lord Duke before this terrible surprise came upon me, but since God has so miraculously preserved to me the life of father and son, I shou'd be very ungratefully wicked did I not endeavour being easy …[28]

The old Duchess of Portsmouth retained her beauty into ripe old age, although she was always in financial difficulties. Neither William III nor Queen Anne would allow her to visit England, and it was not until 1716 that George I repealed the decree and she was allowed to visit to claim her arrears of pension. Being received at court, she still enchanted and delighted everyone by her liveliness and brilliance, although then 67 years old. The story is told that Catherine Sedley, Countess of Dorchester, for many years mistress to James II, was well known not only for her 'want of beauty, but also her hereditary gift of wit which shocked by its indelicacy'. Meeting in a drawing room of George I with the Countess of Orkney (formerly

16 Louise de Keroualle, Duchess of Portsmouth, was Charles II's last and favourite mistress, and mother of Charles Lennox, 1st Duke of Richmond.

mistress to William III) on the occasion of the duchess' visit, she remarked, 'Who would have thought that we three whores should have met here!' The mistresses of three English kings being present together in the rooms of a fourth was certainly a strange coincidence.[29]

However much his mother and grandmother concerned themselves about the young Earl of March's safety, it had little influence on his enthusiasm for horses and hunting. The romantic story of his marriage to Lady Sarah Cadogan, then only 13, has been told many times; how at the Hague on the eve of his departure for the grand tour with his tutor, Tom Hill, the marriage took place to settle a gambling debt between their fathers; and how, nearly three years later in the theatre at the Hague, enquired who was the beauteous young lady sitting opposite, with whom he promptly fell over head and ears in love, he was told she was the reigning toast, the beautiful Lady March! Returning to England with his new wife, he soon settled in to the delights of the chase at Charlton and by this time, the Great Room, to which his father had contributed, was finished.

Harry Budd, kennelman and gamekeeper, who died in 1806 aged 94 testified that he remembered 'when Fox Hall was first built and the Duke and Duchess of Richmond with Lord March, Lady Anne Lennox (later Countess of Albemarle) and Miss Macartney coming to Charlton and having assemblies there'.[30] In fact our poet tells us that the goddess Diana did relax the rules about ladies when the Great Room had been built, and allowed the Duchess of

17 Sarah, Duchess of Richmond with her husband, the 2nd Duke. Their romantic betrothal led to a blissful marriage and 12 children, of whom seven survived infancy.

Bolton and Lady Forrester to join the party, the duchess having made them a present of a weather vane.

> The goddess, thus ador'd, in high delight
> to show her sporting youths her full content,
> abates the rigour of some pristine laws,
> allows chast nymphs sometimes to join her swains.
> Boltona first, where all the Graces shin'd;
> she two wax tapers offer'd at the Dome;
> an altar piece besides she did present
> to shew the winds from ev'ry dif'rent point.
> With her Foresta came, a buxom dame,
> but long alas! were not allow'd to stay.

Of course, they were not allowed to stay long as the gentlemen had to pass the port!

> And Bacchus too, the jolly god of wine,
> had leave sometimes, but never to excess;
> tho' now and then, after a glorious chace,
> the merry god would slyly push the glass;
> the goddess wink'd at that, since she was sure
> that Venus never durst to venture there.

I doubt if Venus could be trusted that much, but there is no doubt that the Great Room often rang out with hunting songs after dinner. Three of them, written by John Budd of Charlton, were known as the Sussex Garland.[31] This one recalls the time when Roper's old hounds Emperor and Fleury were in the pack.

>There were three jolly huntsmen
>   And they would [hunt] a fox,
>And went to find old Reynolds
>   Amongst the woods and rocks.
>With a hoop, hoop, halloa, hark on brave boys,
><u>Hark away!</u> the huntsman cried.
>With a twink, twink, twink and a twivee, twivee twink
>As we from the kennel did ride, boys,
>   As we from the kennel did ride.
>
>We threw into the covert
>   To see what we could find,
>And soon we spied old Reynolds
>   Tripping it down the wind.
>With a hoop, hoop halloa, hark on brave boys,
><u>Tally-ho!</u> the huntsman cried.
>With a twink &c
>And down the wind we did ride, boys &c
>
>The huntsman cried <u>Away, hark, away!</u>
>   The hounds together stuck,
>And bravely they pursued him
>   And crossed o'er the brook.
>With a hoop, hoop, halloa, hark on brave boys,
><u>Hark forward!</u> the huntsman cried.
>With a twink &c
>And o'er the brook we did ride, boys &c
>
>We being brisk and airy
>   Did gallop o'er the plain,
>Whilst Emperor and Fleury
>   The chase they did maintain.
>With a hoop, hoop, halloa, hark on brave boys,
><u>Aye, that's good!</u> the huntsman cried.
>With a twink &c
>And o'er the plain we did ride.
>
>At length we saw an old shepherd
>   As we were ganging along,
>And there we spied old Reynolds
>   The ewes and lambs among.

13 Henrietta, Duchess of Bolton, daughter of the Duke of Monmouth by Eleanor Needham. She was a regular frequenter of Charlton.

> With a hoop, hoop, halloa, hark on brave boys,
> <u>Whooo!</u> the huntsman cried.
> With a twink &c
> And o'er the plain we did ride.
>
> Poor Reynolds being weary
>   Could neither go nor stand,
> And now he must surrender
>   And be at our command.
> With a hoop, hoop, halloa, hark on brave boys,
> <u>Whoo whoop!</u> the huntsman cried.
> With a twink &c
> And so poor old Reynold died, boys,
>   And so poor old Reynold died.

Henrietta, Duchess of Bolton, daughter of the Duke of Monmouth by his mistress Eleanor Needham, was the duke's third wife. She had a special affinity for Charlton and their son Lord Nassau Powlett was successfully recruited to the hunting field by Mr. Roper himself.

> *And now the silvan queen began to think*
> *recruits would soon be wanting to her train.*
> *Young novices she brought inclin'd to sport*
> *and plac'd them all under Ropero's care*
> *to be initiate in her rural rights*
> *and learn of him the practice of the field.*
> *The downy Nassau first she brought, a youth*
> *well made and fair Boltona's chiefest care;*

19 Charles Howard, 3rd Earl of Carlisle. A subscriber to the Great Room at Charlton, he was the builder of Castle Howard in Yorkshire.

Another great architect and builder who frequented Charlton was Charles Howard, Earl of Carlisle. He bred a pack of exceptionally large hounds which he hunted in the wolds of Yorkshire from kennels at Londesborough.[32] He was constable of Windsor Castle until 1730, when the king wished to appoint the Duke of St Albans, but there was difficulty in finding another office of profit for the earl. The Mastership of the Harriers was then vacant, but the earl wished the style to be that of 'Foxhounds.' The post was on offer 'with a salary of £2,000 for yourself, deputy and all the charges attending the same', but the earl declined to accept 'Foxhounds' to be merely added to 'Harriers', so he stayed in Yorkshire and there never was a pack of Royal Foxhounds.[33] He is best remembered as the builder of the famous house at Hinderskelf, now known as Castle Howard, which was the first commission for the famous architect John Vanbrugh. On the strength of his success at Castle Howard, Vanbrugh was later chosen to design Blenheim Palace for the Duke of Marlborough.

Then there was young Lord Pelham, of Claremont, East Sussex, a nephew of the late Duke of Newcastle, whose coming of age party in July 1714, to which many of his Charlton friends would have been invited, sounds a sumptuous affair.

> On Wednesday last came of age the Lord Pelham, and at his seat in Sussex he made them a noble entertainment, when were dressed seven oxen, fifteen sheep, six calves, eight bucks, and so proportionable of fowls &c. There were eighty stands of sweetmeats on the first table and so proportionable on the rest, forty nine hogsheads of strong beer, seven hogsheads of claret, besides champagne, burgundy &c and four hogsheads of bunch [sic] &c the aforesaid feast cost two thousand pounds.[34]

Being a promising young Whig politician in the Lords and a zealous supporter of the Hanoverian succession, which had recently occurred, he was created Earl of Clare in October

20   Lord William Beauclerk, sixth of the nine sons of Charles, 1st Duke of St Albans and grandson of Charles II and Nell Gwynn, was likely to have been a subscriber to the Great Room.

21   Henry Lowther, 3rd Viscount Lonsdale, a subscriber to the Great Room, was appointed Lord Privy Seal in 1733.

and advanced to Duke of Newcastle the following year. He was subsequently Secretary of State for many years while his brother Henry Pelham, also a Charlton man, was First Lord of the Treasury.

Thomas Coke was from an old Norfolk family, who 'wanted to make out all manner of tales about their origin, but who really owe their surname to some excellent ancient caterer whose merits earned him the distinction of the Cook'.[35] In 1718, he married Margaret, a daughter of the Earl of Thanet, who 'is a very agreeable and good lady who brought him £80,000. He was near undone in the South Sea year by that vile scheme, but having recovered his affairs, she has never so much as received of him her pin money. Moreover half a year after her marriage he resumed his debaucheries and continues them with several ladies of quality and fashion.'[36] O dear! Returning from the grand tour in 1732, replete with a vast cache of antiquities and treasures, he conceived and built the magnificent house at Holkham in Norfolk to house his collection. A member for Norfolk for many years, he was created Lord Lovel in 1728 and was later Earl of Leicester.

Viscount Lonsdale and his brother Hon Anthony Lowther were also subscribers. They were zealous Whigs and managed to raise from their native Yorkshire no less than 10,000 men when the Jacobite uprising threatened in 1715.[37] Lord Lonsdale was later Constable of the Tower and in 1733 in the cabinet as Lord Privy Seal.

Lord Brooke, of Warwick Castle, ancestor of the Earls of Warwick, bred hounds in Warwickshire and is likely to have been at Charlton around the time the Great Room was being

22 Lord Brooke of Warwick Castle, ancestor of the Earls of Warwick, who was likely to have been a subscriber to the building of the Great Room.

built. His stallion hound Cocker was warded with Doxy'21 in 1722 and they produced a litter of eight, all of whom were entered in 1724. He died in 1727, so his name did not appear on the definitive list of subscribers drawn up in 1737, as it included only those who were still living. Like several others, therefore, his inclusion as a subscriber is based on circumstantial evidence only.

Roper was now getting very old and, by the time the Great Room was completed, he was over eighty. He would sit at the head of the table in his own special chair, afterwards always known as 'Roper's chair'.[38] Apparently he was getting rather dictatorial to the younger members of the field, judging by a comment from the Duchess of Richmond to the Earl of March, who was still on the Grand Tour.

Goodwood, Wednesday 29th November 1721

… Lord Burford and Lord William with the Marquess of Winchester are in these parts to fox hunt with Mr Roper, but by what I see, Lord Burford does not much approve Mr Roper's laws …[39]

The Earl of Burford and Lord William Beauclerk were brothers, two of the nine sons of Charles, Duke of St Albans, a natural son of Charles II by Nell Gwynn. Two other brothers, Lord George and Lord Henry, were also keen Charlton foxhunters.

Perhaps wisely and maybe realising he was not going to last for ever, Roper decided to take on a joint master for the season 1721/2 to share the burden of running the hunt, although he was still hunting the hounds himself. The person he chose was Charles Powlett, Marquess of Winchester, heir to the Duke of Bolton.

— IV —

BOLTON

When now another noble duke appears,
graceful his air and blooming were his years.
He long a faithful votary had been
and paid due homage to the huntress queen;
but now he begs admittance in her band.[40]

The Powletts, Marquesses of Winchester, were a Hampshire family, whose seat was at Chawton. The first Duke of Bolton, who built Hackwood Park, was known as The Loyal Marquess from his staunch support of William and Mary's accession and his rejection of James II's pretensions to the throne. His grandson Charles, who succeeded as third duke, was born in 1685 to his father's second wife Frances, who came from a Yorkshire family.

His marriage in 1713 to Lady Anne Vaughan, an exceedingly rich heiress, had caused quite a stir. 'There is such a running after my Lord Carbery's rich daughter as you never saw. My Lord Lumley makes the greatest bustle … My Lord Winchester and Lord Hertford[41] are also in pursuit.'[42] A few weeks later, 'My Lord Winchester is to be the happy man that marries my Lady Anne Vaughan. They say it is concluded.'[43]

Unfortunately they separated soon after the marriage and 'my lord made her an early confession of his aversion'.[44] 'Educated in solitude with some choice books by a saint-like governess, crammed with virtue and good qualities, she thought it impossible not to find gratitude, though she failed to give passion and upon this threw away her estate, was despised by her husband and laughed at by the public.'[45]

He was well known as one of the gallants of the period, but had a poor write up in the gossip columns of the day.

Now Bolton comes with beat of drums
Tho' fighting be his loathing
He much dislikes both pikes and guns
But relishes the clothing![46]

'Being as proud as if he had been of any consequence,' wrote Horace Walpole, bitingly sarcastic as always, 'besides what his employments made him; as vain as if he had some merit and as necessitous as if he had no estate; so he was troublesome at court, hated in the country and scandalous in his regiment.'[47] Walpole may have been exaggerating, but no doubt the duke found the wealth he acquired from his estranged wife useful to pay for his new hunting establishment.

23 Charles, 3rd Duke of Bolton, a subscriber to the Great Room and proprietor of the hounds at Charlton from 1721 to 1728. By marrying Lady Anne Vaughan he acquired a large fortune, but his true love was the actress, Lavinia Fenton, the star of *The Beggar's Opera.*.

24 Anne, Duchess of Bolton, a rich heiress from whom the duke separated shortly after marriage.

The first hound list which is extant dates from this time. There were definitely earlier lists, probably going back to the Duke of Monmouth, but tantalisingly they are (so far) missing. In the fly leaf of the *Pedigree of Charlton Hounds*, now in the library at Goodwood, there is written the following:

> This book containing the pedigree of the hounds kept at Charlton in Sussex begins with the year 1721; the books of the preceeding years, having been transmitted to John Anstis Esq, Garter Principal King at Arms, are laid up in the Earl Marshal's office, where any person may have the perusing of them gratis.[48]

Earl Bathurst, lent the book in 1932 by the Duke of Richmond for his studies of the Charlton and Raby hounds,[49] had the Heralds' College searched and enquiries made at the British Museum. The author, who is also grateful to the present duke for the loan of the book, has recently made a similar effort to find them, but regrettably to no avail. The archivist at the College of Arms wrote, 'I have concluded that Garter Anstis never did lay them up in the Earl Marshal's office. They presumably passed instead with his private papers. These are now widely dispersed. It is possible that the pedigree books have survived somewhere, but who is to say where?' Perhaps they will turn up one day.

The first entry is dated 25 November 1721 and lists 15 couple of old hounds in the joint ownership of Mr. Roper and the Duke of Bolton.[50] On this date, the new master's father was still alive, although he died shortly after, on 21 January 1722. Some historians have assumed from this that the 2nd Duke of Bolton was a joint proprietor with Roper, especially as his wife Henrietta had old links with Charlton through her father, the Duke of Monmouth. There is no

A List of Old Hounds 25 Nov.r 1721
Mr Roper & the Duke of Bolton

Betty
Bell
Blewcap
Blewmaid
Curious
Diamond
Dolly
Dolly lame
Doxy
Famous
Fairmaid
Fortune
Folly
Fleury
Jolley
Lovely
Madam
Merrylass
Nancy
Phillis
Pleasant
PROMISE & Ropers. Doxie.
Sr Wm Gorings. Emperor.
Ransom from Lord Carlisle

Rowsey Ld Carlisle
Rockwood
Ruby
Spanker
Stately
Sweetlips
Virgin

other evidence that the second duke was ever master, although that does not exclude the possibility. The slight discrepancy of the list naming the hounds as belonging to Mr. Roper and the Duke of Bolton before the second duke's death could simply be due to the list having been written a few weeks afterwards.

The following season there was a young entry of 12½ couple, including a hound from Mr. Draper of Beswick in Yorkshire, who was a master of hounds from 1726 to 1746. He was not wealthy, but was nicknamed the King's huntsman of East Riding. He is said to have kept his horses, hounds and 14 children on £700 a year! He seems to have taken up foxhunting as a necessity, as good husbandry was his passion and foxes were killing his lambs. One of his daughters was whipper-in and a leathern girdle round his drab coat and a rusty velvet cap were his 'royal' insignia of office.[51]

Numbers were further increased in 1723 by 15 couple bred by the Duke of Bolton, including a litter sired by Mr. Orlebar's Shifter out of Mr. Roper's Promise.[52] Mr. Richard Orlebar of Hinwick Hall established a pack of fox hounds in 1702, giving up in 1727.[53] His hound list is of great interest, being the oldest in existence, starting with three litters of whelps bred in 1708.[54] In September 1722 he gave 15 couple, including Shifter and his sire Tipler, to the Duke of Grafton and later gave another 5½ couple to the Earl of Halifax.

It appears that many working hounds were a first cross between the old Talbot southern bloodhound, originally used in Elizabethan times as a tufter, and the small northern Ribblesdale beagle bred by Sir Thomas Cockaine in the 16th century, the former contributing nose, cry and substance and the latter drive. There is no evidence that these crossbreds were successfully bred from. Well into the 18th century there is an evident distinction between the 21-inch fox beagles, which some masters entered to fox and the larger slower hounds preferred by others. But changes were happening and owners of kennels were responding to the requirements of fox hunting. The small northern hound did not answer without an outcross; it may have been short of cry, it may have been wild, it may have lacked substance and stamina. It may even have gone too fast. The old southern hound was incapable of catching a fox above ground. The solution of a first-cross working hound was both inconvenient and unreliable. Mr. Roper and Mr. Orlebar, Mr. Thomas Noel of the Cottesmore, Mr. Thomas Bright in Yorkshire, Lord Walpole and Mr. Thomas Coke in Norfolk and others therefore developed a crossbred from which they bred.[55] Our poet describes the proper conformation of such a hound:

> *Of middle size, with nostrils wide and red,*
> *the muzzle small and lean, the head and jaw*
> *with open throat, no vives [swellings] along the chawle [jowl],*
> *their crests and shoulders thin, their withers sharp,*
> *too far they can't run backward to the chine [spine],*
> *nor can the fillets [loins] be too broad and round.*
> *An oval even croup [rump], the tail set high,*
> *large ribb'd, close flank'd and cushion'd well behind,*
> *his brisket [chest] deep, his sides both long and full,*
> *his joints well knit, his legs both flat and short,*
> *his feet both hard and round, and rather small*
> *than large, for those no speed can ever show.*

25 *(facing page)* A List of Old Hounds 25 Novʳ 1721. Mr. Roper and the Duke of Bolton.

26 Mr. Roper in his latter years. He is here referred to as Charles, but is clearly the same person pictured on p.10.

Roper seemed to approve of the new acquisitions brought by the Duke of Bolton and by keeping the best in the kennel and strategic placing of his whippers-in, the sport improved.

Fresh troops he brings, all under his command.
Ropero paus'd but liked the kind of hound;
which told, he soon the goddess willing found,
and now they cull the pack, the choicest keep;
they found no fox that ever did escape,
for now against poor Ren, the odds were vast;
at every check two packs there was to cast;
John Gough up wind did always choose to go,
but Harry Barratt down he best did know.

On the following page of the hound book, there is a simple record of Roper's death: 'Mem^m: On the 26 Feb^y: 1722/3 being Shrove Tuesday Mr Roper died at Monckton Furzes'.[56] Our poet described the scene thus.

But lo! the fatal catastrophe draws near;
Ropero quite worn out with years, tho' full
in health, yet all his strength and vigour gone;
at Findon he and Herbert sportsman true

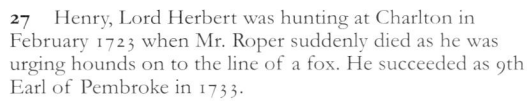

27 Henry, Lord Herbert was hunting at Charlton in February 1723 when Mr. Roper suddenly died as he was urging hounds on to the line of a fox. He succeeded as 9th Earl of Pembroke in 1733.

28 James Graham, 1st Duke of Montrose hunted at Charlton in Roper's time.

> *and Andrew his most faithful friend, went out*
> *to Monkton furzes, fatal was the day!*
> *A fox just found 'Get on!' he cries, and then*
> *that instant fell and life that instant fled;*
> *and thus Ropero died at eighty four*
> *a quick and sudden death and in the field.*
> *Could Julius Caesar e'er have wish'd for more?*

For some reason our poet has made an error, as Monkton Furzes is not at Findon but on the downs above Treyford, as can be conclusively shown by reference to the hunting diaries later kept by the Duke of Richmond. This error has been repeated many times by later historians, who simply copy without referring to the original source! Herbert refers to Lord Herbert, heir to the Earl of Pembroke, and Andrew was one of Roper's long serving whippers-in.

> *Bolton's great duke now him succeeds in all*
> *the whole command of hounds as grosveneur;*

The Duke of Bolton was now sole proprietor, but the position of huntsman needed to be filled with some urgency. In the absence of any other evidence, it can only be assumed that the person appointed was John Ware, who held the post for 11 seasons. Despite Roper's death, Charlton's popularity continued unabated. The Duke of Montrose, Lord and Lady Forrester

29 Lord Forrester, the fifth baron, was an early visitor at Charlton and probably subscribed to the building of the Great Room.

30 Lady Forrester is mentioned as having been allowed to attend the Great Room at Charlton soon after it was completed.

and Generals Honywood and Kirke joined in the sport; Ralph Jenison, knight of the shire for Northumberland, came from the north and 'the stripling' referred to was probably Richard Honywood.

The train increases and the sport goes on;
pleasing were all the Delian virgin's rules
and happy was great George's gentle reign.
And now, Diana's leave first ask't, there came
from different parts, sportsmen of different names.
From Adrian's wall, two northern peers there were;
Montrose the duke and Forester the lord,
with Honywood the gay and Kirk the grave,
a stripling too, who to the first was kin;
sedate he was and sly and hunting lov'd.
The gentle soft and meagre Jenison
from Humber's bank on little Toby came.

People even started coming from far away places and the local cuisine was not without its attractions.

As visitors came full many a one
of Germans, French and Irish one to see
the Sussex sport or taste a Charlton pie.

31 General Sir Phillip Honywood who was a subscriber to the building of the Great Room at Charlton.

In 1723 the Duke of Richmond died and left his son not only titles and estates, but also debts. The young duke had not forgotten that his marriage with Sarah had been arranged to settle a gambling debt, and he was fortunate in having two very sensible uncles, who came to his rescue in the manner that this letter from Uncle Cardigan explains:

Friday 10th January 1724

I am extremely concerned to find by your uncle Brudenell [his mother's other brother] that you have run very much into debt since the death of the late lord duke. I beg leave to make this proposal to your grace, which I find by your uncle Brudenell will be agreeable to you, that is to borrow ten thousand pounds at Lady Day next, your grace appointing two trustees for the discharging of such debts as shall be specified, and for you to assign over £2,500 a year for five years, which will pay off both interest and principal ...[57]

Uncle Cardigan continued to take an interest in his nephew's finances but was also concerned to see the young duke properly mounted for hunting and found a way of helping by offering to repay him for some books in the shape of a horse.

Deene, Saturday 8th February 1724

I am heartily concerned that your debt is so great, but since you are resolved to take it up, I dare say you will soon find the sweets of it; I must beg the favour of your grace to send me a particular of your whole debt and the nature of it and I hope I shall be able to propose something to you that may be of service, in case we should be disappointed in the raising of £10,000, but I do not even despair of getting that sum. I think the allowance you propose for keeping your house &c to be very high; with good economy I am sure it would come to a great deal less. I am glad your grace proposes lessening the number of your servants, they are generally the plague of mankind. If you approve of my looking out for the £10,000, I will do it as soon as I receive your commands.

As I am indebted to you for a parcel of books, I have but one way of paying your grace for them, since you will take no money of me. I have a very fine grey gelding just broke, fit to carry your weight. I should be glad that you would accept of him. If you have a groom that can be trusted in the travelling of him, I wish you would send him down here for the gelding. He must be purged and used to the bit before he will be fit for use, but in my opinion he is a very likely gelding and the sooner you send for him the better.[58]

Ever since his return from the grand tour, the young Duke of Richmond had been a keen supporter of the hunt. He was well acquainted with the Duke of Bolton, since they were both colonels in the Royal Horse Guards, 'The Blues'. Lord Cadogan, Richmond's father-in-law, who was commander-in-chief of the forces, wrote to excuse him from being present at a regimental review, as the duchess was with child.

Causham, Thursday 20th August 1724
I received yesterday the honour of your grace's of the 18th. I design to review your regiment the first of next month and to go the day before to Hackwood. I write tomorrow to the Duke of Bolton who is now at Burly in the Forest to acquaint him of it. If anything should happen to delay the review I shall take care to let your grace know it in time … I am rejoiced to find that the duchess continues in good health; my blessing to her and a thousand assurances of my tenderest friendship. I am sorry the review falls out so near the time she expects to lie in, but your grace is not absolutely obliged to be there and I am certain the Duke of Bolton will dispense with your coming as well as myself, so that your grace needs not be under any constraint as to that point …[59]

Uncle Cardigan continued to be concerned about the duke's hunters and offered him another one.

Deene, Friday 15th January 1725
I forgot in my last to tell you that I have a little gelding … he trots well and a good size for his short legs, his price is fifteen guineas, the horse is now at grass, or rather at snow, for it has been four foot deep; he is not poor, but will soon be in good order when taken up and if you are not too low in pocket the horse is worth the money, but no more promising notes, for I have wrought so hard to get one and to keep myself warm, that I am not able to do more and to attempt it would be but in vain, so that I am afraid you will get my grey horse for nothing.[60]

Hunting at Charlton was thriving. Hunting boxes and stables for more horses were being erected by the Duke of Grafton, the Earl of Halifax, Lord Walpole and Lord Delawarr.

Then Grafton's duke and farming Halifax
and Walpole's lord and Delawarr, once West,
their diff'rent palaces and stables had.

Uncle Cardigan was still looking for hunters for the Duke of Richmond. He must have congratulated himself on making a more thorough examination of the mare before disbursing his nephew's 50 guineas; this was before the days of vetting prior to purchase. Blistered in the sinews would have augured ill for the unfortunate animal's staying powers up and down the hills of Goodwood and the combes and valleys of West Sussex.

Deene, Monday 6th November 1727

I was in hopes I had brought your grace the hunter I recommended to you when I was last in town. I saw her yesterday and I find she has been lately blistered for her sinew. I am very much afraid her leg will not stand hard exercise, therefore I have sent her back again, for I durst not venture to buy her with that leg. I had agreed the price at fifty guineas. Since your grace is disappointed of this hunter, I must await your directions what I must do with the sixty pounds I have in my hands.[61]

The Duke of Bolton wrote to the Duke of Richmond encouraging him to come to Charlton for some hunting and join the party:

Charlton, Wednesday 6th December 1727

As to our sport, we had very good last Friday; we went out on Monday, but were driven home by the rain, so we hunted yesterday and killed a fox that gave us so little running that we intend to hunt today, if the frost will let us. I hope you won't alter your resolution of coming; it is much desired by the whole company, but most ardently by the old general [John Huske], who toasts you every day.[62]

They even had a foot follower! Francis, Earl of Godolphin was the son of Queen Anne's famous Lord High Treasurer who was so supportive of the Duke of Marlborough during his long continental campaigns. He was married to Marlborough's daughter, Henrietta, who later became Duchess of Marlborough in her own right. Our poet would have us believe he was frightened of riding.

> *Godolphin too would once assay to see,*
> *on foot for fear, the side hill chace, the best*
> *when winds set right and foxes take that way.*

However Colonel Charles Churchill liked a good gallop, but was not so keen on hunting. So Diana sent him back to the ladies!

> *And Churchill Charles best rider in new park,*
> *for there is scope to lay his courser out,*
> *but such as he the goddess did disdain,*
> *so gave him back to Venus and the maids.*

A nephew of John, Duke of Marlborough, Colonel Churchill was indeed a ladies' man, being the lover of Anne Oldfield, the celebrated actress, by whom he fathered a son in 1720. A devoted friend of Sir Robert Walpole, Churchill was renowned for his good nature and wit though barely literate. He is commemorated in a sonnet by Sir Charles Hanbury Williams:

32 Francis, 2nd Earl of Godolphin was Charlton's foot follower, being frightened of riding. He was married to the Duke of Marlborough's daughter, who inherited the dukedom in her own right.

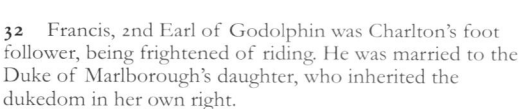

33 General Charles Churchill, a subscriber to the Great Room. His father was a younger brother of John, 1st Duke of Marlborough.

> *None led through youth a gayer life than he,*
> *Cheerful in converse, smart in repartee.*
> *Sweet was his night and joyful was his day,*
> *He dined with Walpole, and with Oldfield lay;*
> *But with old age its vices came along,*
> *And in narration he's extremely long;*
> *Exact in circumstance, and nice in dates,*
> *On every subject he his tale relates.*

But Venus was not satisfied just with Charles Churchill. She wanted to capture the master and lure him away from Diana.

> *The Cyprian queen [Venus] was not content with him;*
> *her thoughts were fix't on Delia's choicest man,*
> *whose breast nor she nor Cupid yet had touch't.*

Is it a coincidence, or would the gradually diminishing number of hounds bred in the kennels have anything to do with love? His breast had certainly not been touched by Lady Anne Vaughan and, although he had acquired from her a substantial estate, he had been estranged now for 15 years. Could he be blamed for being attracted to another lady of charm?

34 Lavinia (Fenton), Duchess of Bolton, the duke's second wife.

From a peak of 26½ couple entered in 1723, successive seasons showed a decline: 18, 15, 11, 7 and in 1728 only 8½ plus two couple donated.[63] For in love he was. Charlton did not suit his paramour at all and the hunting was taking second place.

> *A nut brown wench, with lightning in her eyes,*
> *white teeth her beauty and a warbling voice,*
> *outdid herself in acting of distress;*
> *admir'd by all but most by Bolton's grace.*
> *The queen of love, who watch'd him, smil'd with joy.*
> *'He's mine' she cried, 'I have him, he's my own;*
> *long obdurate he has my laws refus'd,*
> *but he'll repair that crime by constant love.'*

This was the beautiful Lavinia Fenton, whose mother shortly after her birth had married Mr. Fenton, keeper of a coffee house at Charing Cross. She appeared first on the stage when

35 Scene from *The Beggar's Opera* with Lavinia Fenton in the character of Polly Peachum.

about eighteen as Monimia in *The Orphan* and two years later was the star of *The Beggar's Opera* in her celebrated character of Polly Peachum. She acted in 62 performances as Polly before she was finally removed from the stage by the Duke of Bolton;[64] one of her conditions was that he should give up being master of the hounds at Charlton. He persisted for a while, but eventually gave in and finally resigned in 1729, although he did continue to breed hounds, some of whom were later entered at Charlton.

> *Now he to Charlton for a while did come,*
> *unwilling and asham'd to leave the sport,*
> *till forc'd at last by love's resistless power,*
> *resign'd his place and hounds and left the Court.*

Lavinia lived with him as his mistress for 23 years, being the mother of three sons, Charles, Percy and Horatio Armand, born before marriage and all called Powlett.[65] When the duchess died in 1751 and he was free to marry Lavinia he did so, but his life was drawing to a close. He died in 1754.

— V —

RICHMOND AND TANKERVILLE

After Roper's death the Charlton hounds continued to retain their popularity and supremacy in West Sussex, but in the latter part of the Duke of Bolton's mastership a rival pack began to challenge it. The proprietor was the Earl of Tankerville, grandson of Lord Grey, who had kept the hounds at Charlton with the Duke of Monmouth.

> *Near Compton, where Ropero us'd to hunt,*
> *is seen a castle fam'd for prospect fine,*
> *o're sea and land the view does far extend;*
> *Uppark 'tis call'd, thus nam'd from site so high.*
> *Here Tankerville, the friend of Monmouth dwelt.*

Grey's daughter Mary had inherited not only Uppark, but also estates in the north at Warke and Chillingham. She married Lord Ossulstone in 1695, who being a zealous Whig was advanced in the peerage by George I and created Earl of Tankerville, the title formerly held by his father-in-law. Their son Charles, born in 1697, turned out to be a rebellious youth just like his grandfather. At the age of 18 he fell in love with Camilla Colville, the daughter of a butcher in Durham. Meeting her at an assize ball at Newcastle, he pursued her to Rotterdam, whither she had been sent by a prudent father. 'The linden walks there lent their shade to meetings of lovers and his lordship made signals from the street, which Camilla could furtively read in the friendly mirror projecting from the parlour window.' In consequence she was sent back to England, but Lord Ossulstone (as he then was) contrived to secrete himself on board the vessel in a cask and they landed together at South Shields. Soon afterwards they were married at Jarrow church, for ages the resort of young couples seeking to enter the bonds of wedlock without the consent of parents.[66] Ossulstone was living in the north when his father died in 1722, and he immediately came south to claim his Sussex inheritance. Very soon the new Earl of Tankerville had established a pack of hounds and installed them in the kennels which his father had been happy for Roper and the Charlton hounds to use during their visits.

> *And now a noble earl of stature low*
> *and haughty mien, good humour'd tho' when pleas'd*
> *this castle own'd and the same title bore.*
> *His youth with northern sportsmen he had spent;*
> *his father dead, to Sussex straight he comes,*
> *with large estate and vig'rous youth endued*
> *and hounds he'd have without the goddess' leave;*
> *this could not please, because 'twould interfere;*

Tankerville considered it his right to draw whatever coverts he liked, as his grandfather had done 45 years before. As may be imagined, it caused considerable discord in the countryside, and this at a time when hound breeding at Charlton was in decline and the huntsman Ware was proving a disaster. Hardly surprising then that the Duke of Bolton, torn by the entreatings of his lady love, should be contemplating resigning. The Duke of Richmond, ignorant of this, but no doubt fed up with the bickering, decided to give the next season a miss and in September 1728 set off for an extended continental tour.

Aubigny, Thursday 3rd October 1728

… I am here in the centre of France with the Duchess of Portsmouth [his grandmother], who is now completely fourscore years of age, and in humour, figure, spirits, memory and everything, has the appearance of a woman under fifty. My greatest diversion here is partridge shooting, which I have in great perfection, especially for those of the red leg kind. As I have no hounds here, I can take no other diversion of that kind, but as I have great woods here, there are wolves, wild boars and roebucks. In about a week I shall set out for a more southern climate. I shall go first to Orleans, Blois, Poitiers, Bordeaux and Bayonne, and from thence I believe I shall take a trip to Madrid and Lisbon but I have not yet determined that …[67]

He did go to Madrid and Lisbon, and by the summer reached Paris, where his mind turned again to horses and hunting.

Paris, Wednesday 4th June 1729

… As regards the horses, my wife's horse can go out to grass; give the order as soon as possible, but at the same time be very careful that he doesn't catch cold when he goes out, for that is very dangerous for horses. As for the Borrough gelding, he can be sold, but that must be done by you, or a friend, not the groom, for that tempts them too much to swindle their masters. Let them know that as I intend to hunt this winter they must give the hunters sweats and exercise …[68]

And a month later, great concern about his best hunter.

Paris, Sunday 20th July 1729

I am very angry to hear that Bay Bolton is not well; apparently that rascally groom has given him green food when he had a slight cold on him. If that is the case he will certainly become broken winded and then I shall lose entirely the best looking and most perfect hunter in the kingdom and that will plunge me into despair, for then perhaps I shall not be able to hunt for two years. Make enquiries to see if the groom has fed him on grass with a cold or if it is owing to some other neglect, because, if it is like that I will dismiss him on the spot; but meanwhile let every care be taken of the horse. I also wish the groom to take his turn as park keeper or pay for it, or else he can go to the devil; but look to it first that the horse be either got out of trouble or dead, for he is of more consequence to me that all my fat bucks …[69]

Fortunately the horse survived and retired to stud where he became the sire of one of Richmond's best hunters and was used by the Duke of Bolton and many others. This famous stallion, bred by Sir Matthew Pierson in Yorkshire, died at Bolton Hall stud farm in 1736.

Chantilly, Saturday 23rd August 1729

… I am now at Chantilly with the Duc of Bourbon, that is commonly called here in France Monsieur le Duc. We pass our time here extremely agreeably, for in the first place he is one of the best bred men and the easiest I ever knew in my life to live with. We either stag hunt, boar hunt, wolf hunt or go a-shooting every day, of all which diversions the last is what I like most, for the whole country about here swarms with pheasants and partridges and one must be a bad shooter not to bring home twenty or thirty birds of one's own shooting in an afternoon …[70]

The home-coming approaches and instructions are sent.

Aubigny, Thursday 2nd October 1729

I have received, Labbé [his secretary], yours of 27th August. I have also seen your letter to Mr Hill [his old tutor], wherein I learnt of the death of my horse Mars, which I assure you cannot help being a great loss to me, since now I have only my poor Patapon. You must certainly take up from grass my wife's hack and my mare at once. We expect to arrive in London a few days before the king's birthday [30th October], so I beg you will be there about the 20th or 22nd of this month of October with whatever is required for the family; and the mares with the travelling carriage or the coupé carriage, which is at Goodwood …[71]

When he arrived home in late October, things at Charlton had greatly changed. The Duke of Bolton had resigned. There was a serious vacuum and popular opinion amongst the members centred on the Duke of Richmond to succeed as proprietor; so indeed decreed the goddess Diana, observing that lying a-bed making love in the morning should have no right to interfere with the important business of hunting!

Diana, vex'd at being thus beguil'd
by Venus and that wicked imp her boy [Cupid],
resolves to try how Hymen would agree
with early rising and with long fatigue.
Then straight on vig'rous Lennox she does pitch,
who oft from Goodwood near did used to come
to pay her homage at her stately dome.

Many of the frequenters of Charlton we have met already, but others who would gather for an evening of good fellowship in the Great Room had since appeared on the scene and included Richmond's brother-in-law the Earl of Albemarle, married to his sister Anne; Frederic, Earl of Lifford, a naturalised Frenchman and a major general in the Horse Guards; young Philip Honywood; Philip Meadows; Rt. Hon. William Conolly; Thomas Strickland, who owned a covert near Goodwood; Sir Thomas Prendergast of county Galway, the Duchess of Richmond's uncle and M.P. for Chichester; William, Earl Cowper, son of the late Lord Chancellor; the Earl of Scarbrough, Master of the Horse, of Stansted Park and his brother Hon. John Lumley; Stephen Fox, later Earl of Ilchester; Sir John Cope, of Bramshill, M.P. for Hampshire; Richard Edgecumbe of Mount Edgecumbe co. Devon, M.P. for Plympton; Sir Richard Mill, of Woolbeding, M.P. for Midhurst; William Corbet M.P. for Montgomery; Hon. Charles Howard, son of the Earl of Carlisle (a subscriber to the Great Room); the Earl of Rothes,

36 General Hon. Charles Howard was a younger son of the Earl of Carlisle through whom he owed his connection with Charlton.

37 Stephen Fox Esq, created Lord Ilchester in 1741.

colonel in the King's Own Scottish Borderers; Lord Baltimore, a great grandson of Charles II and Governor of Maryland in America whose capital city took his name; and Sir William Middleton, of Belsay Castle, M.P. for Northumberland.

These were some of the friends who encouraged the duke to take the hounds on. The start of the 1729 season was imminent and with no new proprietor, Tankerville seized his chance and began to draw the coverts normally reserved for the Charlton pack. Richmond was faced with a difficult situation, but at least he had popular support. He was heavily committed at court and elsewhere and was naturally concerned he would not be able to give it enough time. Equally he was very keen to do it; in fact it was his cherished ambition! So he agreed, on condition that Lord Delawarr should be master in his absence.

> *He gladly takes the proferr'd place, but begs*
> *that Delawarr subgovernor may be,*
> *to keep her rights and rule when absent he*
> *at Aubigny or George's court must be.*

John West, Lord Delawarr had hunted at Charlton for some years and subscribed to the Great Room. He was an ardent admirer of Mr. Roper, who had originally introduced him the sport.

> *And then tall West of old patrician race,*
> *whose warlike ancestors at Boxgrove lie.*[72]
> *This youth adept to all he undertook,*

48

Richmond and Tankerville

38 Richard Edgecumbe Esq, later Lord Edgecumbe. Between 1446 and 1859, the family of Edgecumbe was represented in virtually every parliament as members for Plymouth.

39 The Right Honourable William Conolly.

40 Philip Meadows, a subscriber to the articles.

soon took to hunting and forsook his book.
The old man, pleas'd with so apt a scholar,
call'd him his son and wish'd for such another.
West in return did all he could to please;
he walk't, he talk't, he dress't, his boots, his sleeves,
nay more, his very shape, was grown like his.

A few years older than Richmond, Delawarr was also a colonel in the Horse Guards and held similar posts at court, being a Lord of the Bedchamber and later Treasurer to the Household. He was delighted to accept the offer and was responsible for starting the tradition of taking the hounds from Charlton to Bolderwood in the New Forest in the spring.

In Rufus wastes he bears despotic sway,
where Bolderwood high elevated stands.
There in the spring the hounds shall always go;
there end the sport and pleasing dreams retain,
while basking in the summer's sun they lie.

After lengthy and acrimonious negotiations, Richmond and Tankerville eventually consented to be joint proprietors for the season 1729/30. Not everyone, including the virgin huntress, was hopeful for the success of this move.

Diana soon foresaw it would not last;
she knew the youth, so flatter'd him awhile;
at last contrives with Lennox he should join.

Seven couple of hounds were entered, including a litter by the Duke of Grafton's Welcome and another by Lord Tankerville's Sober.[73] So began an unhappy episode in the history of Charlton. Not much is found in the records, but nobody writes much when they are engaged in a struggle. Richmond was still short of hunters, but wary of being swindled, even by a fellow duke; and how infuriating that the wine for his table had not come from London. No doubt he needed it, as he told his secretary.

Charlton, Wednesday 18th February 1730
I have agreed with the Duke of Bedford for the horse and I believe he will be sent to town on Sunday or Monday next. You must upon delivery of the horse pay one hundred pounds, either to the Duke of Bedford, or his order, or to Mr Dixie Gregory, his gentleman of the horse, or his order. Matt the coachman must be in the way to see that it is the same horse that I saw at St Albans. I'll send Jess or Will Leggit to town for him, or if they don't come, send him away the next day after his arrival with the second coachman, who can ride him hither in two days and be sure to charge him to take prodigious care of him. As for the money, I take it for granted you have had at least that sum from Mr Bowen.

The wine and the parcel that was directed to Charlton that were sent to the carriers last week when I myself was in town are not yet come, which is an intolerable shame. So for the future Williams the water man must positively see the things put upon the pack horses or into the wagon himself.[74]

Now that he was a proprietor of the Charlton hounds, albeit in circumstances which were far from ideal, Richmond decided he needed to enlarge his estate. Goodwood was a 'mansion house' built by the Earl of Northumberland in the early 17th century which had been used as a hunting lodge and occasional residence, and a small estate, consisting of the immediate park of 200 acres and farms in Boxgrove and Westhampnett. In 1730, he purchased the manors of Singleton and Charlton from the Earl of Scarbrough, which included the forests and the best coverts within easy reach of the kennels. He also decided he needed a hunting box in the village to avoid having to hack over from Goodwood in the early morning. The meet in those days was always at daybreak and, after a good dinner with his friends in the Great Room, it was hardly convenient to have to ride or drive the two miles over to Goodwood only to return in the early morning; so he chose a site nearby and building was started.

With all the quarrelling it must have been a miserable season. At the end of it the parties had become so battle weary that they sought to make peace by drawing up a legal agreement, which was written on a roll of parchment seven feet long, signed by the two parties and witnessed by four dukes.[75]

Treaty of Peace Union and Friendship

between the Most High Puissant and Noble Prince Charles Duke of Richmond and Lennox Earl of March and Darnley Baron of Settrington Methuin and Torbolton one of the Gentlemen of His Majesty's Bed Chamber and Knight of the Most Noble Order of the Garter and the Most Serene and Right Honourable Charles Earl of Tankerville and Baron Ossulstone of Ossulstone Concluded at London on the Eighteenth Day of March in the Year of Our Lord One Thousand Seven Hundred and Twenty Nine.[76]

The preamble explains the squabbles which had been going on for some time between Tankerville and the Duke of Bolton and now with Richmond and Delawarr.

Whereas the above named most puissant and noble peers are disposed towards one another with a mutual desire of making peace and healing now in their own times the miseries that have of late years wasted and destroyed the county of Sussex be it therefore known to all and singular whom it may concern that the most puissant and noble Charles Duke of Richmond &c and the most serene and right honourable Charles Earl of Tankerville &c consulting and providing for (as far as mortals are able to do) the advantage ease and sport of their friends as well as the tranquillity of the said country have resolved at last to put an end to that war which was unhappily kindled and has been obstinately carried on for many years which has been both cruel and destructive by reason of the frequent chases and the effusion of the blood of so many vixen foxes wherefore the said most noble and illustrious Lords (after divers and important consultations had and held in London for that purpose) having at length without the intervention of any mediator overcome all the obstacles which hindered the end of so wholesome a design have agreed on reciprocal conditions of peace union and friendship as follows.

Article 1 smacks of pious hope rather than expectation!

That there be and remain from this day a true firm and inviolable peace, a more sincere and intimate friendship and a strict alliance and union between the said most puissant and noble

Charles Duke of Richmond and Lennox &c and the most serene and right honourable Charles Earl of Tankerville &c the territories they now stand or shall hereafter be possessed of and also their servants so to be preserved and cultivated that the parties contracting may faithfully promote each other's interest and advantage and by the best means they are able to prevent and repel from each other all damage and injury.

Article 2 stipulates that a single pack of hounds only are to be kept:

That a pack of foxhounds be maintained by and between the said Charles Duke of Richmond and the said Charles Earl of Tankerville which shall consist of forty couple at the least.

Article 3 sets out the agreed division of expenses, but also clearly indicates that the hunt shall be under Tankerville's control!

The Earl of Tankerville shall maintain and defray all expenses relating to the hounds and horses of the huntsmen and whippers in, warreners, earth stoppers and all other contingent expenses whatsoever relating thereto, for the sum of two hundred and nineteen pounds and one shilling per annum of good and lawful money of Great Britain, to be paid to the said Earl of Tankerville by the said Duke of Richmond at four equal quarterly payments, the first payment to be made on the first day of August next ensuing the date hereof.

Article 4 kindly allows the Duke of Richmond to retain his own hunt servants and provide them with horses:

The Duke of Richmond shall be at the sole expense of buying horses for his own huntsman and whipper-in.

Article 5 says that of course he also has to pay for their expenses!

The Duke of Richmond is to pay the wages and board wages and to furnish the clothes of his huntsman foot huntsman and whipper-in.

Article 6 sets out the programme for the season:

It is moreover agreed by and between the abovenamed contracting powers that the said pack of foxhounds shall be kept
- from October the 15th to November the 15th at Findon
- from November 15th to January 1st at Charlton
- from January 1st to February 1st at Uppark
- from February 1st to March 1st at Charlton
- from March 1st to April 1st at Uppark
- from April 1st to the laying up of the hounds at Lyndhurst
- from the laying up of the hounds to October 15th at Uppark

These times of removing the hounds to be observed unless otherwise agreed to by the consent of both parties.

Article 7 indicates that Lord Tankerville was not prepared allow his staff to look after the duke's horses when they were stabled away from Charlton!

> It is moreover stipulated and agreed by and between each of the contracting parties that John Ware, huntsman to the Duke of Richmond shall have the care, direction and management of His Grace's horses belonging to the hunt when they are not under the immediate care of His Grace's own groom.

Article 8 does allow the huntsmen to share the responsibilities and perks of the job!

> It is further agreed by and between each of the abovenamed parties that John Ware and Vincent or the Huntsmen for the time being shall have equal care of the hounds and equal profits and share of perquisites either arising by field money or by hounds that are given away or any other manner whatsoever relating to the hunt.

Article 9 is the get-out clause; if either party wished to resign, he had to give all the hounds to the other party.

> This Treaty to continue and remain in full force until the death of one of the contracting parties (which God for many years avert) or until one of them shall give six months notice to the other of his intention to determine this agreement in either of which cases the entire pack with the whelps shall remain to the use of the survivor or party to whom such notice shall be given.
>
> IN WITNESS whereof the above named contracting powers have hereto subscribed their names and affixed their seals of their arms at London this eighteenth day of March in the year of our sovereign lord George the second by the grace of God of Great Britain France and Ireland King defender of the faith &c annoque Domini one thousand seven hundred and twenty nine
>
>   RICHMOND & LENNOX TANKERVILLE
>   Signed and sealed in the presence of
>   GRAFTON ST ALBANS BOLTON MONTROSE[77]

Was there any doubt in whose favour this agreement was drawn up? What alternative was there? Little or none, if the pack at Charlton was to survive. These arrangements were put into effect for the season 1730/1. In addition, for reasons which are hard to fathom, Richmond and Tankerville invited a third master to join them, one Garton Orme Esq of Woolavington.[78] Relations must have been very strained and maybe Mr. Orme acted as a mediator between their lordships. Who knows? The Orme family had been in Sussex for generations, being descended from Giles Garton, citizen and ironmonger of London, who bought Woolavington from the Earl of Arundel in 1578. Garton Orme was born in 1696 and married Charlotte Hanway of Hatton Garden in 1717. He appears to have had considerable financial problems, and his attempt to use his wife's fortune to pay his debts eventually led to litigation. When Charlotte later died in suspicious circumstances, probably from poisoning, Orme married the daughter of Rev. Daniel Laffite, his vicar at Woolavington.

Meanwhile in the summer of 1730, the Duke of Richmond's hunting box was going up and by Michaelmas the walls were finished and covered in;[79] and a welcome winning bet in August helped to pay the bill.

41   Garton Orme as a child at the spinet and his future wife Charlotte. A joint proprietor of the hounds at Charlton for one season with the Duke of Richmond and Lord Tankerville, his childish innocence conceals a murky character who poisoned his wife to obtain money to pay his debts.

Greenwich, Saturday 15th August 1730

As I have had the good luck to win upwards of two hundred pounds at Tunbridge Wells, I send you a hundred and fifty of it, which I know will be welcome; but you must take care to set aside this same sum upon this Michaelmas quarter for to pay for the bricks and timber I have taken up for my building at Charlton, for I promised to pay them upon the Michaelmas quarter and I can now be punctual …[80]

Three weeks later, whilst on court duty, he had bought a new hunter, lost money at the races and borrowed some from, of all people, Lord Tankerville!

Windsor, Tuesday 8th September 1730

I have bought a horse for my huntsman here which has cost me five and twenty guineas; and I have lost my money upon Lord Albemarle's horse that ran for a plate here; so I have been forced to draw some money upon you. The bill is for forty pounds, payable to my Lord Tankerville or order, three days after sight, which I desire you would be punctual in paying …[81]

With the merging of the two packs and some old hounds brought by Mr. Orme, the kennel was full and only two couple of hounds were entered.[82] John Ware was being tolerated as huntsman, but he was never a great success. The duke received from him a bill for services and the spelling is so appalling, that it is reproduced verbatim.[83]

Noumbry 20 1730 his grace the Duk of Richmond bill	
paid for bringn of a hound hom	0-1-0
paid for 2 shows ahonting	0-1-0
paid for n hipcord	0-2-6
paid for riting paper	0-1-0
paid for digen of a fox at findon	0-3-0
paid for bringn of a hound hom	0-1-0
paid for bringn of a teryor hom	0-1-6
paid for 2 shows a honting	0-1-0
paid for a bed at fendon 2 weeks	0-5-0
paid for digen of a fox at findon	0-2-0
paid the smithes bill at findon	0-6-0
paid for a hors hire	0-1-6
paid for a pare of bouts for Jon rowll	0-13-0
paid for a pair of bouts for Richard taylor	0-12-0
	2-11-6

To cheer the place up, the duke decided the headquarters of the sport of kings was surely worthy of a distinguishing flag!

Charlton, Sunday 29th November 1730

Dear Bumbo [nickname for John Russell, Clerk of the Cheque at Woolwich]
We want a proper flag for this place and you know where such things are made. I would have it a fox, red in a green field with the union in the corner and about the size of one of the yacht's ensigns. So pray let me know what it will cost and be so good as to bespeak it and you will oblige.[84]

The sketch arrived a week later, but it was evidently the work of one little versed in the appearance of bold Reynard, for the duke wrote, aghast at the caricature:

Charlton, Sunday 6th December 1730

Dear Bumbo
The enclosed sketch is most sadly drawn. The fox ought to be as big again and take up all the middle part of the flag and the union little more than as quarter as big in the corner. The fox's tail must also be straight out and not hanging down like a horse's; so I beg to have a new sketch of it and the fox must be yellow and not red as I said. Surely £3 10s is a great deal, if it is nothing but bunting as I would have it; but you are the best judge of that. However pray let me have a draft before it is begun.[85]

The flag duly arrived and was erected on a large pole in the middle of the village.

Just in the centre of the village, where
in sacred spot, white palisaded round,
appears a mast erect of monstrous height,
on top of which flies waving with the wind
the emblematic standard of the queen

of woods (Diana), whose fav'rite colour's always green,
in which a golden running fox is seen.

If there was some hope of peace there was not much goodwill. But they had their moments. They installed a weighing scales and on 14 February 1731 started a weighing book. The Duke of Richmond weighed in at 15 stone, Tankerville at 11 stone and Lord Delawarr no less than 16 stone 8 pounds. The weights of 28 others are recorded, a few of whom do not otherwise appear in the hunt records. Michael Broughton was one, a great friend and regular correspondent of Richmond, who tipped the scales at 20 stone 3 pounds! Another was Henry Fox at 11 stone 13, son of the well known paymaster general of the forces, who, according to Lord Egmont, had started life as a footman. He was later to elope with the Duke of Richmond's daughter Caroline causing a great family and court scandal. Their son Charles James Fox was the famous politician after whom our quarry 'Charlie' is named![86]

The accounts of 'The United Hunt' for the season were drawn up by Lord Tankerville and he sent the bill to the Duke of Richmond. Most of the cost of keeping the hounds is for feed and bedding plus coal and Lord Tankerville should be given credit for his remarkably accurate estimate in the agreement, which turned out to be less than £2 out! The expenses were split between Richmond and Tankerville and Mr. Orme does not seem to have contributed. Their lordships also had to buy the kennels at Charlton from the Duke of Bolton for £260. Note the livery charge for the duke's four horses, which works out at 5s. a week![87]

The clue to how the power struggle was resolved lies in these accounts. They cover a period 'from the time they came together viz May 1st 1730 to the time they went to the New Forest viz March 1st 1730/1 viz for 10 months'. According to the agreement, the hounds were supposed on that date to go to Uppark. Lord Tankerville had conceded defeat. He tore up the agreement, ignored article 9, sent the duke the bill, which was promptly paid, took half the pack and resigned. Poor Mr. Orme however found he had to give his hounds and horses to the duke!

About two years this fickle Earl did well,
when on a sudden, he abruptly breaks
all ties of friendship and from Charlton goes;
takes half the hounds, which chanc't to be the best.
While thus distress'd, the goddess vows revenge,
another petty thoughtless squire [Mr Orme] appears
and he fox hounds and coursers too would keep.
Diana soon demolish't all his schemes;
she took away his pack and steeds and all.

The duke was mightily relieved and also thrilled to be the sole proprietor of the most famous pack of hounds in England. Lord Tankerville had left 16½ couple of old hounds and no doubt taken some young ones, Mr. Orme left 9½ couple, Sir Robert Jenkinson gave one hound and 13 couple of young hounds were entered, making a total of 39½ couple in the kennel. For the first time a complete list of the hounds in the kennel was recorded and the exultant entry proclaims:

The Duke of Richmond's Pack of Hounds
WITHOUT ANY CLOG TO HIS GRACE![88]

Richmond and Tankerville

The Charges of the United Pack of Hounds belonging to his Grace the Duke of Richmond and the Right Honourable the Earl of Tankerville from the time they came together viz May 1st 1730 to the time they went to the New Forest viz March 1st 1730/1 viz for 10 months

	£	s	d
By 32 qrters of ground oats to July 26th 1730 at 16 shillings per qrter with chaff carriage and grinding	25:	12:	0
3 chaldron of coals D° time	5:	2:	0
3 load of straw D° time	1:	16:	0
A bill of horseflesh D° time	9:	14:	6
By 15 qrters of oats ground from July 26th to December 9th at the above price	12:	0:	0
By 76 qrters of oats made into oatmeal to December 9th 1730	68:	8:	0
3 Chaldron of coals D° time	5:	2:	0
4 load of straw to February 2nd 1730/1	2:	8:	0
A bill of horseflesh from July 26th to February 13th	12:	6:	6
By another bill of horseflesh ending October 23rd	13:	19:	6
By a bill at Findon	5:	1:	6
By another bill of horseflesh to March 1st 1730/1	12:	12:	11½
3 Chaldron of coals from John Budd	5:	14:	0
A cord of wood from D°	0:	15:	0
For a load of straw and horseflesh from Cole of Havant	1:	16:	0
Mr Hobbs for whey	5:	1:	10
Mr Goodwine for drugs	5:	9:	0
Mr Lardner for D°	4:	1:	6
Earth stoppers bills	24:	9:	6
A horse from John Budd	0:	7:	0
	£221:	16:	9½

Duke of Richmond £110: 18: 4¾
Earl of Tankerville £110: 18: 4¾
£221: 16: 9½

His Grace the Duke of Richmond His account
Dr to the Rt Honble the Earl of Tankerville

	£	s	d
By the Duke of Bolton's Receipt dated May 9th 1730 my Lord paid for the dog kennel at Charlton £260.16.1½ the half of which is £130.8.¾	130	8	¾
By the half of the within bill of charges keeping the hounds from May 1st 1730 to March 1st 1730/1	110:	18:	4¾
By a third part of ten qrters of oatmeal at Charlton	4:	13:	4
By keeping 4 hunters one year which will end the 1st of May next viz 1731	100:	00:	0
	346:	00:	1½ *
My Lord Tankerville allows in part of the above balance a bill of John Budd viz £25:15:9 on my own acct & £7:17:0 on the joint acct of the kennel expenses in all	33:	12:	9
& 2 loads of hay from Goodwood	4:	0:	0
	37:	12:	9
Balance	308:	7:	4½

7 April 1731 Rec'd of his Grace the Duke of Richmond three hundred and eight pounds seven shillings and fourpence halfpenny being the balance of the above written acccount
    Cha: Clarke   Tankerville

* An error in the addition is noted!

(from Goodwood MS 149, A11, West Sussex Record Office.)

The Charlton Hunt

42 The kennels at Charlton, now converted into cottages.

43 The Duke of Richmond's Pack of Hounds without any Clog to his Grace, 1731.

The hunting box at Charlton was making progress, the inside of it being finished at Michaelmas[89] and Andrew Charlton wrote to the duke, who was in London, to report on the sport.

Charlton, Thursday 26th November 1731

The hounds came hither on Saturday last, having been purged that week at Findon before they came away and Jack Ware, expecting to find your Grace here, did not write you an account of it.

We hunted on Monday at Burton, where we fell in with a litter of foxes and our hounds divided. One parcel went over the river and ran a fox to ground about three miles and the other ran a fox to ground at Red Hill near Burton Park. We afterwards ran from fox to fox till we were forced to take off.

On Tuesday we carried the young hounds to Old Park by the sea side, where after running an hour or two, they killed a fox.

On Wednesday, we went with the old and young hounds together to Farm Wood, where we found a fox who came away all the good country through the Tegleaze and was going for East Dean Wood, but Mr Orme, being out shooting there, headed him and put us to a fault, but we hit it off and ran him back the side hills to North Combe, where he got into the earth. Had he not been headed, we had surely killed him. We afterwards went down to Burton and found a brace of foxes and the hounds dividing, one part came up the hill and the other to Bignor Park, but it being late and the weather bad we were forced to take off and made it dark night before we came home.

The hounds are very well (except for a few lame ones) and seem to be very steady, both the young as well as the old. If we had but some rain, I am confident they will show your grace very good sport, but without that, the ground is so dry, it's almost impossible in the hills to do anything and now we have a hard frost that has prevented our hunting today, as I fear it will do tomorrow.

Your horses are very well and you have three of Mr Orme's, which Jack Ware rides sometimes. I hope, though the frost continues, we shall have the pleasure of seeing you here after the masquerade is over. Mr Honywood is much your Grace's humble servant.

PS All the wells here are quite dry and we are forced to send to Cocking for water.[90]

Three miles away! A week later he writes again.

Charlton, Thursday 3rd December 1731

We were yesterday at the Rewell and the minute we came, fell in with a litter of foxes. We were a good while before we could stick to one, at last we did and was very near killing him and unless he got into some hole, I can't imagine how we lost him.

This being in the Rewell is the occasion of my writing to your grace to desire you to speak to the Duke of Norfolk about the ways in the upper part of the wood to be cut, for they [are] grown up so there is no riding. And as Mr Jbitson his old steward is put off, a new one won't do anything without his grace's orders. As I believe there is a good many foxes there, we shall visit that covert often, the sooner therefore we can get the ways cut the better.

We were on Monday at Old Park and ran a fox two or three hours but could not kill him. Now there is a prospect of the weather altering for the better, I am in great hopes of seeing some good sport, for yesterday I thought the hounds performed (considering the weather) as well as could be desired; and I likewise hope soon to see your grace here to be tried,

44 Sir Conyers Darcy, at Newmarket being urged to purchase a horse.

judged (but I hope not condemned) for drawing your forces too near a neighbouring prince's front.

Your horses came hither yesterday. Bay Bolton continues lame and friend John ran away with the boy into a bush and has hurt his eye so much that the groom fears he will lose it. The rest are all well.[91]

No other records of the hunting that season survive, but at last peace had broken out and Charlton was regaining some of its popularity. Many distinguished new members were joining the company, amongst whom were Lord Dursley, heir to the Earl of Berkeley; Colonel Henry Hawley; Lord James Cavendish M.P., brother of the Duke of Devonshire; Lord Ossulstone, Lord Tankerville's heir; Edward Pauncefort of Early Court; William Fauquier; Lord Charles Fitzroy, fourth son of the Duke of Grafton; Lord George and Lord Henry Beauclerk, brothers of the Duke of St Albans; Sir Harry Liddell Bt, later Lord Ravensworth; Sir John Miller of Lavant; George, Earl of Cholmondeley, son-in-law to the prime minister Sir Robert Walpole, himself a keen hunting man (the magnificent house he built at Houghton in Norfolk was

Richmond and Tankerville

45 Henry Herbert was created Lord Herbert of Chirbury in 1743. He was heir to the last Marquess of Powis and expected to be granted his titles, but had to be content with an earldom.

46 Hon. Thomas Villiers was the younger son of William, Earl of Jersey. He became Chancellor of the Duchy of Lancaster and was created Earl of Clarendon.

47 Hon. George Shirley was a younger son of Earl Ferrers.

48 Augustus, 4th Earl of Berkeley, Richmond's cousin.

inherited by Lord Cholmondeley's son, the first marquess, in 1797); Sir Conyers Darcy KB, PC; Major William Elliot; Hon. Charles Feilding, son of the Earl of Denbigh and Desmond; Henry Herbert, later Earl of Powis; Colonel Charles Perry; Hon. Thomas Villiers, later Earl of Clarendon, a son of William, Earl of Jersey; Hon George Shirley, son of Earl Ferrers; and Colonel Richard Whitworth.

All seemed set fair, but unfortunately, early in 1732, the Duke of Richmond met with an accident whilst in London and broke his leg which put paid to any more hunting for that season.

— VI —

DELAWARR

The Duke of Richmond was delighted to be undisputed master and proprietor of the hounds at Charlton, but 1732 was a miserable year. His broken leg was painfully slow to mend and, at least six months after the accident, he wrote to a friend:

Whitehall, Saturday 16th September 1732
The reason of my not writing to you in all this while is that I had actually no account of my leg to give you. That I gather strength I really believe, but it is so slow that it is scarce perceptible. However I get up every day, dress and sit up in my chair, but they do not think it safe to trust too much yet to my crutches, so I have made but mighty little use of them as yet. They have not opened the leg since last Sunday was fortnight and don't think of opening it till next Sunday; so they hope then to find a considerable alteration for the better. On Tuesday next I'll write to you again to give you a further account. I am glad to hear you intend to be so soon in town, which will be long before, I fear I shall be able to stir out of it … but as soon as I am able [I] intend to go down to Goodwood …[92]

While laid up in London he was kept in touch with hunt affairs by Lord Delawarr, who in the summer drew up the estimates for running the hunt in the New Forest for the coming season. The total, excluding warreners and earth stopping (and staff wages), came to £350 and, a deposit of £200 having been paid in March, the rest was to be paid in quarterly instalments.[93]

Our poet offers Lord Delawarr some advice about hound breeding and goes on to describe in some detail how fox hunting in the 1730s was conducted.

That care be his to see them kept all clean;
to view their kennels oft and see them feed;
to register their names and how they're bred,
that incest foul may never once intrude
to spoil the race and vitiate the blood.

He stresses the importance of conformation:

Be it likewise his studied care to choose
the proper shape, well bon'd and wind with nose.
Let not thin beauty ever tempt his mind
to make a nurse of female kind so shap'd,
nor of the males a stallion ere to choose,
because at head he once did foremost run.

Expenses of hounds and hunters

Expenses of Hounds per annum and of hunters	£:	s:	d:
Hay and straw for 7 huntsmen's horses at 6d each/night	63:	17:	6
Two bushels of oats each horse at 15s	68:	5:	0
10 bushels of oatmeal each week at 4s/bushel	104:	0:	0
Physic and shoeing 7 horses at £3/annum	21:	0:	0
Horseflesh for the hounds at 2 horses each week	41:	12:	0
Straw, whey and physic for the hounds	52:	0:	0
	350:	14:	16
Warreners	16:	0:	0
Earthstopping	34:	0:	0
	£400:	14:	6

Mem: Lord Delawarr hath undertaken to defray the expenses of the hunters and hounds all but the warreners and earthstoppers at the above sum of £350:14:6 per annum of which he hath received to begin from Lady Day 1732 £200 per advance for two quarters to Michaelmas next and at Christmas next is to receive £75:7:3 and so at Lady Day next, which £75:7:3 is to be put in the quarterly distribution for him to receive accordingly, and after that he is to receive £87:13:6 per quarter.

(from Goodwood MS 149, A13, West Sussex Record Office.)

> *Let just proportion be in both the rule;*
> *what shapes in this are wrong, let that amend.*
> *In this idea, strong must be his guide*
> *and trust to nature what she will produce.*

When it comes to warding bitches, he gives advice about avoiding in-breeding, selecting sires and dams who are steady in the pack and preferably mating young hounds with old.

> *Let crossing of the kind be most his care,*
> *for hounds incestuous bred will soon be curs.*
> *Nor think a steady pack of hounds to breed*
> *because the whelps by steady hounds were got.*
> *The sexes both must not with age be worn.*
> *A youthful hound of three years old, well try'd*
> *for wind and stoutness and sagacious nose;*
> *when north east wind or frost exhaled leaves*
> *the tainted turfe, or fox got far before*
> *by cunning turn; the scent by youth o'er run,*
> *when they do wildly stare or rattling fly*
> *to every thing they smell or takes their eyes;*
> *then he, if backward, soon he casts to try,*
> *shows innate judgement in a hound so young.*
> *To him a wise old female put, who is*
> *at most but six or seven years, well known*
> *for finding first or hitting faults the same.*
> *Or to a wise and aged steady hound*
> *in foreign pack or in my own remarq'd*

Delawarr

49 John West, 16th Baron Delawarr was a subscriber to the Great Room. He acted as deputy master of the Charlton hounds from 1731 and was given an earldom in 1761 by George III. Known to his friends as Dell, this rather unflattering engraving drawn by Lord Byron in 1719 is apparently the only known picture.

his pedigree and most of all his nose;
to him conjoin a bitch of two years old,
whose blood without a stain long clean has run,
altho' no wisdom yet she e'er has shown.
Her progeny will answer all his care;
both strength and beauty thus will they produce;
whereas old age in both will still deceive his hope.

Our poet warns his grace and others to avoid the trap of breeding hounds too fast for the riders to stay with them when their youth is past! Even the exemplary Mr Roper was guilty of that! Not that Richmond and Delawarr were very old, but they were not lightweights, Richmond being 15 stone and Delawarr 16 stone 8 pounds![94]

> *Beware another error seen too oft*
> *in many sportsmen, when their youth is past.*
> *They breed for speed, when they no more can ride;*
> *prepostrous thing! a boy I could forgive.*
> *All hounds, while young, too hard are apt to run;*
> *they lead with ignorance and burst the rest,*
> *who breathless come to mend the faults they make;*
> *which done, away again they heedless fly;*
> *despise the wiser heads of middle age,*
> *till off their speed or foil'd with sheep,*
> *unwillingly submit to them to guide*
> *the future chace, in hopes of getting blood.*
> *'Tis this with care avoid, tho' his great weight*
> *and even yours should be a reason good*
> *to teach you both what hounds you ought to breed,*
> *but since Ropero and his friend likewise*
> *in this one article did both mistake,*
> *I can't too much enjoin this future care.*

Most of the hunting took place on the downs, as the vale was heavily wooded and difficult to cross. Open downland was (and still is) notoriously cold scented, so with good scenting days a rarity, the nose of the hounds was of paramount importance.

> *Remember this, that scenting days are rare;*
> *the reason why, e'en to my self unknown;*
> *nature's dark works as yet to us untold.*
> *Consider then what hounds without good nose*
> *can do, when cold east winds shut up all pores;*
> *nay more, a bright sun shining day that's warm*
> *will cause the same effect as rising storms;*
> *then speedy noseless hounds will creep or stare,*
> *while right bred vermin kind will hunt*
> *and stick at mark and walk a fox to death.*

A reminder that speed does not depend on conformation but on wind, and ultimately blood.

> *Nor let him think 'tis shapes alone gives speed,*
> *in hounds and horses both 'tis wind does that,*
> *'tis blood gives wind, proportion just the rest,*
> *then stoutness shines, when breathless jades stand still.*

Different types of hunting country require different types of hound.

> *Consult the country first for which you'd breed,*
> *for this or that must diff'rent hounds be bred.*
> *My Sussex hills require short backs and wind,*
> *for no slight boneless baubles those can climb.*

When spring comes, it is time to select which puppies to keep and which to cast. Our poet has very definite views on the colours he prefers.

> *Early in spring let all the puppy's come,*
> *winter starvelings ne'er are worth the rearing.*
> *Then four or five he ought at most to keep*
> *of every litter, they the prettiest mark't;*
> *the spaniel colour or the brown reject,*
> *the black tann'd dog does never take the eye,*
> *the all white hound of snowball kind don't please.*
> *The black py'd dog with bright tann'd edges round*
> *with buff or yellow head and white the ground,*
> *be this their colour, they'll by marks be known.*

Choosing puppy walkers is important, and town dwellers are to be avoided.

> *Let country walks be got when once they're wean'd,*
> *at butchers, tanners, farmers and such like;*
> *where not o're fed they'll keep their shape and grow,*
> *and some small knowledge learn by prowling out;*
> *whereas in towns they're often fools or spoil'd.*

In those days we are told that 10 dams would produce on average 40 whelps, of whom roughly half would be entered to the pack. Back from walk, they were put in quarantine for two months and the final selection for entry to the pack would then be made, the rejected hounds being given to the hunt servants.

> *Ten nurses forty whelps will raise each year*
> *and ten times two will scarce supply the pack.*
> *In spring again collect the scatter'd youth;*
> *in separate kennel let them all be clos'd*
> *two moons at least and blood them all at first,*
> *lest madness, mortal bane to all my hounds,*
> *should lurking lie, yet hid in their young veins.*
> *And here good judgement mostly is requir'd*
> *to choose for bony strength, for shape and size*
> *and all partiality be then forgot.*
> *The slaves who tend the hounds may take the rest;*

Training the young hounds with the old now starts on exercise, followed by cub hunting to enter them to the scent of a fox and avoiding the line of a hare.

> *The season past, the youth be then their care*
> *to make them bold but still obedient too;*
> *to know their names, to come when call'd and this*
> *by daily walking out in couples join'd.*
> *Till autumn does draw near, the game yet weak,*
> *take out some few with them, some steady hounds*
> *to find and guide the yet unknowing fools,*
> *till by instinct, by nature taught, they stoop*
> *and know a vermin scent, for which they're bred.*
> *Avoid the hare; I cannot that approve;*
> *'tis sloth in summer or want of game;*
> *makes northern sportsmen argue wrong, in that*
> *their reason's only this, to make hounds know*
> *when right, when wrong and mind the huntsman's rate.*

When properly entered hounds should not need rating at all and will stop at nothing to follow the line of a fox.

> *My hounds when made, no rate at all should hear;*
> *it frights the guiltless and baulks the old;*
> *conscious they seem, expect the coming lash;*
> *at distance they humbly creep or look dismay'd,*
> *nor anxious more to find, they heedless walk*
> *behind and shew distaste, nor will they beat*
> *the thick grown coverts, whose inwoven shades*
> *the list'ning fox conceal, but pass him by.*
> *Whereas when hounds no other scent do know,*
> *they'll wind him far, they'll dash unaw'd by fear*
> *with emulation fired; they'll drive him out*
> *with vermin scent inspir'd; they'll tear their skins*
> *or lose an eye unfelt, whilst in pursuit*
> *with eager haste they force their thorny way.*

Cubhunting over and the season proper about to begin, it is time for the oldest hounds to be pensioned off and any young ones who are not up to scratch to be cast. This should leave a pack of 60 couple to hunt three days a week and not more than 30 couple would be needed for each hunting day.

> *November come, another draught must be;*
> *he then must cast the oldest worn out hounds,*
> *a thing ungrateful! yet it must be done;*
> *Mars does the same with old tho' valiant men.*
> *The young ones too by this time try'd and known;*

> *which enters not, which cannot run or tires;*
> *away with such, let all be good he keeps;*
> *and three score couple be at least the stock*
> *to furnish hounds for thrice a week to hunt;*
> *and thirty couple at a time's enough.*

Our poet ends with some advice about terriers:

> *Let terriers small be bred and taught to bay*
> *when foxes find an unstopp't badger's earth*
> *to guide the delvers where to sink the trench.*
> *Peculiar is their breed, to some unknown,*
> *who choose a fighting biting cur who lies*
> *and is scarce heard but often kills the fox.*
> *With such a one bid him a beagle join,*
> *the smallest kind my nymphs for hare do use;*
> *that cross gives nose and wisdom to come in,*
> *when foxes earth and hounds all baying stand.*

and warns against the use of beagles for hunting foxes:

> *This beagle blood, for this alone allow'd,*
> *reject it in the pack in every shape.*
> *The ignorant who oft have bred too high,*
> *do falsely think the nose thus to regain.*
> *The cross is wrong, it alters quite the breed,*
> *makes fox hounds hang and chatter o'er the scent,*
> *as vermin blood makes beagles over run.*
> *The beagle for the hare alone design'd,*
> *tho' fox hounds some so falsely term, when small;*
> *if he marks well these hints, he cannot err.*

Delawarr wrote a series of letters to Richmond which give an excellent insight into the way hunting was organised at that time and the problems they had to contend with. The first recounts how the huntsman, John Ware, was very poor at managing the hounds as well as being lazy and ignorant and the kennelman Rowell not much better; and any hound who was ill immediately raised the spectre of rabies (referred to as 'madness') appearing in the pack.

Bolderwood, Monday 2nd October 1732

I came hither last night and have this morning viewed your grace's hounds very carefully. I can assure you there is either very much ignorance or neglect in the composition of Jack Ware, nor do I think Rowell quite to be excused. I separated from amongst the old hounds eight couple thoroughly mangy. They say they have anointed them and given them some aethiops minsralis. So I immediately purged them and with the buckthorn gave them some flower of sulphur, both to take off the griping quality of the buckthorn and so throw the humour out of their blood. When I went from hence I thought such an accident impossible to have happened, for they were very clean. Since that they have had seven times whey and each time two pound of brimstone, which course of physic would have cured the great devil of the mange, and now these have it, but I hope to set them to rights. This was the manner that made him bring in such apothecary's bills and to be sure at this rate, they will want more physic than meat. With the remaining part of the old ones, we shall hunt tomorrow; the ground is soft enough, but if there does not come rain I will not go out again.

The young hounds are still kept apart, neither have they endeavoured to enter any of them. This piece of laziness may be lucky, for one of them called Ruler (bred by Mr Orme), did not care to feed last Friday. He was immediately taken from the rest and locked up. He pined away and I had him dispatched this morning. He never offered to bite, as they say, so that it may be anything else, as well as madness; however this cannot affect your old pack, they never having kept company together. Neither do I think it possible that madness can without showing itself be nineteen weeks in any dog (for so long it was last Friday) since any hound has been mad. This I beg you to talk to some of your surgeons, physicians and philosophers and send me their opinion.

Your horses are very well and in fine order. I shall say no more at present on this subject, but assure you I will do my utmost to set things to rights, but if [Lord] Lovell [formerly Thomas Coke] would recommend two or three couple of truly good hounds to you, I should not be against your buying them, for I do not think three or four of the young ones will do. This is the present state of the case. When will you have them go to Findon? I ordered whenever my panier de gibier [basket of game] comes from France to have it carried directly to your grace; if it is well stocked, spare my mother a brace.[95]

Sounds good! In the next he sends news of a day's hunting.

Bolderwood, Wednesday 4th October 1732

When I assure your grace that I heartily wish you were well enough to make me happy with your company at Bolderwood, I flatter myself that you do not doubt but that my wishes are sincere. I really think we could show you some sport. We had eight hours rain on Monday night so yesterday morning I sallied forth with 21 couple of hounds. We found a brace of foxes and parted, your humble servant, my groom and Kit went with the biggest parcel, Jack Ware and Jo with the others, who running up wind of us, did not hear our parcel. We ran him very handsomely an hour and a quarter and then hard for half an hour more. He had just time to get into a coney burrow, the hounds were so near him that a couple got into the earth and killed him. We dug out fox and hounds in a quarter of an hour and flung him to the pack, for Jack Ware got to us with his parcel just as we earthed. I do not trouble you with the particular names of the places he ran to because I believe you do not remember them. But your hounds performed well and what pleases me much is I did not see a hound run to the water nor lap coming home. I will be as good a negus as I can and hope I shall have the pleasure of bringing them in good order into Sussex and finding your grace there in good health.[96]

It was a strange superstition, which has persisted until quite recently, that hounds (and horses) should not drink while away from home and if they did so it was a bad sign. Lord Delawarr went on to recount how he had to discipline a hunt servant for being drunk!

I have taken upon me a little, but do believe you will not disapprove. You must know that a little before I came down, when they were airing the young hounds, the boys got drunk and Jo was so drunk he fell from his horse, Spitfire, who came home after having drank as much as he pleased, which had like to have killed him. The boy came home some time after in a drunken condition, upon which my old wiszled face Tom rebuked him. Replication ensued and when I came, I was acquainted with this affair, but after I had writ my last. I sent for him and have assured him that if I see or hear anything of the like for the future, I will take your grace's livery from him and send him about his business. He was much astonished and has promised never to do so any more and I believe the rough side of my tongue may have done good. If I went too far, you will excuse me, for I meant it for your service. I will be as little from them as possible till the parliament meets, before which time I hope you grace will be able to hunt, for till their brains are a little better settled, somebody must have an eye over them.

I went out this morning to air the young hounds. They go very quietly and do not so much as look at sheep and will not offer to run at deer. How they will behave when they have found a scent I cannot say.

I hope you have not forgot to write about having the kennel and stables at Findon repaired. Pray order the troughs for the hounds to feed in to be mended if they want, or new ones to be made if these are past repairing. Consider the time draws nigh.[97]

The duke was furious with the wayward behaviour of his huntsman and wrote to tell him so. Lord Delawarr sent his reply.

Bolderwood, Saturday 7th October 1732

I had this morning the favour of your grace's letter with one enclosed for Jack Ware. He was so ashamed of the condition the hounds were in and does obey directions so willingly when I am with him and I think does to the best of his own capacity, that I own I cannot have the heart to give him such a mercurial. I truly think it more for your grace's service not to depress his spirits with a severe reprimand for the fault he is so sensible of. The hounds have done so well with their physic given in that manner that I do not doubt but to bring them as fine as lap dogs into Sussex.

My last gave you an account of our sport on Tuesday last. We went out on Thursday, but when we were gone a mile, a violent storm of rain coming on, so returned and put up the hounds. Yesterday we went out with all the old hounds and two couple of young. We took a drag and hunted to him; it was not a scenting day, but we still kept it moving till we got near him. He would have got into a coney burrow, but he chose so small a one that the hounds pulled him out without the help of any instruments. It was just such a day's work as I could have desired after their physic, for the whole was over in two hours without any rain and I brought them home and fed them at their usual time, so that I do not doubt but they will be in rare trim on Monday. I take very particular care not to let the young hounds come into the same kennel with the old nor feed with them. The pack is likely to be well in blood and to know an earth, which is what I think very lucky, for they used frequently to leave a fox at ground and never lay at the earth. I hope we are very secure from that at present.

Old Driver died yesterday at three o'clock. [Old Driver, by Charlton Bell'21 out of the Duke of Grafton's Shifter, bred by Mr. Orlebar, was entered in 1724.] When we let the hounds out on Thursday, he went very lame in his shoulders, so I had him put back and put by himself. He fed as well as any hound could do on Wednesday; I gave him milk and other meat when he was put up. He lapped the milk and ate his meat and when I came home from hunting yesterday, I saw him myself eat his meat at 12 o'clock and he died at 3 as I said before. I sent for Harry Woods and everybody agrees it is not madness, for he swelled very much, he did not slaver, nor howl, neither would he have chewed his meat three hours before he died had it been madness. He was twelve years old and nobody thought he could have lasted this whole season.

I am very glad to hear your grace mends so fast and hope to meet you in Sussex. I do propose being with the hounds at Charlton the 20th at farthest. If this country should be too wet, I will move them sooner, for I assure you I shall have no consideration in being here longer than is for the benefit of your hounds, for I make no question of persuading my wife to go to London.

Jack Ware told me yesterday (but I hope he is mistaken) that the copper at Charlton belongs to Tankerville: if so has he not taken it away? That is to be looked after, for we shall make a bad figure to come and have nothing to boil our meat in for the hounds. Pray remember the stables and kennel at Findon.[98]

Rabies was widespread in England at the time, and affected not only foxhounds and domestic animals but also wildlife, including foxes. The bite of a mad dog was greatly feared and desperate situations need desperate remedies. In the hound book are two 'Receipts for the bite of a mad dog', one by no less a person than Prince Rupert, a younger son of Elector Palatine Frederick V and Elizabeth, daughter of James I. He was of course best known as 'The Mad Cavalier' in the Civil War, but in later life, while Governor of Windsor Castle, he spent his time on research in chemistry, physics and mechanics, which resulted in improvements in the art of mezzotint. He also invented 'Prince's Metal' and a new type of gunpowder. Here is his receipt, which could also be used to treat a dog.

A large handful of rue, a handful of red sage, a handful of ground liverwort, two heaped spoonfuls of scraped pewter, six heads of garlic, one pound of Venice treacle or mithridate, three quarts of strong ale.

Put all into a well glazed earthenware pot, stop the pot very close with paste, set it over the fire and as soon as it has boiled take the pot off the fire and set it to infuse by gentle heat for 24 hours, then press it and strain it off for use.

To a man give five spoonfuls morning and evening for three days and repeat it at the next full and new moon. The same quantity once a day to a dog. Dress the wound with old mithridate.

The other receipt was from Dr Meads, who was the duke's medical attendant. The medicine is not so drastic, but the thirty seconds immersed in a cold bath sounds bracing!

Lichen cinereus terrestris half an ounce, black pepper two drams. Make this into four doses. To be taken every morning fasting for four mornings in half a pint of cow's milk warm. The patient must go into a cold bath every morning fasting for a month, then three times a week for a fortnight. He must be dipped all over, and not keep his head above water, more than half a minute.[99]

The duke's leg was now sufficiently recovered for him to be able to travel to Goodwood. The hounds were moved to Findon, but Lord Delawarr found there were problems with the local landowners who objected to too much earth-stopping, a practice essential to showing good sport. Sir Robert Fagg lived at Wiston and Sir Cecil Bisshop at Parham, estates to the north of the downs near Findon. They were related by marriage but apparently not on the best of terms.

London, Saturday 4th November 1732

I am sorry to find by your grace's letter which I received this day, that you have not received mine, which I wrote this day sevennight. It was full of my reflections upon the present state of affairs at Findon. Sir Robert Fagg's brutality is what made me so very dilatory in my coming down, for I thought it would be but a dismal life to sit these long nights by myself and to hunt with the earths unstopped. Sir Robert may say what he pleases, but it is to show his ill humour to Sir Cecil in particular, and to the rest of the world besides, for nothing can be more ridiculous than to say that he will let them be stopped when gentlemen are there, but for the interim, he will contrive to have the hounds kept so much from blood, that they will not be able to show sport to anyone that does come.

I have had but one letter from Jack Ware since they have been there, so God knows what they do. Mr Charlton and I intend to be down there before the time for moving the hounds, so that I will march my forces back to their headquarters. The weather has been excessively cold these ten days, so that I fear they have not done much. PS I have this day an India sow from Bengal with pig. Would you have me save you one; they say they are excellent good meat.[100]

Sucking pig certainly is! At last, on Wednesday 22 November 1732, 'The house at Charlton, it was finished and the Duke and Duchess lay in it'.[101] It was conveniently near the Great Room. The Duke of St Albans had also moved into his, which our poet thought was not quite so grand!

> *A warm but small apartment each one has,*
> *the duke's alone appears magnificent,*
> *conspicuously it stands above the rest*
> *and uniform, and nearest to the dome;*
> *the Albian duke the next best palace owns.*

Mention has been made before of other hunting boxes, belonging to the Duke of Grafton, Earl of Halifax and Lords Delawarr and Walpole. The Duke of Devonshire and Lord Harcourt built a double-fronted dwelling next to the public house and installed William Fauquier in the attic storey above the connecting archway.

> *And here a regular front full south appears,*
> *a double palace which three friends did rear.*
> *The strong Cavendo owns the part of one,*
> *Fauquier his friend in attic storey sleeps,*
> *young furious Harcourt did the other build;*
> *and great was the expense and charge of both.*

Next to this was a house occupied by Ralph Jenison from Northumberland and two of his friends from the north.

> *Adjoining this a large old fabric stands,*
> *and three Northumber youths in that do dwell.*

Lord Baltimore had a hut along the road by the river, in which he apparently lived like the Tartars with his horses and servants, one of whom was black (Pompey), all under one roof!

50 William Cavendish, as Marquess of Hartington was an early devotee of the Charlton Hunt and a subscriber to the Great Room. He succeeded as 3rd Duke of Devonshire in 1729.

51 George Montagu, 1st Earl of Halifax subscribed to the Great Room at Charlton and built a hunting box in the village. His brother-in-law was the Earl of Scarbrough of Stansted, Master of the Horse.

52 Robert Walpole was the eldest son of Sir Robert Walpole, the prime minister for 20 years. He was given a seat in the Lords as Lord Walpole when he was 22 and later succeeded his father as 2nd Earl of Orford. He donated hounds to Charlton and owned a hunting box in the village.

53 Charles Calvert, 5th Baron Baltimore, was a great grandson of Charles II and Barbara, Duchess of Cleveland and a nephew of George, Earl of Lichfield, who had subscribed to the building of the Great Room at Charlton. He became Governor of Maryland in America whose capital city was named after him.

Then east of this, close by the Lavant side,
a certain Baltimore has built his hut;
here he, his slaves and strong made coursers all,
with Pompey too, under one thatch to lie.
'Tis thus we're told the Tartars fierce still dwell;
fond of their horses, of their dogs as fond.

Edward Pauncefort of Earley Court, poor chap, had a place in what can only be described as the slums of Charlton. Our poet thinks Diana had banished him there, although he seems to have been nice enough and described as 'discreet, well looking, modest and all that'.

Yes! one there is that must not be forgot,
at distance in the suburbs it is built;
amid the noisy cabarets [huts] it stands,
where all the grooms and hinds do brawling feed,
all loud in talk, ill bred of course, all such;
and there each self sufficient fool is heard
to contradict whats'ever's said or done;

> *with gaping mouth and drivler in his face,*
> *he hourly argues for arguing sake;*
> *and thus with nonsense deafens every ear,*
> *like hog he swills and drinks full pots of beer.*
> *In this polluted fulsome noisy place,*
> *Diana orders Pauncefort to reside;*
> *her reasons for't the rest cannot conceive;*
> *'tis plain 'tis not because he latest came.*

There were more, but our poet thinks them unworthy of mention!

> *There is one since she cares not where he's plac'd,*
> *intruding, he against all rules would come.*
> *Some more there are, but not much worth remark,*
> *where some as little worth do sometimes come.*

Despite the delight at being back in Charlton, Richmond was not at all pleased with the state of things. At least his leg was completely mended and he had finally discarded his crutches. But he wrote two highly critical letters to which Lord Delawarr replied in a somewhat defensive manner.

Charlton, Thursday 30th November 1732

This is to acknowledge the favour of both your grace's letters and I cannot but be very much concerned to find by the first of them, as well as by Mr Charlton's, that the hounds are so very low. The secret of that is hard to unravel, unless you will think that John Rowell is old and lazy and will not feed as he can; and that the other is young and ignorant how to do it. As to what he alleges, that they have not flesh enough, it may certainly be answered. Why have they not? Who hinders it? They have not been controlled these five weeks that I know of, unless it is a grievance to have an account kept of what oatmeal is delivered to them every week; but the quantity is not limited, so that they have taken what they would, only what they have taken is known; and you may see by the account of the horse flesh, which you have by you, that was used in the forest, that they were not sparing; and how their modesty comes to make them err on the other side can proceed from nothing but their not paying those bills themselves. If the servants will not cooperate, it is impossible for any mortal to have a pack of hounds in order. I own I rather think they seem by the accounts I have received that they take pains the other way, for without skill, any dog will be fat that is not worked hard, which is their case, unless you allow that the quantity of medicines they have taken has quite torn their constitution to pieces. As to the poor work they made of the Monday's chase, that I believe may partly proceed from there having been no rain since the frost, and in that case I never saw the scent lay, for the grounds always carry.

As to your grace's second letter, which I received this day, I am sorry any horses were purged without your knowledge, and much more so that any should want it, besides the two that are now purging, which I told you at Godalming were to be purged at Findon, but I suppose the distemper they had there prevented it. I fancy that I may have put them out of condition, for they were all purged before they left Bolderwood and came as clean and as well from thence as any horses in the world, as you saw, if you called at Charlton as your grace told me you would. John Budd said he never saw the horses come in such order for riding in his life. I have been very impatient to wait on your grace in Sussex and I shall come very soon.

As to their being sick with antimony, it is a cursed lie, for they both know they fed well with it and after it. If you give a pound amongst the pack, it will both vomit and purge them, which in some cases is necessary; but three or four ounces mixed with a pound and a half or two pound of brimstone will only open them if it is mixed as it ought with the meat and not given in lumps. But why always physic?[102]

During the year 10 bitches were warded, four with sires from other packs.[103] On 19 December 1732 there were 32½ couple of old hounds in the kennel supplemented by 4½ couple of home bred and 2½ couple of donated young hounds. By 15 May 1733 there were 41 couple, 29½ of old and 11½ of young hounds.[104] Trueboy, a hound given by Sir Thomas Miller, vanished almost as soon as he had come. Perhaps that is why he gave him away!

At the end of May Lord Delawarr was in London ostensibly to procure some foxes which he had sent down to Sussex. In those days it was the common practice to buy foxes imported from France and turn them out in particular coverts which might be short.

London, Thursday 31st May 1733

I had the favour of your grace's letter by the last post and am glad so many foxes got safe to Sussex. Eleven set out of town so one I perceive was lost or died on the road. As to the register book of the hounds, it is in the New Forest. I never trust it from the place where they are, so cannot have it copied till I go into the forest and then will not fail to have it done according to your desire …[105]

London, Saturday 16th June 1733

… The last letters from the forest give a very good account of your hounds and horses. I have three foxes at present in the house. Give me leave to advise you not to have too many at the same time in the pen, for they will die with the stench and for want of liberty.[106]

How appalling! Meanwhile there was business to be concluded about a horse which was considered not up to the duke's weight (he weighed 15 stone).

Bolderwood, Saturday 14th July 1733

I have this day with Mr Andrews [a hound breeder in the New Forest] and Roger Williams [Lord Delawarr's groom] survey'd the horse and we do unanimously agree that he is a very genteel horse and sound, but we do not think him fit to carry more than twelve or thirteen stone at most, his body being lengthy and we are apprehensive he will be a thin carcassed one when drawn. So that unless you send your positive commands to the man, he is not to come to you. I expected my groom this day from Mr Bright's …[107]

Not many weeks had passed before the hounds in John Ware's care were in trouble again.

Bolderwood, Saturday 11th August 1733

I have been here a week and am sorry to tell you I found a great number of your hounds very much tainted and not the old ones only, but some of the most hardy, as Tapster, Kindness

&c; and I am much afraid it will break out still more in the pack. I find they have been fed as high and with as much flesh this hot summer, when they have not stirred as in the winter when they hunt; it is easy to imagine the consequence. I have now lowered their diet and they are in a course of physic, not but they have been very lavish of it, but without knowing how to give it.

I propose to come hither again soon and I doubt not but to get the handsomest pack I ever saw, in order against you do Bolderwood the honour of a visit. I have much to talk over with you, but I have so far ventured as to tell John Rowell that it is expected from him that the hounds are in good order as to their health. He said then they shall if I may [can]. I told him I depended he would and it was expected from him. Your horses are perfectly well and fine. The boys will blow the brass horn well, but Jack Ware is as forward in three weeks as one of the boys was in two days. As their master says it was his desire to learn and not put upon him.[108]

The brass horn refers to an old custom for some of the field to carry French style horns when out hunting, as is still practised in France. Looking at the puppy list that summer, Delawarr thought the duke may have bred too many hounds.

Hampton Court, Monday 20th August 1733

I have sent your Grace an exact list of your pack and of the puppys. Twelve couple [of puppys], besides what your Grace has at Goodwood out of young Madam and Comfort [Drummer, Tantivy, Diamond by Lord Gower's Ranter out of Madam'31; Emily, Drunkard by the Duke of Rutland's Limner out of Comfort'29]. We have no more quarters in the New Forest, except two to be kept at Bolderwood, which I hope will be two of the three you have [at Goodwood] out of Crimson and Cocker. By it you will perceive you are strong and I fear within another year be overstocked if you breed so many. But you are now to consider which bitches you would have spared; I know no benefit that will accrue by them unless it is more hounds to be given to the huntsman. I am sure five or six bitches will breed as many hounds as anybody can want.

I am in great hopes you will do me the honour to come to Bolderwood next month and I should be glad to know what time you would like, for I then would contrive to make that my time for the forest.

I called at Hackwood and the Duke of Bolton bid me let you know you may have the hunter he recommended to you but his price is 150 guineas. That is a great price, so you should be well satisfied about him. I saw him; he is a fine strong horse but I did not see him move …[109]

Of that horse more anon. Lord Tankerville was still at Uppark, brooding at his failure to establish himself as proprietor at Charlton. However an opportunity arose for him to get a bit of his own back. On 25 June 1733 he had been appointed Master of the Royal Buckhounds. He immediately proceeded to exercise his right of access to the New Forest on behalf of the king, but instead of taking the buckhounds, he started hunting fox with his own hounds from Uppark. Lord Delawarr was furious and wrote to Richmond, who was in France at the time.

Bolderwood, Monday 10th September 1733

I never wanted you so much in my life as at present. That dear creature the Earl of Tankerville is sending his foxhounds into the forest. Consequently yours must move, for there is not game for three packs. I came to London about it and only desired him to stay till your grace came over, that you might give orders where yours might go, but to no purpose. So I am returning to go to Lord Lymington's today. This is hard and I think your friend Tanky uses you but very indifferently, for you will not have a whelp entered. If I knew where to send them near Bear forest[110] I would instantly. To Findon would be eternal ruin, because of the sheep in the woods, too great temptation for young hounds. I beg to hear from you and as soon as I get down I will send to see for some place near Bear Forest.[111]

Richmond had turned down the offer of the Duke of Bolton's horse for 150 guineas and his lordship, wishing to be shot of him, offers him for nothing! Perhaps it may not be quite what he says!

Hackwood, Saturday 6th October 1733
I had the honour of your grace's letter which I would have answered the last post, but I was willing to inform myself about the horse of the man that takes care of my stud. He says that your grace has here inclosed. My lord, as he has never been lame in his life and that I think him by much the best and finest horse I ever saw, so I was very desirous to have you have him. I desire you'll keep him and hunt him. His price is what you please, or if you'll do me the honour to accept of him he is at your service …[112]

During the summer nine bitches were warded, two with Lord Tankerville's Clouder. The litter from one pair was destined to be sent to Richmond's friend the Duke of Bourbon in France.[113] For the coming season, 10½ couple of old hounds were cast and replaced with 11½ couple of hounds bred and 2 couple donated.[114] One was from Mr. Thomas Bright of Badsworth in the West Riding of Yorkshire, who had established a pack in 1720. The Duke of Bolton had exchanged hounds with him in 1723 and Mr. Bright sent a couple to Charlton in 1728. The pedigree of Luther is given in considerable detail, as it contained blood from at least seven kennels; Sir John Tyrwhitt of Brocklesby, Mr. Chaworth and Lord Byron who both had packs in South Nottinghamshire, Mr. Vernon of Staffordshire, Sir William Wyndham of Somerset (the Duke of Somerset's son-in-law), Mr. Huddlestone and Richmond's uncle the Earl of Cardigan.[115] This was a part of the process of improving the fox hound breed which was going on at the time and by 1750 large advances had been made for two main reasons. One was this interchange of blood and ideas from kennels at opposite ends of England and the other was the enthusiasm for foxhunting by men of education and wealth, which meant a sophisticated approach to selective breeding backed by copious means.

But things were not right at Charlton. Tankerville was a serious threat in the New Forest and Ware was a rotten huntsman. Diana told Richmond to keep his pecker up. Things would improve.

'*Your slave who guides the pack I don't approve;*
I have one in my thoughts as yet engaged.
With this! I prophesy some dire mischance;
Be not dejected but on me rely;
Nor guides nor hounds nor ought shall wanting be;
whole packs I'll send and that shall be my care.'

The Charlton Hunt

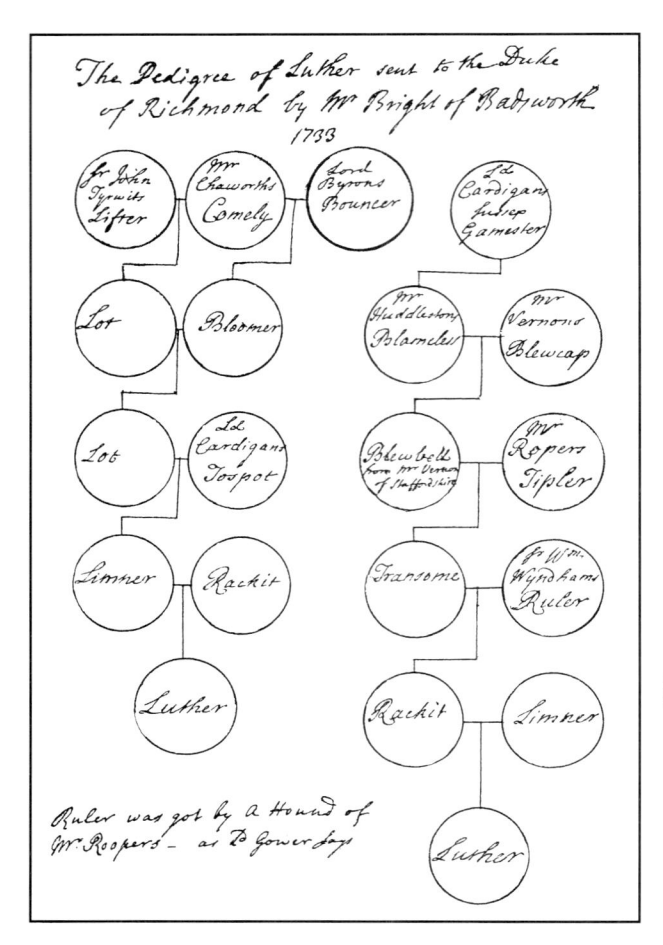

54 The Pedigree of Luther sent to the Duke of Richmond by Mr. Bright of Badsworth 1733.

Richmond's heart overflowed with gratitude.

> *When Lennox thus, with heart o'erjoy'd, replies*
> *'Goddess of woods, tremendous in the chace*
> *of mountain foxes and the savage race,*
> *my constant study it shall daily be*
> *to mind your orders and commands obey;*
> *with awful reverence will your rights maintain;*
> *with hunting songs still celebrate your praise.'*

This song recounts a nine-mile point, 13 as they ran, which took place on Friday 28 December 1733.[116] Jack Ware was hunting the hounds with old Andrew and John Shaw whipping-in. The Duke of Richmond was riding Grey Carey and also out were Lord Delawarr, Ralph Jenison and Brigadier Hawley. The duke definitely did not enjoy the joke when he fell off; and calling Brigadier Hawley a lightweight was fun; he weighed 17 stone. Old Andrew was quite a lad, it seems!

Charlton December twenty eight
      At half an hour past nine
His grace's loitering made it late
      Yet we a fox did find
In East Dean wood; 'twas Kitty cross'd
Hark in, get on or you'll be lost
      With a hark Kitty, hark in hark.

O'er northern down, all up the wind
      So on to Burnt Oak gate,
We all of us just there got in
      The hounds ran a great rate.
Away they went for Herringdean
At Cocking road they turned again
      With a hark forward, hark on hark.

Then down the wind o'er Cocking course
      Each man did push his horse;
To Tegleaze gate where huntsman-like
      We stopp'd to see them cross;
There first came Veny, Luther next,
Young Trojan, Victor and the rest
      With a hark forward, hark on hark.

Then o'er the hills for sheep wash earth
      'Twas stopp'd, it would not do;
From thence to Burton hanger straight
      They ran as if in view;
At Glatting beacon there he came
But there was headed down again
      With a hark Victor, hark in hark.

Of all the hounds of any breed
      Sure Victor is the best;
There he and Trojan took the lead
      And kept it from the rest;
To west Burton and o'er Bury hill
They had no check nor ne'er stood still
      With a hark forward, hark on hark.

But there some sheep did cause a stop
      A minute and no more;
For Victor cast and hit it off
      For Priestcomb on before;
The hounds they heard him and came in
For Houghton cliffs they ran amain
      With a hark Victor, hark on hark.

The Charlton Hunt

Just by the earth poor Ren was seen
      The chase was not yet done;
Jack Ware lept off and straight brush'd in
      But Ren did farther run;
Now all at fault, both man and hound,
Jack would conclude him gone to ground
      With a hoax cross him, hark again, hoax.

Just then we heard a halloa clear
      A mile up wind at least;
Hark halloa, straight get up Jack Ware,
      This trick it is his last;
Away we went to Houghton town
He there had bobb'd all up and down
      With a hark halloa, hark in hark.

Through farmer's yards and their wife holes
      We drove him all about;
We saw him leap o'er pales and walls
      At last he did get out;
Then for Priestcomb again he ran
But at the hedge was at a stand
      With a Whooup, Whooup, Whooup.

His Grace of Richmond then and there
      For to complete the day,
Did get a fall both fine and fair
      From off old Carey Grey
While some did laugh, his grace said nought
But at John Shaw let fly a stroke
      With a hey day, what now, what now.

Now I must tell you who they were
      That rode this noble chase
First then was John, Lord Delawarr,
      I've told you of his grace;
Next Jenison, a northern knight
Of shire, and Hawley, a light weight
      With a hey for Goodwood, hark away hark.

Though last of all, yet first in fame
      Of sportsmen that we know
Old Andrew sure I now must name
      And best companion too;
He knows the hounds and what they do
Can ride and drink and make love too
      With a fal a lala.

— VII —

Tom Johnson

By the summer of 1734, things in the New Forest had settled down and Lord Delawarr, writing to the duke in France, sounded much happier, although Tom Johnson, 'Old Tom', was most upset at the death of the horse he was riding.

Bolderwood, Friday 13th September 1734
I have now good and bad news to send you. The first is that your hounds are well. We have hunted six times and killed six foxes; a brace yesterday, so missed but one day and that was occasioned by a violent shower, for I think they ran harder that day than I ever saw them

The bad is Andrew's black horse is dead. He hunted one day last week, was rid by Tom who rid no faster than I did on Scarborough. The horse came home perfectly well, but lay down in about ten minutes and stretched himself out and died. I am sorry, but Tom is mad for he was a great favourite. But as no neglect or carelessness was the occasion of this misfortune I hope you will not have the worse opinion of old Tom. Especially now Mr Milburn is dead and John Shaw I suppose succeeds, so recommend old Tom to succeed John Shaw, which is not recommending a bad servant, I assure you, but as he has always behaved well, desire his preferment.[117]

As the season approached eight couple of hounds were entered, whelped by the bitches warded in 1732.[118] Three couple came from Colonel Hawley which he had purchased from the Rev. Ellis St John, who bred hounds at Finchampstead in Berkshire; another couple bred from Charlton sires by Lord Cowper came from Hertfordshire; and a further draft of six couple arrived on 8 January 1735 from the Duke of St Albans.[119]

As it happens, that same day, the Duke of Richmond was appointed Master of the Horse and a Privy Councillor; the previous November he had added Duke of Aubigny to his titles on the death of his grandmother and on 22 February the duchess was delivered of a son and heir, who became the 3rd Duke of Richmond. Quite an eventful time!

John Ware had been huntsman at Charlton for 11 seasons since Roper's death and had continually caused Richmond and Delawarr great concern. His eventual dismissal was precipitated by a shameful episode early in 1735 when the hounds ran riot in a flock of sheep.

But oh! mishaps! no pleasure without pain;
the fatal accident she had foretold
at last befell her hounds, so much renown'd!
That vilest slave, the huntsman Ware his name,
alone and drunk went out and let the pack
kill fourteen farmer's sheep all in one day.

55   William, 2nd Earl Cowper. His father, the first earl, was Lord Chancellor under Queen Anne and George I.

Ware was sacked on the spot. 6½ couple from the season's entry (Caley, Cleanly, Darling, Farmer, Fortune, Frolic, Gamester, Lilly, Pyman, Ranter, Snowball, Spanker and Tipler) were put down immediately and another 6½ couple were banished to France where, says our poet, farmers would not bother about dogs killing their sheep! They were Fleury and Spanker, old hounds from Mr Orme who had entered the kennels in 1731, Bowman, Charmer, Climbank, Forester and Molsey from the 1733 young entry, Comely, Dilly, Ranter and Rockwood given by the Duke of St Albans in January and Jugler and Juno from the young entry the previous autumn. Tapster '31, Royal and Sally from the young entry of 1733 and Sherewood '34 were reprieved but were put on probation and had 'sheep' written against their names in the hound book. Luther, the stallion hound given by Mr. Bright in 1733, was the same and not used for breeding again. Emperor is also mentioned, but in the hound book he had no such stigma. Poetic licence, no doubt! He remained in the pack until 1741 when he was given to Sir Rowland Wynne, whose wife Susanna was Mr. Roper's granddaughter by his only surviving heir Elizabeth Henshaw.[120]

Oh! fatal day! and fatal so the next.
Now melancholy scenes each week produc'd;
some hounds were hang'd, some cast and still the best;
to France some went, where farmers ne'er complain.
The best thus lost, the rest of little worth,

56 Hon. John Spencer, ancestor of the Earls Spencer and brother of Charles, 3rd Duke of Marlborough, kept hounds in the New Forest. He recommended Tom Johnson to the Duke of Richmond and sent him to Charlton with a draft of hounds to resuscitate the pack after the disastrous riot on sheep in 1734.

57 Charles Spencer, Earl of Sunderland and 3rd Duke of Marlborough, hunted in the New Forest with his brother Hon. John Spencer.

> *nay Emperor, that fine tho' wicked dog,*
> *was all besmear'd with blood of harmless sheep;*
> *and Luther too kill'd lambs the shepherds care.*

Richmond had to look for a new huntsman and for replacement hounds. He received some advice from Diana via his old friend Colonel Huske.

> *Enrag'd at this, the silvan queen declares*
> *she'll still support the train, new hounds supply.*
> *Her fav'rite Lennox she one night surpris'd,*
> *in Husko's shape she came and thus she spoke*
> *'Cheer up brave youth, for fortune smiles on thee;*
> *the finest boy and noblest post thou hast.*
> *The best old huntsman with no bad hounds I bring;*
> *accept the present, they from Spencer come;*
> *The youth obliges me and gives them you.*
> *To Bolderwood then straight repair and there*
> *you'll find Tom Johnson's hounds and Delawarr.*
> *There try and choose the best and form again*
> *a formidable pack for Sussex downs.*

By the start of the season in 1735 he had engaged Tom Johnson as huntsman and installed him in a cottage near the kennels.

> *And near in verdant field enclos'd, thro' which*
> *the Lavant winding runs and lends his aid*
> *to clean three spacious kennels for the hounds,*
> *who here all walk to stretch their stiffen'd limbs;*
> *and in this field the governor resides*
> *from whence he sees the management of all.*

'Old Tom' was popular with Lord Delawarr. He came with warm recommendations from Hon. John Spencer of Althorp (ancestor of the Earls Spencer) and his brother the Duke of Marlborough, both of whom hunted in the New Forest. He was highly regarded in other hunting circles and was commended by Lord Gower and the Earl of Cardigan, noted hound breeders and joint masters of the Confederate Hunt in Leicestershire.

Mr Spencer bred hounds in the New Forest with Mr. Andrews and they sent Johnson to Charlton with a draft of 21 couple of old hounds.[121] Not only did they make up the numbers but they brought a great variety of blood lines to the kennel, for only one couple was by a Charlton sire (Jockey'28). Apart from the New Forest lines, they came from the Duke of Rutland, Lord Cardigan and Lord Gower in Leicestershire, from Lord Byron and Lord Griffin in Northamptonshire, Lord Craven in Berkshire, Sir Francis Skipwith in Warwickshire, Mr. Noel in the Cottesmore country and Mr. Morley.

Fifty-seven couple were now in the kennels, although two couple (Gamester, Gaudy, Gaylass and Younker) were cast before the start of the season. So with the recovery of Charlton's fortunes, the hunting became ever more popular, the size of the fields increased and our poet took an opportunity to pay his compliments to the duke and duchess and their family.

> *'Twas done; the sport again once more reviv'd;*
> *with transports new the youth came posting down*
> *to Charlton, where new sportsmen daily come*
> *to hunt, to shoot, to dine at Goodwood some.*
> *Goodwood! the place where all exotics are*
> *from cooks exotic to exotic bears [the menagerie];*
> *but there too conjugal affection shines,*
> *the finest duchess and the finest duke.*
> *Hail happy matron, hail most happy wife*
> *still bles't, still lov'd, tho' many years are past.*
> *What am'rous planet reign'd, when this fond pair*
> *were got or born or happily conjoin'd?*
> *The longest honey moon that ever shin'd;*
> *and then their blooming progeny to see,*
> *but Emelia's picture who can draw?*
> *The pretty'st prattling poppet e'er was seen;*
> *petite tripone, jolie mignone des cieuse,*
> *soiez beuite, soiez en toute heureuse.*

58 Lady Emily Lennox (Emilia), Richmond's second daughter, who married the Earl of Kildare when she was fifteen and was later Duchess of Leinster.

New faces were appearing to swell the throng and in particular one Amazonian, nay Herculean, lady of Scottish descent caught our poet's attention. She was apparently waited on by the Duke of Grafton (Fitzroy, 52) and the Earl of Pembroke (46), hardly youths and probably put there to keep her in order, or did they rather fancy her muscular charms?! The duchess' natural friends were more at home letting the men get on with it.

> *Here shine the nymphs in amazonian garb*
> *by Delia trusted to Richmonda's care.*
> *Look how the keen Haralda foremost rides,*
> *attended by a youth on either side,*
> *Fitzroy, Pembroke now comes cant'ring on;*
> *of graceful stature this Hibernian maid,*
> *her size and limbs for Hercules a match.*
> *Some other nymphs at sundry times did come,*
> *but these their beauty or complexion fear'd,*
> *so soon return'd for softer sports prepar'd.*

Others there were to help raise the roof of the Great Room. They included of course John Spencer and Lord Cardigan (who was later Duke of Montagu), anxious to see how the new draft was getting on; young Simon, Viscount Harcourt, just coming of age, a keen newcomer; William Battine of East Marden, Lord Tankerville's agent and a magistrate at

59 George Brudenell, 4th Earl of Cardigan, later Duke of Montagu and Richmond's first cousin. He was one of the masters of the Confederate hunt in Leicestershire.

60 Charles Newby, a noted hound breeder.

61 Hon. Edward Legge, a son of William, Earl of Dartmouth.

Chichester; Charles Newby, a noted hound breeder; M. le chevalier Ossorio from France; Colonel Gregory Beake; Hon. John Mordaunt, the Duke of Bolton's nephew; Lord Diemar; Hon. John FitzWilliam, third son of Viscount FitzWilliam of Merrion; Charles Ellison; Laurence Monk; Hon. Edward Legge, younger son of William, Earl of Dartmouth; Colonel Charles Perry: Sir William Corbet of Stoke, county Salop and last but not least the Reverend Herne, chaplain to the hunt!

All these new faces needed horses and grooms to tend them. The numbers had been growing and there were now a hundred horses stabled in the village with a head groom to supervise the whole operation. Then as now, the grooms not the owners made the decisions!

A hundred speedy coursers now are seen;
by diff'rent names they each distinguish't stand
in sep'rate stalls attended by a boy;
and one sage groom does all those boys command.
Each sportsman has his stalls and groom apart
(who also tries his master to direct).

The evidence that the Charlton livery was blue and gold is contained in the next lines.

More regular than formerly was seen,
the whole in every part does now appear
with velvet caps, in azure vests they're clad
with golden loops, alike they all are made,
and each for use wears couples at his side.

The Duke of Bolton had been away from Charlton for seven years, but he kept up his interest in hound breeding and wrote to Richmond to ask the favour of some stallion hounds.

Hackwood, Thursday 22nd January 1736

You were so kind to say you would help me to some of my old kind of hounds that I may keep up the breed. If you can spare me any of the underwritten doghounds, I shall be obliged to your grace ... Tosser, Trouncer, Ranter, Royal. If you can spare me one running terrier I shall be quite set up ...[122]

Richmond was happy to part with Royal (by Ratler'29 out of Comfort'29 entered 1733) who was on probation for worrying sheep! He also gave him Tosser (by Cocker'23 out of Madam'25 entered 1730). We don't know about the running terrier, but they were so called because it was the practice for terriers to run with the pack (unlike today when they go in the Land Rover).

Little was recorded during the season 1736/7. Tom Johnson was settling in and preparing for the great events to come. They were given two couple of hounds in the following autumn and entered another 17½ couple.[123] The hunting continued to be very popular although there could be a hint that it might be starting to attract the wrong sort of people. Certainly the duke and his friends were constantly on their guard for any malign influence which might interfere with their sport. This letter from a Mr. Peachey in reply to one from the duke suggested he might have been encroaching on their patience.

Newgrove, Wednesday 19th January 1737

I received your grace's of the 16th. I am obliged to you for the just opinion that you entertain of me, that I would not disturb the sport of any gentlemen, to which I must add, still less of any persons of quality and I assure you least of all that of your grace. I keep finders which are half bred spaniels and a brace of greyhounds perfectly for my health and the morning at this time of the year being too cold for old men, I go out in the middle of the day for about three or four hours and that is about three miles southward of my house and never up the hill. I can assure you that my finders cannot hurt a fox nor will they hunt him; nor when I kept hounds did [I] ever suffer them to hunt a fox, well knowing that it spoils harriers. As for my dogs, if they at any time are found running a fox, I desire they may be shot and shall be well pleased with it and if that practice be well followed as it should be, the fox hunter's sport would in a little time cease to be interrupted. My lord I repeat it again that I wish all dogs that follow foxes, except the fox hounds, were shot constantly on seeing it and I give free liberty to any man to shoot mine on that occasion. If I can in anything be assistant in preventing the interruption of the sport of the Charlton gentlemen I shall willingly be serviceable in it, in this or in anything else …[124]

Considering the number of hound breeders active at the time, it is hardly surprising that some of them thought it quite legitimate to let their dogs run at game, including foxes, near their homes. In organising hunting at Charlton (and elsewhere at Findon and in the New Forest) it was essential that 'cowboys' like Mr. Peachey, even if he had formerly had a pack of harriers, should be controlled.

In June peace descended again in the New Forest. Lord Tankerville was appointed a Lord of the Bedchamber and replaced as Master of the Buckhounds by Ralph Jenison, a Charlton member and knight of the shire of Northumberland. He continued to send hounds to Charlton, very likely his cast offs, but we hear no more about quarrels over drawing coverts. Before we leave him, however, there are two things to add. He had made a significant contribution to hunting even though he had quarrelled with the Duke of Richmond and his Charlton friends. He left his 'Instructions' which contain some excellent advice for the hunt servants and the gentlemen in the field as to how they should conduct themselves, all of which is highly relevant today. Bear in mind that this was written some 50 years before Beckford, whose book *Thoughts on Hunting* is generally regarded as the early bible of the golden rules and etiquette of hunting.

LORD TANKERVILLE'S INSTRUCTIONS

The hounds not to be kept behind the huntsman in the morning to whatever country they go, except at times when they are obliged to go through coverts.

The whippers-in to be forward and if any hound or more happens to prole [stray] from the road, they go to call on them, but to use no whip for if they know their names at home they will obey abroad.

When you are come to your beat the huntsman only to speak to the hounds and the less the better.

The whippers-in to have a good look out to stop any hound that steals away with a scent and leaves the body of the pack behind, unless it is a good one and has time to give notice for the rest to be well laid on.

The whippers-in not to speak by way of encouraging any hounds in cover, but in case of riot they shall gently rate them off.

As soon as they have found, one whipper in to go with the huntsman, the other to stay behind to bring any straggling or tail hound or hounds that may be left behind, which will seldom happen, if the two boys know their business and do their duty.

It is not part of the business of a whipper-in at any time to speak to a hound, otherwise than keeping them together; or rate into the huntsman, who should always be with the main body of the hounds.

Neither huntsman or whippers-in to speak to the hounds while running on a good scent; on a middling one the huntsman may encourage his hounds at his discretion without any other persons interfering.

The company always at a distance that the hounds may not be hurried, which is the loss of many a fox, as well as a loss of a great deal of beauty a good pack of hounds will show at a half scent.

When the hounds from running come to a check, the huntsman is not to speak, but allow the hounds to have their first cast; and if after that not cast off, the huntsman to observe the point at which they threw up and then to help the hounds to the best of his judgement, but without hurry; for when a fox is sinking, time must be taken, as he then runs short and is often behind by clapping down.

The gentlemen for their own sakes will observe that a confabulation down wind often heads a fox and endangers the whole day's sport.[125]

The second thing to be mentioned before we part with Lord Tankerville is the poet's revenge. Revenge, that is, for all the trouble he had caused the gentlemen of Chariton, and particularly his grace, whom he revered. It takes the form of a revelation: an illicit affair with a lady who captured his heart and caused him to abandon his wife, house and home, hounds and horses, and flee; the sort of thing that appears in the tabloid press today!

As Homer writes and matchless Pope translates
that gods and goddesses all subject were
to diff'rent passions as we mortals are,
so Delia's [Diana's] breast with deep resentment glows
and meditates revenge on Tankerville,
pert youth who dar'd a goddess to affront.
The Cyprian queen [Venus] one day she thus accosts
'Venus, you're proud of conquests, I am not;
you use your arts my hunters to debauch;
I covet none of all your venal train.
Why cannot we for once here make a truce?'
'The terms? What are they?' Venus quick replies.
'I'll give you Bennet [Tankerville], take him as a bribe;
he does me honour, but he'll do you more.'
Prevailing is the force of wish't for gifts;
the blue ey'd wench then smiling thus consents
'Diana, I do here agree and own
I long have coveted your Tankerville.'a
Both parted pleas'd, impatient each to see
her cunning well laid plots and schemes take place.

62 Hon. Henry Pelham, a subscriber to the Great Room. He was prime minister for nearly twelve years with his brother the Duke of Newcastle as secretary of state.

When straight an am'rous calenture did seize
his guilty head and brain, and Tankerville
forsakes his house, forgets his hounds, distract!
A bailiff does his person seize, his heart
a famous lady keeps, he yields up all
his hounds; Diana takes young Nimrod [a hunter] *too;*
the queen with him to Charlton sends the best;
the rest as trophies thro' the land she sent,
whilst he, Mark Anthony's last steps to trace,
inactive, wastes in Cleopatra's toils,
and for an armful gives his all away.

Lord Tankerville's new amour remained a mystery, until the truth eventually came out. The Duke of Richmond devoted three years of his life to a campaign to stop smuggling in Sussex altogether. As part of the campaign he successfully petitioned for a Special Commission of Oyer and Terminer for the county of Sussex, which was held in Chichester and at which seven of the smugglers—Jackson, Tapner, Carter, the two Mills, Cobby and Hammond were tried and found guilty. Lord Tankerville was suspected of having a romantic entanglement with Mrs. Jackson, the wife of William Jackson, the leader of the smugglers, and this was alluded to in a letter from the prime minister Henry Pelham to Richmond.

London, Tuesday 21st February 1749
… I hope good may come from the encouragement you intend to give Mrs Jackson, and if she should wipe off her guilt in any degree by the justice she shall do her country in detecting such

a set of villains, as your grace speaks of, I should then be curious to know a little of her amours with our friend in her younger more innocent days. I shall hardly look upon Tanky without laughing, and if your grace was present, I would venture his lordship's displeasure rather than lose my joke.[126]

Tankerville resigned as Master of the Buckhounds in 1737 and a year later, after only a year in office, he resigned as Lord of the Bedchamber to the king and went to live on his estates at Warke and Chillingham in Northumberland. Some of his hounds, 13½ couple, he sent to Charlton and thereafter he continued to breed hounds and pass on small numbers of those surplus to requirements. His son, Lord Ossulstone, went to live at Uppark, but the family connection with Sussex came to an end in 1747 when the house and estates were sold to Sir Matthew Fetherstonhaugh.

Camilla, Lady Tankerville, the butcher's daughter from Jarrow, was called by Lord Hervey 'a handsome, good natured, simple woman, to whom the king had formerly been a coquet'! In August 1737 she was appointed a Lady of the Bedchamber to Queen Caroline. In recommending her, the Prime Minister, Sir Robert Walpole told the queen that 'Lady Tankerville was a very safe fool and would give the king some amusement without giving her majesty any trouble'![127]

In November 1737, the Duke of Richmond started to keep a hunting diary, which he continued for 11 years. It began in a modest way, as the early entries were just a record of the horses he and his grooms and servants rode, usually four or five.[128] His equestrian establishments at Goodwood and Charlton were the responsibility of his stud groom William Frederick St Paul, a Frenchman from the family estates at Aubigny. The horses had endearing names: Grey Carey, Royal, Saucy Face, Sir William, Looby, Slug, Gin, Miss Newton, Roger, Sturdy Lump and Cheat! As it happens, his favourites were Sturdy Lump and Saucy Face, whom he rode much more than any of the others!

The exact function of the servants who went out is not clear. They may have been grooms or second horsemen or just attendants on his grace; probably they were all three. For that season they were Tom Durden, Joe Budd, Tom Leaver and Will Macey. He also sometimes mounted Tom Johnson himself, probably because a horse was not available in the huntsman's stable, which was separate; on one occasion he mounted Billy Ives, yeoman pricker to the Royal Buckhounds and sometimes M. de Marpon, a visiting Frenchman.

The hound book had been meticulously kept since its inception in 1721 and the hound lists were entered every year in the same immaculate copperplate hand. During the Duke of Bolton's time, only the young hounds entered and the hounds donated by other breeders were listed. The first complete list of all hounds in the kennel was in 1731 when the Duke of Richmond became sole proprietor and from this time, notes began to be added of how hounds were disposed of, whether cast, dead, lost, gone, leg broke, etc. or given away and to whom. For the next three seasons the young and given hounds were recorded only, but thereafter, from 1735, there were complete lists for each season. Several different people entered annotations or corrections (not always correct!) including the duke himself (whose handwriting is unmistakable), Lord Delawarr and others.

The list in 1737 was written in particularly neat copperplate by our scribe, but afterwards was covered with notes by the duke, mainly filling in gaps in the pedigrees, some of them, it

63 *(overleaf)* A List of the Duke of Richmond's Hounds 20 Dec‍ʳ 1737.

A List of the Duke of Richmond's Hounds 20 Dec'r 1737

Names	how bred	enter'd	
Curious	Lord Walpoles Crimson & old Cocker		gon to Ld Cowper.
§Countess	Comfort & Ratler		
Cocker	madam & Trouncer		
Climbank	Kindness & Trojan		
Carver	madam & Trouncer		
§Careless	madam & Trouncer		
Dashwood	ours Virgin & old Jockey		
Drummer	madam & Lord Gowr's Ranter		
§Diamond	Comfort & Duke of Rutlands Limner		
Emely	Ditto her sister		
Emperour	ours Virgin & old Jockey		
§Gillian	madam & Tapster		
Gamester	Lovely & Jockey		
Kindness	Frisky & Ld Tanks mounter		given to Tom Johnson
Mode	Sally & Luther		
§Mimmy	maiden & Ld Tanks mounter		
Nancy	Young madam & Wildman		dead
Princess	old comely & Trouncer		given to Tom Johnson
Ringwood	old madam & Jockey		
Ringwell	Emely & Gamester		given to Tom Johnson
Suky	Princess & Lord Lovels Jumper		
Trouncer	Frisky & Driver		
Tantwivy	madam & Lord Gowrs Ranter		
Tipler	Sally & Luther		
Topper	old Comely & Trouncer	Jan 2d	shott at Finderton
§Veny	Cruel & Lord Tanks mounter		
Victor	Comfort & Mr St Johns Ranter		given to Tom Johnson
Warriour	Lord Cowper's beagle & old Clowded		

These Fourteen couples of the Dukes own kind

Cruel	Twisdens kind		
Darling	from St John miller		return'd to Ld Craven from whom he was stolen
Driver	Orlebarr, from Chilton at Hampton Court		
Jenny	Noel, gott by Chanter of the Confederate hunt; Chanter was full brother to Ranter		
Luther	Herbert. Racket Limner		
§Phillis	Noel, gott by a son of Mr Tomsons madcap		
Takeher	Ditto		
Ruby	Craven	Jan 26	given back to Ld Craven
Vulcan	St John miller, bred by Mr St John		cast
Wallcot	Noel, gott by Captain		

Continuation of the List 20 Dec.' 1737

Names	how bred	enter'd
Busy	Noels	
Bowler	Cravens. Bridget & Warrior	
Bowner	Ditto. Ld Cravens Crowner & Mr Andrews musick	
Comely	Ditto	— Dead
Daybell	Cardigans. Tom Johnson Carver. Mr Andrews pleasant	— Dead
Dido	Andrews — D. Griffins Sury	
Flurry	Ditto Conqueror & Andrews Juniper	
Gaylass	Ditto. noels ruler, andrews fairmaid	
Jockey	Ditto — D: Richmonds Jockey, andrews's Phenix	— Dead
Jewell	Confederates. D: Rutlands madcap, Ld Gowers Jewel	Colt
Lucy	Newbys. Ld Cardigans wonder	
Mopsy	Andrews.	
Peggy	Ditto — Mr Andrews's Jovial, Tom Johnsons strumpet	
Rachel	Ditto —	Jan 12 given Mr York
Rattler		Colt
Royal	Andrews, Tom Johnsons Clodder, Andrews fortune	— Colt
Rivall	Ditto — Tom Johnsons Conqueror, andrews madam	
Tanner	Herberts, Tom Johnsons Conqueror & Bridget	
Trusty	Skipworths Trusty & a bitch of Lord Byrons kind	
These Nine Couple came with Tom Johnson		
Careless	Minion & Thumper	
Cruel	Sr Wm Twisdens Sempstress & Mounter	
Comely	Mr Pelhams Drinkwell & Trouncer	
Cesar	Bridget & D. of Richmonds Ticket	
Bumper		Jun 20 given to Duke of Bolton
Drummer	Nelly daughter to Fair maid & Wildman	
Daybell	Mr Pelhams Drinkwell & Trouncer	
Doxy	Madam & Mounter	
Dido		Ditto to ye Duke of Bolton
Dolly		
Finder	Nancy, sister to Withers Snowball & Mounter	— Dead
Lilly	Nancy & Withers Finder	
Madam	Old Bonny & Dr Hamiltons Jugler	
Merrylass	Nelly & Old Wildman	
Musick	Cruel & Ruler	
Nelly		
Pleasant	Sempstress & Tipler	
Ruler	Nelly & Old Wildman	
Ransom	Fairmaid & T. Johnsons Conqueror	
Ringwood	Betty & Luther	— Dead
Princess	Madam & Mountain	
Singwell	Pallas & Withers's Snowball	— Dead

Names	how bred	enter'd
Topper	Morley's Dainty & Cludder	
Thunder	Old Bridget & Morley's Victor	
s Virgin	Old Fairmaid & Wither's Snowball	
Young Virgin	Dainty & Tipler	Dead.

These Thirteen Couple & half given by Ld Tankerville

s Bonny	} Blewit & Dashwood	1737
Buxom		
s Cruel	} Comely & Ranter	
Cryer		
Emperour	} Bridget & Emp^r	Cast.
Edmond		Cast.
Kitty	Comely & Ranter	
Lawyer	} Curious & Luther	
Limmer		
s Lewdy		
Pompey	Comfort & Pompey	
Ranter	}	
Rumsy		Jan: 12 given to Ld Verourt
Ringwood	} Daybell & Ranter	
Roister		
Rover	}	
Racket		Cast
Tosser	}	
Tipsy	} Busy & Tosser	
Tattle		
Tickler		
Traveller	Emely & Trouncer	

These Eleven Couple all bred at Charlton & enter'd this Year

The whole Pack Fifty Three Couple

This ends the year: 1737.

Doxey.
Wm Fauquir

has to be said, not consistent with entries elsewhere in the book! The list begins with 'Fourteen couple of the duke's own kind', that is old hounds bred at Charlton; the next is 'Five couple of old given hounds', of whom two couple were new to the pack; then 'Nine and a half couple came with Tom Johnson'; 'Thirteen couple and a half given by Lord Tankerville'; and finally 'Eleven couple all bred at Charlton and entered this year. The whole pack fifty three couple.'

At the bottom of the list is a charming sketch of 'Doxy', a hound from Lord Tankerville, drawn by William Fauquier. Another person with a somewhat illiterate scrawl (possibly Old Tom) has added how some of the hounds were disposed of. Topper, an old hound entered in 1735, 'Jan 2nd shot at Binderton'; Ruby, an old hound whom Brigadier Hawley had bought from Lord Craven in 1735, 'Jan 26th given back to Lord Craven'; Placket, an old hound who came with Tom Johnson, 'Jan 12th given to Mr Horde' and Rumsy, one of that season's young entry, 'Jan 12th given to Lord Harcourt'.[129] Bitches were often spayed and this is indicated in the list by 'S' preceeding the name. Thirteen couple of bitches in this list were spayed. On the other hand gelding was rare (or not recorded); up to 1750 only two dogs in the book were said to be 'gelt'.

The Duke of Bolton was still hunting in Hampshire and wrote on Christmas Eve, delighted to accept an invitation to Charlton.

Hackwood, Saturday 24th December 1737

… I am heartily glad to hear of your good sport and that your hounds do so well. I hope you find the foxes as stout as we find them here, for they have generally run us very great chases before they are killed. I hope you have had better weather than we have had for this fortnight past, for we have been out but three times, but the good sport we had makes some amends. The foxes hereabouts grow scarce so in a week or ten days I shall move and then I will send over to your grace and do myself the honour to accept of your kind invitation …[130]

Richmond was evidently not at Charlton for Christmas and received this account of the sport they enjoyed on Boxing Day from the Duke of St Albans.

Charlton, Tuesday 27th December 1737

I wish I could send you a better account of our sport yesterday or that we had killed a fox which we want to do very much at present, this being the third time we have gone out without killing and the third of Delawarr's going out that I suppose he is not going to see a fox killed. He hunts Wednesday and Friday and Saturday, goes away for the New Forest, that he may possibly hunt five times this year in Sussex, for which 'tis very worth while to keep five hunters.

We found at the Rewell, he came out upon Slindon Common, but was headed in by people at the alehouse or the Brigadier (Hawley) and his boy (Old Tom says he wants as much rating as Bumper or Dolly) but came out again a little lower and so went over the common to Eartham Common over Halnaker windmill hill to Red copse, where 'tis generally thought we changed, from thence through the North hanger over East Dean lane to the Parks, to Strickland's furzes, round Roche's hill to West Dean in a little copse he lay down a hare leaped up and met the hounds as they were running for him which checked them a little with a good deal of halloaing gave Ren an opportunity of getting ground of them went back again to the furzes and going up the hill by Tom Strickland's he was coursed by his dogs, so to my Lady Derby's[131] and then we lost him, a bitter cold day and a worse scenting day could not be. Old Tom went out with us but was not able to ride. We found the want of his head more than once yesterday. Mr. C. Bisshop met us at Madehurst as we were going to the Rewell. It was a pretty hard frost last night and the wind at the north east. I hope we shall see you on Thursday …[132]

The words are a bit difficult to follow and although it may have been a slow hunt because of the poor scent, it was no mean distance. The Rewell is a large wood a mile east of Slindon village, Halnaker windmill is four miles as the crow flies, Red copse a mile to the north, St Roche's hill (the Trundle) two and a half miles west and West Dean another mile or so. Then back to Lady Derby's at Halnaker which again as the crow flies is another three miles. Assuming that the hounds ran a bit further than the crow flies, that would be an eight mile point and 15 miles as they ran. Bumper and Dolly, who are in the list above, whose pedigree was unknown and who apparently required constant rating, were old hounds sent to Charlton by Lord Tankerville who clearly knew they were no good! The scrawl in the hound book reveals that they were given (fobbed off?) to the Duke of Bolton, who cannot have been too pleased to receive them!

As recounted in the first chapter, the Charlton Hunt Club had been formed at the *Bedford Head Tavern* in January 1738. Soon after, having the requisite quorum of three, they invited a visitor to stay for eight days.

Charlton, Sunday 12th February 1738
being the first meeting after the regulating of the society
Present: Edward Pauncefort (in the chair), Duke of Richmond, Duke of St Albans, Brigadier Henry Hawley, William Fauquier
William Fauquier asked the consent of the members present for his brother Francis Fauquier to come down to Charlton for eight days. It was accordingly balloted for in the manner prescribed in the sixth article and it was agreed to accordingly.[133]

A week later they decided to change the rules, which needed a quorum of nine.

Charlton, Tuesday 21st February 1738
Present: Lord Delawarr (in the chair), Duke of Richmond, Duke of St Albans, Lord Harcourt, Brigadier Hawley, Richard Honywood, William Fauquier, Sir Henry Liddell, Sir Robert Guldeford, Edward Pauncefort, Ralph Jenison, M de Marpon.
The following bye-law was proposed and balloted for and carried in the affirmative. That any gentleman of the neighbourhood or any gentleman that shall happen to be in the country may be invited to dinner by any of the members of the society.[134]

It certainly seems reasonable that any member should be allowed to bring a guest to dinner; in the original articles it was the Duke of Richmond's privilege only! The duke had spent most of the season in Sussex and, with the hounds going out three days a week, he had managed to fit in 34 days' hunting. His son and heir was thriving. In the Charlton weighing book it says '24th August 1738. Lord March (in shoes) 2 st 5 lbs being then 3 years 6 months and 2 days old'![135]

— VIII —

A Memorable Season

Undoubtedly the best season in the annals of Charlton was 1738/9. There were many memorable days. They were out three days a week and the duke recorded 45 days in his diary. He began the season with 10 horses in his stable. He still had his favourites Sturdy Lump and Saucy Face; and Grey Carey, Looby, Cheat, Sir William, Slug and Gin were still there. Roger and Miss Newton had gone and were replaced by Fidler and later in the season Infant, presumably a young horse. As in the season before, the duke's attendants would accompany him in the field.

Tom Johnson also had 10 horses in the huntsman's stable, Badger, Frost Face, Post Boy, Pickadilly, Spot, Windsor, Forrester, Crop, Walker and Goliah; they had to carry him and his whippers-in David Briggs and Nim Ives. Nim's brother Billy, yeoman pricker to the Royal Buckhounds, was there for quite a few days, mainly in January, and assisted with the whipping-in; and Mr. St Paul, the duke's stud groom was also out most of the time. The hound list for the season 1738/9 was entered in the book on Friday 24 November. One couple of last year's young entry and 11 couple of old hounds had been cast; 2½ couple were given to Tom Johnson and others were given the odd hound. They were replaced by 12½ couple of young hounds bred at Charlton and one hound given by Mr. Herbert. There were now 53½ couple in the kennel.[136]

They went to the Valdoe, near Goodwood, twice in early November and, although foxes were found, the weather was so bad they could make nothing of it. The next day out the duke mounted a visitor, the Hon. William FitzWilliam, son of Viscount FitzWilliam of Merrion, whose younger brother John was a hunt member; and they had their first kill. The following week they were also successful, running a fox from near Hooksway over the downs to Charlton forest.

That evening there was a meeting and two new members were elected. Lord Delawarr was in the chair and the nine other members present were the Dukes of Richmond and St Albans, Lord Henry Beauclerk, the Hon. Charles Feilding, Sir John Miller, Brigadier Hawley, Mr. Pauncefort, Mr. Fauquier and the hunting parson the Rev. Mr. Herne.

Charlton, Wednesday 8th November 1738
This day His Grace The Duke of Kingston was balloted for and admitted a member of this society. The Hon. Thomas Watson was also this day balloted for and admitted a member of this society.[137]

Evelyn Pierrepont, Duke of Kingston-upon-Hull, had inherited the dukedom on the death of his grandfather when he was only 15, his father having died while he was an infant. His election at Charlton may have been related to his appointment that year as Master of the

64 Elizabeth Chudleigh, 'The notorious Duchess of Kingston', in the character of Iphigenia at the Venetian Ambassador's masquerade at Somerset House. Married to the Earl of Bristol, she was found guilty of bigamy and fled the country.

Royal Staghounds, North of Trent. He later became a distinguished soldier, but he will be mainly remembered for his marriage to 'the notorious Duchess of Kingston'.

Elizabeth Chudleigh, whose father was governor of Chelsea Hospital, was described in the marriage register as a spinster. Twenty-five years before she had married privately Augustus John Hervey, later Earl of Bristol. A divorce *a mensa et thoro* had been granted, which she erroneously considered to have annulled that marriage.[138] George III and his Queen attended the ceremony in St George's, Hanover Square and nothing could exceed the splendour with which this strange marriage was solemnised. The bride was unhesitatingly received at court, though 'it was believed she had sometime carried on intercourse' with the duke.[139] It was rumoured he had previously married Louisa Francisca, commonly called Madamoiselle de Maine, daughter of Lewis Augustus of Bourbon, Duke of Maine and legitimated son of Louis XIV by Louise de la Vallière, although this may have been malicious gossip.[140]

The new duchess had a most beautiful face, although her person was described as 'ill made, clumsy and ungraceful'.[141] Hating prolixity and mock modesty, her maxim was to be short, clear and surprising, so she concentrated her rhetoric into swearing and dressed in a style next door to nakedness![142] The duke died in 1773 leaving her an estate worth £12,000 a year, but his will was contested and, three years after his death, she was tried in Westminster Hall for bigamy before the House of Lords, the prosecutors being Mr. Medows and Lady Frances, his wife, sister of the late Duke.

65 Hon. Thomas Watson, elected to Charlton in 1738 when he was 23, succeeded his brother as Earl of Rockingham in 1745 but died of smallpox only two months afterwards.

The verdict was given according to the usual procedure in such cases. Earl Bathurst, the Lord Steward called upon every peer by his name (119 sat), beginning with the junior baron, asking him: 'Is the prisoner guilty of the felon whereof she stands indicted or not guilty?' Every peer present severally standing up uncovered and answered: 'Guilty upon my honour', laying his right hand upon his breast.[143] She pleaded privilege as a peeress and escaped sentence, left the country and went to live at St Petersburg.

The Hon. Thomas Watson was a less controversial but tragic character. He was the younger brother by a year of Lewis, Earl of Rockingham, familiarly known as Little Rock, who died in 1745 aged 30 from the dreaded smallpox, only to be followed two months later by his brother. The title passed to a cousin, whose son, the Marquess of Rockingham, became prime minister and was remembered by Harry Budd as having hunted at Charlton.

Another visitor was balloted for on Friday 10th, one Richard Meggott at the request of Edward Pauncefort, who was 'admitted for eight days'.[144] On Monday they had a poor day in the coverts to the west of Chichester (Row copse, Oldwick, Stoke, Ashling, Adsdean and Juniper bottom), but a better one on Wednesday up on the downs around Upwaltham, Littleton and Tegleaze, killing a fox back in Charlton forest.

On Friday 17 November towards Arundel they had a poor day and that evening for dinner the company was joined by the new member, Hon. Thomas Watson, and by Ralph Jenison, who had succeeded Lord Tankerville as Master of the Royal Buckhounds the previous June. Hon. William FitzWilliam was balloted for and elected a member.[145] Monday was a rotten day near Chichester; but the day after, heading west towards Stoughton, they had a long day.

Tuesday 21st November 1738
Found at the Wildham, nine couple ran off with Lord Delawarr, over Bow hill to Charlton forest, East Dean wood, Tegleaze and back to Crows Hall.

That was a fair distance, it being seven miles as the crow flies from the Wildham to Tegleaze and another six back to Crows Hall. The rest of the pack had trouble with Lord Tankerville's hounds who were hunting near Uppark.

> The rest went with another fox to the Haslett and because of my Lord Tankerville's hounds made nothing of the scent, so tried back to the Wildham, and from thence to Phillis wood where they found a fresh fox, and ran several rings in the same wood, Monkton park and Lewknor's copse, then over Cocking warren to the Marlows, then back to Lewknor's copse, Sadler's furze, Monkton furze and to Monkton park, where we took off, it being night and all the horses tired.

On Thursday they had better luck, running a fox from the Valdoe near Goodwood nearly to East Marden but, going out on Saturday towards Arundel, foxes were about but the scent was so poor they came home early.

Richmond was a great correspondent. Over the years he was always writing to people and receiving letters. One of his most regular correspondents was the Duke of Newcastle, who was Secretary of State for 30 years. He loved his hunting, which he enjoyed at his estates at Claremont and Bishopstone in East Sussex and, 20 years before, he had subscribed to the building of the Great Room. Since Richmond had become proprietor at Charlton, Newcastle had not been back and it needed all the powers of Richmond's persuasion (and a long letter) to try to get him to come.

Goodwood, Friday 24th November 1738

On Wednesday I received the favour of your grace's letter and I do assure you that if I could be of the least service in the world to you, I would attend you with pleasure. You know very well that before it is long I must go to London, where besides duty I have some business and I hope to contrive to do them both at the same time the week after next and to be back again in about a fortnight, when I shall certainly quit my hounds no more …

The weather is now so fine, the hounds in such order and such a plenty of foxes that I really can spare no time from my sport but what necessity obliges me to. In answer to which your grace may say how are they then to expect to see me at Goodwood or Charlton? I answer because you have promised it for these five years and have never once come, I mean to Charlton, for you have honoured Goodwood, though not so often as I could have wished, but at this time I do beg if you do come westward it may be to Charlton, for this reason, because at Charlton you may be quiet and snug, whereas at Goodwood you know it must be what Jemy Brudenell [his uncle] calls <u>rantum scantum</u>, which would not be proper at this time, for Mrs Brudenell is now here, is so very ill she has kept her bed these six weeks, and I really am in some apprehensions she will not soon get out of it, if ever, for she is certainly in a very dangerous and lingering way.

So noise and company here would not be so proper, but at Charlton, where you are a member, you would make us all vastly happy in your company. We could lodge about six of you very well. Yourself, Honourable Harry [Pelham, Newcastle's brother] and Sir William Gage are of the club. Then as for Linky [Earl of Lincoln, Newcastle's nephew], Colonel Carpenter or anybody else you please to bring, they must either be balloted for or come with me as my guests from Goodwood. I have not a horse you will care to ride except Looby and old Gin. However they are all at your service and I am sure Dell [Lord Delawarr] would with pleasure mount you, whilst you let him ride New York; but why can't you bring a couple of your own horses?

All at Charlton are yours. The company consists in the Duke of St Albans, Lord Harry [Beauclerk], Dell [Lord Delawarr], [Lord] Jemmy Cavendish, [Brigadier Henry] Hawley, [Edward] Pauncefort, [Hon. Thomas] Watson Little Rock's brother [Lewis, Earl of Rockingham] and [William] Fauquier. Jemmy is gone this morning to town and returns on Tuesday. We expect Lord Harcourt, Sir Harry Liddell and the Honywoods very soon, and at Christmas Sir Cecil [Bisshop], but not till then, for at all other times it's dearer living at Charlton than at home, but at Christmas, it is much dearer at home, so at that good time we never fail of his company! If you do come pray let it be either this week next or about the 11th of next month when I shall be back from London. I have written a long letter *a propos de rien* ...[146]

The reply came four days later reporting on a great run in East Sussex, in contrast to the sport being shown at Charlton, but nevertheless Newcastle hoped to be able to accept the invitation.

Bishopstone, Tuesday 28th November 1738

We have this day had as fine a chase as our downs can show. Above ten miles over the best part of our country, as fast as dogs can go and faster than horses went, except for the huntsman's, Linky's [Earl of Lincoln], your humble servant's and his groom's and one more. The Honourable Harry [Pelham], who is just returned from Norfolk and Suffolk (but has not been lately at Charlton) affirms he has seen nothing like this (which by the by he would scarce see at all). Flushed by our chase and being much wanted by a great number of good friends to go to dinner, you must not expect a long letter, though I must send a million of thanks for yours.

As your grace goes to London next week, it will be impossible for me to attend you whilst I stay at Bishopstone, for I am obliged to be in London the week after and Linky gives a ball to the ladies of the Seaford assembly next Thursday, which makes it impossible for me to come this week. However as we courtiers generally do, I will pay the promise or rather ten promises with one more and will endeavour after your return to Charlton to attend you from Claremont and will contrive to send my own horses if I can, otherwise I will ride New York.

We constantly drink your health every day ... The Honourable Harry and Linky are much yours ...[147]

Meanwhile the hounds at Charlton had a busy day starting near Goodwood and ending in the dark at Stansted, seat of the Earl of Scarbrough, whom Richmond had succeeded as Master of the Horse. He hunted regularly at Charlton and was a subscriber to the articles. His sister Mary was married to the Earl of Halifax, who had a hunting box at Charlton and was an original subscriber to the building of the Great Room. It has to be said that some practices which were condoned in the 18th century would be quite unacceptable today, such as taking a live fox home and giving it to the pack two days later.

Tuesday 28th November 1738

Tried the Valdoe, but the hounds did not find, yet a fox stole away from the same covert behind us, and was seen and hallooed by the Duke of St Albans, Lord Delawarr etc; then went and found in Stoke copse, from whence we ran directly to Adsdean, and there to ground. Nim Ives stayed and dug her, a bitch fox, (but she was brought home and given to the hounds on Thursday, her under jaw being broke and the young hounds wanting blood), then we went to the Wildham, found immediately, and ran several rings in the Inholmes, Pitlands, Haslett and back to the

66 Thomas Pelham-Holles, Earl of Clare and 1st Duke of Newcastle, a subscriber to the Great Room and Secretary of State for many years.

67 Henry Fiennes Clinton, 9th Earl of Lincoln, elected by ballot in 1742, was Newcastle's heir and later succeeded as 2nd Duke of Newcastle. He was known as Linky.

Wildham; then back to the Haslett where I lost them, then they went to Stansted forest and there it being dark, they took off the hounds.

On Friday, they met unadventurous foxes near Arundel which ran round and round in the covert and never broke; and that evening in the Great Room, Richard Meggott was proposed by Edward Pauncefort to the members present, of whom there were nine, to have leave to stay eight days longer at Charlton, which was agreed.[148] Richmond was still urging the Duke of Newcastle to come and was prepared to make as much accommodation as he could.

Charlton, Friday 1st December 1738

I am heartily glad to hear your grace has had so good sport. I could wish I might send you the same account from hence, but we have done nothing to brag of this week ... Ten miles in a fine country is sport enough with any pack of fox hounds, if they behave well during the whole time. Mine are at present in perfect order and I must now tell you you may see them if you please to honour us with your company next week, for my journey to London is deferred to the week after.

Linky's ball is a very good excuse for this week and your going to town for the week after next, but you must invent one for next week if you don't come. So pray put us off no more, but make us all happy in your company and I promise you, you shall be perfectly well lodged, mounted, fed and drenched.

68 Richard Lumley, 2nd Earl of Scarbrough, sold the manors of Singleton and Charlton to the Duke of Richmond in 1731. He was Master of the Horse until 1734 when the Duke of Richmond took office in his stead.

My best services attend Linky and the Honourable Harry. I hope they, Sir William Gage and Colonel Carpenter will come with you.[149]

Unfortunately the visit proved to be impossible and it seems doubtful if Newcastle or his brother Henry Pelham ever did go to Charlton again. However their correspondence continued unabated and over the years they wrote no less than 462 letters to one another.

Bishopstone, Saturday 2nd December 1738
As I cannot make a good excuse for not waiting upon you next week and must make one, I must depend upon your goodness for allowing it. Every post brings us accounts that Lord Essex thinks of coming down to Bishopstone and therefore I might say I cannot be absent lest he should come at that time, but the truth is, if I come to Charlton next week, I cannot return hither before I go to London and then I shall lose almost the whole week here, which I should be very unwilling to do, considering how much real pleasure I take with my own friends and how seldom I am able to see them.

Don't reproach me, though you justly may; I will if possible contrive to come from Claremont and will endeavour to settle the time with you when you come to town the week after next. Pray my compliments to all the good company at Charlton.[150]

The Valdoe was one of the most popular draws and an almost certain find. This time the fox took them up to the Benges where they killed:

Monday 4th December 1738
Found in the Valdoe, ran through Heberden's fields round to Lavant, quite through the street and back to the Valdoe, through it to the Redvins, then through Lady Derby's rook wood, the

two Winkins to Stricklands furze, then through the Winkin again to Red copse, North hanger, Selhurst park, the Benges and just beyond it in a hedgerow killed a bitch fox.

and on Wednesday the fox ran from the downs to Stedham near Midhurst, when everyone except the huntsman and Lord James Cavendish were left behind and lost. Friday was one of those tedious days, familiar to woodland huntsmen, when foxes run in circles and hounds keep changing. Three days later they had a better day, but only a short point, ending with the fox going to ground and being pulled out in full view of the pack and hunted again. This is another practice which is now unacceptable. The next day Tuesday 12th they found in the vale at Burton and ran up the downs but the scent failed.

For some reason none of the duke's attendants was with him on Friday. The morning was completely blank. They hacked for fully 20 miles and the hounds drew eight coverts without finding anything. They may have been about to give up, but going back nearly to Charlton they found in the park above the village and had a good four-mile point, 15 miles as they ran.

Friday 15th December 1738
Beat the Tegleaze, North comb, Farm wood, Glatting hanger, Priest comb, Dawtrey's hooks, Benges and Red copse without finding, then found in Charlton copse, ran through East Dean park, both Winkins, Halnaker park and garden, Redvins, the Valdoe, Goodwood park and grove, the Valdoe again, Heberden's fields, Haye's bushes, Binderton down, old warren, up St Roche's hill, down to Strickland's furze, over the road to Halsteds down, and there killed her, an old bitch fox.

On Wednesday they found a fox in the vale near Graffham and ran it up the downs and down the south side where it went to ground. They still run up the downs but very rarely these days do hounds hold the line down the other side.

The duke went to London the next day, which he had been going to do ever since his abortive invitation to the Duke of Newcastle. While he was away, he received a present of some hounds from an aunt. Mary, Lady Molyneux was his mother's elder sister, whose husband Richard, Viscount Molyneux had died very recently on 12 December. They kept a pack of hounds in Cheshire and, wishing to dispose of them, she sent her huntsman John Eastom down to Sussex with 10½ couple. Many of the lines came from the Confederate hunt in Leicestershire where Lady Molyneux's nephew the Earl of Cardigan, son of Richmond's 'Uncle Cardigan', was one of the masters. The pedigrees are meticulously described and recorded, as was the custom; serious hound breeders were continually trying to improve the hunting qualities of the hounds in their kennels. One of the new acquisitions was considered too old to keep, so was sent back with the huntsman; another is noted to have been discarded for running at sheep. Of this new entry, two dogs, Rockwood and Finder, and two bitches, Duchess and Lilly, were later used for breeding at Charlton.[151]

Richmond spent Christmas in his house in Whitehall and notes that Tom Johnson also went away for Christmas, back to his family and friends in the New Forest. However Billy Ives hunted the hounds on Boxing Day and the duke wrote an account of their excellent day's sport in his diary, although he was not out himself. Finding in Stoke copse (now known as Stoke Clump, a famous landmark), they had a six-mile point from Ladyholt in the north to Emsworth in the south and ran for at least 25 miles across country now containing the main Portsmouth railway line and large towns like Emsworth and Havant; these days completely unhuntable.

69 Mary, Viscountess Molyneux, Richmond's aunt, who donated 10½ couple of hounds in 1738.

Tuesday 26th December 1738
Found in Stoke copse, ran to Adsdean over the end of Bow hill, to Watergate hanger, from thence to the Haslett, to the woods above West Marden, to Compton down for Lady Holt, headed back, through the Markwells to Stansted new cut pieces, through Stansted park to Rowlands castle, into Bear forest to Mays copse, Emsworth common and almost to Havant, then back through Westbourne, to Rowlands castle, round Stansted park, to the new cut pieces and there killed him, a very old dog fox.

A frustrating last day rounded off the year 1738, but January 1739 proved to be a red letter month. Hounds hunted on 13 days and caught 11 foxes. It was the exception to account for more than one fox each time out, as normally a kill marked the end of the day's sport, like stag hunting today. On New Year's day, hounds found near Chichester but, although they caught the fox, it was otherwise an unexciting day. Billy Ives was riding 'Lord Delawarr's ball'd face', whatever that means!

They were not out again until Friday, when the duke's horse Sturdy Lump was ridden by 'a boy'. He obviously didn't bother to find out the boy's name! The hunt was short, about five miles and the next day they had a five-mile point, but lost the fox apparently from a false halloa (as far as we know, there were no antis out in those days!). The Harroways is now the straight at Goodwood racecourse.

Saturday 6th January 1739
Found in Trumley copse, ran to Cuckolds lee, Crows hall, up Bow hill by Bradley bushes, almost to the Wildham, but turned short back round by Mr Knight's summer house, down through West Dean warren, then up the hill between Binderton and Midlavant, there cross the Lavant up to the windmill upon St Roche's hill, then down St Roche's hill to the Valdoe, from thence to

Westerton, Seeley copse, Hat hill, down through Strickland's furze, to Charlton copse. There by a false halloa lost the scent, being then at a dead fault, though tried over the Harroways to the Valdoe, Goodwood park, Strickland's furze, East Dean park and Charlton copse, but could never recover the scent. It was afterwards thought that the fox went to ground amongst the elder trees by Goodwood park lodge, which was likely enough, because the hounds carried no scent beyond the corner of the park pale by the Valdoe.

The consistent scenting conditions continued for the next fortnight, although not all the foxes were as adventurous as was to be the case later in the month. However the hounds were very persistent in sticking to the line.

Monday 8th January 1739
Found in the upper Tegleaze, ran through the lower Tegleaze to East Dean wood, from thence out at the corner along the side hills into the Tegleaze again, then back again to East Dean wood, took a ring there, and a brace of foxes came out and through the lower to the upper Tegleaze, but the hounds were kept to one scent and in the Tegleaze the fox went to ground in a rabbit burrow, where he was dug out with a bill and killed, a dog fox.

Nine members were present for dinner in the Great Room; Edward Pauncefort, in the chair, Richmond and his uncle James Brudenell, Lord Henry Beauclerk, Sir Cecil Bisshop over from Parham, Sir Robert Guldeford, who was now 78 and still hunting, Sir John Miller from Lavant, Brigadier Hawley and Richard Honywood. They elected Richard Meggott, who had been to Charlton as a visitor on two occasions that season.[152]

The next hunting day was Wednesday when they went back to Trumley Copse beyond Lavant. After some local hunting the fox broke and ran back almost to Charlton. They went back there on Thursday and drew Stoke Clump, which is very near Trumley, but the fox ran away to the west and the hounds stuck to the line with great tenacity, all around Stansted, Westbourne and Adsdean.

Thursday 11th January 1739
Found in Stoke copse, ran through Stoke coney copse to Adsdean wood, down by Racton farm to Bourne, Bourne common, Stansted forest, so far the scent was tolerably carried on, but then the coldest scent that ever was round Stansted forest, the new cut pieces, Stansted forest again, Stansted park, over by Old lodge, where the scent began to mend, then to Watergate hanger, where in a hedgerow we entapised [this means lurked or lay hid] him, and ran him very hard by Lordington wood to Stansted park, Stansted forest, the new cut pieces, to Bourne common again, back to Stansted forest, over the earth at the Syndals to Racton farm, then by Lordington, up Adsdean down, to Adsdean copse, down again to Racton park, back again by Lordington meadows, up to the down and into Adsdean copse and there they killed him, an old dog fox.

On the following Monday, they went back towards Stoke copse again and the day looked as if it might be blank, were it not for a country yokel halloaing a fox away from a hedgerow near Adsdean, but he was caught after a short run. On Wednesday they found a brace in Red copse near Goodwood and the pack split.

David went off with 10 couple of hounds with one, and everybody else followed the rest after the other fox into North wood, as hard as hounds could run. There they viewed her and killed her, a bitch fox. Then as we missed David and ten couple of hounds, we got as fast as we could to Halnaker and got into them, and then with the whole pack we ran him … up to Eartham common fields, where in a hedgerow they killed him, a dog fox.

Two days later they killed a brace again, the first at the Duke of Norfolk's back door! While hacking home hounds happened to hit on another line, giving them a hunt of about seven miles as they ran.

Friday 19th January 1739
Found in Heberden copse, ran to the Rooks leaving the Rewell on the left hand, through Arundel park to Arundel castle hanger, by the postern gate, there killed a bitch fox. Then coming back through Arundel park the hounds fell upon a fresh scent, carried it into the Rooks, from thence directly through the Rewell to the Rewell hill, to Sherwood from thence down to South wood, then to Houghton hangers, Bury steeps, up to Priest comb, there headed, but came up again by Bury chalk pit, along Arundel course, down West Burton hanger, and there in a hedgerow killed him, a dog fox.

Monday was another memorable run of 20 miles and an eight-mile point at just under eight miles an hour between Coney copse above West Dean and Stopham, where they killed.

Monday 22nd January 1739
Found in East Dean wood, ran the side hills over Heyshott hanger to the north gate of Charlton forest, but came out immediately by Lord Montagu's copse to Herringdean, into the forest again by Foxley copse, over Cocking highway, through the Marlows to Coney copse, from thence back again through the fields over Cocking highway, to Cocking course into the forest again, through the forest and East Dean wood, along the side hills, over Woolavington down, Duncton highway, up through Duncton chalk pit, down Barlavington hanger, through Burton park, Old park, Red hill to Coates, leaving Waltham park just on the right hand, over Midhurst river by Fittleworth bridge, where we crossed over the common to Stopham common, where the fox was found dead, we believe killed by a greyhound and some curs, an old dog fox. We ran two hours and thirty eight minutes, and the hounds behaved extraordinarily well.

Lord Montagu, who is mentioned as owning a covert on the downs near Cocking hilltop, lived at Cowdray Park in the beautiful Elizabethan house, now a ruin. His ancestor Sir Anthony Browne, Master of the Horse to Henry VIII, had been granted the manors and lands of Battle Abbey at the dissolution; he was left the Cowdray estate by his elder brother and completed the building of the house. His son was created Viscount Montagu by Queen Mary (the family were catholics), and in August 1591 he provided six days of sumptuous entertainment for Queen Elizabeth. The nuns of Easebourne Priory, it was said, had put a curse on the family that they would perish by fire and water. That is precisely what happened. On the night of 24 September 1793 the magnificent family seat was totally destroyed by fire and shortly afterwards the eighth viscount died unmarried aged 24, being drowned in attempting to shoot the falls at Schaffhausen on the Rhine. The title passed to a cousin who died four years later without issue when the title became extinct. The last male descendants of the family, two sons of the eighth Viscount's sister, were also drowned in sight of their parents 22 years later in July 1815.[153] A tragic story!

70 Anthony Browne, 6th Viscount Montagu of Cowdray Park.

Wednesday was less satisfactory; the pack split, they kept changing foxes and deteriorating scent and weather put an end to the day. That evening at dinner they were joined by Cornet Philip Honywood and invited another visitor for eight days, Arthur Gore, at the invitation of William Fauquier.[154] In the morning the duke and duchess paid a visit to the old Duke of Somerset at Petworth, who insisted on giving them some rather strange physic for the hunters.

Petworth, Friday 26th January 1739

The most exceeding kind visit the Duchess of Somerset and I received yesterday morning from the Duchess of Richmond and from your grace is now and will upon all occasions be acknowledged with a true sense of it and this day we desire to have the satisfaction to know that both your graces returned safe and well to Charlton, as I did perceive by the looks of the Duchess of Richmond's horse to be very well rode by so noble and so great a huntress to the very death of many foxes and so entirely to her grace's satisfaction. I do therefore take liberty to send your grace the receipt to make cerstial balls to be given night and morning to this horse and to your grace's hunters after every chase. The very same balls I have more than fifty years practised and my horses used to receive very great benefit from them as I hope yours will find the same good effect upon using them. I send your grace a small pot of the balls to be used until the receipt does produce more by your own apothecary.

We wish both your graces good weather which will add to the pleasure and agreeableness in every fox chase now and at your return from London. In the meantime we do presume to flatter ourselves with hopes of the honour to see both your graces here some hours longer than yesterday.[155]

Whether they took his advice we shall not know, but after the old duke's complimentary remarks about the duchess and her hunter, she was up betimes in the morning ready for the day's sport, which turned out to be truly remarkable.

— IX —
THE GRAND CHASE

The hunt on Friday 26 January 1739, which lasted from a quarter to eight in the morning to ten minutes to six in the evening, was measured with a wheel and reckoned to be over 57 miles as they ran. It was actually a 12-mile point; that is, the distance between the furthest points to which hounds ran was 12 miles, from Colworth down in the west to the river at South Stoke in the east. Many have said they must have changed foxes. Maybe, but there is a comment in the account which pointedly states that at Puttocks copse above West Dean the fox 'missed the earth'. The hunting diaries contain many references to the hounds changing foxes, so whilst it remains a possibility, their claim to have chased one fox for that distance should, in the author's view, be allowed to stand.

It was called The Grand Chase by the Duke of Richmond; the greatest chase that ever was, he wrote in his diary. He appears to have started writing shortly after getting back to Charlton. There are some crossings out and hesitation in the wording. Perhaps he started writing that evening, but exhaustion and wine frustrated his endeavours! He continued later, but the account for some reason ends before the kill. The section in brackets completes it, had he continued it to the end, and is taken from the measure of the run which follows later.

THE GRAND CHASE
Friday 26th January 1739

Slug	Myself	Badger	Tom Johnson
Looby	Joe Budd	Pickadilly	David
Sturdy Lump	Tom Leaver	Walker	Nim
then at Goodwood I took		Frost face	Billy Ives
Saucy Face	Myself		
Sir William	Billy Ives		

Here is the account of the greatest chase that ever was.

At a quarter before eight in the morning, the hounds found a fox in East Dean wood, and ran an hour in that cover, then into Charlton forest, up to Punters copse, through Herringdean to the Marlows, up to Coney copse, back through the Marlows to the west gate of Charlton forest, over the fields to Nightingale bottom, Drought house, up Pine pit hanger, over by Downley ruins, through Lady Lewknor's Puttocks, by Colworth down, through old Read, all along Venus wood, to the Hacking place, through the Marlows, cross Cocking road to Herringdean copse, then into Singleton forest, where they ran several rings for near an hour in that covert and Punters copse, and were several times at a fault, then from Punters copse they ran through Charlton forest and East Dean wood to the lower Tegleaze, Buckleys, down between Graffham and Woolavington, through Mr Orme's park and paddock, Northwood farm, over the heaths to

The Charlton Hunt

1738/9 **The Grand Chase**
Fryday: Jan: ry 26.

Slug. — — My self.	Badger. — — Tom Johnson.
Looby. — — Joe Budd.	Pickadilly. — David.
Sturdy lump. — Tom Leaver.	Walker. — — Nim.
then at Godwood I took	Frost face. — Billy Ives.
Saucy face — my self.	
Sr Will m — Billy Ives.	

22.
†

Here is the account of the greatest Chase that ever was.

Fryday: 26: Janry 1738/9.

At a quarter before eight in the morning, the hounds found a fox in East Dean Wood; & ran an hour in the Cover, then into the Charlton forrest, up to Puntys Cops, through Hering=dean to the marlows, up to Coney Cops, back through the marlows to the West gate of Charlton forrest, over the feilds to nightingale bottom. Drought house, up Pine pitt hanger, over by Downly ruins, through Lad Lewknors Puttocks, by Colworth down, through old Rea all along Venus wood, to the hacking place, through the marlows, cross cocking road to Hering dean Cops,

71 The Grand Chase. The duke's own account.

The Grand Chase

~~East Dean Wood the Lower Teglees~~
~~Charlton Forest~~
~~Through Charlton Forest, Puntys Cops, East Dean~~
~~Wood~~
Then into Singleton Forest, where they ran several rings, for ~~above~~ near an hour, ~~in~~ that Cover & Puntys Cops, & were several times at a fault, then from Punty's Cops, they ran through Charlton Forest, East Dean Wood, To the Lower Teglees, Buckleys, down between Graffom & Woollavington, through Mr. orms's Park & Paddock, northwood farm, over the heaths to Selham Furs's, Freilders hop garden, by Selham barn, through the ~~enclosed~~ feilds belonging to Selham & Ambersham, To amersham Fuzzes, Totham Fuzzes, over the brook by Dunford farm, to authers Furs, cross Cocking ~~high way~~ Causway by the lime Kiln to Paddocks wood, Henley Cops, half penny wood, then cross Cocking high way, up by Heming Dean barn, to huncoombs, over Cocking curse to Puntys Cops, ~~through the~~ into Charlton Forest at the north gate ~~by the Table~~ mite through the forest by the stone Table, to Nightingal bottom to Drought house, up Pine Pitt hanger, by Downly riing, to Whistling alley Cops, Heydon Barn, Cross the south end of Weedean Warren, down to Binderton Farm, cross the Lavant up Binderton down, through Hays bushes, Bickley bushes, cross the enclosures into Valdy, through Goodwood Parke where the fox was seen, out at the upper charlton gate to Stretting road upon the downs, through Salley Cops to Lady erbys Rookwood, over by Halnaker windmill to Tebligg farm, over long Down.

113

Selham furze, Fielder's hop garden, by Selham barn, through the enclosed fields belonging to Selham and Ambersham, to Ambersham furzes, Todham furzes, over the brook by Dunford farm, to Aukers furze, cross Cocking causeway by the lime kiln to Paddock wood, Henley copse, Halfpenny wood, then cross Cocking highway, up by Herringdean barn, to Suncombe, over Cocking course to Punters copse, into Charlton forest at the north gate, quite through the forest by the stone table, to Nightingale bottom, to Drought house, up Pine pit hanger, by Downley ruins, to Whistling Alley copse, Heydon barn, cross the south end of West Dean warren, down to Binderton farm, cross the Lavant, up Binderton down, through Haye's bushes, Bickley bushes, cross the enclosures into the Valdoe, through Goodwood park, where the fox was seen, out at the upper Charlton gate, to Strettington road upon the downs, through Seeley copse to Lady Derby's rook wood, over by Halnaker windmill to Seabeach farm, over Long down, (Eartham common field, quite through Mr Kemp's high wood to the railed piece, through the enclosures to Slindon in-down, to Madehurst parsonage, over Madehurst down to Fairmile, through the enclosures to Madehurst church and so to Houghton forest, cross the road by the waypost, over Houghton down to South wood, through the enclosed fields of South Stoke down to the brooks, where they killed her, a bitch fox).

Monday produced another excellent hunt, with the hounds continuing to perform extremely well. They scored a six-mile point and a good twelve as they ran at a speed of almost ten miles an hour. This rather dispels the notion, often raised by modern fox hunters that hunting in those days was very slow. On that particular day, it certainly was not, although it does help if hounds run that far without a check, which is very unusual in any country.

Monday 29th January 1739
Found in Dawtrey's hooks, ran through Kemps high wood, up Long down, all the length of it to Eartham bushes, from thence the length of Halnaker hill, through Red copse, North hanger, the Bubholts, East Dean park, Charlton copse, the Harroways, cross the green lane to old warren, down to Singleton, up to Downley and then in Cobdens pine pit hanger killed him, a dog fox. He ran an hour and nineteen minutes, and the hounds ran hard and were never at a check.

The grand chase had caused great excitement at Charlton and in the hunting world outside. It had to be the longest chase ever and, to make sure it was fully documented, the duke ordered his men to set off with a cart wheel and measure it. They omitted the first three hours of the hunt, which was all in covert and estimated to be 20 miles. They started at the point where they reckoned the fox finally broke covert from East Dean wood, which was shortly after the duke noted they had been several times at fault in Singleton forest and Punters copse.

The first day they managed to walk nearly 25 miles carefully counting the revolutions. The second day took in the remaining 11½ miles.

The measure of the Fox Chase that was run Friday 26th January 1738/9
Wednesday 31st January 1739
Began from the east side of East Dean wood to the lower Tegleaze, Buckleys, Mr Orme's park, Northwood farm, Selham furzes, Feilder's hop garden, by Selham barn, through the enclosed fields belonging to Selham and Ambersham, to Ambersham furzes, over the brook by Dunford farm, to Aukers furze, cross Cocking causeway by the lime kiln, to Paddock wood, Henley copse, Halfpenny wood, then cross the London road, up by Herringdean barn to Suncombe,

over Cocking course to Punters copse, through the forest by the stone table to Nightingale bottom, through the hangers to Drought, up pine pit copse to Downley house, Whistling alley copse, Heydon barn, cross the south end of West dean warren, by Binderton farm, up the downs by Hayes bushes, cross the enclosures into Valdoe, through Goodwood park ands cut at the upper gate, the whole in length

                            24 miles 6 furlongs 31 rods

Thursday 1st February 1739
Began from Goodwood upper gate, cross above Seeley copse to Lady Derby's rook wood, over by Halnaker windmill to Seabeach farm, over Long down, Eartham common field, quite through Mr Kemp's high wood to the railed piece, through the enclosures to Slindon in-down, to Madehurst parsonage, over Madehurst down to Fairmile, through the encloures to Madehurst church and so to Houghton forest, cross the road by the waypost, over Houghton down to South wood, through the enclosed fields of South Stoke down to the brooks, where the wheel could not follow him.

The whole in length	11 miles 3 furlongs 24 rods
Allowed for the brooks by Mr Gideon's opinion	1 mile
Allowed by Billy Ives for the three hours running in cover	20 miles
	57 miles 2 furlongs 15 rods[156]

  The distance of 36¼ miles measured with the wheel can be checked on a map and confirmed to be pretty accurate. The whole chase took 10 hours and five minutes and by subtracting Billy Ives' three hours in covert and the brooks at the end, the measured part of 36¼ miles would have taken about seven hours; that is, a little over five miles an hour. On this basis, the 'three hours running in cover' of 20 miles would be an over-estimate and should be more like 15½ miles, making the total distance, including the mile 'allowed for the brooks' at the end, about 53 miles. Still a very long hunt!

  On Sunday 4 February 36 members gathered for the annual dinner in London at the *Bedford Head Tavern*.[157] There is little doubt about the topic of the moment. The members who had been out at the grand chase were all there, except Brigadier Hawley and Lord Ossulstone. Also present were the Dukes of Grafton, Bolton and Devonshire, the Earls of Berkeley, Albemarle, Cholmondeley and Cowper, Lords George Beauclerk and James Cavendish, the Hons. George Shirley, Thomas Watson and John FitzWilliam, Sir Conyers Darcy, Generals Honywood and Kirke, Colonels Huske and Whitworth, Majors Elliot and Beake, William Conolly, Henry Herbert, Richard Honywood, Stephen Fox, William Corbet, Charles Perry and Richard Meggott.

  Richmond gave the assembled company his account of the run, interrupted no doubt by frequent interjections from the others who were out. Having left Charlton at half past seven, they hacked to East Dean wood and found a fox which ran in covert on the downs until about eleven o'clock. Hounds then went in a wide anticlockwise circle to the north nearly to Midhurst, returning at about two o'clock to Charlton forest not far from where they found. From here hounds ran to the west along the downs past West Dean, turned left handed to Goodwood, which they reached at about half past three and continued eastwards past Halnaker and Slindon to the river near Arundel, where they caught the fox just before six.

  Most of the followers had only one horse. Lord Harcourt said his first horse blew up at 11.30 and his second horse nearly expired going up Cocking hill at two; he was got home to Charlton with difficulty! Mr. Fauquier retired at the same time. Sir Harry Liddell gave up at

Binderton at three. Lord Henry Beauclerk retired at 3.30 near Goodwood and his horse was so tired he had to drive it back to Charlton! Ralph Jenison, Cornet Honywood, Tom Johnson and Nim Ives reached Seabeach farm at 4.30, but had had enough and returned to Charlton. The Duke of St Albans had a fall early on at 9.30 near Drought; he took a second horse at Goodwood at 3.30, gave him to Billy Ives at 4.30 at Kemp's high wood and hacked back to Charlton. Edward Pauncefort on Tinker was with Richmond at Goodwood, caught up with hounds at Houghton forest at five, but could go no further.

The Duke of Richmond said he took a second horse from Goodwood at 3.30. He had a fall shortly afterwards in Seeley copse and caught up with the hounds in Houghton forest at five. He was in at the death. Brigadier Hawley took his second horse near Charlton forest at two. He was with Richmond at Goodwood and caught up with hounds in Houghton forest at five. He was also in at the death. Billy Ives had three horses and was with the pack almost the whole way. He took a second horse belonging to Sir Harry Liddell near Charlton forest at two and took over the Duke of St Albans' horse at Kemps high wood at 4.30, catching up with the hounds at Madehurst soon after five. He was with the Duke of Richmond and Brigadier Hawley at the death.

'Prosperity to Charlton and several other healths were drank' but before 'the Society adjourn'd as usual', someone made a proposal that an official account of the grand chase, surely the longest in the annals of hunting, should be prepared and widely publicised. So a scribe duly obliged and produced a definitive version, which included comments of the personal experiences of those who were out. The document was distributed abroad and in some cases framed and hung in the houses of the neighbourhood.

One of these copies used to hang in the *Fox Inn* in Charlton and is still in the possession of the landlady now retired.[158] It is written in very neat copperplate on parchment and framed in oak from one of Nelson's flagships. There are four other manuscript copies in West Sussex Record Office, which are slightly different in some of the spelling, but otherwise accurate copies.[159]

It begins with a flowery but defiant statement claiming the supremacy of Charlton in the fox hunting world, of which the virgin huntress would surely have approved. (Dymoke is the family name of the Champions of England, whose office it was to ride up Westminster Hall on a coronation day and challenge anyone who disputed the right of succession.)

A full and impartial account of the remarkable chase at Charlton on Friday 26th January 1738/9

It has long been a matter of controversy in the hunting world to what particular county or set of men the superiority of power belonged. Prejudice and partiality have the greatest share in their disputes, and every society their proper champion to assert the preeminence and bring home the trophies to their own country—even Richmond park has its Dimmock [Dymoke]. But on Friday the 26th of January 1738/9 there was a decisive engagement on the plains of Sussex which after ten hours struggle has settled all further debates and given the brush to the gentlemen of Charlton.

<u>Present in the Morning</u>
The Duke of Richmond
The Duchess of Richmond
The Duke of St Albans
The Lord Viscount Harcourt
The Lord Henry Beauclerk

The Grand Chase

72 Charles Beauclerk, Earl of Burford, seen here as a budding young fox hunter, was later 2nd Duke of Saint Albans and a grandson of Charles II and Nell Gwynn. He was a regular visitor at Charlton where he owned a hunting box.

The Lord Ossulstone
Sir Harry Liddell
Brigadier Henry Hawley
Ralph Jenison Esq, Master of His Majesty's Buck Hounds
Edward Pauncefort Esq
William Fauquier Esq
Cornet Philip Honywood
Richard Biddulph Esq
Charles Biddulph Esq
Mr St Paul
Mr Thomson
Mr Peerman of Chichester
Mr Johnson of Chichester
Tom Johnson, Huntsman
Billy Ives, Yeoman pricker to His Majesty's Hounds
David Briggs, Whipper In
Nim Ives, Whipper In

The account starts almost word for word with the duke's version.

At a quarter before eight in the morning the fox was found in East Dean wood and ran an hour in that covert, then ran into the forest up to Punters copse, through Herringdean to the Marlows, up to Coney copse back to the Marlows to the forest west gate, over the fields to Nightingale bottom, to Cobdens at Drought, up his pine pit hanger,

Here begin the frequent interjections which tell us what happened to the followers and their horses.

73   Charles Bennet, Lord Ossulstone, was present at the Grand Chase of 1739. He succeeded his father as 3rd Earl of Tankerville in 1753.

    (there his Grace of St Albans got a fall)
through Lady Lewknor's Puttocks and <u>missed the earth</u>, through West Dean forest to the corner of Collar [Colworth] down,
    (where Lord Harcourt blew his first horse)
crossed the hacking place, down the length of Coney copse, through the Marlows to Herringdean into the forest, Punters copse,

    The duke's version had a significant variation at this point. He said 'Then into Singleton forest where they ran several rings for near an hour, and Punters copse and were several times at fault'.

East Dean wood, the lower Tegleaze, cross by Cocking course, down between Graffham and Woolavington, through Mr Orme's park and paddock, over the heaths to Feilders furzes, to the Hurlands, Selham, Ambersham, through Todham furzes over Todham heath almost to Cowdray park, there turned to the lime kiln at the end of Cocking causeway, through Cocking park and furzes, there crossed the road and up the hills between Bepton and Cocking.
    (here the unfortunate Lord Harcourt's second horse felt the effect of long legs and sudden steep, the best thing belonging to him was his saddle which my lord had secured, but by bleeding and Geneva [contrary to the act of parliament], he recovered and with some difficulty was got home; here Mr Fauquier's humanity claims your regard, who kindly sympathised with my lord in his misfortunes and had not power to go beyond him)

The Grand Chase

74 General Henry Hawley was present with the Duke of Richmond and Billy Ives at the end of the Grand Chase. A celebrated soldier, he earned the title of 'Hangman Hawley' from his ruthless severity to the Scottish rebels after the battle of Culloden in 1746.

At the bottom of Cocking warren the hounds turned to the left across the road by the barn near Herringdean, then took the side hills to the north gate of the forest,
> (here Brigadier Hawley thought it prudent to change his horse for a true blue that stayed upon the hills; Billy Ives likewise took a horse of Sir Harry Liddell's)

went quite through the forest and ran the foil, through Nightingale bottom, to Cobdens at Drought, up his pine pit hanger to my Lady Lewknor's Puttocks, through every meuse she went in the morning, went through the warren above West Dean,
> (where we dropped Sir Harry Liddell down to Binderton farm, here Sir Harry sank)

up to Binderton down, through Haye's bushes, Bickley bushes to the Valdoe, through Goodwood park.

The duke's account notes that the fox was seen in Goodwood park.

> (here the Duke of Richmond chose to send three lame horses back to Charlton and took Saucy Face and Sir William that were very luckily at Goodwood. From thence at a distance Lord Harry [Beauclerk] was seen driving his horse before him to Charlton)

The duke took Saucy Face and gave Sir William to the Duke of St Albans.

The hounds went out at the upper end of the park to Strettington road by Seeley copse
> (where his Grace of Richmond got a somerset)

through Halnaker park over Halnaker hill to Seabeach farm,

119

75 William Fauquier Esq., a member of the Dilettante Society, in whose costume he appears in this portrait.

> (there the master of the stag hounds, Cornet Honywood, Tom Johnson and Nim Ives were thoroughly satisfied)
>
> *up Long down, through Eartham common field to Kemp's high wood.*
>
> (here Billy Ives tired his second horse and took Sir William, by which the Duke of St Albans had no great coat, so returned to Charlton)
>
> *From Kemp's high wood the hounds broke away through the Gumworth warren, Kemp's rough piece, over Slindon down to Madehurst parsonage,*
>
> (where Billy came in with them)
>
> *over Poor down, up to Madehurst down, Houghton forest,*
>
> (where his Grace of Richmond, Brigadier Hawley and Mr Pauncefort came in, the latter to little purpose, for beyond the Rewell hill neither Mr Pauncefort nor his horse Tinker cared to go, so wisely returned to his impatient hungry friends)
>
> *up the Rewell hill, left Sherwood on the right hand, crossed Offham hill to Southwood, from thence to South Stoke to the wall of Arundel river, where the glorious twenty three hounds put an end to the campaign and killed the old bitch fox ten minutes before six.*
>
> *Billy Ives, his Grace of Richmond and Brigadier Hawley were the only persons at the death, to the immortal honour of seventeen stone and at least as many campaigns.*

What the last statement means is obscure, but knowing that the duke weighed 15 stone, could it refer to Brigadier Hawley's weight and military record? One of the versions ends differently: 'to the immortal honour of 17 stone and three score.' The meaning of that is also a mystery!

In three of the manuscripts, there follows a list of the hounds, all of whom were on at the end.[160] In the hound book, the duke marked them with a cross to distinguish them for posterity.

76 General Philip Honywood. As Cornet Honywood he was present at the Grand Chase of 1739.

THE GLORIOUS TWENTY THREE HOUNDS

Old Hounds		Young Hounds
Pompey	Lawyer	Buxom
Doxy	Cruel	Ruby
Taker	Veny	Rifle
Jenny	Edmund	Bloomer
Peggy	Walcut	Goodwood
Dido	Cryer	Lady
Music	Traveller	Crowner
Ringwood	Drummer	

Many of the company were back in Charlton by Thursday and 10 more days hunting were to come before the end of February. The first five days were amazing. On successive days out, the hounds scored points of 7½ miles, 15 as they ran; 4 miles, 13 as they ran; 4½ miles, 15 as they ran; 6 miles, 14 as they ran and 4 miles, 17 as they ran, killing a fox each time, except for the first day, when it went to ground and was dug out and set free.

Thursday 8th February 1739
Found in Punters copse, came out by the north gate of the forest, but headed back by a country man, down to Herringdean, cross Cocking highway to the Marlows, back again to Herringdean, the forest, came out by Punters copse to the side hills, ran along them to the lower Tegleaze, over East Dean common, down to Littleton, up Littleton bottom to Noman's land, through Dawtrey's hooks, Kemps high wood, Eartham common fields to Slindon park, there earthed in a coney burrow, dug for a quarter of an hour and got her, a bitch fox. So she was brought home alive and well in order to be turned out again.

77 Map of West Sussex by Philip Overton and Thomas Bowles, 1740.

[Historical map of Sussex, England, showing an area including Petworth, Arundel, and surrounding hundreds. Place names visible on the map include:]

- Fordly Castle, Fordly Comon, North Heath, Woolveding, Buding-ton, Upper Street, Basebourn, Lavant, Cowdry Park
- Lingfield, Lodsworth, Godsworth wood, LIBERTY OF LODSWORTH, Limbo, Ifold, Lodg
- Burls cops gate, Woods Com, Iladeland, HUNDRED OF ROTHERBRIDGE, Kirdford, Linfold bri, Linfold Green, Ifoldhurst
- Tillington, Netherland, Petworth, Gretham, New Grove, Cross lane Cross, Hallgate, Egdean, Rother bridge, Battlehurst, Moore, Hampshurst Com, Parsonage, Palingham, Blursbury, Banquetting house, Dee Farm, Wharf, Stopham
- Kilsham, Horsebare Gt, Cowderyhall Mills, Egdean, Coates, Bynorth Street, Common, Stopham, Parva, Old Place, Hardham
- Hyle Place, Parsonage, Keyshot, Graffham Marsh, Graffham, Collaying, Duncton, Burton, Burton Engine or raise Water, Fulling mill, Barlavington, Bignor Park, Bignor, Sutton, Watersfield, Hardhamsbro, Herringham, Gritham, Hurst, Wiggonhill, Parsonage
- Cocking Race, High ditch Woods, Charlton Woods, E. Dean, Singleton, Charlton, Upwaltham, HUND. OF BURY, Bury, Bignor, Buriton, Bury Parsonage, Amberley Ruins, Gritham, Racomb, Parham
- Selhurst Park, Cops Lodg, Rooks hill, Habrecker Win, Halnaker Win, Warehead, Eartham, Stoney Stor, Nore Hill, Gundove's Trottvo, Thornwait, Madshurst, Gobles Corner, Houghton, Houghton bridges, N. Stoke
- Boxgrove, Cocker hole, Fulkross hole, Aldingbourn, HUND. OF HALNECKER, Slindon W., Slindon P., Slindon Park, Slindon, Herbedon, Arundel Park, Stoke, Offham, Oppering, Burpham
- Peastree, Laingmeer, Knightan, Aldingbourn Pl, Estergate, Walberton, Torlington, Arundel, Arundel Castle, Dadnor, Street, Warningcamp, Tortington Park, Angmer
- Oveing, HUNDRED OF ALDRIE, Merston, Boars bridge, Lagnergh, Poole, Yapton Place, Barnham W., Barnham, Shrip Street, Binstead, Marsh Farm, HUNDRED OF AVISFORD, Ford, Clymping, Ford dock Sluce, Hollicon, Black Dyke, Courtweek, Poleing, Woodhouse, Decoypond, Old Pla, Angmering

Saturday 10th February 1739
Found in East Dean wood, ran into Charlton forest, after a great ring there back through East Dean wood, out at the white gate, along the side hills to Woolavington hanger, down there to Mr Orme's park, cross the avenue, up the hill again between the sheep wash and Duncton hill, turned on the right hand over Woolavington hill, to the Tegleaze, East Dean wood and Charlton forest, and there in the Delawarr riding killed him, a dog fox.

Monday 12th February 1739
Hit upon a drag in Littleton bottom and carried it to Dawtrey's hooks, there we found and came away through Kemps high wood, St Mary wood, over Noman's land, Glatting beacon, by the lone beech, over the downs to Mr Butler's farm,[161] through Houghton forest, cross Fair mile, up the Rewell hill, through the Rewell wood, into the furze field by the lime kiln, cross Arundel road, there the hounds viewed her into the Rooks, and there killed her, a bitch fox.

Tuesday 13th February 1739
Found in the Valdoe, went out for the sand pits but turned short back to the Valdoe, through Goodwood park, over Halsteds down, through the Winkin, North hanger, cross the East Dean road, up the Tegleaze hill, through both upper and lower Tegleaze to East Dean wood and Charlton forest, there we changed, and after some turns to Herringdean, out by the barn, all along the downs, over Cocking course, Hessiod down, Woolavington down, and up Duncton hill to the chalk pit, down Barlavington hill, by Duncton street to the common by Burton park, there were at a long fault, and Nim with ten couple of hounds had gone down before to Woolavington park, and was also at a fault, then the fox was halloaed up the hill, and both parcels coming up, carried the scent into East Dean wood, from thence to the lower Tegleaze, where she went to ground, and a terrier killed her, a bitch fox.

Thursday 15th February 1739
Found in the Valdoe, ran through Goodwood park to Strickland's furze, over the Harroways to East Dean park, from thence to Charlton copse, back again to East Dean park, the Bubholts, North hanger, Red copse, the Winkin, East Dean park again, Charlton copse, back to East Dean park, Bubholts, North hanger, and Red copse again, so far a very cold scent, but from thence the hounds ran as hard as hounds could run to Halnaker park, the Redvins, down between Boxgrove street and Feilkens's hole, by Crockerhill, the back of Norton, down to Aldingbourne, and between that and Lidsey, they killed her, a bitch fox.

After that things became much quieter and the last five days were largely local hunting and no foxes were killed.

Saturday 17th February 1739
Found in the Rooks, ran several rings there, then over Arundel park to the Rewell, across Arundel park again, up to the Castle hanger, and there came to a fault, and Tom Johnson made several casts, of which the last was to South wood, Houghton hangers, Priest comb, and so to West Burton hill, but could not recover him, so came home.

Tuesday 20th February 1739
Found in East Dean wood, ran some rings in that covert and the forest, then down the hill to Graffham, there earthed in a hedgerow, dug out a dog fox, put him a sack, brought him home, and turned him out: but whilst they were digging, we went and beat Punters copse where we ran a martin for nearly an hour, then tried Singleton forest without finding, so over by the Marlows to Lewknor's copse, there found and ran several rings, a brace of foxes being on foot, Tom Johnson went off with one as far as Coney copse, but brought him back again to Lewknor's copse, then all the hounds together ran a ring through the Sovereigns, Venus copse, the Hacking place, and Marlows, then back again through Stubb copse, to the same Lewknor's copse, where we ran for three hours, and the hounds threw up all at once, from whence it was concluded that the fox went to ground, so we took off and came home.

Eleven members were at dinner that night, exhausted and exhilarated after such a purple patch, including the grand chase.[162] Edward Pauncefort in the chair, William Fauquier, Lord Henry Beauclerk, Cornet Philip Honywood, the Duke of St Albans, the Duke of Richmond and Brigadier Hawley had all been out that memorable day. The company agreed to an extension of Arthur Gore's visit and another visit by Francis Fauquier, William's brother.

Thursday 22nd February 1739
Found in Charlton forest, ran directly over Cocking highway to the Marlows, there turned back again over the same road to Herringdean, Lord Montagu's copse, where a brace of foxes being on foot, the hounds tried the side hills, and from thence were brought into Punters copse, from whence Tom Johnson tried the whole forest, and East Dean wood to no purpose, and the day being allowed to be a very bad one as to scent, we took off and came home.

Saturday 24th February 1739
Found in the Row copse, ran through the Rifles to Ashling, back through the Rifles to the Rows, down to the ditch under the north wall of Chichester, to the Broyle copse, over the sand pits to little Oldwick, up to Trumley copse, Cuckolds lee, Crows hall, over the Lavant to old Warren, up to - - - - - copse, and from thence could make nothing of it, so concluded he went to ground.

Another meeting was held to make sure hosts to visitors paid for their guests. It rather looks as if Mr. Fauquier was not paying up, exactly like some members of the present Charlton Hunt Club!

Charlton, Sunday 25th February 1739
The following bye-law was proposed and balloted for and carried in the affirmative: that every member of the Charlton Hunt that has been at Charlton any time during the hunting season and every new member is to pay his proportion of the extraordinary that year, and in case the new member does not come, the person that proposed him to pay for him.[163]

Monday 26th February 1739
Found in the North hanger, the fox was seen, halloaed, and the hounds ran him very fairly for about half a quarter of an hour, and then threw up at once, and were never able to hit it more, then drew for three hours, without finding so returned home.

The last diary entry for the season is the duke's summary of the finds and the kills.

Killed	Dog foxes	11
	Bitch foxes	16
	In all	27 foxes
	Missed killing	20 foxes
but as four foxes were killed in twice going out, we hunted in all		45 times
	NB 16 weeks and four days at three times a week makes	50 hunting days
and the hounds being purged did not go out for 8 days		
	so deduct	4 days
	remain	46 days

There may have been frost in March and hounds may have gone to the New Forest early. Certainly they spent much more of the year there than at Charlton. Of the total cost to the duke of £841 15s. 5d. for the season, £464 16s. 11d. was spent in the New Forest and £376 18s. 6d. at Charlton. The largest items were oatmeal £206 18s. 4d. and oats £82 9s. 6d., much more than flesh at £35 11s. 2d. Hay and straw came to £79 6s., wood for heating the copper £41 13s.; the farrier charged £19 1s. 4d. for shoeing 20 horses for the year (that is £1 per horse!), the saddler was £12 17s. 6d. and the apothecary £10 5s. Candles and brooms (mostly at Charlton) cost £22 0s. 6d., the gelder, who presumably also spayed the bitches, was paid one guinea and bricklayers and carpenters cost £6 5s. 3d. The earthstoppers and warreners (almost all at Charlton) were paid £63 15s., staff wages were £169 0s. 3d. and the huntsman's bills £35 7s. 9d.[164] Can you imagine these days spending much more on oatmeal for a pack of hounds than the wages of all the hunt staff?

— X —

THE HUNTING DIARIES

Spurred on by the great sport shown in the 1738/9 season, the Duke of Richmond continued to keep a record in his hunting diary of the events of each day. We know from the account of the grand chase that hounds would leave Charlton at dawn, which in mid-winter was around half past seven. The furthest draws were about seven or eight miles, or an hour's hound jog and thus the country extended from the Hampshire border in the west to the Rother and Arun rivers in the north and east and the sea to the south, a 15-mile square with Charlton in the centre. We find also that the articles of the regular society were not rigorously applied. People who lived in the neighbourhood were allowed to join the field with the duke's permission without having to be voted in as a visitor, unless they wished to stay in Charlton and dine in the Great Room. The Duke of Grafton wrote to his cousin at Charlton to say how sorry he was not to be hunting there in the coming season.

London, Autumn 1739

I am quite unhappy that I cannot accept your offer of being at Charlton this year, but as we have hunted but little at Croydon we might lose the right of being there should we go away at this time when we have a good many foxes; likewise the hounds are out of order and some of the servants' horses are not fit to ride your country. These you know are considerations in our trade and therefore pray believe that I am quite unhappy that I don't wait upon you when the case is that one loves both the country and the governor of it, I need not say. My compliments to the Duke of St Albans and I wish you good sport and better weather …[165]

There is an old tradition that the Duke of Grafton was the first to urge that a bridge should be built at Westminster, as he objected to crossing the river with his hounds and horses by ferry boat. It was eventually built in 1750, a bit late for him to take full advantage of, as by then he was well over sixty-five. He it was of whom George II said, that with the duke's great corpse of 21 stone weight, no horse could carry him within hearing, much less within sight of his hounds![166] Despite that, he did continue to hunt until 70, when as a result of a fall, he was confined to his room till he died three years later. It was said he 'usually turned politics into ridicule, he had never applied himself to business and as to books, he was totally illiterate; yet from long observation and great natural sagacity, he became the ablest courtier of his time with the most perfect knowledge of both king and ministers'.[167]

So your friend booby Grafton I'll e'en let you keep,
Awake he can't hurt and he's still half asleep,
Nor ever was dangerous but to woman-kind
And his body's as impotent now as his mind.[168]

78 Charles Fitzroy, 2nd Duke of Grafton, known to his friends as Old Puff, was a subscriber to the Great Room. He kept hounds at Euston in Suffolk but also brought them across the Thames to hunt in Surrey and Kent.

Lord Delawarr wrote from the New Forest in September telling Richmond he needed more horses.

Bolderwood, September 1739

According to your grace's orders Tom Johnson attends you. I fancy if you take him to Lewes races he may possibly find a horse there. In short you want five horses, Tom Johnson 2, Nim Ives 1, Kitt Budd 1, David 1. Tom will let you know how these are wanted.[169]

His advice was taken, as by November there were five new horses in the huntsman's stable; Cardigan, Worsley, Jersey, Whitestockings and Harcourt. Crop and Goliah had been pensioned off leaving 13 in all. Tom Johnson still had David Briggs and Nim Ives as whippers-in, assisted by Billy Ives on many of the days. There were also three new horses in the duke's stable, Bamfield, Granby and Jumper; and with Saucy Face (one of the duke's favourites) and Fidler gone, he had 11 in for the season. His attendants were Jemy Gardiner, Will Macey, Joe Budd and Will Green and Mr. St Paul was also out on most days. Lord Delawarr goes on:

If I have kept Doxy when you sent for her, you must excuse me, but I thought she would be fed enough and her bed good enough in the hall here and I know you do not suffer a hound to come in your parlour at Goodwood, but if you will have her I will send her. I shall say nothing about the glorious number of hounds you have because you know it, but why sixteen couple of young ones; and the madness amongst those left at Charlton; why will you not make quick work where there is infection?

1   Diana, the virgin huntress and moon goddess.

*In this sweet vale by hills and downs enclos'd,
an age ago Diana fix't her court
and thus resolves! 'I'll be ador'd by men,
by Britons bold, where nymphs shall ne're resort;
the wily fox their furious chace shall be
and Charlton is the place where I will fix
my temple, where my votaries shall hunt.'*

11 *Fox Hall, Charlton, the Great Room, completed in about 1722 to the designs of the Earl of Burlington and used by members of the hunt as a banqueting hall.*

III *Charles Lennox, 2nd Duke of Richmond, sole proprietor of the Charlton hounds from 1731 'till his death in 1750.*

A FULL and IMPARTIAL ACCOUNT of the remarkable Chace at

It has long been a matter of Controversy in the Hunting World to what particular County or set of Men the superiority of Power belonged. Prejudice and Partiality have the greatest share in these Disputes, and every Society their proper Champion to assert the preeminence, and bring home the Trophies to their own Country. Even Richmond Park has its Dommock. But on Friday the 26th of January 1738/9 there was a decisive Engagement on the Plains of Sussex which after ten Hours struggle has settled all farther debates and given the Brush to the Gentlemen of Charlton.

Present in the Morning

The Duke of Richmond
The Dutchess of Richmond
The Duke of St. Albans
The Lord Viscount Harcourt
The Lord Henry Beauclerk
The Lord Ossulstone
Sir Harry Liddle
Brigadier Henry Hawley
Ralph Jenison Esq. Master of His Majesty's Buck Hounds
Edward Pauncefort Esq.
William Fauquier Esq.
Cornet Philip Honywood
Richd. Biddulph Esq.
Charles Biddulph Esq.
Mr. St. Paul
Mr. Thomson
Mr. Peerman } of Chichester
Mr. Johnson }
Tom Johnson, Huntsman
Billy Ives, Yeoman Pricker to His Majesty's Hounds
David Briggs } Whippers In
Nim Ives }

At a quarter before Eight on the Morning the Fox was found in Eastdean Wood and ran an Hour in that Cover then into the Forest up to Puntice Coppice thro' Herringdean to the Marlows up to Conry Coppice back to the Marlows to the Forest West Gate over the fields to Nightingale Bottom to Cobden's at Draught, up his Pine Pit Hanger (there His Grace of St. Albans got a fall) thro' Lady Lewkner's Paddocks and missed the Earth thro' West Dean Forest to the Corner of Collar down (where Lord Harcourt blew his first Horse) over the Hacking Pace down the Length of Coney Coppice

thro' the Marlows to Herringdean, into the Forest and Puntice Coppice, Eastdean West the lower Teglees, cross by Cocking Course down between Grafham and Woolavington thro' Mr Oras Park and Paddock over the Heath to Fielder's Furzes, to the Hurlands, Iltham, Amersham, thro' Totham Furzes, over Totham Heath almost to Cowdry Park then turned to the Lime Kiln at the End of Cocking Causeway thro' Cocking Park and Furzes and there crossed the road and up the Hills between Bepton and Cocking (here the unfortunate Lord Harcourt's second Horse felt the effects of Long Legs and a sudden Steep, the last thing belonging to Him was His Saddle which My Lord had secured by Bleeding and Geneva (contrary to act of Parliament he recovered and with some difficulty was got home, here Mr Fauquier's humanity claims your regard who kindly sympathised with My Lord in His Misfortunes and had not power to go beyond Him) At the bottom of Cocking Warren the Hounds turned to the left across the Road by the Barn by Herrindean, then took the Side Hills to the North Gate of the Forest (here Mr. Hayley thought it Prudent to change his Horse for a True Blue that stayd up the Hills Billy Ives likewise took a Horse of Sir Harry Liddle's) went quite thro' the Forest and in the Foil thro' Nightingale Bottom to Cobden's at Draught, up his pine Pit Hanger to my Lady Lewkner's Paddocks thro' every meuse she went in the Morning went thro' the Warren above Westdean where we dropt Sir Harry Liddle down to Binderton Farm) where Lord Harry sunk) up to Binderton Down thro' Hays Bushes Beckley Bushes to the Valdoe thro' Goodwood Park here the Duke of Richmond chose to send three Lame Horses to Charlton and took Saucy face & Sir William that were very luckily at Goodwood) from thence at a distance Lord Harry was seen a driving His Horse before Him to Charlton) the Hounds went out at the upper End of the Park up to Strettington by Sealey Coppice (where His Grace of Richmond got a Somerset thro' Halnaker Park over Halnaker Hill to Seabeach Farm (where the Master of the Stag Hounds Cornet Honywood Tim Johnson and Nim Ives were throly Satisfied) up Long down thro' Eartham corn Fields, and Kemps High Wood (here Billy Ives tired his Second Horse and took Sir William by which the Duke of St. Albans had no great Coat so returned to Charlton) from high Wood the Hounds took away thro' the Gumworth, thro' Kemps Ruff Piece over Slendon Down to Madehurst Parsonage (where Billy came in with them) over Poor Down up to Madehurst then down to Houghton Forest where his Grace of Richmond Br. Hawley and Mr. Pauncefort come in the latter to little

...rlton on Friday 26th January 1738/9

...rose) far beyond the Ruel Hill neither Mr Pauncefort or His
... Tinker Cared to go (so wisely returned to His Impatiant and hungry
...nds) up the Ruel Hill left Sherwood on the right hand crost
...am Hill to Southwood from thence to South Stoke to the Wall
...brundel River where the Glorious twenty three Hounds
...t an End to the Campaign and Killed the Old Bitch Fox
... minutes before six. Billy Ives His Grace of Richmond &
... Hawly where the only Persons at the Death to the immortal
...our of seventeen Stone & at least as many Campaigne.

The Glorious twenty three Hounds

Old Hounds
Pompy
Dovy
Saker
Jenny
Peggy
Dido
Musick
Ringwood
Lawyer
Crewel
Veny
Edmund
Walnut
Cryer
Traveller

Young Hounds
Buxom
Rifle
Ruby
Bloomer
Goodwood
Lady
Crowner
Drummer

IV 'A Full and Impartial Account of the remarkable Chace at Charlton.'

V   *View of Uppark from the south west in the early 18th century. The hounds are probably those of the 2nd Earl of Tankerville who came to live there in 1722.*

VI   *Bay Bolton, a hunter belonging to the Duke of Richmond from 1728 to 1731; in the background a view of Halnaker hill and windmill. The inscription on the stone reads 'Bay Bolton, got by the famous Bay Bolton', a stallion bred by Sir Matthew Pierson in Yorkshire, who died at Bolton Hall stud farm in 1736.*

VII *Tapster'31 by Lord Tankerville's Mounter out of Frisky'25, painted in 1733, the year of the disastrous episode when the hounds killed 14 sheep. Tapster was one of the culprits (along with many others), but was spared and remained in the kennels till 1736.*

VIII *Grey Carey, son of Grey Ramsden, a hunter in the Duke of Richmond's stable for three seasons till his death on 10 December 1740. The groom in red undress livery is probably Will Macey, one of the duke's attendants in the hunting field.*

IX *Grey Cardigan, a hunter in Tom Johnson's stable for the season 1739/40. The servant in the duke's yellow and scarlet livery is probably Nim Ives, a whipper-in and Tom Johnson with the Charlton hounds is seen through the ruined archway.*

X *Sultan, a chestnut hunter in the duke's stable for three seasons 1740 to 1743. The groom in state livery is probably Jemmy Gardiner; in the background a view of Carné's seat at Goodwood. The inscription on the stone reads 'Sultan, given by His Majesty to Prince Charles of Lorraine, 1743.'*

XI Red Robin, bay hunter in the Duke of Richmond's stable for the season 1742/3. The groom in state livery is probably Jemmy Gardiner; in the background Chichester Cathedral and harbour with shipping. The inscription on the stone reads 'Red Robin, given by His Majesty to Prince Charles of Lorraine, 1743.'

XII Sheldon, a chestnut hunter in the Duke of Richmond's stable in 1743. The groom in blue and gold undress livery is probably Joe Budd; in the background a view of old Goodwood House with the Temple of Minerva and Neptune.

XIII *Charles, 3rd Duke of Richmond and his brother Lord Geroge Lennox with the Charlton Hunt, c.1759. The painting owes little to traditional hunting scenes and is unusual in that it represents not a moment of triumph in the hunting field, but a scene of disorder and confusion. The hounds have checked and o not know what to do next and the duke is equally at a loss. He was no doubt involved in the choice of subject, yet he did not use the opportunity to glorify himself, but rather to point out the problems that can arise when hunting the fox. (Venetia Morrison in* The Art of George Stubbs, *1989)*

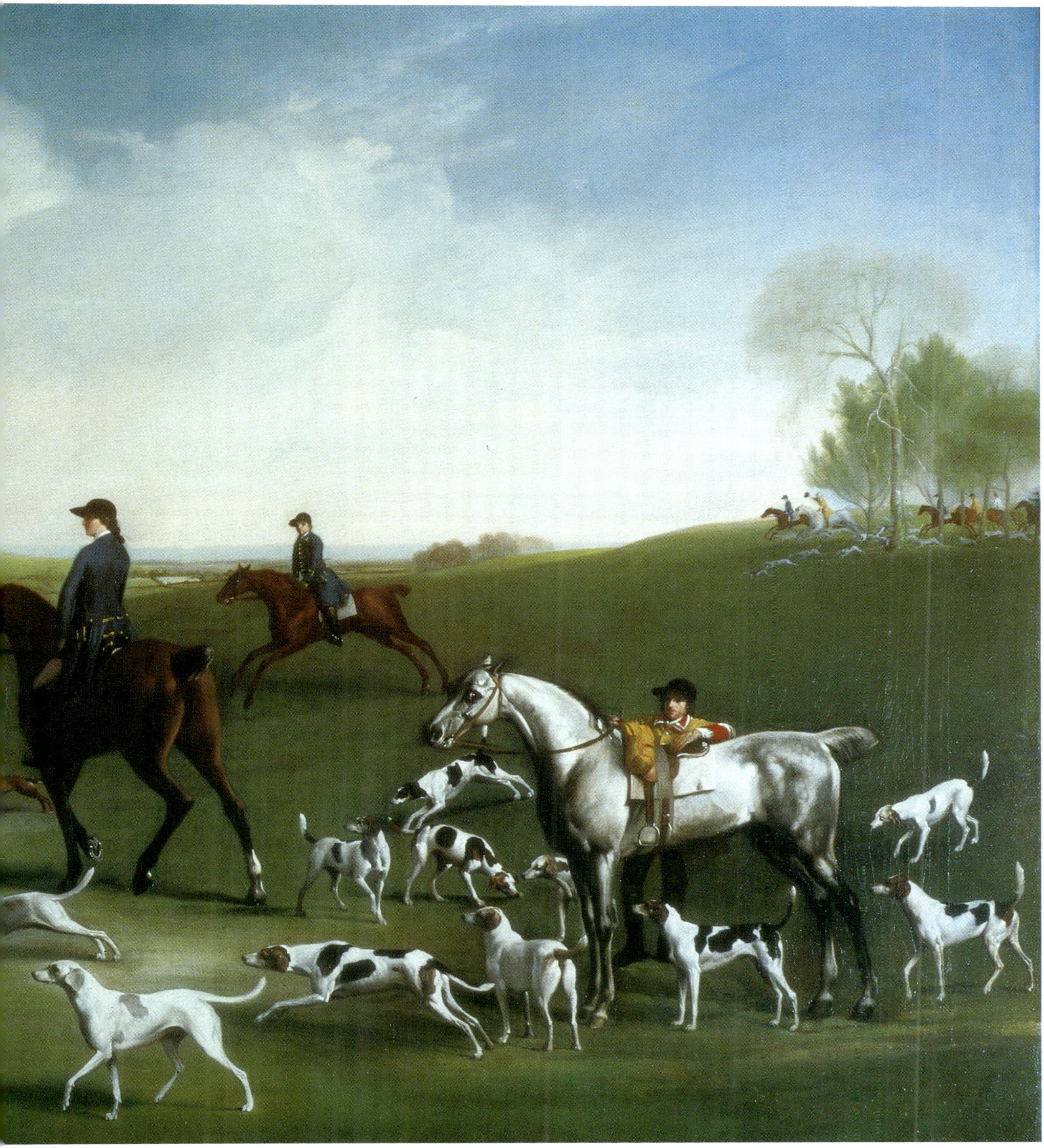

XIV *Mary, Duchess of Richmond and Lady Louisa Conolly née Lennox watching racehorses exercising (detail).*

Doxy was a great favourite who had been out at the grand chase, an old hound given by Lord Tankerville by his Mounter out of his Madam, entered at Charlton in 1737 and given to the Duke of St Albans in 1740. In the kennel, the duke heeded Delawarr's advice and reduced the young entry to 12½ couple. Seventeen couple of old hounds had been cast, leaving 28 couple of old hounds bred at home, 7½ couple given by Lord Tankerville in 1737, 3 couple left from those who had come with Tom Johnson, 5 couple from the 10½ couple given by Lady Molyneux the previous December and 3½ couple of other old given hounds (of whom Blossom by Lord Craven's Jirker out of the Duke of Bolton's Blossom and Clouder by Mr. St John's Ranter out of his Henny were new to the pack), making a total of 59½ couple.[170] They hunted next on Thursday 1 November, but had a poor day. In the evening they admitted a visitor after dinner in the Great Room, attended by the Dukes of Richmond and St Albans and Major General Hawley with Edward Pauncefort in the chair. The minute is written in Richmond's hand.

Charlton, Thursday 1st November 1739
This day the Hon Charles Roper Esq was proposed by the Duke of Richmond to the members present to have leave to come to Charlton for eight days; he was balloted for according to the sixth article and [a great smudge, I wonder why, crossing out 'admitted!'] leave granted for eight days.[171]

The author has searched the peerage and failed to find a record of the said gentleman. However, he went on to enjoy five days' hunting mounted from the duke's stable on Gin or Slug, stayed another eight days, was elected a member and continued to hunt on one of the duke's horses until Christmas. Was he by any chance a relative, maybe a grandson, of the great Mr. Roper and dubbed 'the honourable' in deference to his grandfather's revered memory? Could well be so.

The next day was disappointing, with foxes going to ground, and on Monday the hounds were trying very hard but the scent and the weather were not in their favour, although they ran a fox from Goodwood to Walberton, a distance of five miles. The next day they managed to catch a fox on the edge of Burton mill pond after both fox and hounds had taken to the water, an unusual event then and certainly so today.

Tuesday 6th November 1739
Found in Hammer pond tail, and killed immediately a bitch fox, and in the same instant another went directly out of the same covert to the Merryfields and to Kelsom pond tail, and ran for an hour from one furze covert to another, and then back to the great pond in Burton park, where the hounds viewed him, he took the water, and the hounds swam after him, and killed him in the sedges, a dog fox.

In the Great Room on Wednesday with Edward Pauncefort in the chair and the Dukes of Richmond and St Albans, General Hawley and Sir John Miller, they extended Charles Roper's stay and admitted two more visitors.

Charlton, Wednesday 7th November 1739
This day the Right Hon the Lord Conway was proposed by the Duke of Richmond to the members present for leave to come to Charlton for eight days. He was balloted for according to the sixth article and leave granted accordingly to come for eight days.[172]

Francis Seymour-Conway was then 21 and had succeeded to the title as a minor. He first took his seat in the House of Lords on 15 November 1739, so can barely have stayed his allotted eight days!

> The Duke of Richmond also proposed the Hon. Charles Bentinck in the same manner and he was accordingly balloted for and leave granted him to come for eight days.

He was the Duke of Richmond's brother-in-law, his wife being the duchess' younger sister Margaret, whom he had married the previous January. He represented another of Richmond's Dutch connections, his father being Hans William, Earl of Portland, who, like the father of Richmond's other brother-in-law, the Earl of Albemarle, was a page of honour and later confidential adviser to William III.

Thursday was a poor day near Graffham and no more hunting was recorded until after the third annual dinner held in London on Sunday 18 November 1739 at the *Bedford Head Tavern*.[173] Twenty-seven members were present with Lord Delawarr again in the chair. Also present were the Dukes of Richmond, St Albans, Bolton, Marlborough and Kingston; the Earls of Berkeley, Albemarle and Lifford; Viscount Harcourt; Lords George Beauclerk and James Cavendish; Lords Walpole and Baltimore; the Hons. Charles Feilding and Edward Legge; Sir Henry Liddell; General Kirke; Colonels Huske and Whitworth; Captain Philip Honywood; Ralph Jenison, Richard Honywood, Henry Herbert, Edward Pauncefort, William Fauquier and William Corbet.

Sir Robert Guldeford, now an old man of 79, had kindly lent the club a picture which hung in the Great Room. He had hunted regularly at Charlton in Roper's time and, although also a subscriber to the articles agreed two years earlier, he thought he would like his picture back. No such luck!

> The Duke of Richmond read a letter from Sir Robert Guldeford Bart praying that his original picture now in Foxhall at Charlton might be taken down, the said Robert Guldeford offering to give another in its room. It was accordingly proposed and the question being put it was carried in the negative. Adjourn'd as usual.

The Duke of Somerset offered some hounds, but there is no record in the hound book that they were accepted.

Petworth, Monday 19th November 1739
… I am very glad that my hounds have behaved themselves so well to your grace's satisfaction, therefore pray try them again that they may be, as their landlord, entirely at your commands to have the pleasure to become more and more useful to your sports and satisfaction next year and to know that these seven young hounds are at the head of your old pack in all your fox chases. As the weather has been of late very favourable for hunting, I do not doubt but your grace has had the satisfaction to enjoy many good and long chases to the death of many foxes.[174]

Hunting resumed later in the week but the first few days showed little in the way of sport. Tom Johnson (says a note in the diary) had an attack of gout and was out of action for a week and the hounds were hunted by the first whipper-in, David Briggs. The scent was poor on Wednesday 28th but on Friday they had a better day, scoring a seven-mile point, 12 as they ran;

79 Francis, Lord Conway, later Marquess of Hertford, had been elected at Charlton as a youth of 21 in 1739. He married a daughter of the Duke of Grafton and had a distinguished career abroad and at court.

Friday 30th November 1739
Found in the lower Tegleaze, went along Woolavington hill, cross Duncton highway, there had a long fault, but recovered it near Farm wood then to North comb, Glatting hanger, along the side hills by Bignor and West Burton hangers, to Priest comb, from thence over the fields to Houghton steeps, then up through South wood, to Offam hill, quite the length of Offam down, through Herons wood to Offam hanger, there he went to ground but dug him and killed, an old dog fox.

Beaten by bad weather on Saturday, the next week they went to try the western end of the country. On Monday they lost a fox to ground at Adsdean, but returning on Thursday, the scent improved and hounds ran for about eleven miles before they lost the line, a six-mile point.

Thursday 6th December 1739
Found in Ashling woods, ran across Juniper bottom up to Adsdean copse, from thence down Walderton hill, through Walderton, up to Stansted park through that and Stansted forest to Rowlands castle, into the forest of Bear, and through the holt to Blendworth, there they came to a fault, but so far errant running, then picked a cold scent back over Glanville corner, Broad halfpenny, by Idsworth park, Well copse, Hucks wood and through Lady Holt park, from thence across the road to Compton down, and there the scent died away, and they could make nothing

of it. Tom Johnson thought he went to ground in some rabbit burrow, of which there were many by the road side.

On Tuesday 4th the company had been joined by Lord Harcourt and William Fauquier and they invited Charles Bentinck to stay another eight days.[175] By Friday the members present had swelled to nine giving them a quorum to elect Lord Conway and Charles Roper members.

Charlton, Friday 7th December 1739
Present: Edward Pauncefort (in the chair), Duke of Richmond, Duke of St Albans, Lord Harcourt, Hon Edward Legge, Sir John Miller, General Hawley, William Fauquier and Thomas Strickland.
This day the Rt Hon Lord Conway was balloted for and admitted a member of this society.[176]
The Hon Charles Roper was also balloted for and admitted a member of this society.

Lord Conway later had a distinguished career in parliament and at court. Like many frequenters of Charlton, he was a Lord of the Bedchamber to the King and a Knight of the Garter, but his other posts included Ambassador to Paris, Viceroy of Ireland, Master of the Horse and Lord Chamberlain. He married a daughter of the Duke of Grafton and was created Earl and later Marquess of Hertford.

Then William Fauquier Esq proposed to the members present that Sir Robert Smyth Bt should have leave to come to Charlton for eight days. It was accordingly balloted for and carried in the affirmative.

Sir Robert, now 31, had succeeded to his father's baronetcy when he was eight. He had a seat at Isfield in East Sussex and is pictured in a charming family study by Andrea Soldi. The sport on Saturday and Monday was unremarkable, with unadventurous foxes running in large circles, but on Tuesday they had a long busy day ending with hounds scattered all over the country.

Tuesday 11th December 1739
Found a brace of foxes in the Wildham, Tom Johnson with one and two brace and a half of hounds went directly over Bow hill to Germanleith, the rest of the pack went off to the Hasletts, to Watergate, then turned back to the Inholmes down by the Pitlands, up to Long hill, the whole length of that, cross the Winchester road, through North Marden fields, there by Germanleith came into Tom Johnson; through Germanleith to Phillis wood, back by Phillis farm and Hill Lands to North Marden, from thence over the downs and Lord Tankerville's warren, into Uppark; there by the kitchen garden wall, turned back over Harting hill, then up to Harting beacon, and to Germanleith again, Phillis wood and Monkton park, back through Phillis wood again to Germanleith and there came to a dead fault, but Tom Johnson upon a cast to the Winden, either hit it off again, or found a fresh fox in the Winden, and from thence they ran down almost to Chilgrove, round the enclosures there, and back again to Phillis wood, Monkton park, through the Winden to Lewknor's copse; there they had so many scents on foot that they were forced to take off, though not without very great difficulty, for the hounds were dispersed all over the whole country; Tom Johnson was forced to go to Charlton forest where some of them had carried a fresh fox from Lewknor's copse; and Nim Ives went back as far as Phillis wood to take

80 Sir Robert Smyth Bt of Isfield, elected to Charlton in 1741, with his wife Louisa, daughter of John, Earl of Bristol and their son Hervey.

off another parcel that had also carried a fresh fox thither, and David Briggs with difficulty got off the rest in Lewknor's copse.

The next day out was near Slindon, where they put a fox to ground, hunted another and changed foxes only to be stopped by fog and heavy rain. The duke spent the next week in London and missed only a moderate day on Monday, but on Wednesday after a busy hunt between Upwaltham and Cocking hilltop, most of the pack changed to a fresh fox which flew along the downs to the west past Harting hill and Uppark to Ladyholt going to ground at Ditcham park, a seven-mile point.

Wednesday 19th December 1739
Took a drag above Waltham at the beginning of Randall's bottom, which lasted half an hour to the farther side of East Dean wood, there he went off round the outside of the forest, through Herringdean, was headed at Cocking road, came back through the fields to Nightingale bottom,

from thence to Broadham, through the bottom of Charlton forest, and East Dean wood, took a large ring in the lower Tegleaze, and came back along the side hills, the outside of Charlton forest, through Herringdean, across Cocking highway, up the Marlows as far as Colworth down, thereabouts the hounds parted, about sixteen couple came back almost to Coney copse, and thereabouts they changed. The fresh fox flew at once for Cocking chalk pit, turned there for Sadlers furze, but went by them and crossed for the side hills, and for the Winden, kept up by the outside, and by Monkton park, through the fields by Germanleith crossed then other fields at the bottom for Treyford earth, from thence kept the steeps up the trundle to Harting beacon, there the company saw him, the hounds did not view him, over Harting windmill hill into Uppark, by the kitchen garden and dog kennel close by the house, there there was a short check, then crossed him again close by the front of the house, from thence to Lady Holt park gate, turned there over the hill for Harting down, and then for Ditcham park, by the wood side they had a check, and whilst they were trying, a man told them he saw him go into the main earth, which proved true, so they came home.

Two good days' sport followed before Christmas, the first being a five-mile point, [13] as they ran

Saturday 22nd December 1739
Took a drag in the Redvins, and carried it over the earth at Goldings copse to the Valdoe, there either he or a fresh fox flew up St Roche's hill, cross Goodwood warren, through Stricklands furze field, East Dean park, the Bubholts and North hanger, down by Droke house, across the lane, up the hill, over Dell bottom, up to the Tegleaze road, across down by the Stony house, and to East Dean wood, round of the inside of Charlton forest, down to the Drought common or west gate of the forest, then up again to East Dean wood, and there lost him; it was believed he went to ground.

and the second a hunt of about six miles.

Monday 24th December 1739
Took a drag in the Tegleaze, but as it went to East Dean wood we took off, and a fox was halloaed in North comb, the hounds were immediately layed into him and ran down through the covert and took a ring in the fields between Barlavington and Sutton, then up the hill through Farm wood, through Glatting hanger, up over Glatting beacon, into the Gumworth, cross Slindon down, into Mays bottom along Trotrow, by Madehurst, to Fair mile, and there was headed back, and in a field by Madehurst church they killed him, a dog fox.

After that there was a long frost and the company did not reassemble until March as the duke records in his diary:

During the long frost the hounds were only aired, but as I could not come down before Saturday the first of March, Tom Johnson went out five times with the hounds, and earthed a brace of foxes.

They managed four days the first week, with a poor day on Monday and a little better on Tuesday accounting for a dog fox. On Friday they found on the downs and running eastwards ran down the hill to catch the fox near Barlavington church.

Friday 7th March 1740
Found in East Dean wood, and went off directly over Cocking course to Woolavington hanger as hard as hounds could run, there we had a check of a quarter of an hour, then took the scent again over Duncton highway to Duncton chalk pit, over Barlavington hill to Farm wood, tried the earth there, and then back again over part of Barlavington hill, and down through Barlavington parish, and there three fields beyond the church we killed him, a dog fox.

Saturday was disappointing and the four days in the following week gave the company moderate sport, but nothing exceptional. However the last day of the season was extraordinary.

Monday 17th March 1740
Found in the Marlows, ran up to the Hacking place, through Coney copse, then back again through the Marlows cross Cocking highway to the field by Herringdean, then I saw the fox and halloaed him back again to Cocking warren, into Coney copse, to the Sovereigns, Venus copse, through Lewknor's copse, Monkton park, Winden, Phillis wood, Germanleith, to Up Marden, along Up Marden down to Harting beacon, thence to the earth at Treyford, went to ground and in the meanwhile a fresh fox came up the hill, through Germanleith, and along the hills, leaving all the covers on the right hand till he came to Lewknors copse, there we had a dead fault but recovered it again in Monkton park, for he was headed back by workmen, then we carried the scent as far as Germanleith, but could make it out no farther, so Tom Johnson cast to Treyford earth, and round the Lewknor's copse, and there found Peggy who had run him back by herself. Then we had several rings upon a cold scent that at last we could make nothing of it, so came home, but Walcut and a terrier, ran him by themselves to the Warren house at Cocking, where they say he leapt up atop of the house, and came down the chimney, and they called in the two dogs and caught her and brought her here, a bitch fox with whelp. David went off with 13 couple of hounds and had a fine run along the side hills to Twines, but there in the dry fallows could make nothing of it.

That was the end of the season at Charlton. The hounds had accounted for 15 foxes in 29 days. In the spring they went to the New Forest for a few bye days. The Duke of Bolton was also there and wrote to the duke at Goodwood. Lord Delawarr was not at Bolderwood as he was preparing for active service (England was at war with Spain), so Bolton asked Richmond to join him as he had only Colonel Charles Perry (a member at Charlton) for company. The shortage of foxes was worrying and perhaps the forest was being over hunted.

Burleigh Lodge, New Forest, Friday 28th March 1740
I came to this place yesterday, my hounds came here on Tuesday, the ground being so dry at Sombourn that I could not hunt there. They hunted on Wednesday and killed an old dog fox at Lynwood. Your hounds had a very great chase on Monday and earthed in the Nodes; they did not find on Wednesday on the low country. I find foxes very scarce in the forest; I went out today and drew a great deal of likely ground without finding.

As I hear that Lord Delawarr's warlike preparations will prevent his coming here this season, if your grace has a mind to see your hounds, you will do me great honour and pleasure if you will come to this place with whatever company you like to bring with you. Here is good wine but no French cook, five beds and only Perry who can eat more than any two people.

If your affairs won't admit of your coming, I should hope that you would order your hounds to hunt no more. It is no more than what my hounds will do when I leave them, for I think if we both hunt separate[ly] we need not think of coming here next year. The forest is in good order, but the weather is very cold. I had a visit from Mr Johnson this afternoon …[177]

A final word about the season's expenses. They had gone up by over £200 to £1,061 5s. 8d., almost entirely from a great increase in the consumption of oatmeal and oats, which were now costing £440 13s. 2d.[178] It makes one wonder whether the surfeit of flesh fed to the modern fox hound really enhances their hunting qualities.

— XI —

Ringwood '41

A new scribe made his appearance in the hound book in 1740. His writing is exceptionally neat and the entries are less inconsistent from one season to another with fewer mistakes. Seventeen couple of old hounds were cast, 1½ couple of old hounds were given and 21½ couple of young hounds entered, making a total of 65 couple in the kennel.[179]

They started hunting on Wednesday 5 November when the duke, who had hunted at Charlton for over 20 years, noted he had his first blank day! On Monday they found in the Valdoe and ran to Selhurst park via Halnaker where the fox turned and ran back almost exactly the same way to the Valdoe where they finally lost it, despite persisting for a long time. This was a four-mile point, over 12 as they ran.

There is a note that Grey Carey, one of the duke's favourite hunters, had died that morning.[180] How long he had been in the duke's stable is uncertain, but he features first in the list of horses in November 1737 and had been pensioned off before the start of 1740 season. Granby, Cheat and Jumper had also gone and a new horse Sultan had appeared, leaving the duke only eight horses. Three had also been pensioned off in the huntsman's stable and no new ones brought in, leaving him 10 for the season.

Wednesday 12th seems to have been blank again; on Friday they hunted a fox which, unusually for an old dog, ran in circles before being overtaken by the pack; and Saturday was better, but the pack were slow to leave the Broyle copse near Chichester until they had accounted for a badger, after which they had a reasonable hunt, fast at the end, of five miles, catching the fox in East Dean park.

Unfortunately, several pages of the hunting diary for November, December and January are missing, although a comment in one of the letters mentions a period of frost before Christmas. The annual meeting in London was also not recorded; the minute book reads 'There was a meeting in the year 1740 at the Bedford Head Tavern but no minutes of it remain'.[181]

By Christmas Lord Harcourt was planning a visit to join the hounds who were due to go to Findon, although he was having some difficulty persuading his Charlton friends to come. He wrote to the duke who was at Goodwood and referred to a Mr. Green, a resident of Findon who provided accommodation and hunted with the Charlton pack.

Henrietta Street, Thursday 25th December 1740

The Duke of St Albans, having laid aside all thoughts of going to Findon, has been so kind as to offer me the use of his house and stable that was taken for him. I wrote by last post to my friend Green, desiring him to procure me a stable at Findon, but since the duke has been so obliging as to let me have that which was designed for him, I must entreat your grace to let Mr Green know it, that he may give himself no further trouble upon my account. I should not trouble your grace

81 Simon, 2nd Viscount (later Earl) Harcourt was a regular at Charlton. He was later Viceroy of Ireland and lived into his sixties when he was accidentally drowned in a well. His dog had fallen in and in attempting to recover him, lost his balance and fell in himself. His dog was found alive sitting on the body of his dead master.

upon this occasion, but that I think you are likely to see him before he can probably receive a letter from me.

Pauncefort will scarce come down this time, for he only talks of a possibility of coming down on Wednesday next. Hawley has quite given up the Findon expedition and I don't yet hear whether Mr Fauquier is determined to go. However I have sent to offer him a conveyance to Guildford on Sunday next, which for my own sake I hope he will accept of. Were these gentlemen extravagantly fond of sport, I don't believe they would be so terrified with the apprehensions of a tedious and dangerous march to Findon or the inconveniences that are to be encountered in that place.

I have no news or even lies to trouble your grace with, but ... I think I shall be able to bring your grace a budget full of good or bad news by next Sunday evening, if I have the pleasure of seeing you then at Charlton ...[182]

The Duke of Newcastle also wrote to Richmond on Christmas day inviting him to East Sussex:

Bishopstone, Thursday 25th December 1740

I conclude the thaw has brought you to Charlton as it has done me here. I wish you would be so good as to honour me with your company ...[183]

to which Richmond replied:

Goodwood, Friday 26th December 1740

I shall certainly wait upon you next Saturday at Bishopstone and will stay with you on Sunday. Sir John Miller who is now with me will also certainly attend you and we will pick up what friends we can; nobody of consequence in this part of the country is against us, but this is a time that they choose to stay at home, however we will do what we can.

On Thursday we hunt by the way and dine at Findon, where we stay till Saturday, hunt that morning and after hunting go to Bishopstone, so very likely we mayn't arrive till night. Sir John [Miller] will hunt with you on Saturday. We shall have no Charlton people but Harcourt and Pauncefort with us and I shall certainly bring them. Sir John will be with you on Tuesday.

We have had a very fine chase today, nobody but Dayrolles[184] with me, who will also attend you with your leave. I shall employ Green to get what people I can.[185]

Newcastle wrote back to Richmond pointing out his proposed arrangements did not suit, not least because he was threatening to bring more people than the house would accommodate!

Bishopstone, Tuesday 30th December 1740

I am very much obliged to you for your kind intention of coming to Bishopstone, but as you can't be with us 'till Saturday night and we all decamp from hence on Sunday to be in London on Monday, I must beg you would not give yourself the trouble to come this time unless you can be here on Friday, which I conclude from the dispositions you have already made will be disagreeable to you.

For the same reason you will be so good as to stop Green and company. We had yesterday twice as many people as this house would hold ... We go to Lewes tomorrow, lie there tomorrow night, hunt on Thursday and dine here that day and shall have a ball for the Seaford ladies on Thursday night. On Friday we all dine at Firle with Sir William Gage[186] and return hither at night, hunt on Saturday and go towards London on Sunday. I beg you would desire Sir John to meet us at Sir William Gage's on Friday and he shall go home with us in my coach ...[187]

Unfortunately Richmond's youngest daughter had been taken ill, so he was undecided what to do.

Goodwood, Wednesday 31st December 1740

My situation at present is very disagreeable and uncertain. My youngest daughter [Lady Margaret, born 16 November 1739] is very ill, that is she has a fever and we don't know what the consequence may be; so if I go to Findon tomorrow, the Duchess of Richmond stays here. From thence I can soon return if the poor child should be worse; but if it should be better on Friday, I'll try to wait upon you at Bishopstone either Friday or Saturday, tho' you do go away on Sunday. I assure you I always wish to be with you, however don't expect me for fear it should not be in my power.

There is only Lord Harcourt and Dayrolles with me. Sir John Miller can't go for my Lady Miller is extremely ill ... If I come on Saturday it will be by dinner, but will be with you if possible on Friday ...[188]

In the event he did not get there by Friday but wrote from Findon.

Findon, Friday 2nd January 1741

My attending your grace tomorrow at Bishopstone or not will depend upon two circumstances. The first whether my little girl is better or worse, which I shall hear tonight; that is but too good an excuse. The other (which I hope you will be so good as to indulge me in) is hunting tomorrow, but if it should be so very bad a day that we can't hunt, I'll attend you if you desire it, tho' I should be wet to the skin. I should certainly not think of so trifling a thing as hunting if my going to Bishopstone could be of the least real service to you or if it was necessary to show the world how sincerely I love and esteem you, but I hope that is out of all doubt … We had a very fine chase yesterday and ran to ground. Sir Cecil [Bisshop], Sir Charles Goring [of Highden near Washington] and John Middleton were out with us …[189]

He notes later in the letter that 'poor Kirke is dying or dead', the General Kirke who was an original subscriber to the articles and a regular attender of the annual meeting in London. As to the little Margaret (whom Newcastle mistook for her elder sister Emily), progress was slow. The other children had been moved to Charlton so as to be away from the infection.

Goodwood, Tuesday 6th January 1741
… My poor little girl has got the confluent kind of smallpox which is very dangerous, 'tho no bad symptoms as yet appear, however 'tis but the fifth day so nobody can tell yet how it will go with her …[190]

Goodwood, Wednesday 7th January 1741
… My poor little girl goes on but slowly. She can't be out of danger before Saturday and happy it will be if she is so then, for she has a very bad sort. I do my best to smother my anxiety, but 'tis a most cruel situation. 'Tis Margaret, my youngest daughter, not Emily; she with her two brothers (Earl of March and Lord George Lennox) are at Charlton and as yet in perfect health. But I dread what in all likelihood may come.[191]

Sadly the poor little thing died shortly afterwards. The next entry in the hunting diary is at the end of January when the hounds were at Findon, but they returned to Charlton after hunting near Arundel on the way back. They were out again near Arundel on Wednesday and Friday and caught two foxes and a martin! The next day hounds went to draw near Chichester and ran a fox to Slindon, a point of seven miles, turning back to Selhurst park where they killed.

Saturday 7th February 1741
Found in the Broyle copse, ran a leash of foxes, but one at last broke away to the Valdoe and ran through Goldings copse by Goodwood park to the Redvins, Halnaker park, over by Halnaker windmill, Seabeach farm, Long down, Eartham common, Slindon park where we had an entapis and a view, down into the fields on the north side of Slindon park, up by the windmill, through Bay comb, up the Rewell hill but not quite into the wood, down again by Heberden farm, over Slindon down to Slindon park again, to Eartham over the common fields and Long down, to the bushy field by Selhurst park and there killed her, a little bitch fox.

The start on Monday was slow, but Wednesday's hunt was 18 miles as they ran and a 5½-mile point.

Wednesday 11th February 1741
Found in East Dean park, ran over Selhurst park, Gumworth, Bay comb, Slindon park, the common to Walburton, back over Eastergate common, Slindon park again, up to Nore hill,

through North wood to Bushy field, by Seabeach to Halnaker park and garden, there viewed her by a faggot pile, through the garden, down into Halnaker street and fields, into the corner of the Redvins and there killed her, a bitch fox.

Finding in East Dean wood the next Monday, hounds ran almost to Petworth, although they would have had to cross the river to get there. Tuesday was a poor day and the last notable day of the season was from East Dean park when hounds ran for 20 miles without going far from the find, so it was probably a vixen which they finally lost and the horses had had enough.

Thursday 19th February 1741
Found in East Dean wood, ran by the Stony house over Dell comb, down by Waltham, up through Selhurst park to North hanger, the Winkin, to Halsteds down, through Strickland's furze, over the Harroways, through East Dean park, the Bubholts, down cross the road by East Dean, up to Court hill, East Dean wood, upper Tegleaze, back by Stony house again to East Dean wood, Charlton forest, out at the north east gate, back through Punters copse into the forest, to East Dean wood, up to the Stony house, over Dell comb, down by Waltham, up Selhurst park to North wood, back through Selhurst park, cross the road by Droke house, up through Dell comb to Stony house, East Dean wood, through Charlton forest to Herringdean, there the hounds lost the fox and most of the horses blown up.

To round off the season, they had a meeting in the evening at which Lord Tankerville rather unexpectedly turned up, having not been to Charlton for ages.[192] He may have been collecting a bitch hound called Cruel whom he had given to the duke in 1737 and from whom they had a litter which was entered at Charlton in 1741. Since his visits were so infrequent, the company thought it politic to invite him to take the chair. Also present were the Dukes of Richmond and St Albans, Lord Harcourt, Sir Harry Liddell, Sir John Miller, Messrs. Jenison, Honywood, Fauquier and Strickland and Captain Honywood. They elected Sir Robert Smyth, who was staying in Charlton at the time, and Solomon Dayrolles members.[193]

Solomon Dayrolles was the godson and secretary of Philip Stanhope, Earl of Chesterfield, well known as sponsor of the bill to introduce the Gregorian calendar into England, which was enacted in 1752. His other claim to fame was as the author of 'Letters to his Son'. His only child was born to Elisabeth du Bouchet, a Huguenot lady with whom he had an affair while suffering from acute boredom as Ambassador to the Hague. The child was born in England in 1732 and was called Philip like his father. Marriage to the mother was out of the question, although he set her up in a house in Marlborough Street. The following year he married Melusina de Schulenberg, Countess of Walsingham, an illegitimate daughter of George I. She was immensely rich and settled his financial affairs admirably and they lived quite amicably in separate apartments in Grosvenor Square. George II was furious at the match, dubbing him 'a little gossiping tea table scoundrel' and the next year Chesterfield was banished from court owing to his indiscreetly 'having offended the queen by paying court to Lady Suffolk, the king's mistress'! The 'Letters to his Son' were not intended for publication and by them he hoped to enable the boy to reach the triumphs in life he himself had failed to grasp. Dr. Johnson famously remarked that they 'inculcated the morals of a strumpet and the manners of a dancing master' and of the earl himself he added that he was 'a wit amongst lords and a lord amongst wits'.[194] Regrettably the letters failed in their purpose as Philip died in 1769 at the age of thirty-seven. Chesterfield then began another series of letters to Dayrolles his godson, who was something of a celebrity, his social qualities having gained him the important post of Gentleman of the Privy Chamber to the King and Master of the Revels. He was the recipient of Lord Chesterfield's last articulate words. Polite to the end, on his death bed in his 79th year on Wednesday 24 March 1773 at Chesterfield House, his magnificent mansion in Mayfair he said, 'Give Dayrolles a chair!'[195]

Before we pass to the next season, the accounts in 1741 show very little change in the total hunt expenses, which came to £1,067 5s. 4d.; except a rise in the staff wages by about ten per cent to £184 16s. 6d., still way below the expenditure on oatmeal for the hounds at £232 19s. 8d.![196] The duke acquired four new horses; Lord Mayor, Roger, Sir Harry and Justice and having lost Royal and Looby, he now had 10 in his stable. Walker and Frostyface had gone from Tom Johnson's stable; they had a new young horse, Bumper; and Windsor had been brought back after a season's rest. The duke's attendants remained much the same, but Nim Ives, who had whipped-in to Tom for many years, and Billy his brother, who was a hunt servant to the royal buckhounds, both left Charlton at the end of the 1740/1 season. David Briggs was still there and Jack Row was the new second whipper-in.

In the kennels the numbers were drastically reduced from 65 to 49½ couple by casting 26½ couple of old hounds and entering 11 couple of young hounds; 9 couple bred at Charlton and 2 couple given.[197]

Charlton's most famous hound, Ringwood'41 by Lord Craven's Drunkard out of Ruby'38, was entered that season. He hunted with the pack for five seasons, no doubt with great distinction, and was sent to Mr. Charles Pelham of Brocklesby in Lincolnshire for breeding in 1746. His pedigree went back to Mr. Orlebar's Tipler'17, the sire of his Shifter'19 which he gave to the Duke of Grafton. Shifter was the sire of the Duke of Bolton's Maiden'22, who was dam of his Wildman'25, who sired Lord Tankerville's Ruler, an old hound given to the Duke of Richmond in 1737. Ruler was the sire of Charlton Ruby'38, the dam of Ringwood. Mr. Pelham warded Ringwood with Lovely, Sally, Cleanly, Cloudy and Tipsey in 1746; with Famous, Dolly, Cloudy (again), Frisky, Rachel, Lilly, Marvel and Famous (again) in 1747; and with Famous (again), Daphne and Cloudy (again) in 1748. From the 16 litters, they produced 38 couple of hounds, many of which were drafted to other kennels.[198] His blood can now be found in practically every kennel in England. Ringwood was returned to the duke in 1748 and 'sent from Whitehall to the New Forest on 23rd March' along with one couple of his progeny, Crispin out of Cloudy and Tansey out of Famous, both of whom were entered at Charlton that year.[199]

Hunting on four days the first week of the season, they had two hunts of about seven miles, killing on each occasion; followed by a four-mile point on Thursday, 15 as they ran with the fox going to ground; and a blank day on Saturday.

Thursday 5th November 1741
Found in Dawtrey's hooks, ran through the Gumworth, Mays farm, Abraham walls, back over Slindon down, through North wood into Dawtrey's hooks again, there faulted for three quarters of an hour, then hit it off in a cold scent through Waltham bottom and had an entapis in a hedgerow near Waltham, ran up through the upper Tegleaze, along the side hill to Barlavington hanger, North comb and Farm wood, down to Sutton, to Bignor park, to Burton park, up Barlavington hanger to Farm wood and there ran to ground in the great earth.

The next week they were out on three days. Monday was spoilt by the weather and Wednesday was only a short run, but on Friday they had a terrific hunt from Winden wood on the

82 Charles Pelham, ancestor of the Earls of Yarborough and proprietor of hounds at Brocklesby in Lincolnshire. He bred 16 litters from Charlton Ringwood'41, as a result the blood of the Charlton hounds can be found in practically every kennel in England.

downs down past West Dean, Binderton and Lavant to Chichester, a 6½-mile point, 17 as they ran. Additional excitement was provided by the fox pretending to enter a brewhouse near Lavant and later dipping in a hog trough at Graylingwell (now a mental hospital) to try to throw hounds off the scent!

Friday 13th November 1741
Found in the bramble piece by the Winden, ran through the Winden to Lewknor's copse, to Coney copse, through Cocking warren, up the hill back to the Winden, back again to Lewknor's copse, over Colworth down, there helped by a halloa, over to the Warren house in West Dean warren, over the hill to the copses above West Dean, there was a second halloa at Preston corner, then down to Preston farm, along the road and by Binderton orchard almost to Midlavant church, there another halloa, to the plantation by Raughmere, there we thought he had got into the brewhouse for all the hounds threw up there, but soon after hit it forward and ran to Grayling well, there they saw him go through a hog trough, hit it off again to the Broyle house, over the fields below the house to the fields above the Row copse, there in a hedgerow killed him, an old dog fox.

The third week produced three excellent hunts. On Monday they had a five-mile point, 14 as they ran; and on the other two days, remarkably straight running foxes took hounds for eight miles on Thursday and 10 miles on Saturday.

Monday 16th November 1741
Found in Ashling woods, ran through Stoke copse and back again through Ashling woods, up through Down farm, over Stoughton down, through Stoughton fields up almost to the Hasletts, round the Wildham wood, over Bow hill, down to Chilgrove, over the fields by North Marden to Phillis wood, Monkton park, all along the side hills to Cocking warren, to Coney copse and there killed him, a dog fox.

Thursday 19th November 1741
Found in the Broyle copse, ran through Raughmere copse and cross the fields to the Valdoe, over Goodwood warren by the corner of the park, up through Molecomb furze, through the Winkin to North hanger, over Selhurst park, through the Benges, over Noman's land, Glatting beacon to Glatting hanger, there turned short back again over Glatting beacon, down almost to Littleton farm, up above Twines to North comb, Barlavington hanger and Duncton hanger, then down to Burton park and over the fields, several times backwards and forwards and at last in a hedgerow by Barlavington common killed him, a very old dog fox.

Saturday 21st November 1741
Found in the Row copse, ran all the lower way through the fields by Hampnett below Westerton to Feilkens's hole, by Boxgrove and Halnaker street to Eartham bushes, over Eartham and Eastergate common and Slindon common to Heberden copse and Watson's piece, and there in full view the hounds lost him, though we tried four times round the covert and in every part of the cover, so we imagine he must be gone to ground in some little hole.

In the last week in November, Tuesday was a good day, although very cold, and the Thursday fox took to the sea at high tide near Dell Quay to escape and hounds failed to follow. Saturday's hunt was a four-mile point and hounds ran for 15 miles without a check in two hours and 10 minutes, an average speed of seven miles an hour, which is quite fast.

Tuesday 24th November 1741
Found in the Broyle copse and went directly to ground in the sand pits. Then went and found in Newman's copse below Adsdean wood, ran up to Adsdean, over Black bushes and back again to Stoke coney copse, from thence through Stoke copse, Ashling woods, the Rifles and Row copse to the Broyle copse, there they ran the foil for above two hours and a fresh fox just came into the covert at the same time; and the day changing into great cold, the hounds could make nothing of it and lost the fox.

Thursday 26th November 1741
Found in Row copse and ran down to Bosham and ran several rings there for above five hours and lost him, but afterwards found that the fox had crossed the water above Dell quay at high water and gone into the Manhood.

Saturday 28th November 1741
Found in the Rewell, took a turn in the Deans, up by the Rewell chalk pit, all along the Rewell through Sherwood, over the hill into South wood, over Houghton steeps, Priest comb, along the side hill, then over Bignor hill to Glatting beacon, to Noman's land, a turn in Littleton bottom, back up through St Mary wood, North wood and over the top of Nore hill to Slindon windmill, through Bay comb to Heberden farm, up to the Rewell again, down into Watson's piece, there killed him, an old dog fox. Ran two hours and ten minutes and hardly ever at fault.

Early December saw a lull in the activity and the duke was in London for the week. However when he came back, they had a very hard day. A short hunt to start with, followed by a hunt of 9½ miles to Merryfields near Burton park where they changed, followed by a third hunt of 10 miles to Glatting hanger where they had to take off in the dark, although, says the duke, the hounds were still fresh. Lord Mayor was the only horse not knocked up and guess who was riding him. The duke, of course! The Biddulph brothers, Richard and Charles, both of whom had been at the grand chase, peeled off before the end, their horses not fit enough.

Monday 7th December 1741
Found in the Rewell, ran a fox several rings in the Rewell and Deans and earthed him in the main earth in Heberden copse. Then found another in Walberton copse, ran him through Slindon park, over Nore hill, Kemp's rough piece, Gumworth, Dawtrey's hooks, Glatting beacon, along the side hills to Bignor hill, there down the hill to Bignor park, to Red hill, to Burton park, the Merryfields they changed, came up Barlavington hill, over by Twines, up to Dawtrey's hooks, over the Gumworth, the rough piece, over Slindon down, there the two Biddulphs knocked up, down by May's farm, over Madehurst common down, by the lone beech, to Bignor hill again and along the side hills, they came to a check at Glatting hanger, there it being almost night, we took off, the hounds fresh, but all the horses knocked up, except Lord Mayor; the hardest day's work for hounds and horses that I ever saw, except the famous long chase upon the 26th January 1738/9.

There were three more days before Christmas, Thursday being a seven-mile point, 15 as they ran and Saturday a hunt of about eleven miles.

Thursday 10th December 1741
Found in East Dean wood, ran several rings there and in the forest, then broke covert and ran through the Tegleaze to Duncton chalk pit, Barlavington hanger, North comb, Farm wood, Glatting hanger, over Glatting beacon, Gumworth, over Gumworth corner to the Coneygates, up to Abraham walls, here an entapis, down through Ashlee, over Slindon down to the rough piece, through Gumworth again, up over Glatting beacon, along the side hill to Bignor hill, there crossed and went over the top of Bury hill, where we viewed him all the way up the hill, the length of Bury hill, then down into a little copse called East Dare just by Bury village, there killed him, a dog fox.

Saturday 12th December 1741
Found the instant we threw off in Burton pond tail, ran up to the Merryfields, turned short back, by the mill to Shopham bridge, back again through the meadows to the Merryfields again, over Duncton common, through Burton park, up Burton hill, over Barlavington hanger, North comb, Farm wood, over Farm hill by Haslecomb, Twines, by Littleton farm, up the hill to the upper Tegleaze, along Woolavington and Duncton hills, cross Barlavington hanger again and into North comb, there went to ground, but dug to him and let him bolt, ran several rings in North comb and went to ground again in the main earth in North comb, so took off and went home.

A select company were at Charlton on Wednesday 23 December, although there is no mention of hunting. Perhaps it was frosty. However they admitted one John Butler as a visitor with leave to stay for eight days.[200] Hunting resumed in January, when they had one day from Charlton and the hounds then went to Findon, where they enjoyed reasonable sport for the first week.

One of the people who often joined them there was John Cheale, a resident of Findon. He was an intimate friend of the Richmonds and was often to be found amongst the house parties at Goodwood. Out hunting he was certainly no thruster and mounted on his hunter old Findon he preferred to jog along in soberer fashion than his more youthful companions, for he was of maturer years and portlier presence than they. His geniality made him universally popular with the young ladies at Goodwood. He had recently been engaged in the preliminary ceremonies which were to qualify him for the post of Norroy King at Arms, of which he gives an amusing description.

London, Tuesday 17th November 1741

I have been in a great hurry ever since I have been in town to get the patent for a herald passed, for nothing can be done in the other till I was made a herald, which I was last night at Lord Effingham's house. In the first room was Norroy and the heralds and pursuivants in their habits, who went all into the inward room, except two heralds who stayed with me. Then word was brought that all things were ready, then the two heralds took me under each arm and told me I must do as they did. The first thing I saw was the earl sitting very majestically in a great chair with his hat on and the marshall's staff in his hand. Norroy stood on one side and a herald on the other with a cup of wine in it; and the rest ranged themselves according to their order around a table (which was set before the earl) whereon was laid a bible and a sword across the bible. As soon as the door of the room where the earl sat was opened, we three made a very low obedience, then went three or four steps further and did the same and then knelt down. Then I put one hand on the bible and the other on the sword. Then Norroy read the oath, which was pretty long; amongst other things I was to succour ladies in distress, not to frequent taverns, not play at dice. Then the earl got up and took the coat and put over my head and the collar of SS and then took the cup and poured the wine on my head and said 'Arundell'. So ended the ceremony [but] there is a good deal more ceremony to be used when Mr Lake and I are crowned Kings at Arms, which is performed at the Heralds Office. Then the sword that the Duke of Norfolk fought with at Flodden Field where he killed the King of Scots is brought out, but I don't know what is to be done with it … I hope your grace had good sport, tho' the weather with us is very cold …[201]

Newcastle warned Richmond whom he could expect to be joining the party at Findon, with instructions to look after his nephew.

Claremont, Saturday 2nd January 1742

… Lord Harcourt and Linky [Lord Lincoln, Newcastle's nephew and heir] meet you at Findon tomorrow. I beg you would not let Linky drink. He has not been very well and is a poor tender creature; but don't let him know I have given you this hint. My service to all your good company …[202]

Monday 4th January 1742

We set out from Charlton at seven o'clock and as soon as we crossed the water at Houghton, threw off in the Wildbrook and found and ran a fox immediately to ground by Parham common, left people to dig and found another just by Rowdel, but he had stole away a great while before the hounds and they brought a very cold scent up the hills and carried it by High down, Muntam, over to Black patch, by Mitchell grove, up to Mitchell grove woods, there several foxes were immediately on foot, so with great difficulty we took them off and went to Muntam hedgerows where our dug fox was turned out, but the hounds ran her up in seven minutes and killed her at Cobden farm, a bitch fox.

Wednesday 6th January 1742
A very rainy morning, however we went out and found in Steyning holt, but the day was so bad, that as soon as the hounds came to a fault, we took off and came home, to hunt the next day.

To hunt a fox to the sea is unusual in itself, but then to see a cur dog continue the chase into the sea before the hounds caught her must be unique in the annals of hunting.

Thursday 7th January 1742
Found in Juniper bushes by the Stony Deans, ran through the Stony Deans and up round Chanctonbury hill, down to Wiston malthouse, then up by the Lyons bank and Steyning holt to Mawdelin, over all the downs away to Applesham, down to the bank of the river, then turned up by Lancing windmill and then down to South Lancing and through the common field to the sea beach, there after a fault a cur dog was seen to course her into the sea and they swam together and then out of the sea and over the beach, where they stood at bay and the hounds came up and killed her, a bitch fox.

After the first week the duke rather lost interest and for the last few days he even forgot which horses they took out! No more entries in the diary are to be found for the rest of the season, no doubt due to a severe prolonged frost. The annual meeting in London was on Friday 26 March 1742 at a new venue, the *Fountain Tavern* in the Strand, and attended by 32 members with Lord Delawarr in the chair.[203] The Dukes of Grafton, Richmond, St Albans, Devonshire, Kingston and Newcastle were there, all staunch Whigs and no doubt wondering what the future held after the resignation of the prime minister Sir Robert Walpole the month before. In the event, Walpole went to the Lords as Earl of Orford and within a year had reunited the Whigs and eased them back in power with Henry Pelham (who was not present at the meeting this time) as prime minister and his brother the Duke of Newcastle as secretary of state. Their ministry was to last until Pelham's death 11 years later. The Earls of Berkeley, Albemarle and Cowper were also there; Lord George Beauclerk, Viscount Harcourt, Lord Conway, the new member and Lord Ossulstone, Tankerville's heir. There were five baronets, William Gage, Henry Liddell, William Corbet, William Middleton and Thomas Prendergast; three Honywoods, the soldiers Huske, Perry and Beake; William Conolly, Ralph Jenison, Edward Pauncefort, William Fauquier, Lawrence Monk and Solomon Dayrolles. The minute concludes, 'Prosperity to Charlton and several other healths were drank and the society adjourn'd as usual'.

The duke's expenditure on the hunt was down on last season from £1,067 to £850, mainly by cutting down on oatmeal consumption (and wages) in the New Forest.[204] He was there in the spring and the last inkling of sport was a line in a letter to Newcastle.

Bolderwood Lodge, New Forest, Wednesday 14th April 1742
… this is the last fox hunting I can possibly have this whole season, that is 'till November next, and that the weather is excessive fine, I would fain stay out next week …[205]

The next day came an invitation for the Master of the Horse, the Duke of Richmond, with some of his Charlton friends to join the Groom of the Stole, the Earl of Pembroke, for a little dinner at Wilton. Lord Pembroke was not a member at Charlton, but had been hunting with Roper on the day he died in 1723 and had been there on one or two occasions since.

Thursday noon, 15th April 1742

… Saturday noon … I hope you will meet me. Dinner shall be ordered to be ready at three o'clock. Not a French dinner, but such as it is. Your honour, Mr. Pauncefort and Sir John Miller shall be extremely welcome, as your honour and your company will always be. Don't send your man back to tell me you can't come [on] Saturday, for we like to dine at 4, 5 or 6 as well as any other hour. Shall wait till then. Come therefore and stay as long as you please, the longer the better, the more the merrier, of honest fellows, I mean. Then do not mistake me, a word to the wise is enough …[206]

— XII —

Roper's Chair

Come the new season, 12½ couple of old hounds were cast and replaced by one couple of old and 14 couple of young hounds, bringing the total for the season up to 53 couple.[207]

There was quite a turn around in the stables. Two old favourites, Sir William and Gin, were retired from the duke's stable, having both done five seasons; and Sir Harry and Justice, who had been brought in only a year before, were no good and also had to go. Five new ones replaced them, Tetlow, Spider, Red Robin, Commode and Smith, and a grey gelding is also mentioned. In the huntsman's stable Jersey, Windsor, Postboy and Forrester were pensioned off and replaced by Castle, Drewet and Trueblue. Both stables now had 10 horses.

The season began on 1 November and the first fortnight produced little sport of note and no hunt of any length. Going out four days each week they managed to catch only two foxes. On 9 November Richmond wrote to Newcastle hoping that a meeting of their dining club could be arranged to cheer up his forthcoming visit to London.

Goodwood, Tuesday 9th November 1742

I have nothing to trouble your grace with but to tell you we have had no sport and to ask whether the Bridge club meets as usual at the Bridge tavern in Palace Yard on Tuesday next. If you like it should be so, the Duke of St Albans and I will attend you, but then you must be so good as to send to the man to summon the other members of the club for that day and I take for granted if you do it in time you will have a pretty full club, but if you don't care for it, 'tis very easily let alone. I shall be in town early enough on Monday … I have received a most impertinent letter from Orme; such a one as none but a true ungrateful country gentleman could incite.[208]

Garton Orme of Woolavington had of course been a joint proprietor of the hounds with Richmond 12 seasons before, so one wonders what he can have written to have so irritated his grace! They were out again on Thursday 11th which was only a short hunt and on Saturday they were beaten by the weather. The duke duly went to London for various parliamentary and court duties and returned to Charlton the following week. Monday and Tuesday were dull days, but Wednesday was a day of real persistence, hounds going round and round in circles for over seven hours and failing to catch a fox. Men were of sterner stuff in those days! On Saturday they had to do without Old Tom who had an attack of gout. After a hunt of about eight miles they changed foxes and just failed to catch the hunted one.

Richmond hated going to London when he could be hunting, but felt a bit guilty in his next letter to Newcastle (who was after all the Secretary of State):

Goodwood, Sunday 28th November 1742

… I must trouble you a little about myself. In the first place I am delighted to see things go so well in the House of Commons. Then as to the House of Lords I take for granted any attendance will be unnecessary and as for cabinet councils they are quite out of fashion, so that all the business I can have in town is waiting upon my royal master which I ever was and ever shall be ready to do, when there is any duty that calls me … but I own I can't help preferring foxhunting and being with my family to what may be called fiddle-faddle waiting, so I could wish to be excused going up till after Christmas. Now I know you'll be in a passion, but don't be really angry with me, for rather than suffer that I will go up at any time … I had certainly rather not go up at all. However if I am to go, I should choose it about next Sunday or Monday; that is if the king should go to the house any day that week, so pray be so good as to let me know whether you think he will go that week or no …[209]

but Newcastle was not cross at all and, basking in the luxury of a large parliamentary majority, replied

Newcastle House, Tuesday 30th November 1742

… tho' I am always glad to have you with me or near me (if you will forgive the familiarity of the expression) I must own I would not now interrupt your country sports when there is no absolute necessity. As we carry everything by such majorities in the House of Commons and bring on Tory elections and postpone Whig ones as we please by great majorities, I conclude we shall have nothing to do in the House of Lords, at least for some time, and most likely not till after Christmas, so you and all your good company (to whom pray my kindest compliments) may hunt at your ease and I wish you better sport than I am afraid you have yet had … My compliments to Goodwood and Charlton …[210]

Meanwhile Richmond was enjoying his sport (although the scent was still not good), but in early December there was a long frost and hunting was cancelled for nearly three weeks. Lord Harcourt wrote to commiserate and to recommend that Hon. John Mordaunt should be invited to dinner at Fox Hall. He was already a member, but not having been to Charlton for some time, he seemed to need the duke's approval before being allowed to come.

London, Saturday 18th December 1742

I received the letter your grace honoured me with and I most heartily condole with your grace upon the badness of the weather. We had a fog last night which is not yet quite gone off, but the weather is milder than it was and the wind is got a little more southward, which may perhaps bring about a thaw … If the weather should allow us to meet your grace at Charlton you may depend upon my best endeavours to muster as many of our members as possible, tho' I despair of bringing the whole number together. I saw Jack Mordaunt yesterday and he seems very desirous of going to Charlton. He says he has been there with the Duke of Bolton, which he hopes will entitle him to a seat in Fox Hall. However I believe nobody will pretend to give an opinion in an affair so important till your grace shall declare your sentiments …[211]

In the event, John Mordaunt attended the annual meeting in London in February and came to Charlton for some hunting later that month. The duke obviously kept a close watch on who was allowed to join the party in the Great Room. They had not admitted any visitors or

83 General George Keppel, Viscount Bury, later 3rd Earl of Albemarle, was elected in 1745. He was Richmond's nephew.

new members for a year, but one person who heard he might be coming up for election soon was young Lord Lincoln, Newcastle's nephew whom he had adopted as his heir. He was by all accounts a cheeky youth. Horace Walpole wrote to a friend, 'You will laugh at a comical thing that happened to Lord Lincoln. He sent the Duke of Richmond word that he would dine with him in the country, and if he would give him leave, would bring Lord Bury with him. It happens that Lord Bury is nothing less than the Duke of Richmond's nephew. The duke very properly sent him word back that Lord Bury might bring *him* if he pleased.'[212] In anticipation of his election at Charlton, Linky was a bit worried about the prospect of a quorum but not at all worried about being black balled!

Whitehall, Saturday 18th December 1742
I wrote you a letter last post full of despair about the cursed frost, but as thoughtless as Jack could be for his soul, forgot to send it. The frost I thank my stars is over, so instead of a long stupid desponding letter, I will tell you the contents of it in a very few words. I began with making apologies to your grace for not answering your letter sooner (which to be sure I should have done); however I laid the fault upon the Duke of Newcastle who constantly told me we should have business in the House of Lords which would oblige your grace to come up to town. I then said a thousand civil things to you for your kind offer of a bed at Charlton, thanked you over and over for the pains you have been so good as to take about the ballot, and concluded with railing most damnably at the weather. But now all is well, for it thaws most delightfully and I flatter myself I shall soon have the pleasure of being a member of Charlton. I fancy we shall be able to make up nine; if so I shall have impudence enough to take it for granted I shall be chose and come down immediately …[213]

84 William Battine junior was elected in 1742 and later became a lawyer. His father, also William, of East Marden was mayor of Chichester and agent successively to Lord Tankerville and Sir Matthew Featherstonhaugh, owners of Uppark.

After a three-week gap hunting resumed with a day of heel lines, fresh foxes, a split pack and a final muddle on meeting other hounds belonging to William Battine junior.

Wednesday 22nd December 1742
The hounds hit upon a drag at the bottom of St Roche's hill and carried it through old warren to Preston corner, but it growing worse and worse, we found that they took it the wrong way, so as it was back to East Dean park and a very fine morning, we went to Ashling woods and there found a fox that went over between Down farm and Adsdean, up Juniper bottom and the black bushes and the whole length of Bow hill, but above Chilgrove, a fresh fox started up out of a single bush. 22 couple of hounds with Tom Johnson and Jack Row stuck to the old scent and the hounds ran very hard through the Wildham wood, the Hasletts and almost to Stansted forest and back again to the Hasletts and there, as Tom thought, ran him to ground; whilst David with 13 couple of hounds and the rest of the company ran the fresh fox in view by Chilgrove, through Phillis wood and all Lewknor's copses, the Marlows and Charlton forest to Punters copse, there, by the help of young Battine's hounds, they divided, ran hare, rabbit and everything but fox, so we lost our scent and came home.

Young Battine must have been unpopular, but the duke was not cross for long as in the evening there was a meeting in the Great Room and he was amongst those elected. As Linky had feared they barely had a quorum and Mr. St Paul, the duke's French stud groom, who had not been to the Great Room before, was hastily summoned to make the numbers up to the requisite nine. By way of light relief, they put Solomon Dayrolles, Master of the Revels at court, in the chair.[214] Lord Harcourt had come down, the Duke of St Albans (of course), Sir John Miller and Ralph Jenison were there.

Also present were Hon. Edward Legge in support of his brother Henry; and William Battine senior in support of son William. Relations staring at you are a great discouragement to putting in a black ball! Lord Lincoln was balloted for first followed by young Battine and, both being present, they were invited to join the party. Also elected were John Butler, a visitor from last season; Captain Ruddeyard of the Coldstream Guards; Hon. John Boscawen, younger son of Viscount Falmouth, a cornet in His Majesty's Regiment of Horse, and Hon. Henry Legge, younger son of the Earl of Dartmouth.

Henry Legge later became a prominent statesman, being Chancellor of the Exchequer in Newcastle's last ministry. In the typical idiom of the day thrown at successful politicians, Lord Holland wrote, 'He sacrificed every honest consideration to selfish cunning. He had no sooner got preferment from one patron than he looked to his adversary and probable successor for the preservation or augmentation of it.'

The last new member was John Cheale of Findon, Norroy King of Arms, whom we have met before and more of him later, for we have the next day out with the hounds on Christmas Eve; another poor day and two days after Christmas little better, although they managed to catch the fox.

William, Earl of Home joined the party in the evening as a visitor.[215] Mr. Jenison proposed he should stay, knowing that, having married a rich widow on Christmas day, one Elizabeth, daughter of William Gibbons of Vere, Jamaica, he was desperate to get away from her. The reason was simple. She was delighted with her title and he with her money, and living together was never the intention. Lord Home was there for eight days and returned later in the season for more hunting, having by then deserted his Jamaican wife for good and, no doubt, appropriating some of her fortune. He was a soldier and became governor of Gibraltar where he died in 1761.

Wednesday was frustrated by fog, Thursday was too cold for the gentlemen of the field, so they left Old Tom and the whippers-in digging, but missed a good hunt when the fox bolted, and on Saturday they lost the hounds and missed another very good hunt!

Saturday 1st January 1743
Found in Red copse a brace of foxes and ran them both into East Dean park, and one of the scents was carried into Charlton copse and then out upon the rough ground between the parks where they came to a fault and a halloa was heard towards Charlton, but as it was an excessive bad day in every respect, but particularly for hearing, we followed the halloa for near half an hour, then heard that about ten or twelve couple of hounds had gone full cry over North down and we tried to follow them in vain for above two hours, so were obliged to come home; but we heard afterwards by Daniel Treges the earth stopper and Mr Biddulph's keeper who was most part of the time with them, that they went over the Tegleaze and down by Duncton chalk pit, through Burton park to Red hill earth, tried that and so to Watersfield warren near Greatham bridge, came back by Red hill through Burton park and Fountains copse, where they found a fresh fox, who went away to Farm wood with about three couple of hounds and the others, about four couple stuck to the hunted fox and ran him into Charlton forest, from whence they came home.

The next week started with a blank day, but they caught a fox on Tuesday after a moderate run. Five of the new members were in Charlton on Wednesday 5 January enjoying the sport, including Henry Legge, Lord Lincoln, John Boscawen, John Cheale and young Battine.

85 Robert Darcy, 6th Earl of Holdernesse, was elected in 1743 and became Secretary of State for the North. He was a member of the Dilettante Society.

On Wednesday they elected another member, Robert Darcy, Earl of Holdernesse, then a youth of 24.[216] He married a Dutch lady later that year, but their family life was tragic as both their sons died in infancy and on his death the earldom became extinct. He did however have a successful political career, being appointed at the age of 32 Secretary of State for the South and subsequently the North in succession to the Duke of Newcastle, a post which he held for 10 years. But to revert to the hunting. A greyhound had the temerity to catch the hunted fox on Thursday (it seems amazing today that summary justice was considered necessary) and Saturday produced an excellent seven-mile point, 15 as they ran.

Thursday 6th January 1743
Found in the Rewell, ran through the Deans, Heberden copse, Bay comb and tried Butt hill earth, then back again through Bay comb, over Fair mile and up again to the Rewell, over Arundel park, cross the road to Tortington common and back again to the Deans where a greyhound caught her, a bitch fox. N:B: The greyhound was immediately hanged.

Saturday 8th January 1743
Found in the Broyle copse and the instant the fox was found he broke covert and went directly over the old Broyle, through the Moutenes, the Rifles, Stoke copse, Ashling woods, Down copse, by Down farm, up Bow hill, through black bushes, the whole length of the course upon Bow hill, down Chilgrove hanger, over the fields to Phillis wood, through Monkton park, out upon the downs till we came to Lewknor's copse; there about seven couple went away with a fresh fox down the hill, but near thirty couple stuck to the first scent and in Lewknor's copse killed him, a dog fox.

Frost intervened at the end of the next week but there was a good day on Wednesday when they encountered a straight running fox who gave them an eight-mile point, nine as they ran.

Wednesday 12th January 1743
Found in the Bubholts, ran through East Dean park, over the Harroways, through Strickland's furze, over Halsteds down, by Lord Derby's lavender garden, up through Halnaker park and the wilderness, the Redvins, cross the fields through Eagly copse down by Shopwyke, through the meadows to Leethorn and down to Hunston farm, there about a quarter of a mile below the farm the hounds had an entapis at him in a thick hedgerow and viewed him cross three meadows and killed him, a dog fox.

The hounds went to Findon on Monday 17 January and returned to Charlton on Saturday 12 February, in which time they killed four brace of foxes. The duke did not go himself and was in London to attend the annual dinner which was held at *Lebeck's Head* in Chandos Street on Thursday 3 February with Lord Delawarr in the chair and 23 other members;[217] the Dukes of Grafton, Richmond, St Albans, Devonshire and Newcastle, the Earls of Lincoln, Berkeley, Holdernesse, Cowper and Lifford, Lords Harcourt and Conway, the Hons. Edward Legge, Henry Legge, John Boscawen, John Mordaunt and Henry Pelham, Sir Henry Liddell and Sir William Corbet, William Fauquier, Ralph Jenison, Solomon Dayrolles and John Butler. The minute was brief as usual: 'Prosperity to Charlton and several other healths were drank and then the society adjourn'd as usual'. A few days later the company were back in Charlton for more sport, but the scenting conditions were poor. Going out on four days the next week they accounted for a brace of foxes and thanks to old Beauty, one of the hounds that came from Lady Molyneux in 1738, they also killed a badger, but none of the runs was of any note. The scent continued to be poor, 'so bad a scenting day was hardly ever seen' said his grace on Monday, but it improved by Saturday when they had a twelve mile hunt mostly in the fog.

Saturday 26th February 1743
Found in Burton pond tail and ran over the Merryfields and over Duncton common and ran to the eastward of Woolavington park and up the hill by the sheepwash earth, there almost everybody was thrown out in the thickest fog that ever was seen, but Sir John Miller and David followed the hounds by the ear, for they never saw them until a quarter of an hour after they earthed, but when they were up the hill, they went by Tegleaze corner, then down the hill between Twines and Waltham, then up the hill to the eastward of Waltham hanger to the Gumworth corner, from thence over the Coneygates earth leaving Abraham walls on the right hand, down through Houghton forest, up the hill and all along Bury course, then turned down the hill beyond Priest comb and ran by Bury to the right hand of Bignor park to Fittleworth common and earthed in an enclosed ground there called Mallards Berry and dug him out in less than an hour and killed him, a dog fox.

The next day out they hunted on the downs and never went far from East Dean wood, hunting two foxes and catching the second. Determined to catch the first fox, hounds went back to East Dean wood again on Thursday for the last day of the season, but they were again foiled by fresh foxes, this time not by one but three.

The expenses for the season were about the same as 1741/2 at £901 4s. 1d.; £544 0s. 8d. for the New Forest, £349 3s. 5d. for Charlton and £8 rent for the kennels at Findon.[218]

In April 1743, many members of the hunt including Richmond as Master of the Horse accompanied the king to the continent to fight the French in the War of the Austrian Succession. They and their allies were successful at the battle of Dettingen on 27 June, the last in which a reigning sovereign led his troops into battle. They did not return until November, so the first entry in the hunting diary is in December, although the duke notes that the hounds had been out before but had killed only one fox.

There were several new hunters in the stables. In the Great Stable there were Slug, Bamfield, Sturdy Lump, Smith and Lord Mayor, all old favourites, especially Slug and Sturdy Lump who had now done seven seasons. To these were added Splints, Boss and Sheldon. The three-stall stable had Bijoux and Ashburnham, both new, along with Irish Pad, who had been around for a bit. There was also a new horse called Tom. The hack stable, horses used for going back and fore to Goodwood, had four horses new to Charlton; Grey Tatler, Biddulph, Salamanca and Roper. Old Tom's horses were unchanged except for one newcomer called Dick and on one day he rode a horse called Kingston whose name does not appear in the stable list. A few had gone, notably Pickadilly, who had carried the whipper-in David Briggs for four seasons, and Sultan whom the duke had ridden a number of times. Bumper, Commode, Red Robin and Tetlow had not been there long and were moved on. The total compliment was now 12 in the duke's stable, 10 in the huntsman's stable and five hacks. The hound list was entered in the book in December. Twenty-two couple of old hounds had been cast, a motley collection of seven couple had come from Lord Tankerville and 12½ couple of young hounds were entered, making a total of 50½ couple in the kennel.[219]

The first day was marked with a hunt of over seven miles ending at St Roche's windmill, a prominent landmark; Wednesday was overtaken by the weather and Thursday was a day marred by changing foxes, but they hunted the third fox for nearly eight miles before losing it.

Monday 5th December 1743
Found in the Valdoe, ran over Goodwood warren, through Molecomb into East Dean park and Charlton copse and back again to East Dean park, and having hung near an hour in those two covers, she went back again over St Roche's hill to the Valdoe and then out over Lavant fields to St Roche's hill windmill and there killed in view, a bitch fox.

Thursday 8th December 1743
Found in the Rewell, ran through Heberden copse into Tortington woods, there the hounds after several rings came to a fault and then were carried off to a halloa up to Slindon windmill, but not being able to make anything of it, were carried down to Slindon common where about six couple of hounds were running a third fox; there they were laid on and after several rings in Walburton copse, broke covert over Slindon common, up to Nore hill, through North wood, St Mary wood and Noman's land, through West wood bottom, over Waltham down and Waltham hanger, over Glatting hill to Glatting hanger, where as the weather was excessive cold, they lost the fox, so we took off and came home.

They must have had a good evening in the Great Room for the duke wrote to Newcastle the next day and commented at the end of the letter, 'I have a cursed pain in my right arm, occasioned I believe by too much drink'.[220] However that did not prevent him hunting the next day when they had a fast run of seven miles in 44 minutes, that is 9½ miles an hour.

Saturday 10th December 1743
Found in Punters copse, took a short ring there and then directly through Charlton forest, East Dean wood, the lower and upper Tegleaze, down the down between Randall's bottom and Twines, through the fields by Waltham, through West wood bottom, over Waltham down, into Waltham bottom and there killed her, a bitch fox. Not one check in the run and it lasted 44 minutes.

The second week in December they were out on Monday and had a run from Ashling woods to the Valdoe of about six miles in just under an hour. Hounds went out next on Wednesday when they had a slow hunt, again from the Valdoe, of about nine miles in two hours and on Friday they ran some seven miles in 2¼ hours.

The duke received a letter from Lord Harcourt to say he was coming to join the company and hinting he would need to borrow a horse.

London, Thursday 15th December 1743
I had the pleasure of waiting upon the Duchess of Richmond the night before last and of finding her grace perfectly well. She told me that she expected your grace in town on Saturday next, which tempted me to put off my journey to Charlton till about Tuesday next, when I am informed your grace proposes to return to Charlton, at which time I shall be glad of the honour of attending you. I propose to stay a fortnight at Charlton, which the Duke of St Albans will scarce believe. What I shall do there is another question, for I don't know whether I have a horse to ride, for I have had but a bad account of a horse I had from the Duke of Bolton, upon which I had great dependence. However, let that be as it will. The company of my friends, good punch and a pipe of tobacco will make Charlton go down very well …[221]

The duke did go to London, but missed a long hunt of 19 miles on Monday, although they failed to catch the fox; and on Friday old Tom took out the young hounds, who managed to put their fox to ground after a short run.

Monday 19th December 1743
Found in the Wildham, ran over Bow hill course through the black bushes over the top of Kingly bottom down to Adsdean earth, over Newmans down to Down Frame copse into Ashling woods, there he headed and came back the foil to Adsdean, then down to Hambrook common, to Racton park and from thence to Bourne common field, crossed the river over to Aldsworth common, there he was headed by Yarrall Johnson and came back some part of the foil and crossed over to Woodmancote, through Racton park and Racton grounds, up to Adsdean down, into the copse, by the end of Juniper bottom over Newmans down, into Down farm copse, crossed the way into Ashling woods and an entapis about the middle of the wood, then straight through the grounds of Great Oldwick, Little Oldwick and behind West Lavant to Mundean hedgerows, by Trumley copse, over Sir John Miller's down, Compton's down, Oldwicks down and Stoke down into Bradleys bushes, made a point to Crows hall, but turned up the steep of Crows hall hanger, over the top of Bow hill to black bushes and to the Wildham wood, up Haslett hanger to the end of the Hasletts, where they think they ran him to ground, as the

hounds ran very hard thither and then threw up at once and there were a great many coney burrows.

The duke was back by Christmas Day and Lord Harcourt was there as well. In the evening they had a meeting and elected three new members. The court jester Solomon Dayrolles was in the chair again, and significantly the minute reads that he sat in 'Roper's Chair'. The grand old man, who had now been dead for 20 years was still remembered with awe and reverence.[222] Present were the Dukes of Richmond and St Albans, Lords Lincoln, Berkeley and Harcourt, Sir William Middleton, Charles Roper, Ralph Jenison and Battine father and son. He became a frequent visitor to Charlton and later built his own stables in the village. Next was the Earl of Home, of whom we have heard before, and thirdly Colonel Robert Carpenter. They hunted on Boxing Day, but the fox proved very unadventurous.

There were three days recorded in January. After a quiet day on Saturday, Monday 16th was unusual as, after a hunt of 13 miles in two hours, the fox ran in covert for the next three before breaking and returning to the covert, where she was caught; the following Wednesday they had a four-mile point, 16 as they ran.

Monday 16th January 1744
Found in Lewknor's copse at nine o'clock, ran through them directly back to the side of Sadlers furze, thence to the side hills by Treyford and Didling hanger, cross the Beacon hill to my Lord Tankerville's warren close by the pale of Uppark, then turned back through the copse by the warren, over North Marden down to Phillis wood, Monkton park, Lewknor's copse again, the Hacking place, Marlows, to Pine pit hanger over the Hat, then cross the highway between Singleton and West Dean, up the hill towards old warren, but then turned to the left over Cocking highway, through Yewtree bottom, over Charlton down and up to Charlton copse and East Dean park, so far by eleven o'clock, then there she ran the foil for near three hours, the scent growing worse and worse and a brace of other foxes being on foot in the parks at the same time, however the hunted fox at last broke covert and went over the Harroways, through Molecomb furze, out by the great chalk pit, through Goodwood warren, back over the Harroways to Charlton copse again and East Dean park, where at about five minutes before two we killed her, a little bitch fox.

Wednesday 18th January 1744
A fox stole off from the Merryfields and was halloaed by Mr Orme's north gate of his avenue, so the hounds were laid on there and they ran it very hard up the steep part of Graffham hanger, over the Tegleaze to Randall's bottom, cross the road up to the Benges and from thence to Dawtreys hooks, over Waltham common, by the lone beech and up to Houghton pound and to Priest comb, there the fox headed and turned back and ran all the side hills to Farm wood, North hanger and Barlavington hanger, there he went down the hill and ran by Sutton to Bignor park and Waltham park and then back to Farm wood where he went to ground in the main earth, so he could not be dug.

Then the frost descended and the duke wrote:

I went to London and the hounds were out but three times as it was a hard frost, and in the three times of going out, they did not find once or had even a touch of a fox; they beat twice below the hills by Midhurst, Feilders furze, Burton and Bignor park and once at Chidham.

86 Sir William Middleton, Bt., M.P. for Northumberland. He took the chair at the annual meetings in 1744 and 1747.

While in London, the company held their annual meeting on Thursday 26 January 1744, this time back at the *Bedford Head Tavern*. There was a good attendance of 35 and Sir William Middleton, M.P. for Northumberland, was elected to take the chair. The Dukes of Grafton, Richmond, St Albans, Bolton and Newcastle head the list, followed by Lords Lincoln, Cowper, Lifford, Effingham, Home and Harcourt. A welcome attendant was Count Maurice of Nassau, an original subscriber to the Great Room in 1720, who had not been seen since the inaugural meeting of the society six years before. The Prime Minister, Henry Pelham, was there, the Hons. Thomas Villiers, Henry Legge, John Boscawen, Charles Roper and John Mordaunt, baronets William Gage, Henry Liddell, Richard Mill and William Corbet, Colonels Honywood, Carpenter, Whitworth and Beake and Messrs. Honywood, Fauquier, Pauncefort, Conolly, Jenison, Dayrolles, Butler and Perry.[223]

Some of them were back in February for the last two days of the season, when there is the one and only mention of hunting a bag fox (now quite illegal). Having lost two foxes, Sir John Miller appeared from Lavant with his hounds and the bag fox. Presumably the packs joined forces and they proceeded to hunt the poor creature for over 20 miles, eventually losing it near Stoughton. It surely deserved its brush.

Friday 3rd February 1744
Found in Lewknor's copse, where after several rings, we lost him. Then went to the Wildham where we found and ran up through the Haslett to the Pitlands and there we lost that fox also, it being an excessive bad day. Then we tried Adsdean copse and Juniper bottom, where Sir John Miller had brought a fox with his hounds, then we laid on to him and ran it over the top of Bow hill and the black bushes, then down Kingley bottom through Stoke coney copse to Stoke copse, Ashling woods, the Moutenes, Row copse and the Broyle copse, then he turned

87 John, 2nd Duke of Montagu, Richmond's neighbour in Whitehall, who objected to the stench of Lord George's pet fox.

short back again through the Row, the Rifles and so over to Bosham and all over Hambrook common, up to Racton park, by Lordington to Stoughton down, up Bow hill to the black bushes again, then down the hill to Downley farm and Ashling woods again, where after a turn he came back by Stoke coney copse and up Kingley bottom again to the top of Bow hill again, and then upon Stoughton down, we lost him, tried all round and could never hit it off again, so came home.

Old Tom had not being enjoying the best of health and had had the odd day off with the gout. During the summer he became worse and sadly 9 February 1744 was the last he had with his hounds.

In the spring the duke received a singular complaint from the Duke of Montagu, his neighbour in London.

Montagu House, Whitehall, February 1744
There is a gentleman that has been *attaché* to your family for some years and for whom I have a very great regard, as I have for all his relations, some of whom pretend to have been ill used by you, tho' he can have no reason to complain of ill usage himself, but quite the contrary; for you have really been a father to him and in great measure he owes his life to you. Tho' I have not the happiness to be personally acquainted with him, I can't help being concerned for his health which I fear must be greatly impaired by his living always in town, and I am persuaded if he was at liberty to follow his natural inclination he would lead a country life, and I am persuaded that Goodwood air would be much better for him than that of London, provided he could have a safe and easy carriage down into the country, for by his having lived the greater part of his life in London, I fear he would be very unable to travel any other way than in a wheel carriage; and as

83 Lord George Lennox was Richmond's younger son and father of the fourth duke.

I really wish him well with all my heart—nay, I may say, I love him—I should be very sorry to have him put to any inconvenience, or that anything should happen to him that might make him the least unhappy or uneasy. I must own that altho' I say so much about him and that we have been neighbours for some years, I have no personal acquaintance with him; I have indeed had the pleasure of seeing him several times in company with Lord March and Lord George and have been pleased with his pretty behaviour in their company, and to be sure he is a very agreeable pretty gentleman, and one whom I should be very glad to do any good office to, and therefore it is (without his having said one word to me about it I do assure you) that I wish you would let him go into the country; I have not seen him lately, but since I have lived a good deal in my new room, as that is very near his lodgings, I have smelt him extremely, and I am sorry to say an unmannerly thing of so honest and agreeable a person, and one I love so well, but the truth is he stinks like a fox and is enough to poison the devil, and as I know his inclination is a rural life, if you would let him go into the country I am sure it would oblige your faithful servant and slave Mr Renny as much as it would

    Yours sincerely   Montagu[224]

The pet vixen, for so it was, belonged to Lord George Lennox, Richmond's younger son, then aged seven. Whether the offending creature was at once removed is not known, but that she eventually took her departure there can be no doubt and at considerable risk to her personal safety, as we shall see in the next chapter.

— XIII —

Death of Old Tom

House parties provided entertainment during the summer when there was no hunting. The Richmonds went to Bishopstone in East Sussex, one of the Duke of Newcastle's country seats. Newcastle wrote to thank for the return invitation.

Claremont, Saturday 25th August 1744
I intended to thank you by this post for your kind and agreeable visit at Bishopstone. I am now glad to add my acknowledgements for your invitation to Goodwood, which I shall with the greatest pleasure obey. I have not seen or heard from old Puff (the Duke of Grafton) this month, so know nothing of him, and I want no inducement or other company. It will no doubt be too soon to come next week as I have lately been absent for some days, but I hope in the course of next week to let you know when I can attend you and I shall wish and desire to find you alone, unattended by my very good friends in your neighbourhood. You may imagine I don't mean literally, for I must beg you would let me wait on you to make a visit to my good friend Sir Ian (Sir John Miller of Lavant) …[225]

Richmond also asked Henry Pelham, who declined; and the Duke of Grafton, who accepted. Richmond wrote to Newcastle:

Goodwood, Sunday 2nd September 1744
I shall be overjoyed to see you whenever 'tis convenient to you to come and if you can come on Friday I hope you will, for the sooner we see you the better, and for that reason I wish you could have come with the Duke of Grafton tomorrow. However if anything should happen to hinder your journey on Friday, I hope it will at least be the week after. I am glad to hear dear Linky [Earl of Lincoln] will come with you, and I can tell you, you both flatter your Queen [the Duchess of Richmond], as you call her, extremely for she looks upon this intended visit as to her …[226]

and received a reply.

Newcastle House, Tuesday 4th September 1744
My Lord Lincoln, Jemmy [Hon. James Brudenell, Richmond's uncle, now aged 64] and I intend ourselves the honour of waiting upon your grace and the Duchess of Richmond on Friday next. As Jemmy is a sort of invalid, he cannot travel without help and therefore he begs you would send a chaise for him to Liphook on Friday morning and we will take care to convey him thither. Linky and I, hail strong fellows [Newcastle was then 51], ride from Godalming [25 miles] and propose to be with you by dinner. We conclude you will not dine before three …[227]

Newcastle evidently enjoyed his visit.

Newcastle House, Thursday 13th September 1744

I must begin by returning your grace and the Duchess of Richmond my most sincere thanks for your kind and agreeable reception and entertainment at Goodwood. It is always a pleasure to me to wait upon you, but never so much when I can do it as I have done it this last time … My compliments to all at Goodwood and Lavant …[228]

The Duke of Grafton had been a keen supporter of Charlton in his younger days, but was much taken up with his own hounds which hunted not only on his estate in Suffolk, but also south of the Thames. He attended the annual dinner in London regularly and was much attracted by the new member Solomon Dayrolles, who must have been highly amusing and well suited to his post as Master of the Revels at Court. Visiting the duke at Euston for some hunting, Dayrolles wrote to Richmond to report on the sport, not forgetting the mishaps which overtook him.

Euston, Saturday 6th October 1744

According to your grace's directions I would have taken the liberty to trouble you before this time with a letter, had anything occurred worth intruding upon a few moments of your leisure. There was ne'er a good fox chase that I could give you an account of and it would have neither moved your pity nor given you any entertainment had I informed your grace of the exquisite and unaccountable pains I suffered in one of my feet when I lay at Chesterford on my way to Euston, and told you the discourse I had with a physician that happened then to be in the house, who declared to me (tho' he did not say it to frighten me), that it was the forerunner of some dreadful distemper and that the shortest and safest method to cure my complaint would be to apply directly a caustic to my foot. This terrible sentence did not however prevent my coming here and it has had no other bad consequence than the loss of a very good chase this day sennight. Since that I have been out three times.

The first day we found two foxes but lost them both in a very little while. The second day we killed one in his kennel, ran another about five miles and then lost him. This morning we had a chase of about an hour and very hard running but the fox was headed and lost. Here I must again make mention of myself and perhaps move your grace's compassion, tho' the Duke of Grafton had no more bowels than a flint: *tout au contraire*, express choler; but this was more owing to his disappointment than to my misbehaviour. As I was galloping over one of his heaths, my horse struck into a coney burrow, fell down flat upon his side and flung me some yards before him with my side against an old mole hill. It was such a bang that I was speechless for some time; however I mounted my steed again and when his grace came up with me, I was comforted in the same manner as Job was by his friends.

After this we tried for another fox, but my pains increasing I went home to be doctored a little; but finding myself better after some inward and outward applications, I returned to the company when in my way I spied Renny, who had stolen away from behind the hounds. I then gave them a view halloa, brought them back, ran him for an hour and a quarter over the finest part of this country and killed with the whole pack at his brush. This has made his grace unknit his brow and curse the rabbits and their burrows. Tomorrow he sets out for London and is to be here again next Monday. For my part I remain here. We have had Mr [Baron] Hardenberg[229] here this week on his way to my Lord Orford[230] and my Lord Lovel[231] *qu'il est bien aise de connoitre* …

89 Thomas Coke of Norfolk was a subscriber to the Great Room in 1720. He donated hounds to the Duke of Bolton in 1723, was created Lord Lovel in 1728 and was later 1st Earl of Leicester.

My Lord the Duke of Grafton, My Lord Bishop of Llandaff and Baron Hardenberg desire their compliments to your grace and the Duchess of Richmond.[232]

The first recorded event in the new season at Charlton was a meeting on Monday 5 November when they admitted two visitors, Captains Carpenter and Norris.[233] Eight horses had gone from the stables, notably Badger, who had been Old Tom's horse for six seasons. Irish Pad after five seasons went from the duke's stable and Trueblue, Smith, Boss, Kingston, Sheldon and Tom, who had not been there long, had also gone. They were replaced by Black Jack, Bruin, Foxhunter, Little John and Pig, and four new hacks.

An innovation by the duke in his diary was a note of who was in the field each day. The Duke of St Albans was out every day except one, Mr. Jenison was there until Christmas and returned in February, Mr. Pauncefort came in December and stayed till the end of the season, Lord Harcourt and our friend Dayrolles had a few days, as did Sir John Miller. Mr. Thomas Hill, the duke's tutor, who had been with him since he was 11, was out occasionally and some others who appeared later were elected members. The Biddulph brothers and Mr. Yarrall Johnson from Chichester were frequent visitors and other locals included Mr. Mellish, Mr. Cobden who lived at Drought farm, the Rev. Mr. Pinnell and Mr. Henry Wells. The fields were quite small, not more than 12 plus the huntsman, two whippers-in and two grooms in attendance on his grace.

It was a season badly affected by the weather and they lost many days, notably six weeks in January and February because of frost. Only one day's sport was recorded in November when they had a local hunt in the woods above West Dean. In the absence of Old Tom, David Briggs carried the horn with Jack Row and Moses Wing whipping-in.

After that in November, the hounds were out five times, but the weather was so bad that they had no sport but one day, and then, by Mr. Jenison's account, they had a pretty run and ran a fox to ground and killed him, a dog fox. The next proper hunt was from East Dean wood in early December when they had a 6½-mile point, 12 as they ran.

Friday 7th December 1744
Found in East Dean wood and after a quarter of an hour's run there, over the lower and upper Tegleaze, Sheepwash earth, Duncton chalk pit, Barlavington hanger, North comb, Farm wood, Glatting hanger, Glatting beacon, corner of the Gumber, Madehurst common, Madehurst fields, Houghton forest, cross Fair mile and there upon the Rewell hanger viewed him back to Houghton forest and killed him, a dog fox.

The duke was not happy with David Briggs as huntsman, so the next day out he asked Jack Woods, who had not appeared at Charlton before, to hunt the hounds until a replacement for Old Tom could be found. His first day proved to be a memorable one, and the duke's own account was later embellished with some asides (in parentheses).

Monday 10th December 1744
Found in the Valdoe, ran over the Valdoe corner, Goodwood warren, the upper corner of Molecomb to East Dean park, several rings there (during which Mr Dayrolles drank tea at the ?), then a halloa away between the two parks, cross the East Dean lane and up the forty acres, over the side of North down, cross to Levin down, over the top of it, then turned short to Broadham, Singleton forest and over Cocking highway, through the Marlows, Hacking place, Cocking coney copse, then by Lewknor's copse lower gate and over the bottom of Colworth down, cross the grounds to the warren, all through West dean warren, headed into Crows hall grounds, cross Binderton lane, through Preston farm yard, up over West Dean down, through Old Warren (there Lord Mayor of London, his brother mayor being on foot, got a fall), down through the grounds close by Singleton, up by the Hat and Pine pit hanger, through Ware hill hanger (where the Master of the Revels [Solomon Dayrolles himself] got a fall), up the long slip and Coney copse, in Cocking warren, cross the warren then up the bottom of it to Sadlers furze, over the hill by Linch hanger, then along the side hills to the bottom of Cocking warren again (where the fox was viewed), cross it, up to Cocking coney copse again, the Marlows, cross Cocking highway (from whence Lord Mayor went home fully satisfied with 18 stone and the day's diversion), up through Singleton and Charlton forest to East Dean wood great gate, then along the side hills above Woolavington, Duncton chalk pit, Barlavington hanger and North comb, above which in a hedgerow they killed him, a dog fox.

N:B: the chase lasted 5 hours and 11 minutes, of which above 2 hours of it was cold hunting, almost every horse knocked up, however David (getting a fresher horse), Lord Harcourt, Sir John Miller, Messrs Pauncefort, Dayrolles, Fletcher and Hill were in at the death.

In distance the run was second only to the Grand Chase of 1739, being a 6½-mile point, over 25 as they ran, at an average speed of five miles an hour. The next day the duke wrote to Newcastle, with a copy to Grafton:

Death of Old Tom

Charlton, Tuesday 11th December 1744

... We have had better sport than we any of us ever remember. Old Puff has an account sent him of a most prodigious chase ...[234]

The hound list was written in the book on Saturday 15 December when 16 couple of old hounds had been cast and 11 couple of young hounds entered, making a total of 48½ couple in the kennel.[235] The next day out they ran a fox to ground but left him and two days later ran only a short distance before killing.

That same day a sad entry appeared in the hound book.[236]

> **Mem^m.**
> **On Thursday: 20: Dec^r.**
> **1744**
> **Thomas Johnson**
> **dyed at Charlton**
> **& was buryed in the**
> **Church at Singleton**

Everyone at Charlton had thought the world of Old Tom. He was sorely missed. His 10 seasons had been immensely successful. The duke in particular held him in very high regard, so much so that he decided to erect a monumental inscription above his grave in Singleton Church.

Near this place lies interred Thomas Johnson who departed this life at Charlton December 20th 1744. From his early inclination to Fox Hounds he soon became an experienced Huntsman. His knowledge in this Profession, wherein he had no superiour and hardly any equal, join'd to his honesty in every particular recommended him to the service, and gain'd him the approbation of several of the nobility and gentry. Among these were the Lord Conway, Earl of Cardigan, the Lord Gower, the Duke of Marlborough and the Honourable Mr Spencer. The last master whom he serv'd and in whose service he died was Charles, Duke of Richmond Lenox and Aubigny, who erected this monument to the memory of a good and faithfull servant, as a reward to the deceased and an incitement to the Living. Go and do thou likewise. St Luke, Chap x, Ver xxxvii.

> *Here Johnson lies what hunter can deny*
> *Old honest Tom the tribute of a sigh*
> *Deaf is that ear which cought the op'ning sound*
> *Dumb is that tongue which chear'd the hills around*
> *Unpleasing truth death hunts us from our birth*
> *In view and men like foxes take to earth*

After the funeral Old Tom's ghost was out in the countryside. No foxes were to be found for several days, but things picked up and indeed after Christmas the first day was marred by too many foxes.

Wednesday 26th December 1744
Crossed upon a drag upon North down and ran it into East Dean wood and there round and after several rings there and in Charlton forest, he went down the hill by Graffham and cross

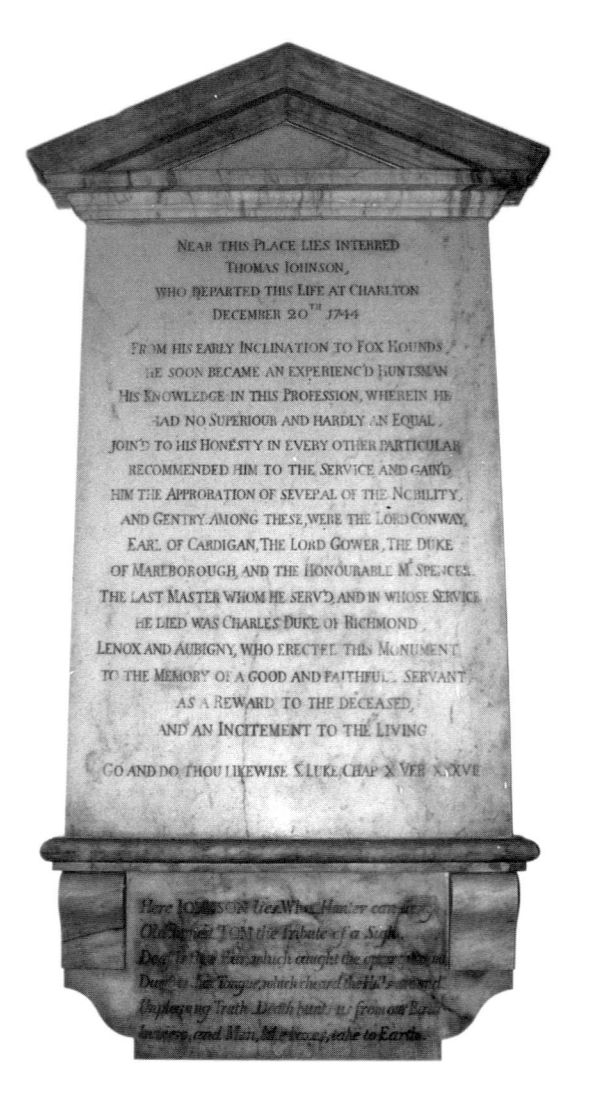

90 Monument erected in Singleton church by the 2nd Duke of Richmond in memory of Tom Johnson, huntsman at Charlton from 1734 to 1744.

Graffham common, there in some furze fields came to a check, but was halloaed off by those that stood upon the hill; for 2½ couple of hounds had carried another fox through the forest and Broadham fields, Foxley copse and Herringdean, then along the side hill and into East Dean wood, when the other hounds being halloaed up the hill were laid on, and they ran him several rings there, then they divided into several parts and four or five foxes were on foot in East Dean wood and Charlton forest at the same [time], it being also an excessive bad scenting day and the hounds come to a dead check, we took them off and came home.

On Friday there was nearly a catastrophe. The hounds almost caught Lord George's pet vixen Fanny. Having been allowed to leave her comfortable quarters in London, she escaped from Goodwood. Fortunately, as the pack were pressing her hard, another fox got up in Bubholts and gave them a great run right down to the coast of well over twenty miles, although they changed foxes again on the way.

Friday 28th December 1744
Whilst the hounds were beating of Red copse, a fox was halloaed out of a hedgerow by East Dean lane and as we were going to lay the hounds upon it, they crossed upon a drag and found in East Dean park and ran down the fields between East Dean and Charlton, then turned to East Dean street where the fox was halloaed, and by their seeing a collar and link of a chain about his neck, it proved to be Lord George's fox, but the hounds ran him so hard, they could not be taken off and ran him into the Bubholts where we certainly changed to a fresh fox who went across North hanger, Selhurst park, all along the west side of Long down, through Eartham bushes and the fields to Boxgrove common, cross Teen wood, by Crocker hill, cross the high road and meadows by my Lady Derby's decoy where we think we changed again, then to Aldingbourne, and from thence through Eastgate to Yapton and from thence down to Bilsom and down to Elmer copses by the seaside and then turned up to Bourne wood where, he being a great way before them, we lost him.

The next week the only hunt was on Tuesday when they killed after a run of about eight miles.

Tuesday 1st January 1745
Found in East Dean wood and ran directly over Cocking course, up by Duncton chalk pit to North comb, Farm wood, then turned short over Farm hill by Hasle comb and back by Duncton chalk pit and down by Barlavington hanger through Burton park and pond tail and to Red hill, there he ran to ground in a coney burrow and was dug and killed, an old dog fox. N:B: the 8th dog fox killed and no bitch this season.

More frost descended and it was not until the following Saturday they were able to go out again when they had a very fast hunt of over 15 miles at an average speed of over 10 miles an hour. Nobody can claim hunting was slow in those days.

Saturday 12th January 1745
Found in the Rewell and took a round by the Deans, the Rooks and through Binsted parish, back through Heberden copse and the Rewell, then down the Rewell hill, cross Fair mile bottom, Houghton forest and over the downs to Glatting beacon, through Glatting hanger, Farm wood, North comb and down by Barlavington to a little copse below the village called Barlavington coppice where she went into a coney burrow and was dug in five minutes and killed, a bitch fox. The chase lasted one hour and 25 minutes.

That day the Duchess of Richmond and Lord George accompanied by John Cheale were paying a visit to Claremont, where they were joined by the Earl and Countess of Albemarle (she was Richmond's sister). Newcastle wrote:

Claremont, Saturday 12th January 1745
I will begin with what I am sure you will be the most pleased. Lord Albemarle arrived last night and was with me this morning in high spirits and health. We were just as when I last saw him and I own I had so much pleasure in seeing one I so sincerely love that I forgot everything that had passed, which at the time gave me uneasiness. I dined yesterday with the Duchess of Richmond and Cheale. You may imagine your health was not forgot. I drank it once to the Duchess of

91 William Cavendish, Marquess of Hartington, was elected at Charlton in 1745. As 4th Duke of Devonshire he was, for a period of eight months in 1756, First Lord of the Treasury and Prime Minister.

Richmond in a common glass and afterwards to Cheale in a bumper. The same company dine with me on Wednesday with the addition of the Albemarles. I can't say I wish you here for as I know you like hunting and I really think it so right for your health, I never would call you from it when there is not a real occasion; and as the Duchess of Richmond assures me she has no call for you, our insipid political situation don't require your presence till something more particular or material happens than at present seems likely for some time …[237]

Such news was always a relief to the duke who resented being dragged away from his hunting. So they were out again on Monday, but were frustrated by people heading the fox; first some soldiers (surely they were not training on the downs!), then some ploughmen. After that more frost kept them in for some time.

At the end of the week, the company was still at Charlton hoping for a turn in the weather, so on Friday 18 January, there being a quorum of nine in the Great Room, they held an election and admitted six new members. Present were the Dukes of Richmond and St Albans; the Earl of Home, his ugly Jamaican wife long forgotten; Sir John Miller; Battine father and son and Messrs. Pauncefort, Carpenter and Jenison, who was in the chair.[238] The first to be balloted was Captain Benjamin Carpenter, a visitor earlier in the season. Next was William Cavendish, Marquess of Hartington and heir to the Duke of Devonshire. He was then 25 and M.P. for Derby. He married shortly afterwards the 17-year-old Elizabeth, Lady Clifford, daughter and heir of the Earl of Burlington, who brought him Bolton Abbey and immense estates in

92 Brice Fisher Esq, elected at Charlton in 1745, was a director of the ill-fated South Sea company and M.P. for Malmesbury.

Yorkshire and Derbyshire, Chiswick and Burlington House and extensive property in Ireland. At the time of the wedding, Lady Mary Montagu enthusiastically wrote, 'I do not know any man so fitted to make a wife happy. With so great a vocation for matrimony, I verily believe if it had not been established before his time, he would have had the glory of the invention!'[239] Some invocation, but sadly, very sadly, the marriage was short lived as she died six years later at the tender age of twenty-three. He went on to pursue a distinguished political career, being briefly, for seven months, prime minister, due to William Pitt's refusal to serve under the Duke of Newcastle.

Third in the ballot was John Campbell, Earl of Loudoun, a representative Scottish peer in the House of Lords. We shall hear more about him, as he featured prominently during the Jacobite rebellion later that year. Also elected were Edward Phipps, Viscount Bury, son and heir to the Earl of Albemarle and Richmond's nephew and Admiral Isaac Townsend, a rear admiral of the Red, about whom a bard at Charlton wrote the following ode:

> *Th'adventurous admiral next my muse would sing*
> *Whose thund'ring arms made Cartagena ring.*
> *See him at Charlton ride 'thout fear or care*
> *Following the fox upon his flying mare.*
> *Nought can the fury of his course restrain*
> *Nor fox by land, nor Frenchman on the main!*
> *No clime or country will he ere forgo*
> *After a fox, or after Europe's foe.*[240]

Lastly, at the suggestion of Lord Harcourt, they invited Brice Fisher as a visitor.

93 Admiral Isaac Townshend, a rear admiral of the red, was elected at Charlton in 1745.

From 14 January till 23 February there was so much frost that the hounds hunted but twice and killed a bitch fox by the Rifles. With no hunting for so long, a record number of 39 turned up for the annual dinner at the *Bedford Head Tavern* on Monday 28 January 1745. The Duke of Richmond took the chair and with him were the Dukes of Grafton, St Albans, Devonshire and Newcastle; Lords Lincoln, Albemarle, Rothes, Home, Lifford, Effingham, George Beauclerk, Harcourt, Conway, Herbert of Cherbury, Hartington, Loudoun and Bury; they welcomed back M. Chevalier Ossorio, who was an original member, but had not been seen for some time; the Hons. Henry Pelham, Charles Feilding, John Mordaunt, Henry Legge and John FitzWilliam were there; Sir Henry Liddell, Sir William Corbet, Sir Phillip Honywood and Sir John Cope; Admiral Townsend, Colonels Honywood, Elliot and Carpenter; and Messrs. Conolly, Fauquier, Pauncefort, Jenison, Cheale, Perry and Carpenter. The brief minute reads 'A motion was made that Mr Edward Sedgwick [the duke's agent at Goodwood] should be appointed Secretary to the Club and the question being put it passed in the affirmative. Prosperity to Charlton and several other healths were drank and then the society adjourned as usual.'[241]

Back in Charlton another two weeks passed before the duke wrote in frustration:

Charlton, Sunday 10th February 1745
… This cursed frost has hindered us hunting; however I shall persevere one week more and no longer … Don't answer this for I am gone, as Roper used to say …

94 Francis Scott, Earl of Dalkeith, was heir to the Duke of Buccleuch and a descendant of the Duke of Monmouth. He was elected at Charlton in 1745 and tragically died of smallpox in 1750.

In the event he did persevere but had to wait nearly a fortnight, by which time he had decided to appoint John Smith as the new huntsman. David Briggs stayed until the end of the season but then was heard of no more. He had been at Charlton as whipper-in for at least eight seasons, certainly from before 1738 when his name first appeared in the duke's diary. One hopes he went on to better things. The bad weather gave the new huntsman a few days to get used to the kennels and the hounds before taking them out for the first time. After putting a fox to ground, they hacked for no less than eight miles to the next draw, from Woolavington hanger to the Broyle copse near Chichester.[242]

Saturday 23rd February 1745
Found in Charlton forest, ran through that, Punters copse, East Dean wood, through the lower Tegleaze and down to Woolavington hanger where she went to ground and was dug out and saved, a bitch fox. Then it being a cold frost upon the hills, we went down to the Broyle, Row copse and Oldwick and did not find.

After that it snowed which kept them firmly indoors, but having still a quorum, six more members were elected on Sunday 24 February. The company was the same except that Lord Home had gone and Lords Lincoln and Harcourt had arrived.[243]

'The Duke of Richmond proposed that the Earl of Dalkeith should have leave to dine at Foxhall, which upon ballot was granted.' Lord Dalkeith was a great grandson of the Duke of

95 John Lindsay, 20th Earl of Crawford, was elected at Charlton in 1745. He was the veteran of many continental campaigns and died of his wounds in 1749.

Monmouth, his father Francis, Duke of Buccleuch being Monmouth's grandson and heir. After dinner at that meeting he was of course elected and thereafter became a regular member of the field at Charlton.

Lord Chedworth was the next. He hailed from the Cotswolds and owned a pack of hounds which he later sold to the young Duke of Richmond in 1757. Baron Hardenberg we have met before at Euston in the company of Dayrolles and the Duke of Grafton. Brice Fisher, later M.P. for Malmesbury, had been a director of the South Sea company. Considering how many Charlton members must have lost money in the venture (rather like Lloyds today), it seems surprising he would have been acceptable at Charlton.

The fifth candidate was Lord Crawford. John Lindsay, the 20th in line, was generally known as the gallant Earl of Crawford and had served with the allied forces on the continent, joining the Imperial army in 1735 and fighting in the battle of Clausen in October of that year. He went on to serve with the Russian army against the Turks in April 1738 and, in the battle of Krotzha near Belgrade in July 1739, his horse was killed under him and he himself was desperately wounded. Returning home he saw action at Dettingen in 1743 and Fontenoy in 1745 rising to the rank of general, and later took part in the suppression of the Jacobite rebellion of

1746. He married secretly in 1747 a daughter of the Duke of Atholl, who was greatly annoyed, as Crawford was much older and deeply in debt. However she died of a fever six months later and he, poor fellow, succumbed himself in 1749 in great suffering, his wound of 10 years earlier breaking down for no less than the 29th time. What a debt civilised nations owe to the gallant defenders of their liberty! One more candidate came up for ballot that night. Edward Sedgwick, the secretary who was duly appointed a member of the club.

They were still there a week later, patiently waiting for the thaw. The duke wrote to Newcastle:

Charlton, Sunday 3rd March 1745

… You made Harcourt mighty happy with your kind letter; he, the Duke of St Albans and Linky, who plays at whist from morning till night, are all your humble servants. We have not been able to go out once in the last week and the snow now is deeper than any I have ever seen in England since the year 1709, I think it was [the duke was then eight!]. We shall however weather it out this week, but propose to be in town to dine with my Lord Lincoln at all events on Sunday next …[244]

The locals, Sir John Miller and Battine father and son, had gone but with the addition of the new members Lord Chedworth, Baron Hardenberg and Brice Fisher they could muster a quorum to elect Sir John Peachey of West Dean, another local squire, who was M.P. for Midhurst.[245] By Tuesday it had thawed sufficiently to take the hounds out, but the sport was poor and on Wednesday the duke decided to finish the season.

In the spring of 1745 the duke was compelled to spend some weeks in London, his presence being required both at St James's and in the House of Lords on matters of international importance. The duchess and her children remained at Goodwood and Lady Emily, aged 14, was wont to write letters for her mother now and then. John Cheale was at Goodwood, a great favourite of the children, to whom he was a never failing source of amusement.

Goodwood, March 1745

… As I have always some ridiculous story of Cheale, if dear papa is not tired of them, I will tell him another, which is that this evening in mama's room, as he sat in a very high chair and was pretty warm in discourse, according to usual, we saw him all at once break down the chair and fall with his heels over his head, which set us all a-laughing most prodigiously; but he said the leg of the chair was so weak and he so heavy that that caused his fall.

I dined with my lady and Cheale today. We waited dinner for Lord Lincoln till past five. Cheale was extremely impatient and I believe never wished so much to see him in his life, but to make it up, besides the quantity he drank at dinner, he dispatched two bottles afterwards while we were drinking coffee … I forgot to tell dear papa that to stay his stomach, Cheale ate a whole roll and drank two bumpers of white wine before dinner.[246]

Away from London by April, the duke managed to fit in his usual spring hunting as was hinted in a letter he received in May from a friend in Scotland.

Fortwilliam, Tuesday 14th May 1745

I am glad to find your grace has not left off fox hunting, which I suppose is your diversion in the New Forest. Nobody is more strongly prejudiced for bodily exercise than myself, who has always used it and I fancy it has preserved my agility and vigour beyond many I see younger and of better constitution than myself …[247]

The letter was from Colonel Edmund Martin of Wolfe's Regiment, a native of Sussex and an old friend of the duke, who was stationed in the highlands of Scotland, where the army maintained a garrison. Little did they know of the plans for the Jacobite rebellion which struck when Bonny Prince Charlie, encouraged by a significant defeat of the allies at Fontenoy on the continent, landed at Moidart on 25 July 1745. From the largely disastrous involvement of our forces in the continental war, the military effort had suddenly to be switched to events at home.

This is not the place to reiterate the history of the '45, but to mention that many of the gentlemen of Charlton were actively involved in the fighting. Richmond himself went to Lichfield where he was in command of the cavalry under the Duke of Cumberland, waiting for the arrival of the rebels. In the event, they gave them the slip and advanced to Derby, but thereafter retreated north and captured Carlisle. Cumberland's army followed them, the duke with them, where they laid siege to the city in December, the rebels finally seeking a truce at the end of the month. This was the last part which Richmond played in the war and he was welcomed home at Goodwood early in January.

The first recorded event of the hunting season was the entry in the hound book on Monday 30 December 1745. Fifteen couple of old hounds had been cast and 11½ couple of young hounds bred in Charlton were entered. In addition Lord Tankerville gave 9½ couple, the Duke of Bolton two couple, Mr. Newby one couple and Sir John Miller and Mr. Pelham of Lincolnshire one hound each, making a total of 58½ couple in the kennel.[248]

There were three new horses, Harlequin, Richmond and Star, but of Sturdy Lump, Drewet, Keeper, Ashburnham, Dick, Bruin and Pig we hear no more. Sturdy Lump had done his bit; nine seasons and 69 days out including the Grand Chase. Roger, Slug, Bamfield, Lord Mayor, Spot, Harcourt, Whitestockings, Castle, Splints, Black Jack, Foxhunter and Little John were still there, a total of 15 horses in.

The annual dinner was held at the *Bedford Head Tavern* on Thursday 23 January 1746 with his grace of Richmond in the chair. The numbers were down to 29 owing to the absence of the military in Scotland, but as usual the Dukes of Grafton, St Albans and Devonshire were there; Lords Hartington, Lincoln, Berkeley, Albemarle, Rothes, Lifford, George Beauclerk, Harcourt, Bury and Conway; Hons. Henry Pelham (this year without his brother Newcastle), Henry Legge, John Boscawen and John Fitzwilliam; Sir William Corbet and Sir John Peachey; and Messrs. Ellison, Perry, Conolly, Fauquier, Meggott, Butler, St Paul, Carpenter and Sedgwick. 'Prosperity to Charlton and several other healths were drank and then the society adjourned as usual.'[249] Straight afterwards Richmond and his friends repaired to Sussex, but on the first day out they met with too many foxes.

Monday 27th January 1746
Found in East Dean wood at least three brace of foxes, so could have no sport for the hounds divided, one was run to ground, one killed down by the forest house, a dog fox and another killed down by Graffham as said, but never brought home, and another took a ring round the Tegleaze and all along the side hills from the upper Tegleaze to Charlton forest and so back to East Dean wood where we conjectured him also gone to ground, so gave the fox that was killed by a handful of hounds at the forest house to be worried by the pack. The first that was run to

ground was also dug out of a rabbit burrow, a dog fox, but as the hounds had blood enough, we saved him.

The campaign against the insurgents was still in progress up north. After what proved to be their last successful skirmish, which was at Falkirk against the royal forces under General Hawley, the Jacobites retreated north and crossed the Forth on 1 February 1746. They were pursued by the Duke of Cumberland, now given supreme command, who set off after them three days later on 4 February. Meanwhile in Sussex the frost had caused a temporary cessation of hunting, much to the duke's irritation:

Goodwood, Wednesday 5th February 1746
… If this damn'd weather lasts I shall be in town on Saturday night …[250]

but hearing good news from Scotland, he vented his spleen to Newcastle on the Jacobites in Scotland:

Goodwood, Thursday 6th February 1746
I am excessively obliged to you … for the very good news you sent me, tho' to have heard that these villains were totally destroyed would have been still better. However 'tis all I expected, tho' you used to scold me for despising them, but I always did and always shall despise them as the scum of Scotland, which is certainly the sink of the earth; and I always said that it was but only looking these rascals in the face and I was sure they would never stand their ground. This the late Lord Cadogan [his father-in-law] always said and I have since been an eye witness of it, but indeed if our people run away at the sight of them, they must be beat even by the Westminster scholars [his son, later the 3rd duke, entered Westminster school that year!]; and what did that panic come from but their hearing that these were desperate fellows with broad swords, targets, lochaberaxes and the devil knows what, that was eternally preached up by the Scottish Jacobites, even at Whites and St James's, stuff actually fit to frighten nothing but old women and children.[251]

By Saturday it was thawing, so he put off his visit to London to hunt on Monday, but came home early feeling unwell. The weather continued unfavourable and another week went by before they could go out again, and then to no avail. The next day out their quarry escaped, the hounds running into a pack which had hunted a deer from Parham.

Thursday 20th February 1746
Found in Red copse and after a ring by the Winkins and parks and it being a bad day on the hills, they lost him and we tried Molecomb furze and found directly and took a ring by the Redvins, Valdoe, side of St Roche's hill, East dean park, over Selhurst park, Benges, St Mary wood, Noman's land and into Littleton bottom, there we ran into Capt Turner's hounds that had just killed an outlying doe of Sir Cecil Bishopp's, so our day's sport was at an end.

Mr. Jenison brought a visitor for eight days, a Mr. Taaf who enjoyed a day's hunting on 26 February.[252] It was not a good season. Foxes were either unadventurous or too numerous, but in the last week of the season there was a nice day's sport on Tuesday and a short run on Wednesday.

Tuesday 4th March 1746
Found in the Valdoe and ran by Goldings copse and cross Goodwood park by Waterbeach gate and through Seeley copse, up the Winkins where the fox was halloaed, down North hanger, cross the road above East Dean, through Dell comb to East Dean wood, Charlton forest, Punters copse and Herringdean, there the hounds being as we thought at a fault and a very bad scenting day, we came home and ordered them home; but Jack Row and my Lord Dalkeith with him was gone off with eight couple of hounds to the Marlows, Cocking coney copse, Sadlers furze, down Cocking warren then up again through Monkton park and Chilgrove to the bottom of Bow hill, there the hounds which were but eight couple, came to a fault and Jack Row took them off and came home.

Wednesday 5th March 1746
Drew Droke hanger, Dawtreys hooks, Littleton bottom, Glatting hanger, Farm wood, North hanger, Burton pond tail, Merryfields and Feilder's furze without finding, then found in East Dean wood and took several rings in Charlton forest, Punters copse, Herringdean and back to East Dean wood, where everybody were thrown out but the Duke of St Albans, Lord Dalkeith and Sir John Miller, then they ran through the lower and upper Tegleaze and ran to ground in Woolavington hanger where they dug three foxes and killed an old dog and a young bitch, but they saved an old bitch with cub and turned her out again.

Meanwhile the Duke of Grafton had scored a very long hunt with his hounds, as Newcastle reported to Richmond. Unfortunately no details survive, neither do we know where it was.

Newcastle House, Thursday 6th March 1746
… My kindest compliments to the Duke of St Albans and Linky. Old Puff killed a fox yesterday after the finest chase of six hours and a half. Can we say as much in Sussex? …[253]

Two more days were left and the season ended on Saturday 8 March with the company being caught in a storm. The Duke of St Albans with Lords Hartington, Dalkeith and Lincoln had joined the duke at Charlton for the last fortnight of the season. Sir John Miller and Mr. Jenison were also there and other names mentioned include Captain Bull, Mr. Yarrall Johnson, Mr. Thomas Hill, the duke's tutor, Mr. Brice Fisher, elected last season, Parson Peckham, Mr. Whitburn and Alderman Norton. The duke was very taken with Lord Dalkeith and told Newcastle so.

Charlton, Sunday 9th March 1746
Linky is gone off this morning in high health, spirits and vigour, so woe be to your neice tonight … I must tell you how we are all in love with my Lord Dalkeith. Linky will give you a full account of him. He is as honest as any of us and vastly derirous to be in parliament. Now surely it would be a credit to a ministry to bring him in … He as eldest son you know can't be chosen in Scotland, so his brother will be chosen for the county of Tweedale. He says he is ready to spend a thousand and would be glad to be chosen by the interest of <u>this</u> administration, so indeed I think it worthwhile to talk to Mr Pelham about it; for the having and encouraging a man of his quality, property and good character is an honour to a party, and tis upon that footing merely I mention it. He is gone up with Linky and without reflecting upon anybody, I fancy my Lady Dalkeith will be almost as well pleased as other ladies may be tomorrow morning …[254]

96 John Campbell, 4th Earl of Loudoun was elected by ballot in 1745. Despite rising to the rank of general, his military career was rather undistinguished.

97 General William Keppel, 2nd Earl of Albemarle, was Richmond's brother-in-law and in command of the cavalry at Culloden. His father had been page boy to William III on his arrival in England in 1688 and was later appointed Master of the Buckhounds.

Not many years afterwards tragedy struck poor Lord Dalkeith when he contracted smallpox and died at the young age of thirty.

In March 1746 the Jacobite insurgents retreated towards Inverness whence they were pursued by Cumberland and his troops. The Earl of Loudoun had raised a regiment of highlanders *ex parte regis* and was harrying the rebels near Dornoch firth, when they were attacked during the night of 19/20 March in a thick fog and routed. The earl escaped and was obliged to flee to the mountains with a few servants only in attendance. The decisive battle was fought at Culloden moor on Wednesday 16 April 1746. Many Charlton members had taken part in the campaign. Lord Albemarle was in command of the front line at Culloden, General Huske the second line and General Hawley commanded the cavalry. The Duke of Kingston commanded his own regiment of Light Horse, Lord Crawford was in command of a brigade, Lord Herbert of Chirbury had raised a regiment of Fusiliers in Shropshire. Also serving were the Earls of Rothes and Home, the Hons. Charles Feilding, John FitzWilliam, Charles Howard, John Mordaunt and John Boscawen; Colonels Philip Honywood and Charles Perry, Major Ruddeyard and Captain Richard Meggott. News of the victory was conveyed to London by Lord Bury, Albemarle's son and heir, who was a Lord of the Bedchamber to the Duke of Cumberland. Richmond was hunting in the New Forest when he heard the news from Newcastle's secretary.

98 John Leslie, 10th Earl of Rothes.

Whitehall, Thursday 24th April 1746

Lord Bury arrived this morning with a full confirmation of good news that I had the honour to send your grace last night. He was dispatched by his royal highness immediately after the action, but as he came by sea and met with contrary winds and bad weather, he was glad to be able to land on Monday last at North Berwick, from whence he came post to London. He brought only a short letter from his royal highness to the king, which confirms the particulars received yesterday from Edinburgh, with little variation or addition … General Hawley and Kingston's Horse are highly commended and all the troops in general behaved perfectly well, though I apprehend they could not all be engaged …[255]

Richmond replied and as usual resented that business in London was about to interfere with his hunting, which he was enjoying in the company of his friends Linky and Dell.

Bolderwood, Friday 25th April 1746

A thousand thanks to the Duke of Newcastle and yourself for the exceeding good news I received from you last night and the confirmation I had of it this morning. It has given us all the greatest pleasure … Lord Lincoln, Lord Delawarr and myself will certainly attend the House of Lords if we have timely notice, but we hope and beg of all things that it may not be before Thursday …[256]

— XIV —

The Sun Begins to Set

The duke's hunting diaries are missing from now on. It seems unlikely he stopped keeping them, as the sport continued and the duke was at Charlton no less than was his wont, and the agreeable company too. On Wednesday 10 December 1746 a quorum of nine were in the Great Room to elect new members. With the duke were Lord Harcourt, Sir John Miller, Ralph Jenison, Battine father and son, Solomon Dayrolles, Brice Fisher and, for the first time for six years, Lord Tankerville.[257] He had not just come on a casual visit from Northumberland. He sat himself at the head of the table in Roper's chair and called on the assembly to ballot the first candidate, who was none other than his younger son George! Knowing the potential ignominy of being black balled, the long journey south was deemed essential to keep an eye on the voters!

Next in the ballot was the Marquess of Granby, heir to the Duke of Rutland, who had served in his father's regiment of foot in the campaign against the Jacobites. Rutland was master of his own pack in the shires and in the 1730s the Earls of Cardigan and Gainsborough and Lords Gower and Howe also had their own hounds, though not all entered to fox. They amalgamated their countries for fox hunting, formed a combined pack and styled themselves the Confederate Hunt. Many of the hounds drafted in to Charlton after John Ware's disaster with the sheep in 1734 were by Confederate sires and dams, including some which Tom Johnson brought from the New Forest; and many of the hounds given to Charlton by Lady Molyneux in 1738 were bred by Lord Cardigan.

The Confederate pack was kennelled at Croxton Park from mid-October until the end of November, at Cottesmore in December and January and at Thawston until the end of March. They had a standard height of only 20 inches (they were really fox beagles), but larger hounds were drafted to the private packs which each confederate still kept. Lord Gainsborough was the first to leave the confederacy and hunted part of the Cottesmore country on his own and by the 1750s the Belvoir country had become established with the Marquess of Granby as acting master. The pack was entered solely to fox in 1762.

Lord Granby married Lady Frances Seymour, a younger daughter of the Duke of Somerset, born to his second wife when he was sixty-six. She was 'one of the great heiresses of old proud Somerset. She has £4,000 a year and he is in debt £10,000. She who never saw nor knew the value of ten shillings while her father lived [he died when she was 20] and has had no time to learn it, bespoke away so roundly that for one article of the plate, she ordered ten sauceboats! Besides this, she and her sister have squandered seven thousand apiece on all kinds of baubles and frippery.'[258] She had no difficulty in squandering her wealth, leaving her husband in severe financial trouble at her death 10 years later at the age of thirty-two.

Granby died in 1770 and William Pitt wrote 'the loss to England is irreparable'.[259] 'As a divisional leader, he was unquestionably a splendid soldier. He was brave to a fault, generous

99 John Manners, Marquess of Granby, elected to Charlton in 1746, was a military commander who was very popular with his troops. Many public houses are called after him.

100 John, 2nd Earl of Ashburnham, was elected to Charlton in 1746. A courtier in the reign of George III, Horace Walpole wrote of him, 'A most decent, reserved and servile courtier who did not want sense but it all centered in self interest'.

to profuseness, careful of his soldiers and beloved by them. In the days of political power, he warmly opposed the principle of dismissing military officers for their political opinions.'[260] His popularity in the kingdom is shown by the frequency with which his name occurs on the sign boards of country inns and public houses. He died heavily in debt, but these were wholly discharged by his son who succeeded as 4th Duke of Rutland in 1779.[261]

Next to be elected was the Earl of Ashburnham, a young man of 22 who became a prominent courtier in the reign of George III. 'I have the greatest opinion of his judgement in the conductive part of life. I really believe if any man went through life with consummate discretion, it has been himself and he has preserved his reputation at the same time.'[262] For the company in the Great Room he sounds rather dull!

Colonel Hon. John Waldegrave, a son of Earl Waldegrave who had served in Scotland, may have been better, but Colonel Thomas Noel was definitely a hound man. Three hounds which had come with Tom Johnson in 1735 were from his pack, as well as Jenny, Phillis and Taker entered in 1736 and Walcut in 1737, a notable dog hound who was in at the kill on 26 January 1739 at the Grand Chase. Later his stallion hounds Dolphin and Pilgrim were used to sire litters of Charlton hounds entered in 1748.

Thomas Noel was a cousin of Lord Gainsborough of the Confederate Hunt and had acquired a pack of hounds from Viscount Lonsdale (a subscriber to the Great Room in 1720), who, by an old family tradition, used to bring his hounds each year from Lowther Castle in Yorkshire to Fineshade Abbey in Northamptonshire. Mr. Noel's hounds hunted the Cottesmore country with Lord Gainsborough and at his lordship's death in 1751 he married his widow, a

101 Sir James Peachey of West Dean was elected to Charlton in 1746. He was created Lord Selsey in 1794.

102 James Fitzgerald, Earl of Kildare, was elected at Charlton on 1 January 1747, the day after Richmond had consented to his engagement to his daughter Lady Emily. He was created Duke of Leinster 20 years later.

daughter of William Chapman, the gamekeeper on the estate. After Mr. Noel's death in 1788, Sir William Lowther, later Earl of Lonsdale, bought the pack back from his heirs and successors and restored it to the Lowther family.

Fifth to be balloted was James Peachey, younger brother of Sir John, of West Dean, elected the previous season. He was an M.P. for many years and held various posts at the court of George III, being eventually created Lord Selsey (after whom the public house in West Dean is now named). Last was Josiah Iremonger, a brother-in-law of Sir Matthew Fetherstonhaugh, who bought Uppark in 1747 and became a member at Charlton shortly afterwards.

A week later, on Tuesday 16 December, the duke at Goodwood noted in a letter that 'we have glorious sport',[263] but there are no details. However, if there were no records of the hunting, the hound list was kept up to date and entered in the book. Eighteen couple of old hounds had been cast, 7½ couple of young hounds entered and one old hound was given by Lord Tankerville (perhaps as a thank you for not black balling young George Bennet!). This left the kennel with 48½ couple, rather less than a year ago, but still an adequate number to hunt three days a week.[264] Hunting being temporarily suspended by frost, a quorum was present on Thursday 1 January 1747 in the Great Room for more elections, including Lords Lincoln, Hartington, Bury and Dalkeith, John Cheale, John Waldegrave and William Conolly, who was in the chair.[265] 'The Earl of Kildare was balloted for and admitted a member of this society and his lordship being present balloted for the next candidate.' A black ball was clearly not expected! James Fitzgerald, Earl of Kildare, later created Duke of Leinster, had succeeded to the

Irish earldom as the 20th in line two years before and had recently been betrothed to the Duke of Richmond's second daughter Emily. The marriage took place on Saturday 7 February 1747 at St Margaret's, Westminster. The bride was then 15 years old and she bore him no less than nine sons and eight daughters. When he died in 1773, she married again, bore three more daughters and lived to the ripe old age of eighty-two.

The other candidates elected that day were Henry Vane and William Varey; and thirdly Ambrose Crowley, who came from a wealthy city family and whose sister Elizabeth later married the Earl of Ashburnham, bringing him a fortune of £200,000 and extensive estates in Suffolk. However dull company he may have been at Charlton, he was certainly not poor! Newcastle sent his greetings to cheer them up in bad weather.

Newcastle House, Thursday 1st January 1747
My best wishes of happy years etc to all the good company at Goodwood and Charlton. My humble respects to the cofferer.[266] I lament the frost which is come so unluckily … I drank your health today with my good lady and old Puff.[267]

Goodwood, Friday 2nd January 1747
… We are all locked up here with a confounded hard frost. The cofferer is extremely well, but I think a little tired of our company last night, for all Goodwood dined and supped yesterday at Charlton and he'll have more of us for they all dine here today. I propose being in town about the latter end of next week …[268]

They were still there on Sunday and elected Percy Wyndham O'Brien a member.[269] He was the younger son of Sir William Wyndham and a grandson of the Duke of Somerset. He had added the name of O'Brien after that of Wyndham after inheriting the estates of Henry O'Brien, Earl of Thomond, the late husband of his mother's elder sister Elizabeth. He was an M.P. for many years, held various posts at court and was later created Earl of Thomond in his own right.

The annual dinner that year was more popular than ever. It was held on Sunday 25 January 1747 at the *Bedford Head Tavern* and attended by 43 members. Sir William Middleton took the chair. There were five dukes and four heirs to dukedoms: Grafton, Richmond, St Albans, Devonshire and Kingston; and Lords Hartington, Granby, Dalkeith and Lincoln.[270] Also present were Lords Holdernesse, Rothes, Tankerville, Effingham, Ashburnham, Kildare, Harcourt, Bury, Ossulstone, Herbert of Cherbury and Baltimore; the Hons. Henry Pelham, Charles Howard, George Bennet, John Boscawen and John Waldegrave; baronets Henry Liddell, Robert Smyth, William Corbet, John Peachey and Thomas Prendergast; Admiral Townshend and Colonels Ellison and Honywood; and Messrs. Conolly, Fauquier, Jenison, Dayrolles, St Paul, Fisher, Peachey, Vane and Sedgwick (secretary). For the first time there appears in the minute a toast to the grand old huntsman Mr. Roper. He had been dead for 25 years and there were only a few who actually remembered him. Grafton, Devonshire and Henry Pelham had been subscribers to the Great Room in 1720 and St Albans had complained in 1721 that Roper was too dictatorial in the field; Richmond of course knew him from his childhood and Ralph Jenison had first come to Charlton around the time of his death. The rest were too young.

Prosperity to Charlton, the memory of Mr Roper and several other healths were drank, and then the society adjourn'd.[271]

103 Percy Wyndham O'Brien, elected at Charlton in 1747, was a grandson of the Duke of Somerset who inherited the estates of his uncle Henry, Earl of Thomond and was later given his title.

Edward Pauncefort had been unable to attend and confessed the reason why. Presumably the letter means he had a mistress of three years standing rather than three years old!

Early Court, Sunday 25th January

I have just now received a printed summons to meet the gentlemen of the Charlton hunt or send an answer by Friday. The latter was impossible for me to perform; the former indeed I might, was I not grown desperate enough to own that I could not stay longer in town from a young mistress I keep in the country of three years old; and my mother who I had left not so well as I could wish. I must therefore make an apology for not waiting on your grace on Wednesday (tho' as yet have had no summons) since had I stayed in town it would have prevented me the pleasure of attending your grace at Charlton, which I propose soberly to perform; that is only to be drunk once a day after dinner with your grace and then go write. Pray warn Mr Conolly out of my stables; I shall fill the whole.[272]

They were back in Charlton by Sunday 1 February, including Mr. Pauncefort Richmond wrote a long letter to Newcastle, typical in the time of the Pelham ministry, trying to persuade him to recommend Lord Berkeley (Richmond's nephew) to the king for appointment as Lord of the Bedchamber, in preference to Lord Cardigan (his first cousin) and Lord Ashburnham (whom they had just elected at Charlton). Typical because, it has to be said, the sole aim of the Pelhams was to keep political peace and secure places for their friends and relations![273]

Later in the week the Duke of Grafton (old Puff) arrived at Charlton with his hounds. The old members were joined by those recently elected and on Monday 9 February 17 members assembled in the Great Room for dinner with the Duke of Grafton in the chair.[274] They elected George Bridges Brudenell (a relation of Lord Cardigan), Lord Robert Manners (younger son of the Duke of Rutland) and Colonel Charles Fitzroy (a cousin of the Duke of Grafton). Later in the week the duke reported to Newcastle:

Charlton, Friday 13th February 1747
… Now as to our Charlton affairs, which you know are of no small consequence. The Puff hounds and mine have each had a good chase, but to both our shame have been baffled by a true gallant Sussex fox that seems to despise us both. However old Puff is set upon his death and the first time we attack him, either he or all our hounds are to die. We are now twenty inhabitants of Charlton besides chance comers and a jolly set we are …[275]

John Budd wrote a song about this gallant fox who defied the duke, at the same time giving a strong hint as to who the 'chance comers' at Charlton might be![276]

Come listen awhile
Of foxhunting I will sing
Which on our Sussex downs
Is sport for any king.
And to Sussex we will go &c

That all men are sportsmen
I hold for to be true
For some scent or another
Each man he doth pursue.
And a-hunting we will go &c

Some hunt after riches
While others honour hunt
But they who love a stronger scent
Will hunt a rousing cunt.[277]
And a-hunting we will go &c

All on a morning fair
To East Dean wood we went
To hunt a captain fox
It being our intent.
And a-hunting we did go &c

This fox having defeated
A duke I shall not name,
We were resolved to hunt him
For to revenge the same.
And a-hunting &c

In case there should be any doubt who were the jolly set of 20 inhabitants enjoying the favours of the 'chance comers', they are listed in the minutes as follows. The Dukes of Grafton and Richmond; Lords Harcourt, Lincoln, Effingham, Hartington and Dalkeith; Sir William

186

Corbet and Sir John Miller; Hon. John Waldegrave, Edward Pauncefort, Ralph Jenison, Colonel Honywood, Captain Benjamin Carpenter, Brice Fisher, Josiah Iremonger, Ambrose Crowley, William Varey, Percy Wyndham O'Brien and George Bridges Brudenell! On Monday 16th they welcomed a French visitor, the Marquis de Bellegarde and he was 'balloted for according to the sixth article and admitted for eight days'.[278]

In April the duke was to be found at Bolderwood for some spring hunting in the New Forest with a few friends. Lord Delawarr wrote from London, where he was on military duty.

London, Friday, 17th April 1747

I have as great happiness as I can (when deprived of waiting on your grace) in hearing that everything within doors at Bolderwood has been to your satisfaction and that Nanny has played her part well as to the sorts of provisions you like, being very desirous that whatever place I have anything to do in may be agreeable to you. I am glad you approve of the new building. I think it will make the whole very convenient and prevent your being so much strained another season; but when I think how uncertain modern sportsmen are. I then imagine any [no] house will be large enough … I hope you have had as much rain as we had last Wednesday evening; that and the wind now changing will contribute to your sport, which I wish quite to your grace's satisfaction. To be sure, new hounds in a pack never show at first, but I have always heard from those that used to crack them up, only of their very hard running, which caused me to doubt with myself whether they were good nosed ones and good beaters. Your grace will let me know that, for I never saw them in my life. I desire my compliments to all your company …[279]

Next month the earth stoppers sent the duke their report:

The Earth Stoppers account of young foxes given on Saturday 30th May 1747
    a litter in East Dean wood
    a litter in the Marlows
    a litter in Farm wood
    a litter in North comb
    a litter in the Sheepwash earth
    2 litters in Priest comb and the Oars
    a litter near Bignor park
    a litter in the Wildham
    a litter in the Haslets
    a litter in Stoke lithe

They believed there were a great many more in other places, but the above is all they are certain of.[280]

As the next hunting season approached, Lord Delawarr reported that all was well with the pack in the New Forest:

Bolderwood, Saturday 2nd August 1747

… All your hounds here look perfectly well; I have been a great while this evening in the kennel and examined them very attentively.[281]

But from another quarter the duke was again in trouble for being a country bumpkin:

Claremont, Friday 5th September 1747

… Old Puff and somebody else [i.e. Newcastle himself] who are your very good friends were blaming you extremely for having been two months in the country and during that time not come up one Saturday to attend the king at Richmond. Old Puff comes every Saturday from Northamptonshire and returns on Monday. Your coming here cannot be a secret and I had rather punish myself with your absence than be any ways instrumental to your doing anything that can be blamed, as I really fear this would be and with some sort of reason. And to be serious: why can't you come to London of a Friday … wait upon the king on Saturday at Richmond and come hither at night. You see what liberty I take with you, but when I think anything for your service, I can't help saying it, tho' as in this instance I may suffer by it, and after this do as you will …[282]

Richmond did go to Claremont, but whether he waited on the king at Richmond, history does not relate. He wrote next to remind Newcastle he owed him some money and revealed that quarantine regulations for imported cattle were in place at that time.

Goodwood, Friday 2nd October 1747

Since I saw your grace I have had nothing to make a letter of and this of no great consequence, only to tell you you owe me £8 7s 4d for two Alderney cows that I have by your own commands got for you, but by his majesty's commands in his last proclamation, they are and must be prisoners in the field they are now in for three months. However they are in good pasture below Chichester at a farm of our friend Sir John Miller and the best care will be taken of them; and when the time of their quarantine is out, you shall have them paying for their keeping …[283]

Hunting opened at Charlton in early November and a fragment of paper contains a record of 29 days, although only the finds and kills are recorded. Hounds were out regularly three days a week apart from a gap in early December, presumably because of frost. Three new members were elected during the season. Granville Leveson-Gower, Viscount Trentham was balloted on Sunday 27 December.[284] He was heir to Earl Gower, a joint master of the Confederate hunt in the shires and one of the people who had recommended Tom Johnson to the Duke of Richmond in 1734. His mother was a sister of the Duke of Kingston. Before entering the Lords, he was a Tory M.P. until 1749 when he defected to the Whigs. His ratting caused peculiar resentment, so much so that Dr. Johnson in his dictionary, when explaining the word 'renegado', wrote 'one who deserts the enemy, a revolter, sometimes we say a Gower', but the printer struck this out![285] He later held important offices of state, including Lord Privy Seal, Master of the Horse, Lord Chamberlain and Lord President of the Council, being advanced to Marquess of Stafford by George III.

The second to be elected was Sir Matthew Fetherstonhaugh who had acquired Uppark from the Tankervilles the year before. His father of the same name had purchased Fetherstonhaugh Castle, the ancient Northumbrian seat of the family, in 1711. Their wealth derived from the coal and wine trades and in 1710 he married Sarah Browne, who upon the death of an only brother became heiress to a large fortune. Matthew Fetherstonhaugh the elder was twice Mayor of Newcastle and lived to the age of one hundred and two. Matthew the younger was adopted as heir to a childless kinsman Sir Henry Fetherston, second and last

104 Sir Matthew Fetherstonhaugh Bt. was elected at Charlton in 1747 shortly after purchasing the house and estate at Uppark from Lord Tankerville.

105 Henry Pleydell Dawnay, 3rd Viscount Downe, was elected at Charlton in 1748. He was mortally wounded in battle in 1760.

baronet of Hassingbrooke Hall, Essex, on whose death in 1746 he inherited the estates and a fortune of £400,000. He petitioned for a baronetcy, as his benefactor had wished, and this was granted on 3 January 1747. A week before he had married Sarah Lethieullier, whose father was a director of the Bank of England. She bore him a son Harry, who lived to the age of 92 and enhanced and embellished the family home at Uppark, leaving it much as it is today, a jewel in the crown of the National Trust.

The hound list written up on Thursday 31 December 1747 showed that 17 couple of old hounds had been cast, 6½ couple, some young, some old, came from the Earl of Orford (formerly Lord Walpole), who as early as 1723 had first donated hounds to Charlton; a couple of young hounds came from the Duke of Grafton's pack, who were resident in Charlton at the time, and 13½ couple of young hounds bred at home were entered, giving a total of 53½ couple in the kennel.[286]

Another ballot was held on Sunday 3 January 1748 when Henry Pleydell Dawney, Viscount Downe was elected.[287] He was an Irish peer and eligible to sit in the House of Commons. Returned unopposed for York, a wag wrote, 'Lord Downe is returned from his unopposed election in Yorkshire and instead of sighing at the ladies' feet in Arlington Street, sets out instantly for Paris and hopes to preserve firm peace between the two nations by running his hands immediately up the coats of Madame de Pompadour, alert and assuré like any Frenchman, but without the language'.[288]

The second candidate that night was black balled. He was Charles Churchill, a relation of the Marlboroughs and a dissolute young man of seventeen. No doubt the duke disapproved of him, but he became a well-known satirical poet before dying in his early thirties. Educated at Westminster school where the Earl of March was also a pupil, he had recently effected a clandestine marriage and in 1756 was ordained priest 'through need not choice',[289] but after a bankruptcy, a formal separation from his wife and a course of unclerical dissipation, he gave up the church. His satirical poems became the terror of actors and the scourge of Dr. Johnson, William Hogarth and other well-known figures of the time. He lacked the chief essential of true satire, a real insight into the heart of man, but possessed volubility in rhyming, boisterous energy and an instinctive hatred of wrong. When he was proposed for membership again a year later, the duke relented and he was duly elected.

Hunting was off because of the frost, as the duke commented to Newcastle, making his usual excuses about not going to London.

Charlton, Sunday night, 3rd January 1748
… I observe also in your letter that you say you wish I was in town … but … I cannot conceive what use my being in town could be of, but if you think it may, I certainly will attend you upon the first call as I told you in my letter this morning; tho' if it thaws I shall be sorry to leave the country.[290]

The duke did go to London, if only to attend the annual dinner on Sunday 17 January at the *Bedford Head Tavern*.[291] A welcome visitor was Lord Cardigan, Richmond's cousin, who was an original member, but had not been before. He lived at Deene Park in Northamptonshire and still hunted in the shires. His wife was a daughter of the Duke of Montagu, on whose death he changed his name from Brudenell to Montagu and became Duke of Montagu himself. Not many of the original members still came; in fact at that gathering there were only eight out of the 26 who attended; Grafton and Richmond, Lord Harcourt, Sir Harry Liddell (now Lord Ravensworth), Sir William Corbet, John FitzWilliam, William Fauquier and Mr. St Paul. Another visitor of note was Lord Loudoun, recounting his escape to the mountains after being defeated by the Jacobites during the '45. He later went to America as commander in chief of the forces but was soon recalled. He was not a natural leader and was described by a wag in Philadelphia as 'like St George upon the signposts; always on horseback, but never advancing!'[292]

The frost relented and two days later the hounds went to Findon and hunted on seven days. The duke was pleased with the last day, as he recounted to Newcastle that evening:

Goodwood, Tuesday 2nd February 1748
… A glorious chase today. Found after a drag of an hour and a half by Mitchell grove and killed this side of Houghton bridge.[293]

After that there was yet more frost, and Newcastle wanted Richmond's advice:

Claremont, Saturday 6th February 1748
… If the frost lasts, I hope you will come to London, for I want the advice and assistance of my best friends. I say of you 'of my best friend.'[294]

But the duke was at Charlton and made a note of who was there and where everyone's horses were stabled. Mr. Pauncefort did have his own lodgings in the slums of Charlton, but the duke took pity on him and had him to stay. One hundred and forty three is a fair number of horses for 19 people, although in addition to the hunters, some would have been hacks and others carriage horses.

Quartered in Charlton, Sunday 7th February 1748
Duke of Richmond, Mr Brudenell and Mr Pauncefort at the Duke of Richmond's
Duke of Grafton and Sir William Corbet at Chitty's
Colonel Honywood, Sir Matthew Fetherstonhaugh and Mr [Wyndham] O'Brien at John Budd's
Lord Lincoln, Mr Vane and Colonel Carpenter at Lord Lincoln's
Lord Harcourt at Lord Harcourt's
Lord Downe at Lord Delawarr's
Lord Trentham at Lord Effingham's
Lord Ravensworth at Moll Rudd's
Mr Crowley and Mr Varey at General Hawley's
Colonel Waldegrave and Mr Fisher at Dearling's
Quarters for horses
Duke of Richmond - 8 and 3 in his own stables, 10 in huntsman's stables, 8 hacks at Mr Bilsom (oats, hay and straw to be furnished from Goodwood)
Duke of Grafton - 10 at Mrs Hayley's stable, 14 at Chitty's (oats, hay and straw from John Budd)
Sir William Corbet - 7 at Chitty's (oats, hay and straw from John Budd)
Colonel Honywood - 5 in Mr Dayrolles' stable (oats, hay and straw from John Budd)
Sir Matthew Fetherstonhaugh - 6 in Mr Iremonger's stable (oats, hay and straw from John Budd)
Mr [Wyndham] O'Brien - 6 at Lord Halifax's (oats, hay and straw from John Budd)
Lord Lincoln and Colonel Carpenter - 8 at Lord Lincoln's (oats, hay and straw from John Budd)
Lord Downe - 8 at Lord Delawarr's (oats, hay and straw from John Budd)
Mr Crowley and Mr Varey - 8 at General Hawley's (oats, hay and straw from John Budd)
Mr Brudenell - 4 at the Fox (oats, hay and straw from John Budd)
Lord Trentham and Colonel Waldegrave - 8 at Glover's (oats, hay and straw from Glover)
Lord Harcourt and Lord Ravensworth - 6 at Lord Harcourt's (oats, hay and straw from Dearling)
Mr Vane or Lord Trentham - 8 at Lord Effingham's (oats, hay and straw from Dearling)
Mr Fisher and who he pleases - 16 at Dearling's (oats, hay and straw from Dearling)
    Total   143[295]

There may have been more, as no mention is made of Mr. Pauncefort's horses, which were presumably in his own stable, to which he had previously referred. The frost continued and the duke was beginning to think he could no longer avoid going to London as Newcastle had requested. The bad weather seemed to be getting at him!

Goodwood, Tuesday 9th February 1748
… If the frost lasts I will go to town; not that I can be of any service. I can't help giving my advice by letter, tho' I am very diffident of my capacity in giving it; but I know that when I give advice that is liked it will be taken, and when I offer such as is disliked it will not be taken, which is a very good reason for not giving myself the trouble of a journey, whereas paper advice may be used in a water closet. Don't think I am testy now, tho' you know you made me damnably so last time I was at Newcastle house, and be sure I never can be so with you, but when I think you are hurting yourself …[296]

Newcastle was grateful for the letter, but there was no sign of the duke in London.

Whitehall, Friday 12th February 1748

I am infinitely obliged for your most kind letter; these marks of friendship always make the right impression on me …[297]

There was still no hunting, but the duke was waiting patiently and rather pleased he had an excuse to stay where he was.

Goodwood, Wednesday 17th February 1748

I had thoughts of going to town today, but the snow is so deep, that I dare not carry up the Duchess of Richmond till the roads are a little better; but Saturday or Sunday at farthest I believe we shall be in town if this weather lasts.[298]

It seems unlikely he did go and he wrote next from Charlton, where there is mention of Colonel Carpenter, Sir John Miller, Grafton and Lincoln still being there.

Charlton, Wednesday 2nd March 1748

Carpenter told me that you said you had received my letter … Sir John Miller has been with me … We are now kept home by the rain which is better than the frost, for as soon as it hold[s] up we are now sure of sport. Old Puff is finer than ever he was in his life and Linky is a comical and as testy.[299]

There are no records of any more hunting days at Charlton that season. As usual the duke went to the New Forest in April and let Newcastle know his plans in case he was needed in town.

Bolderwood, Wednesday 20th April 1748

… Though I have as much diversion here as fox hunting can afford me, I shall at any time return to town upon the first summons from you; and if the king should go to the house or the parliament be up soon, I beg you would let me know it; but if I hear nothing from you that requires my going up, I propose staying here all next week and then going for two or three days only to Goodwood and to be in town about the 5th or 6th of May.[300]

Lord Delawarr was in London on military duty and wrote:

London, Thursday 21st April 1748

I had the honour of your grace's from Bolderwood and am glad you found that place in such tolerable condition as to make me hope the continuance of your favour to it. I can assure you, and I flatter myself you think me sincere, that one of the greatest pleasures in the additions I made to the house was proposing by that to be able to accommodate your grace rather better than with what you had been so good heretofore to take up with. I think it now enough and convenient and hope to have some comfort there, tho' as yet [I] have had very little pleasure from the uncertainty of the times for some years past. If peace should come, I wish it may soon; I may then hope to have again some merry hours with your grace in the forest and at Charlton, and if a birthday does not fall out regularly at Bolderwood we must make one; and Charlton I believe generally every day is such [the duke's birthday was 18 May and Delawarr's 4 April].

106 George, 3rd Viscount Howe was elected at Charlton in 1748. He was slain in a skirmish with the French in 1758.

I am glad to find Nanny keeps in your good graces; I dare answer she had your bed well aired and hope she will take care you want not calvered salmon or anything else that country affords.

As to your proposal of planting, put in as many trees as you please and where you will, though it is to be sure the worst place in the world for that sport. I have planted hundreds without any success and therefore would advise planting them in baskets. I have tried every other way.

The Earl of Lincoln set out this day in order to hunt with you on Saturday; I beg you keep him in some order, for killing a heath hen or partridge on the heath at this time is destruction. And tho' I do not look on his lordship as a very excellent shot, yet I know by experience that a gun is a very dangerous instrument; for I remember to have seen a gun go off in the late Lord Sussex's (Totty Sussex we called him)[301] hand and he killed a partridge, tho' he was looking another way and did not see the couvée.

I must own your grace was very alert to sally forth immediately on the going off of the snow. I hope now the wind is come to the west you will have better weather and better sport; and should that lead the earl into a bog, I hope you will not conceal it from me. Who have you got with you? If Pauncefort, I then suppose he takes up his habitation in the library, which I believe he does not think an unpleasant room.[302]

The season of 1747/8 had come to an end and the duke recorded the final tally.

107 Hon. Augustus Keppel, elected at Charlton in 1748, was a sailor and, as Viscount Keppel, became First Lord of the Admiralty in 1782.

>   In the New Forest in autumn - 16 foxes
>   In Sussex in the winter - 19 d°
>   In the New Forest in spring - 19 d°
>   In all - 54 - 27 brace[303]

Very little else is recorded of the events at Charlton. The company were there on Saturday 24 December 1748 and elected Lord Howe, Augustus Keppel and Charles Churchill (at the second time of asking). Lords Lincoln, Dalkeith and Trentham, Battine father and son, Sir Matthew Fetherstonhaugh and Messrs. Carpenter, Iremonger and Vane were the duke's companions.[304]

George Augustus, Viscount Howe was an officer in the Guards and ADC to the Duke of Cumberland, whose father had been one of the masters of the Confederate Hunt in the shires. His mother was an illegitimate daughter of George I by the Countess of Darlington. By the age of 33 he had risen to the rank of brigadier general, but in 1758 was slain in a skirmish with the French while serving in America under General Abercrombie. He was universally popular in the army and tributes poured in from many quarters. 'His life was long enough for his honour, but not for his country. He was the first to encounter danger, to endure hunger and to support fatigue. He was rigid in discipline but easy in his manners and his officers and soldiers readily obeyed the commander because they loved the man.'[305] A monumental inscription was erected in Westminster Abbey by the Province of Massachusetts.

Augustus Keppel was a sailor, the second son of Lord Albemarle and Richmond's nephew, who became an admiral and First Sea Lord and was created Viscount Keppel in 1782.

The hound list written in the book on Saturday 31 December 1748 recorded that only eight couple of old hounds were cast and 13½ couple of young hounds entered, increasing the total to 59 couple.[306]

Thirty-six attended the annual dinner at the *Bedford Head Tavern* on Sunday 5 February when Lord Delawarr was in the chair and the usual toasts were drank.[307] The duke was in the New Forest in the spring as usual where he again recorded the tally for the season:

> In the New Forest in autumn - 18 foxes
> In Sussex in the winter - 26 d°
> In the New Forest in spring - 11 d°
> In all - 55 - 27½ brace[308]

The duke served a brief term as ambassador to Paris in summer of 1749, returning in the autumn. He received this letter from Lord Eglinton, who had acquired a residence in the New Forest and a pack of hounds.

Somerley, New Forest Sunday 29th October 1749

I am extremely glad to hear of your grace's safe arrival in this country, as it renews our hopes of seeing your grace in this wild part of the world before the fox hunting season is quite over. I have been out with your grace's hounds and have the pleasure to assure you they are rather better than last season, if that is possible. Those your grace had from Sir Charles Goring are remarkable good hunters, but I am apt to think there are some of them which will not run so hard as your grace's old sort towards the end of the day.

There are a couple of old bitches which Smith and John Row think too much wore out to breed out of and not able to run. If your grace thinks them neither an ornament nor of use to your pack. I should be extremely obliged to your grace to place them in mine, where they may still make a figure, at least in the way of gallantry; as I am of the opinion (notwithstanding what those learned gentlemen say) that the chip of an old block is often as good as the sprouts of a young tree.[309]

December came and the duke and duchess sent an invitation to their son-in-law Henry Fox and his family to pay a visit to Goodwood. It had taken some time to be reconciled after he had outraged the family by eloping with their daughter five years before.

Goodwood, Sunday 17th December 1749

… There is a cursed hard frost, which is very hard upon foxhunters and planters. You are one of those I know that don't comprehend anybody's loving hunting, so must entertain you with a question. She [Lady Sarah Lennox aged 4] asked her mama upon my being gone out on a bad rainy day 'Esceque Papa est obligés d'aller à la chasse, ou escequ'il en a envie?'[310]

The Earl of Dalkeith had been a regular member of the company at Charlton for several seasons and, having his seat at Adderbury near Banbury, was a neighbour of Mr. Selby (whose family were masters of hounds until 1920 in what eventually became the Whaddon Chase) and Lord Leigh of Stoneleigh Abbey in Warwickshire. He was grateful for the duke's offer of some hounds.

Adderbury, Sunday 17th December 1749

Since I had the honour of seeing your grace, I have laid aside for the present the scheme I had of hunting fox with my harriers, in performance of a promise I made to Mr Selby (who has a house within two miles of this place) not to hunt upon Edgehills after Lord Leigh's death, which country Mr Selby, out of compliment to Lord Leigh, never went into, or more properly, out of compliment to Lord Leigh's huntsman, as Lord Leigh never came upon the hills himself.

I am very much obliged to your grace for thinking of me and return you a great many thanks for your kind offer. A present of the same sort will be very acceptable to me, if Mr Selby should at any time grow tired of his hounds or of this country.

I am extremely glad to hear your grace has had good sport and I should think myself very happy if it was in my power to wait on you this Christmas. I fully intend to have the pleasure of attending your grace at Charlton in February …[311]

The duke had noted the contents of Lord Eglinton's letter. He gladly gave him the bitches he had requested (after the huntsman had advised him they would be no loss), but had not been best pleased with the cavalier way in which this young upstart had moved in to his treasured territory, as the next letter from Lord Eglinton implies.

Somerley, New Forest Friday 29th December 1749

I return your grace a thousand thanks for the two bitches. Your grace may be sure they shall be taken particular care of, both on account of their own merit and the person who gave them.

I am sorry your grace should have been told that I have been destroying your hunt. I promised your grace I would not hunt that part of the forest and as I have most religiously kept my word, I cannot help thinking that I am the only person [that] has reason to complain, as your grace seems to credit such information. Were I by chance, my lord, to kill one of your foxes, I do assure you I would be the first person to acquaint your grace of it myself. 'Tis true there has been a brace of foxes killed in the upper part of the forest by my hounds, but they were neither of them found there and I dare say your grace is too keen a sportsman to desire I should not follow them. I shall not trouble your grace any further about this affair at present, but shall do myself the honour to wait on your grace the moment I come to town; and make no doubt I shall satisfy you as to that matter. Meanwhile I hope your grace will do me the justice to believe that there is nobody to whom I should be more sorry to give cause of complaint …[312]

As alluded to above, the duke had been given some hounds by Sir Charles Goring, which Lord Eglinton had said were going well and in fact he had given four couple of old hounds. Mr. Thomas Bright of Badsworth, from whom the duke had not heard for 20 years, gave 2½ couple and Mr. Wyndham O'Brien gave one couple. Twenty couple of old hounds had been cast and in the hound list entered in the book there were 58½ couple in the kennel.[313]

The duke and his friends were in Charlton on Tuesday 2 January 1750 when they elected Captain Hon. William Keppel (the Albemarles' third son), the Earl of Sussex (son of 'Totty' Sussex of shooting fame), Captain Henry Norris and a visiting Italian soldier, Lieutenant General Count Luchesi.[314]

The annual dinner that season was at the *Kings Arms Tavern*, Pall Mall, where they had not been before. Thirty-three members came and for the first time the Duke of Richmond took the chair. The Duke of Grafton was the senior by far, now 66, Delawarr was 56 and Richmond forty-nine. The recently elected members were young and keen, mostly in their twenties, and

108 General Hon. William Keppel, who was elected to Charlton in 1750, was appointed commander-in-chief of the forces in Ireland in 1773.

jealous of their privilege of being a member at Charlton. So much so that there was still concern that the ballot should be conducted fairly and undue pressure should not be put on the members to vote in favour. So a motion was put:

> That from and after this 28th day of January 1750, no person shall be balloted for to be member of this hunt according to the 3rd article that shall be within twenty measured miles of Charlton at the time of such ballot, unless his habitation should be within that distance, and in that case, he may be balloted for according to the 3rd article if he is not within the village of Charlton during the time of the said ballot, nor any time in the day on which such ballot is to be made. And the question being put, it was carried in the affirmative, nemine contradicente.
>
> Prosperity to Charlton, the memory of Mr Roper and several other healths were drank … and then the society adjourn'd.[315]

Lord Dalkeith was as good as his word and was in Charlton in February, with Lord Harcourt, Lord Lincoln, Lord Downe, Lord Robert Manners, Sir John Miller, Ralph Jenison and a few others and they elected Sir Thomas Sebright and his son and Mr. Offley[316] The duke was not there, the first minuted meeting he had missed. And there were no more. His last day's hunting was in March when he wrote to his wife:

197

109 Sir Thomas Sebright Bt, almost the last person to be elected to Charlton in 1750.

Charlton, Friday 9th March 1750

I have just come home from an exceeding fine chase, but by the excessive dryness of the fallows, we were forced at last to give it up without killing the fox, so I comfort myself with the thought that it was a bitch fox. This finishes the hunting season in Sussex for the time and everybody but myself goes away tomorrow when I shall go and stay quite alone at Goodwood at least till Wednesday …[317]

The duke died at Godalming on his way from London to Goodwood on Wednesday 8 August 1750 and after that the Charlton hunt began to die too.

— XV —

Goodwood and After

The world was stunned. The loss of such a popular man at only 49 was hard to bear. The duke had possessed a kindliness of disposition and a personality which invited the confidence of his fellow men to a remarkable degree. He was at ease with all ranks and every profession, from the great officers of state to the raw recruit in the regiment. Weaknesses of course he had; they are the common lot and to err is human! But he had at all events one great redeeming point. He never forgot a friend and took special delight in collecting round him those whose company he enjoyed.

Court functions, soldiering, sport and the administration of his estates, together with a considerable amount of magisterial work, occupied his time to the full. He was not fond of politics and as we have seen actively resented being dragged away from his hunting to go to London. But he was a zealous supporter of the Whig ministry and his help and advice was valued by many of those in high office.

His fame as a sportsman, and that best of all sportsmen, a genuine lover of the chase, had hardly an equal. He loved his horses and his hounds and his letters were full of anxious enquiries as to the welfare of his favourite hunters and his precious hounds. The Charlton Hunt club, 'The Regular Society', had been his creation and the members were to a man his close friends. No one wanted to take on the responsibility for the hounds. In any case, without the duke it could never be the same. So hunting at Charlton ceased altogether, the hunting boxes were deserted and Fox Hall was dead. Charlton was silent, the glory had departed. The hounds were dispersed to other packs, a part being bought by Lord Eglinton, who hunted in the New Forest. Where the rest went is not known.

Seven years passed until the horn was heard at Charlton again. The young duke was only 15 when his father died but, being filled with enthusiasm to perpetuate the tradition which his father had loved so deeply, when he came of age he set about starting the pack once more. He turned first to Sir John Miller of Lavant, an old friend of the family, who had spent many days hunting at Charlton and dining in the Great Room. Sir John acquired a number of hounds from various breeders, including Lord Eglinton, Mr. Taylor, Lord Newburg, Mr. Norton Pawlett, a distant relative of the Duke of Bolton,[318] and Lord Granby, who was now master of the Duke of Rutland's hounds at Belvoir Castle. These he gave the young duke to start his pack. The second person he turned to was Lord Chedworth, an old Charlton member, who kept hounds in the Cotswolds near Cirencester and was giving up, maybe because of ill health as he died four years later. Mr. Edward Gibbon,[319] a resident of Buriton near Petersfield, also contributed some hounds and, together with a few more that came directly from Lord Granby, by the start of the season in 1757 the young duke had collected a pack of 51½ couple.

110 Charles Lennox, 3rd Duke of Richmond, restarted the Charlton pack in 1757 when he came of age and remained master till his death in 1806.

    He naturally tried to get back as much of the old Charlton blood as possible,[320] and succeeded in acquiring 4½ couple descended from Mr. Roper's Promise out of his Doxy by Sir William Goring's Emperor, who appeared in the hound list of 1721. There were in fact seven blood lines which could be traced back to Promise. Modesty, an old yellowish py'd bitch, was one of the hounds given by Sir John Miller 'from Lord Eglinton's pack out of Mode in the part he bought of the late Duke of Richmond's pack'. Mode was by Merryman'46 out of Julian'42, one of the large litter of 11 entered at Charlton in 1749. She had three lines back to Mr. Roper's Promise as follows: Mode'49 by Merryman'46, out of Ruby'43, out of Racket'40, out of Buxom'38, by Emperor'34, out of Comely'34. Emperor'34 was by Jockey'28, by

Dashwood'22, out of Mr Roper's Promise. Comely'34 was by Goodwood'31, by Jockey'28 as preceding. The third was from Mode's dam Julian'42 who was by Carver'38, out of Kindness'31, out of Frisky'25, out of Mr. Roper's Promise. Modesty had two litters by Lord Granby's Farmer, of whom two couple, Finder, Fleesom, Merrylass and Mode, were entered at Charlton in 1758.

The next two lines relate to a litter of three, Fudler, Flurry and Frolic who came from Mr. Gibbon and were 'by Mr Norton Pawlett's Boxer out of the late Duke of Richmond's Rowsey.' Rowsey was by Mr. Noel's Pilgrim out of Rifle'45 and had been entered at Charlton in 1748. Rifle'45 was by Ringwood'41 out of Veny'42. Ringwood'41 was out of Ruby'38, by Ruler'37, by Wildman'25, out of Maiden'22, out of Mr. Roper's Promise, the sire being Mr. Orlebar's Shifter. Veny'42 was out of Comfort'38, out of Kindness'31 who went back to Promise as in Mode's line above.

The third link with the old pack relates to a young hound entered the following season. Crowner, a yellow py'd dog, was from Lord Eglinton 'of the late Duke of Richmond's Turpin sort'. This was Turpin'48, by Turpin'42 out of Tansey'45, who was given to Lord Dalkeith in 1749. He had two lines back to Mr. Roper's Promise. His dam Tansey'45 was out of Bell'41, by Bouncer'38 who was by Emperor'34 out of Comely'34. These had the same two lines back to Mr. Roper's Promise as for Mode above.

So the 4½ couple descended from Mr. Roper's Promise were Modesty, Fudler, Flurry and Frolic who were taken to Charlton in 1757, and Crowner, Finder, Fleesom, Merrylass and Mode entered in 1758. There may have been one more, which is Rifle, an old hound from Sir John Miller bred by Mr. Pawlett, who was taken to Charlton in 1757 and in the list of old hounds in the kennel on 1 October 1758, the scribe has written 'descended from Mr Roper's Promise'. That may be so, but no hound lists of Mr. Pawlett's pack survive to be able to substantiate it and anyway by October 1759 he had given all his remaining hounds to Mr. Spencer.

The pack took some time to settle down and, although in the first few seasons old hounds were replaced with young ones bred in the kennel, by 1761 there was a need for some other old hounds to steady the pack. Accordingly, a draft was obtained from Mr. Ashton Curzon of the Dunstable Club of 16 couple in November 1761, a further 23 couple in April 1763 and 11½ couple of young hounds in October 1763. Most of the unwanted hounds were given away to other breeders, but a number were drafted to hunt hare, some to the pack of hare hounds kept at Goodwood, but others also went to hunt hare in France, possibly to a pack kept by the duke at Aubigny. A few hounds in the 1780s were even sent to the East Indies! Another interesting feature of the hound list is the practice of earmarking certain old hounds whose job it was to hunt with the young ones until they were steady enough to join the main pack.

The duke was very proud of Charlton's pre-eminence in the hunting world and in early 1759 commissioned the promising young artist George Stubbs to paint the Charlton hounds and the racing stud which he was busy acquiring. They are wonderful portrayals of the times and are now famous for their depiction of fox hunting before the golden age which was about to erupt in other parts of England. Perhaps the duke wanted to recreate the glories of Charlton and hoped that by commissioning the paintings he might further his objectives. But Melton was stirring and Hugo Meynell at the Quorn was changing the face of hunting. The sportsmen had moved to the shire packs, which were now exclusively entered to fox, as the Duke of Beaufort's had done in 1762. True, Richmond never stinted in his commitment to his hunting establishment and, judging from the wonderful hound book, he must have kept an orderly

111 The stable block at Goodwood built by the 3rd Duke of Richmond to the designs of William Chambers and erected between 1757 and 1761.

establishment of which his father would have been proud. But the support of fashionable society had gone and, as the years passed, Charlton was forgotten and the pack became known as the Duke of Richmond's hounds.[321]

He was a great builder and much of the Goodwood we know today is his creation. The first major work he put in hand was the stables, which were of breathtaking magnificence, to this day quite the most beautiful building at Goodwood. They were designed by Sir William Chambers, who was responsible for Somerset House and erected between 1757 and 1761. They form a huge hollow square, about as big as Goodwood House itself, built with Sussex flint and dressed with stone with a magnificent triumphal entrance arch. And when he decided in 1787 to move the hounds from Charlton to Goodwood, he built kennels so palatial that nothing so grand for the housing of the canine species has been seen before or since. They moved there in 1790 and had the luxury not only of ample space but a sophisticated central heating system as well. 'This building, both from extent and singular arrangement, is unequalled by any other in England destined for the same purpose'[322] and 'exceeds in magnificence and conveniences of every kind, even to luxury, any structure perhaps ever raised before for the reception of such tenants.'[323]

The hound books were meticulously kept and are a model of exquisite calligraphy. From the first entry in 1757, for each season there is a list of old hounds remaining, followed by the young hounds entered.[324] The annual recapitulation summarises numbers of dogs and bitches, whether spayed or open, and a total of hounds disposed of, whether cast, died, given away, lost, sent to hunt with the beagles at Goodwood or to France.[325] No records survive about the

112 The old kennels at Goodwood built by the 3rd Duke of Richmond and completed by 1790

sport or the hunt servants, except that the last Charlton huntsman before the pack moved to Goodwood was a Mr. Budd, several of whose family had been attendants on the old duke. Some of the members of the field were recorded in a series of crayon portraits drawn about 1790. They include five of the Goodwood ladies: Mary, Duchess of Richmond, Lady Louisa, Lord George's wife and their daughter Mary, Henrietta Le Clerc, the duke's illegitimate daughter and her friend Louisa Bunbury, Lady Sarah Lennox's daughter by Lord William Gordon. Others who hunted were Lord Chichester, Sir John Davis and Sir Godfrey Webster, the Steele brothers, the Tredcrofts, Lord King's family, Colonel Teesdale, Mr. Peckham, William Hamilton, Mr. and Mrs. Leeves, Mr. Smith of Ashling, the Reverend Moses Toghill and the Reverend Alcock. Sir Harry Fetherstonhaugh, who had succeeded Sir Matthew in 1776, would come over from Uppark and of course Lord Egremont came from Petworth. But we must first turn to the events which had been happening in that neighbouring country.

Although the Duke of Somerset had made an abortive attempt in the early 1700s to establish a pack of hounds in opposition to Charlton, when he built kennels on the downs at Twines near Upwaltham, there are no records of hounds at Petworth until 1773. Ten years before the Petworth estate had passed to 12-year-old George Wyndham, Earl of Egremont, a grandson of Sir William Wyndham and Lady Catherine, the Duke of Somerset's second daughter. On attaining his majority, the earl bought Sir Thomas Gascoigne's hounds from Yorkshire and took the country which the Duke of Somerset had tried to hunt, but had been frustrated by Mr. Roper and the gentlemen of Charlton. Luke Freeman came with the hounds; he and they were an enormous success and over the years numerous sires from

LIST of the FOX HOUNDS when taken to CHARLTON on the 16th October 1757.

Names.	When Enterd	Colours, & Marks	Dog or Bitch	S or G	From whom had.	How Bred.	How Disposed of.
Bowler		White with a Black Spot on his Side	Dog		Lord Chedworth		Given to Mr Herne
Brilliant		White with a Yellow Spot on her Side	Bitch		Lord Chedworth		Dead
Brusher		Yellow Py'd	Dog		Lord Chedworth		Dead
Belman		Yellow Py'd	Dog		Lord Chedworth		Cast
Bluebell		Blue Py'd	Bitch		Lord Chedworth		Dead
Carver		Yellow Py'd	Dog		Lord Chedworth		Dead
Croney		Black Py'd	Bitch	S	Lord Chedworth		Cast
Cocker		Black Py'd	Dog		Lord Chedworth		Cast
Driver		Blue Py'd	Dog		Lord Chedworth		Dead
Danger		Yellowish Py'd	Dog		Lord Chedworth		Cast
Drummer		White	Dog		Lord Chedworth		Dead
Damsell		Yellowish Py'd	Bitch		Lord Chedworth		Dead
Diamond		Yellow Py'd	Dog		Lord Chedworth		Cast
Forrester		Blue Py'd	Dog		Lord Chedworth		Cast
Frater		White	Dog		Lord Chedworth		Given to Mr Herne
Foreman		Black Py'd	Dog		Lord Chedworth		Cast
Frollick		Yellow Py'd	Bitch		Lord Chedworth		Died
Fairmaid		White	Bitch	S	Lord Chedworth		Cast
Fidler		Brown Py'd	Dog		Lord Chedworth		Cast
Famous		Grey Py'd	Bitch	S	Lord Chedworth		Dead
Gamester		Blue Py'd	Dog		Lord Chedworth	Got by Old Blue Cap	Dead
Jenny		Yellow Py'd	Bitch		Lord Chedworth		Dead
Jovial		Brownish Py'd	Dog		Lord Chedworth		Cast
Luter		Blue Py'd	Dog		Lord Chedworth		Given to Mr Herne
Lusty		Blue Py'd	Dog		Lord Chedworth		Dead
Lively		Blue Py'd	Bitch	S	Lord Chedworth		Given to Mr Herne
Music		Black Py'd	Bitch		Lord Chedworth		Given to Mr Herne
Madam		Yellow Py'd	Bitch	S	Lord Chedworth		Died
Maiden		Blue Py'd	Bitch	S	Lord Chedworth		Cast
Maukin		Blue Py'd	Bitch		Lord Chedworth		Cast
Nancy		Yellow Py'd	Bitch	S	Lord Chedworth		Died
Polly		Yellow Py'd	Bitch	S	Lord Chedworth		Cast
Phillis		White	Bitch	S	Lord Chedworth		Cast
Phœnix		Blue Py'd	Bitch		Lord Chedworth		Cast
Pleadwell		Yellow Py'd	Dog	G	Lord Chedworth		Given to Mr Barber
Redcap		Black Py'd	Dog		Lord Chedworth		Given to Mr Barber
Ransom		Blue Py'd	Bitch		Lord Chedworth		Dead
Ratler		Black Py'd	Dog		Lord Chedworth		Dead
Ranter		Black Py'd	Dog		Lord Chedworth		Died of Old age
Ruby		Black Py'd	Bitch		Lord Chedworth		Died
Roman		Brown Py'd	Dog		Lord Chedworth		Cast
Sober		Black Py'd	Dog		Lord Chedworth		Died
Sylvia		Black Py'd	Bitch	S	Lord Chedworth		Died
Traveller		Grey Py'd	Dog		Lord Chedworth		Kill'd by Accident
Trojan		Yellowish Py'd	Dog		Lord Chedworth		Died
Tipsey		Black Py'd	Bitch	S	Lord Chedworth		Cast
Virgin		Black Py'd	Bitch		Lord Chedworth		Died
Windsor		Yellow Py'd	Dog		Lord Chedworth		Died
Brusher		Black Py'd	Dog		Sr Jno Miller	From Lord Granby's Pack	Dead
Dido		Black Py'd	Bitch		Sr Jno Miller	From Ld Eglintownes Pack	Dead
Dancer		Grey Py'd	Dog		Sr Jno Miller	From Lord Granby's Pack	Dead
Farmer		Brown Py'd	Dog		Sr Jno Miller	From Lord Granby's Pack	Dead

113 List of the Fox Hounds when taken to Charlton on the 16th October 1757.

114 George O'Brien Wyndham, 3rd Earl of Egremont. He inherited the Petworth and other estates when he was 12 and lived to the ripe old age of 86. He started a pack in 1773 which was carried on by his successors and hounds are still kennelled in Petworth Park.

Petworth were used to infuse new blood into the Duke of Richmond's hounds and no doubt others as well.

When in 1800 Lord Egremont decided to give up, the story goes that he sent the pack with Luke Freeman to the duke whose kennels were now at Goodwood. The hounds were examined and hunted but the duke could not decide which were the best, so after a fortnight the duke said: 'Well, Freeman, I have tried the hounds and you may select the youngest and the best of them and leave me the rest'. This was just what he wanted, so losing no time in making the necessary selection, he prepared to leave Goodwood. Meanwhile the duke had ridden round to the park gate through which Freeman would have to pass and meeting him as he approached, he observed:

'So, Freeman, you have got all the youngest and the best hounds?'

'Yes, please your grace, all the youngest and best.'

'Then,' rejoined the duke 'would you be good enough to conduct them back to my kennel and you can take the remainder!'

The duke died in 1806 at the age of 71 and was succeeded by his nephew Charles, the son of Lord George Lennox, who had died the previous year. The new duke was a soldier and started his career as secretary to his uncle who was then Master General of the Ordnance. He was a hot-headed youth and in 1789 had survived two duels, the first with HRH the Duke of York, who coolly received his fire and then fired into the air.[326] 'Poor Lennox,' wrote Edmund

115 *(following 8 pages)* Map of West Sussex, 'The Great Survey' by Thomas Yeakell and William Gardner 1778.

COMPTON
EAST MARDEN
UP MARDEN
West Marden
Ileworth Farm
Lodge Farm
North Wood
Broad Reed
STOUGHTON
STANSTED FOREST
THE PARK
Stansted House
Lumley Seat
Woodlands Farm
Walderton
Racton Common
Mays Coppice
Bourn Common
Aldsworth
Racton Park
FUNTINGTON
WEST BOURN
Woodmancote
HAMBROOK
COMMON
Brick Kilns
Inlands
Emfworth
Hermitage
Printfted
Nutbourn
Mill
Turnpike Road from Portsmouth

West Dean Warren
Singleton
West Dean
Binderton
Preston F.
Rooks Hill Trundle
Crowshall Fm
Kingley Bottom
The Marsh
West Stoke
Mid Lavant
West Lavant
East Lavant
Stoke Common
East Ashling
Densworth Fm
Ryefields F.
Mid Lavant Common
Raw Mare
The Old Broil
The Broil
Woodcote Farm
West Hampnet
Hampnet Place
Knap Farm
Colworthy Common
PORT

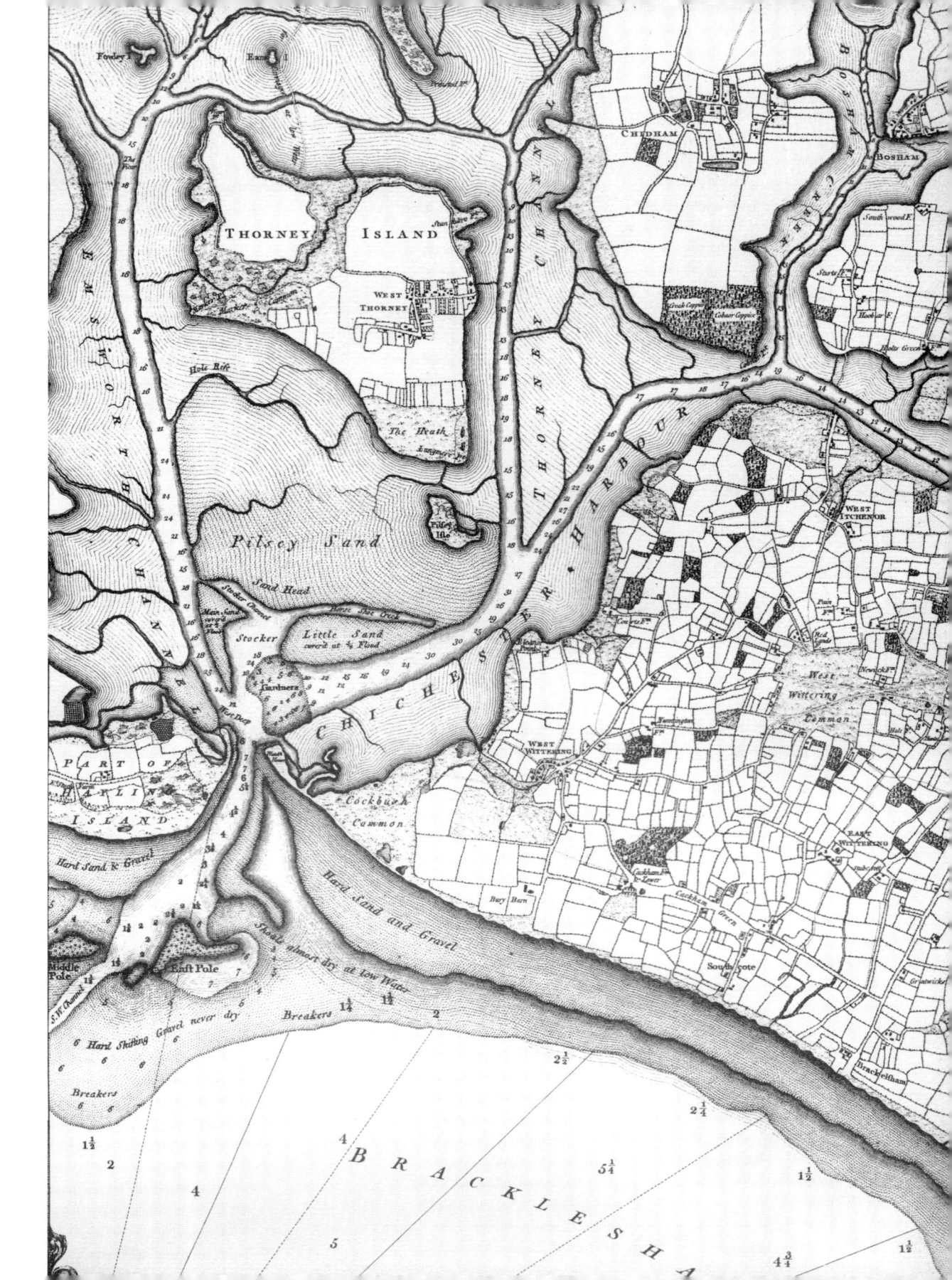

(Map)

Old Fishbourn
Walton
Fishbourn
Chichester
Rumboldsweek
Kingsham
Appledram
Old Park F.
Del Key
Old Park
Donnington
North Mundham
Runcton
Hunston
Birdham
Cowdry Farm
Common
Siddlesham Common
Brimfast
Fishers
South Mundham
Siddlesham
Carthagena
Somerly
Highley
Pagham Harbour
Pagham
Ham
Earnly
Thorney Marshes
Earnly Marshes
2½

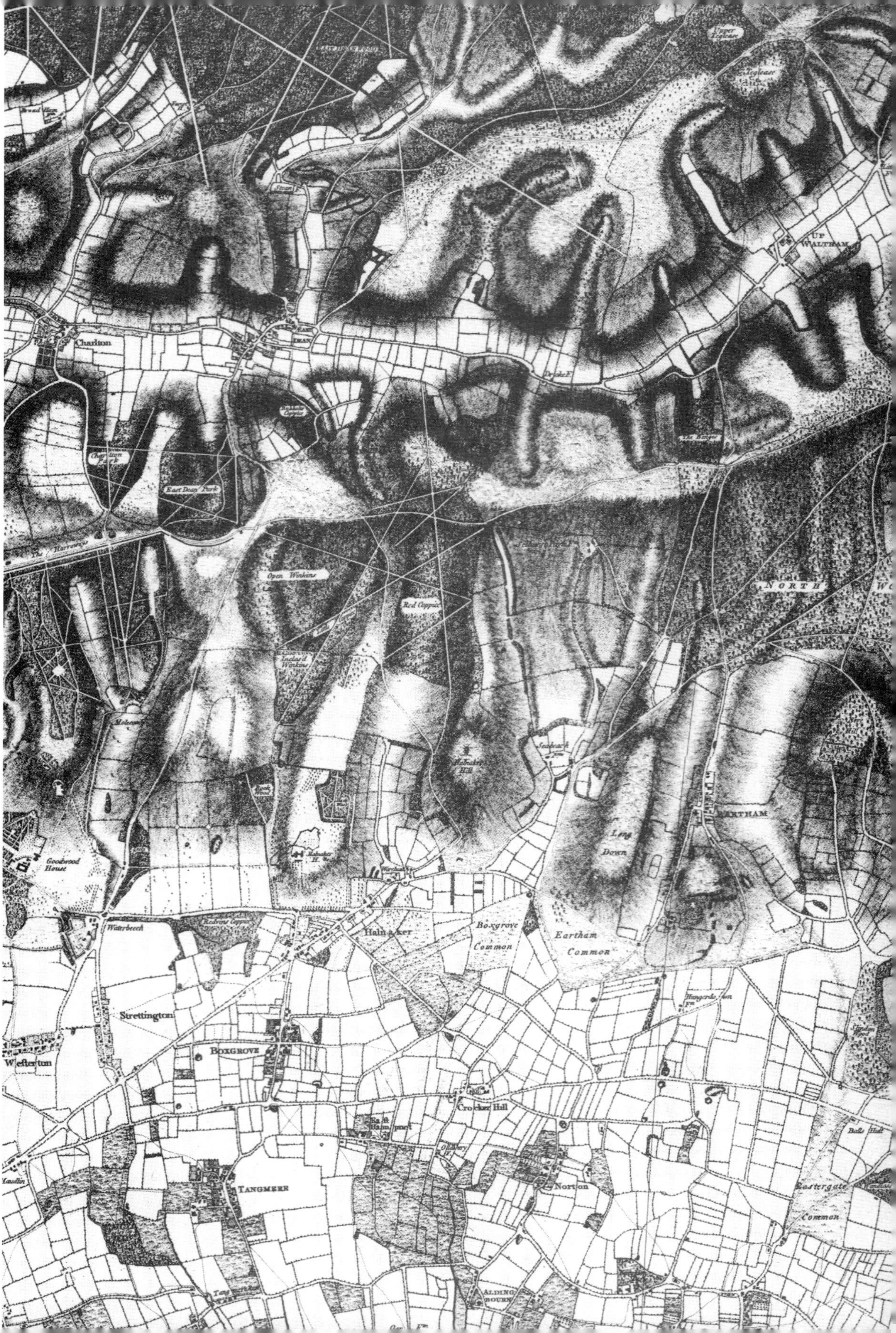

Up Waltham
Charlton
Charlton Park
East Dean Park
Open Winkins
Red Coppice
Halnaker Hill
Long Down
Eartham
Goodwood House
Waterbeech
Halnaker
Boxgrove Common
Eartham Common
Strettington
Boxgrove
Westerton
Crocker Hill
Tangmere
Norton
Eastergate
Common

SUTTON
BIGNOR
West Burton
BURY
Bignor Hill
Bury Hill
HOUGHTON
Houghton Hill
NORTH STOKE
SOUTH STOKE
ARUNDEL PARK
ARUNDEL
Common
BINSTED
WALBERTON

OVING
Westergate
EARTERIDGE

MERSTON
Colworth
Ladfey
Shripney

Lagnefs
ParkF
North Bersted
Chalkrofs F
SOUTH BERSTED
FELPHAM
Aldwick
Great Bognor

BOGNOR ROCKS

Barn Rocks

1
1¼
1½
1
1½
2
2
2½
2¼
2½
3
3½
3
2¼
3
4
4
5
4¼
5¼
3½
3

2½
2½
5

2
2¾
3¼
5½
4

TORRINGTON

YAPTON

FORD

Court Week Fm

Court Week

CLIMPING

LEOMINSTER

LITTLE HAMPTON

Bilson

Park Fm

Battle Court F.

Ancton

Atherington

Fort

Elmer

MIDDLETON

ARUNDEL HAVEN

Middleton Ledge

Shelly Rock

2
1½
5

2
2½
2
2½

3

3½
2¾
3
2½

2½

3½
3½

4½
4
3½

4
4½
4½

5½
5¾
6
5

5

6¼
6
6½
4¼
4½

116 Charles Lennox, 4th Duke of Richmond, lived most of his life abroad and gave the Charlton hounds to the Prince Regent in 1813.

Burke 'has paid the forfeit for his imprudence, which has been such as I believe has had few examples, even at his imprudent time of life.'[327] (He was twenty-five). He was immediately expelled from the Coldstream Guards and enlisted in the 35th Foot. Shortly after, Theophilus Swift wrote a pamphlet which reflected on Charles Lennox's character, and he also was challenged to a duel. Swift was hit in the body, but fortunately the wound was not fatal; Lennox was uninjured.[328] Two months later he was married to Charlotte, eldest daughter of the Duke of Gordon, perhaps the best thing to happen to a hot-headed young man! He seems to have taken little interest in the hounds at Goodwood, but this was mainly because he spent very little of his life there. A year after succeeding to the dukedom he was appointed Viceroy of Ireland and went to live in Dublin Castle. The duke and duchess maintained a household of regal proportions and spent so much that they could never afterwards afford to live at Goodwood and in 1813 took up residence in Brussels. The kennels were closed down and the hounds were given to the Prince Regent, who installed them with the Royal Buckhounds at Windsor. On 15 June 1815 the duchess gave the famous ball in a coach maker's depôt in the Rue de la Blanchisserie in Brussels, the night before the battle of Quatre Bras (three days before Waterloo). At Waterloo the duke was in Wellington's suite and was to have commanded the reserve had it been formed.[329] His next assignment was in 1818 when he was appointed Governor General of Canada, but a year later he tragically died of rabies, apparently from the bite of a pet fox.[330]

The kennels at Petworth had been in abeyance since 1800, but Freeman had managed to retain a few of the best hounds and in 1812 Lord Egremont decided to restart the pack with a draft containing some of the old Egremont blood from Mr. Pawlett in Hampshire. The hounds were managed by the earl's heir George Wyndham, who was then in his late twenties and an officer in the 27th Foot. He moved them away from Petworth to new kennels at Drought house (now Drovers) near Singleton and hunted the old Charlton country, taking them from

117 Tom Grant, last huntsman of the Charlton hounds, pictured in 1827.

time to time to kennels at Findon. Meanwhile his younger brother Henry, who was also a keen hound man, started a separate pack to hunt the northern part of the estate. He built kennels at Sladelands near Kirdford and hunted what is now the Leconfield country.

The last huntsman of the Charlton hounds at Goodwood was Tom Grant, who was interviewed in 1827 by the artist Mr. R.B. Davis, who also drew a pencil sketch.[331]

'Well,' said I to Grant one day as I met him sauntering from his garden to his house at the kennel between two dogs blind from age and services. 'Well, and how goes on the world with you—how are you, Tom?'

'Why,' he replied, shaking himself, 'I don't know but I am not so young as I was, and I am so very deaf and mopy like - I miss hunting sadly. The colonel[332] don't let me know when he comes nigh hand. A few hours with the hounds sets me right for some days.'

'Why, September, you know, is early, Tom,' I replied; 'too much sunshine for foxhunting yet; the regular days are not fixed of course.'

'Aye, that's true,' said Grant; 'but I don't fancy them out near hand and not to know it. His grace[333] gives me a run for my hunter and he is not up from Halnaker Park yet. My pony would carry me well enough in the coverts for a few hours; besides I am quite sure the colonel wants my help, though he don't think so. You know he has lost Robert, so I am sure he wants assistance, though I don't dare tell him so. Aye, they may say what they please, Mr Davis, but there is no hunting now. Lord bless you! 'tis all very well if the hounds can kill their fox alone; if not your gentlemen huntsmen get mad - they'd damn the hounds, the weather, the people and the country and all is in fault but themselves; they know more of hunting and the country than I do, after riding over it for fifty years. Mr Davis, our old friend Mrs Dorrien[334] still rides well and egad looks quite young again. She is always very kind to me; but poor Mr Bingham Newland is gone. You remember him well; he was game to the last; he hunted a few days before he died. A great pity, Mr Davis, that this place (pointing to the kennel) is not kept in better order. I should like to see hounds in it once again. Not a nicer man in all England, sir! (pointing to Goodwood House), that fall was a sad one for us all.'[335]

'Well, Mr Grant, will you oblige me with a few particulars of your late hunting establishment?'

'I will tell you all I can,' he answered, 'but if my name is to be put in print, don't put it down *Mr* or *Thomas* Grant, but plain *Tom* Grant, because everybody knows me as *Tom*. Why even the ladies and children at Goodwood call me *Tom* Grant. I like it best so; use, you know, is everything.' We sauntered into his house and sitting ourselves snugly together in his back room without the aid of any inspiring beverage (for Tom, like myself, was never a disciple of Bacchus), he began his reminiscences.

'I was born at Lyndhurst in the New Forest in the year 1754. I suppose you don't want to know what my father and mother were or what they did. I took to hunting very early and never rode above ten stone in my life. I have had many a day with the king's staghounds before I was nine years old. I got into service as whipper-in to Sir Philip Jennings, who hunted the New Forest. I learned little there, and so hired myself to Lord Castlehaven, whose hounds were hunted by that noted man of his time, Abram Booker, a real good one, depend on't, master. That was in the year 1771—the hounds were kept at Groovely in Wiltshire. I lived there about six years and then came to the third Duke of Richmond to whip-in to Mr Budd, the very best day's work I ever did. The pack was then kept at Charlton, just handy over the hill. The hunt had a club or lodge, as they called it, and many a good bout I have known there. Few alive now, sir, that used to meet us in the field earlier than some of our sportsmen go to bed now; that was the time for fox hunting. You must know that the third duke bought the pack of Sir John Miller about the year 1757, but then they were different from what you can remember them. There is a picture of hounds and the people painted by Mr Stubbs at the house; but they were a different sort of hound, for when his grace brought them from Charlton kennel to this in the year 1790, a great improvement took place.

'I was made huntsman in the year 1791[336] and persuaded his grace to make some farther alterations in the appearance of his pack. This country don't require a large heavy hound; a neat close shape, showing fine breeding and not exceeding twenty one inches is the thing for us. They will beat anything, depend on't. Our pack was a good deal improved by getting drafts from Lord Egremont and Mr Pawlett. When his lordship gave up his hounds we had a fine choice to mend ours; they were originally from Sir Thomas Gascoigne, a real thoroughbred foxhound, and old Luke Freeman was a clever huntsman, though an immense weight for a horse to carry; in fact as good as ours they might be, but there could not be better in all the world.

'Oh, what a pity, sir, that they should come to what they did! I thought I should have died when I was told that his grace had given them to his present majesty to hunt calves or donkeys with—poor fun that to my thinking—this was in November 1813. They tell me that they enjoyed reynard if he crossed them and that they continued good and handsome up to the unfortunate time when madness got into their kennel; for in the summer of 1821, nearly the whole pack was destroyed at Brighton, when down there—for the benefit of their health, I suppose. I never went to see them after they left Goodwood, although they often invited me up, and I have no doubt but that they would have made me welcome. I was at Sir John Cope's[337] last season—aye that's the best pack I have seen for some years—they manage things there uncommonly well.'

'Well, Tom,' I replied, 'I am obliged to you for so much and we shall I hope see it in black and white; and perhaps you will someday give me a copy of that celebrated run hanging against your wall,[338] as it may be deemed worthy in a corner in some number when they lack matter, so thank you for so much.' And away I trotted, dwelling on the delights which remembrance gave me of Tom Grant and his pack in their best time.

Two years later Colonel George Wyndham's bitch pack of 1829/30 was described in glowing terms.[339]

Perfection, they tell us is denied to man, and it is idle therefore to expect absolute faultlessness in the kennel of any one. The most fastidious judge in Christendom, however, could find but little to alter in Colonel Wyndham's bitch pack. With the most undeniable and fairy-like symmetry and elegance, they possess in a very eminent degree that indispensable property of fox-hounds— strength. And as to legs and feet, I have scarcely ever in any kennel I have been in, seen a better display. The head that they carry in the chase is killing in the extreme, yet with all that delightful dash to the front which maintain is the life and soul and glory of the sport and without which it ceases to be fox-hunting. They can turn if they choose exceedingly close, or, if their game runs short, hunt him to death with an indifferent scent, as well as burst him with a good one.

The huntsman also comes in for some fine praise.

Both in field and kennel, Colonel Wyndham possesses a most admirable servant in his huntsman Arber. His hounds can never beat him. Go where they will, he is always, not after them, but with them. Yet with all this hard riding, so quick is his eye, so excellent his hand and so cooly but determinedly does he set to work, that nine times out of ten in a run across the country, his horse shall be as fresh at the finish as those who have seen scarcely a tithe of the affair.

A fine pack and a fine huntsman indeed, if only they were hunting in the right place, for the scribe continues.

They are indeed far too brilliant to be buried where they are, for Sussex with its accursed wood and water and mud and hill and ten thousand baffling obstacles in the way of sport, is anything but the arena they should be destined to exhibit! This Colonel Wyndham knows, his huntsman Arber knows, in fact everyone person who has ever been out with them knows; and the best proof of their knowing is the fact that they are going to introduce the blood from some of the best slow packs into their kennel.

And on the subject of horses, he has some harsh things to say about the Sussex yeomanry.

Colonel Wyndham's people as well as himself are at all times very effectively mounted, and his stud comprises some very first rate hunters, including a lot of particularly handsome and sporting-like greys. However, with all the opportunity afforded by the horses at Petworth and the extremely liberal encouragement given to breeding by Lord Egremont[340] very little indeed of what I call hunting stock is to be met with in Sussex. The farmers go to work completely in the wrong way and when they breed at all, pick out the very worst description of mare conceivable for their purposes. The prices too which they have usually the modesty of demanding are preposterous in the extreme. In this immediate neighbourhood I have been repeatedly asked seventy or eighty guineas for a raw unmade flippertygibbet of a four-year-old, perhaps to ten stone over the turf, when completely furnished and come to his strength!! As to weight-carriers, there is no such to

217

be had, as far as I can judge, for love nor money in the county; and he who means to hunt in Sussex, if he ride anything above a catch-weight, must bring his stud with him from some other market. It is truly lamentable to see the facilities so patriotically, I may say, afforded by the venerable owner of the Petworth stud thus completely thrown away. But until there is a total change in the system of breeding, as pursued by the tenantry, even his efforts to ameliorate and improve the style of horse amongst them will be utterly in vain.

When the Earl of Egremont died in 1837, he left the estate to his heir Colonel George Wyndham. Relations with his brother Henry, later General Sir Henry Wyndham, must have been rather cool, for as soon as he became legal owner of the estate, George refused to allow Henry to draw the coverts around Petworth. In fact he resorted to shooting the foxes and other unneighbourly acts. The position became so acrimonious that, following an exchange of letters in the sporting press, it became impossible for Henry to continue and in 1840 he gave up his hounds and went to live on his estate in Cumberland.

The coverts around Petworth were then not hunted until 1848, when Colonel Wyndham brought his hounds from Singleton back to the kennels at Petworth. For a few seasons he hunted the hounds himself, but then engaged the services of Squires, who was an excellent huntsman celebrated for his very fine voice. However Squires was unable to keep on friendly terms with the other hunt servants, and in 1862 left to hunt the Lanark and Renfrew country, where he eventually broke his neck galloping down a ride. Colonel Wyndham was elevated to the peerage in 1859 and the hounds became known as Lord Leconfield's. Ten seasons later he died and the title and estates passed to his second son Henry, then aged 39, the elder son George having died aged 20 some time before.

The country Lord Leconfield hunted over with his new huntsman Shepherd was immense. It embraced not only the whole of the old Charlton and the Petworth country but, for several seasons, the Findon country as well. Shepherd did good service and eventually retired in 1896 at the age of 79 after 34 years' carrying the horn. In his *Impressions and Memories*, Lord Ribblesdale says of Lord Leconfield, 'He hardly ever spoke in the House, but his idol was land in all its complexions and aspects, speaking with authority from practical contact and knowledge. Cool, critical and shrewd, he looked on the personal administration of his great estates as a profession.' And great estates they were, in Sussex, Yorkshire and Ireland totalling 109,935 acres worth £88,112 a year.

In 1879, at the request of the landowners, the Findon country was taken over by the Crawley and Horsham, and the hunting country shrank further in 1883, when the Duke of Richmond decided to re-establish a pack at Goodwood, with the Earl of March as master. It had taken Lord March almost a year to complete the groundwork before he could even start building kennels or acquiring hounds for the new pack. There was one particular area of dispute which took the Masters of Foxhounds Association over a year to resolve. The coverts in question, Lordington wood and Watergate hanger were on the Stansted Park estate which Walter Long, master of the Hambledon, claimed Lord Leconfield and his predecessors had allowed them to hunt unmolested for 80 years, but which Lord March asserted was old Charlton country. Neither was disposed to give way and the obvious suggestion that the county boundary should be the dividing line was unacceptable as it ran straight through several coverts and would therefore render them neutral and available to neither pack exclusively. On and on the argument went, both sides intransigent and settlement was not in sight by the time the hunting season was due to open in November.

Another problem had arisen with a tenant on Lord Egmont's Cowdray estate at Midhurst, who preferred to shoot foxes rather than let them be hunted in the usual manner. Lord Leconfield had written about it to Egmont in past years. 'These woodlands supply with foxes the only good bit of grass below the hill that exist in my country and very good sport we used to have in it. But since your shooting tenant has been there the foxes have almost disappeared from it.' Egmont, who was a shooting rather than a hunting man, replied guardedly:

> I can assure your lordship I will do what I can to show sport to hunting men, but I do not think it sport to find nine foxes in our woods in one day. Sometime back, I asked your father to let me the shooting of a fir plantation of about six acres adjoining your lordship's woods, as our birds would draw there as we have so few trees. We could not have it as it was let to the Duke of Richmond. In my application I said if we could have that we could preserve both foxes and pheasants. In consequence of the 'ifs', I am afraid we have the credit of killing all the foxes.

A year later Leconfield asked Egmont to allow him to rent the land, adding 'As Mr Hollis only preserves pheasants, poultry and rabbits for the market, he is never likely to allow a fox to live. In fact my best country is destroyed by him. My reason for asking is that if the same destruction is to continue, I must reduce the number of my horses and hounds.' Though Egmont undertook not to let the property again without mentioning it to Lord Leconfield, the lease did not expire till 1883. By then it was March who was interested and he took up the battle.

> You have a tenant of the name of Hollis who has the shooting of the Marlows etc. I believe he is a yearly tenant and I am sorry to say that foxes do not thrive under his keeper. The worst of it is that not only are the foxes on that particular beat affected, but a strange fox wandering there suffers equally and consequently a large proportion of the woodlands on the downs, as well as those below the hill, are denuded of foxes. Am I asking too much of you if I ask you to let me have the refusal of the lease before it is renewed to your present tenant? My father having given me the management of the hunting I am writing in the interests of a good many besides myself.

Despite all this, new kennels were built at Goodwood in the winter of 1882/3 modelled on Lord Leconfield's in Petworth Park. The superb old kennels at Goodwood dating from 1787 had since been put to other uses, being for a time the home of John Kent, the fifth duke's racing trainer, and later, as the race meeting expanded during Victorian times and more and more police were needed, to providing attic dormitories, for which the roof had to be raised on jacks. The building was now enlarged and adapted to provide flats for the huntsman, first whipper-in, stud groom and kennelman. There were 34 hunters in the magnificent stables at Goodwood, which had not seen a hunter for 70 years, and 55 couple of hounds purchased from Lord Radnor were in the new kennels in the charge of George Champion, the renowned huntsman of the Southdown, who had been engaged to hunt the new pack.

At the opening meet held on Monday 5 November 1883, the gentlemen of the hunt were expected to appear in Charlton blue coats and the huntsman and whippers-in were attired in the old Lennox hunting livery of yellow coat with scarlet collar and cuffs. In the event the colour of the occasion was enhanced further by the scarlet coats of the visitors from Petworth. 'What Derby day is to the Londoner' wrote a reporter, 'the first meet of the Goodwood hounds upon this occasion was to the folk of West Sussex. All the countryside seemed to have turned out, noble and simple, pedestrians and equestrians, ladies and gentlemen, the old and the young.' The attendance was so vast that the Valdoe copse, where hounds were put in to draw, was engulfed. The first fox could find no way out and was immediately chopped in covert and the second could offer no better a chase and was cornered in the timber yard behind the house. 'Although these two short runs', continued our reporter, 'did not afford much sport for the old fox hunters who were well mounted, it was a most enjoyable day for the novices and enabled many to proclaim they were in at the death, which proud position they never enjoyed before nor have probably since. The noble master, having offered so much sport for the general public, trotted off with the pack to Boxgrove common to try and afford good sport for the habitual sportsmen. Unfortunately, this effort failed for some little time, as not only was Boxgrove common blank, but Bines furze and Slindon common also. At last Dale Park contained the object sought for, and after a tolerably good run, another fox was run into upon the lawn in front of Dale Park house, only about 25 sportsmen being in at the death. Thus terminated the ever-memorable day of the re-establishment of the Goodwood or, as it was anciently written, the Charlton Hunt.'

The dispute over the coverts at Stansted had still not been resolved and in July 1884 the case was heard by the Masters of Foxhounds Association, which was as good as a high court trial. Counsel were briefed, the evidence and history printed in fullest detail. It seemed to the adjudicators that the dispute hinged on the nature of the permission given by Lord Leconfield to the Hambledon in regard to the area in question: had Lord Leconfield abdicated his rights at Stansted, in which case the Hambledon could after all that time reasonably feel the country was theirs, or had he only lent the country for the time being? Whichever it was—and Leconfield had apparently volunteered in 1871 to call Stansted neutral—March said he had no right to do so, since Leconfield himself was only there by permission of the Duke of Richmond. The fact that all the parties involved in that permission were long since dead did not ease the resolution of the matter. Walter Long was producing old men who distinctly remembered their fathers telling them this, and March was quite sure that his great-great grandfather had said that. Leconfield was summoned to Tattersalls for the grand inquisition, and though again it was a question of what his father had done, it was finally decided that the Goodwood hunt could no longer regard Stansted as their exclusive province. When it was all over, reason returned to banish the obstinacy of the participants, and Long offered several coverts to March for the next season, making the boundary between them not the county border but the railway line from Rowlands Castle to Petersfield—which is what March had suggested 18 months earlier!

By the final decade of the century, large landowners were feeling the pinch, as the *Banffshire Journal*, which circulated near Richmond's Scottish estates, explained:

> From the time of its establishment, the duke has maintained the pack at his own expense. He cannot do so any longer, not from any want of will, but simply because of the enormous shrinkage in the value of his estate, in common with other landed property all over the country. An effort to keep up the kennels by subscription fell through, simply because many of those who enjoy the benefits and privileges of hunting want to get their sport for nothing. The dissolution of the Goodwood pack is not a good sign of the times. It is sad to think that the ancient traditions and customs of the country should be sacrificed.

The last meet of the Goodwood Hunt took place on 13 April 1895. There was a strong east wind under a clear sky as the 70 horsemen assembled at Goodwood. The day was unremarkable initially, but later they found a fox which ran from the Valdoe to Boxgrove Priory, Woodcote, Aldingbourne, Boxgrove and Tangmere

> where the quick eye of the noble master discerned the sleek coat of Master Reynard glistening in the afternoon sun as he reclined at his ease in a furrow. The angelic smile on the face of Fred White, the excellent first whip was a picture. He evidently thought it most amiable of the fox to have located himself just where he did. Such a scurry ensued as has seldom been seen in that locality, for Reynard betook himself to the road, where the going was easy, and was followed by the whole hunt pell mell. We have heard of a fox having a dusting, but we doubt whether one was seen so completely dusted before.

The West Sussex roads were evidently not yet blessed with Macadam's attention. Just the same, the fox was too good for them and went to ground near Aldingbourne.

A second fox gave them a run round what later became Tangmere airfield and on to Oldbury farm at East Hampnett, where they found 'a yawning ditch full of water and big enough to engulf a waggon and horses, in the high back of which Reynard had ensconced himself as a last resort'. Thus ended the last run of the famous Goodwood hounds. Then there was a long pause and someone said, in a hushed voice, 'This is the funeral'. Everyone seemed reluctant to move from the spot, but five was the hour, and at length, slowly and sadly, by two and by threes, the members of the hunt melted from the sad field.

Among the many letters of regret received at Goodwood was this one from the Duke of Norfolk at Arundel Castle:

> I was very sorry to get your letter telling me you did not see your way keeping on the hounds. I cannot pretend I am surprised. When I got your letter, I had just had my lawyer urging upon me the necessity of drastic reductions in my expenditure and I almost wished I had a pack of hounds to cut adrift. I seem to have dropped out of hunting altogether, but I am none the less grieved you are going to give up. What is to be the end of it all for all of us is a depressing consideration.

On 10 May 1895 the Goodwood pack was sold at Tattersalls along with the hunters and saddlery. Every generation has its apocalyptic moments. 'What changes!' said *The Field*, 'What a different England we now exist with! Was this event portentous? Was it the precursor of that universal bankruptcy which appears to overshadow agriculturalists and all who obtain their living from the land? Alas! we fear it may be so.'

Lord Leconfield died in 1901 after a long illness, leaving the estate to Charles his second son, the eldest son George having succumbed to typhoid fever some six years previously. Charles Wyndham, the new Lord Leconfield, was born in 1872 and, after serving in the Boer War, returned to Petworth to hunt the bitch pack two days a week, while his huntsman Charles White, who had succeeded Shepherd, carried the horn with the dog pack. The old Charlton country which had been vacated by the Goodwood hunt remained unhunted for 10 years until Lord Leconfield reannexed it in 1905, starting at its eastern end, but gradually penetrating west until, two years later, it all came under his control. Then for six seasons, until the outbreak of war in 1914, his hounds were hunting six days a week.

At the end of the war in 1918, he reduced the hunting days to four, still carrying the horn himself, but the country was still too large and he was happy to accede to a request in 1921 from Lord Cowdray's sons Hons. Harold and Clive Pearson to take over the old Charlton country and start a new pack. Lord Leconfield accordingly reduced his hunting days to two but continued to carry the horn himself until 1931. In that year the Leconfield became a subscription pack and in 1942 Lord Leconfield gave up the hounds all together, arranging to lend part of the country to the new amalgamated Chiddingfold and Leconfield.

The Cowdray hunt kennels were at Balls Farm just across the river from Cowdray House under the care of Will Shearman, the kennel huntsman. Hounds were hunted by the masters and the opening meet was held in November 1922. Hon. Harold Pearson succeeded as Viscount Cowdray in 1927 only to die suddenly six years later. His brother Clive continued for two more seasons and retired in 1935 when the Cowdray too became a subscription pack. A second amalgamation took place in 1973 to form the Chiddingfold, Leconfield and Cowdray hunt, as a result of which the hounds kennelled at Petworth were once again hunting the same large area covered by Lord Leconfield's hounds in Edwardian times.

> *We have no wish to exaggerate*
> *The worth of the sports we prize,*
> *Some toil for their church and some for their state*
> *And some for their merchandise;*
> *Some traffic and trade in the city's mart,*
> *Some travel by land and sea,*
> *Some follow science, some cleave to art,*
> *And some to scandal and tea;*
> *And some for their country and their queen*
> *Would fight, if a chance they had.*
> *Good sooth, 'twere a sorry world, I ween,*
> *If we all went galloping mad;*
> *Yet if once we efface the joys of the chase*
> *From the land, and outroot the stud,*
> *Good-bye to the Anglo-Saxon race!*
> *Farewell to the Norman blood!*
>
> Adam Lindsay Gordon

Appendix 1

Fox Hall, Charlton

The most conspicuous building in Charlton today is a charming early Palladian three-storied house on the south east corner of the village known as Fox Hall. We heard in Chapter 3 how in 1720 some 28 members of the hunt, at the suggestion of the Duke of Grafton and the Earl of Burlington, subscribed towards the building of a banqueting hall, which Lord Burlington designed and which was known as the Great Room, referred to in the poem as the Dome and later called Fox Hall. We also know from Chapter 12 that on Christmas day 1743, the chairman sat in 'Roper's chair', so this gives a clear indication that it must have been completed before Roper's death in February 1723. Some architectural opinion has suggested it was more likely to have been designed by Roger Morris, Burlington's assistant who later worked independently, based on its similarity to the Council House at Chichester, which was his work.[1,2] Others have accepted it could easily have been, and probably was built to Lord Burlington's design.[3,4,5] The house consists of three small rooms downstairs and a single large room with a high ceiling on the first floor, occupying almost the whole area of the building; ideal for a banqueting room. An architectural study of eighty banqueting houses in England concluded that Fox Hall was a building 'undoubtedly used for gatherings at which food and drink, probably in large quantities, was consumed'.[6] Daniel Defoe in 1738 referred to there being at Charlton 'a large room which was designed by the Rt. Hon. the Earl of Burlington where the gentlemen foxhunters dine every day together during their stay in the village'. In the minutes, the greatest number of people present at a meeting was twenty, on Monday 16 February 1747. The author has dined in the room with his hunting friends on many occasions and it will comfortably seat twenty or more people. It was still standing in 1777 on the evidence of Tom Grant, the last huntsman of the Charlton hounds, who was appointed whipper-in in that year. He stated (see Chapter 15) that 'the pack was kept at Charlton, just handy over the hill (from Goodwood); the hunt had a club or lodge as they called it and many a good bout I have known there.' There can be little doubt therefore that Fox Hall is the original Charlton hunt banqueting hall.

In 1863, the waters were muddied by T.J. Bennett, who wrote an article on the Charlton hunt in which he stated that 'Fox Hall was pulled down; the residences of the various noblemen in the village have disappeared (the Duke of Richmond's lodging only remaining), with all the vestiges of the Charlton Hunt, once so famous'.[7] He probably based this on an estate map of 1731 by Thomas Bucknall (fig.118) in which Fox Hall ('Z') is referred to in the key as 'Ld Duke's House'; and another map in 1765 by Yeakall and Gardner (fig.119), where Fox Hall (L1) is called 'The House in a messuage belonging to the Duke of Richmond'.

Now it is perfectly true that the 2nd Duke of Richmond did build a lodging or hunting box in the village. In 1730, by now master and proprietor of the hunt, he purchased the manors of Singleton and Charlton and started to build his hunting box (see Chapter 5). A note in the

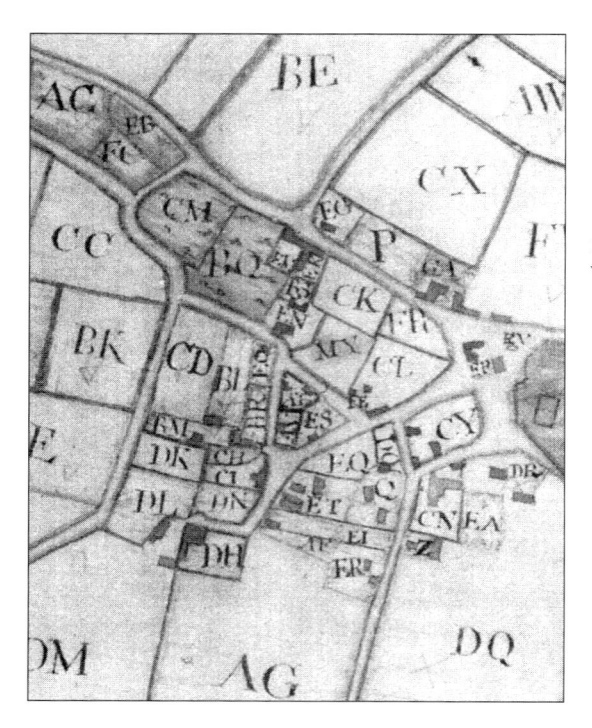

118 Goodwood estate map of 1731 showing Fox Hall ('Z') which is referred to in the key as 'Ld Duke's House'.

119 Goodwood estate maps of Charlton by Yeakell and Gardner. The map of 1765 (left) shows a house immediately north of Fox Hall (L1) [arrow] which is not there on the map of 1767 (right).

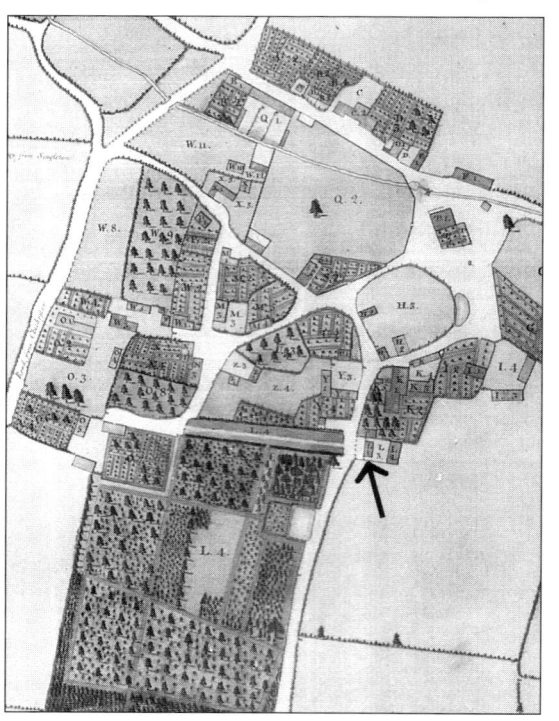

Adsdean document states 'The house at Charlton, walls finished and covered in at Michaelmas 1730; the inside of it was finished by Michaelmas 1731 and it was furnished and the Duke and Duchess of Richmond lay in it November 22nd 1732.' The next reference is in the poem where, referring to members' hunting boxes, it says that 'a warm and small apartment each one has, the duke's alone appears magnificent, conspicuously it stands above the rest and uniform, and nearest to the dome'. From this it can be seen that the duke's hunting box was the nearest building to the Great Room and that it was not occupied until 1732.

The map of 1731 had been commissioned by Richmond to show the 1730 additions to his estate and may well not have shown his new building under construction. Fox Hall could therefore have been called 'Ld Duke's House' simply because Richmond owned not only the hunt but the land as well. However a careful look at the map of 1765 does show a building very near Fox Hall, just to the north across the pathway to the courtyard. This could well be the duke's hunting box, but on a slightly later map of about 1767 (fig.119), it has gone. The 2nd duke had died in 1750 when his son was a minor and hunting in Charlton was not revived until 1757, when the 3rd duke started building his magnificent stable block over the hill at Goodwood. Clearly there was no longer any use for a hunting box in Charlton and after 17 years of neglect, the 2nd duke's old hunting box must have been in a state of decay. It therefore seems reasonable to assume it was pulled down.

After the hounds moved to Goodwood in 1790, nothing is known about Fox Hall until the last quarter of the 19th century, when Mr. Thomas Foster, who started the sawmill in Charlton, lived there as a tenant. Various structural alterations had been carried out to adapt it for this purpose, including a passageway across the yard, which shows in the 1874 Ordnance Survey map. The inside was still ornamented with decorations relative to the chase, wall coverings patterned with foxes and carvings of foxes and hounds on the ceiling (added evidence for the building being for hunt gatherings), but these, along with a fine marble fireplace, were later removed to Goodwood. Mr. Foster's daughter lived there early this century and thereafter it continued to be associated with the sawmill, with the manager's office on the ground floor and living quarters on the upper two floors. The last person to live there was Mr Tinniswood, buyer of timber, who began there as a tenant and became the owner after the Goodwood estate sold it to him in 1961. After his death in 1979, his daughter, Mrs Hampden-Smith, put the house up for sale by auction and it was bought by the Landmark Trust, who have since carried out a sensitive restoration and returned it to something approaching its original appearance and arrangement.[8]

Notes

1. Charlotte Haslam (personal communication).
2. Richard Hewlings (personal communication).
3. Rosemary Baird (personal communication).
4. Christopher Pringle (personal communication).
5. Colvin's *Biographical Dictionary of British Architects*.
6. Christopher Pringle (personal communication). Banqueting houses started life as little buildings on the top of Tudor mansions, came down off the roof at the end of the 16th century, when they were generally in the corners of gardens, and then when garden fashions changed around the 1720s, became independent buildngs frequently of great architectural merit. Their original function was to provide a place away from the Great Hall where senior guests would repair to partake of 'banquetting stuffe', which was the early form of dessert, while the hall was being cleared.
7. Bennett, p.79.
8. Haslam, 1994.

Appendix 2

MEMBERS OF THE CHARLTON HUNT

ALBEMARLE, 2nd Earl of. William Anne Van Keppel b 1702 styled Viscount Bury succ 1718 as Earl of Albermarle d 1754. Subscriber to the articles. S and h of Arnold Joost 1st Earl by Gertrude de Quirina da and h of Adam Van de Duyn Lord of St Gravenmoer in Holland and Master of the Buckhounds to William III. Lieutenant General. Ambassador to France. KG 12 July 1750. Groom of the Stole. M 21 Feb 1723 Anne 2nd da of Charles Lennox 1st Duke of Richmond by Anne widow of Henry 2nd Baron Belasyse da of Francis Brudenell styled Lord Brudenell s and h ap of Robert 2nd Earl of Cardigan.

ALBEMARLE, 3rd Earl of. George Keppel b 1724 styled Viscount Bury succ 1753 as Earl of Albermarle d 1772. Elected by ballot 18th January 1745. S and h of William Anne 2nd Earl by Anne 2nd da of Charles Lennox 1st Duke of Richmond. General in the army. KG 25 July 1771. M 20 Apr 1770 Ann yst da of Sir John Miller of Chichester 4th Bart by Susan da of Matthew Combe of Winchester MD.

ASHBURNHAM, 2nd Earl of. John Ashburnham b 1724 styled 1730 Viscount St Asaph succ 1737 as Earl of Ashburnham d 1812. Elected by ballot 10th December 1746. S and h of John 1st Earl by his 3rd wife Jemima 2nd da of Henry de Grey Duke of Kent. Master of the Great Wardrobe. Groom of the Stole. M 28 June 1756 Elizabeth da of John Crowley of Barking Suffolk by Theodosia da of Rev Joseph Gascoyne DD.

BALTIMORE, 5th Baron. Charles Calvert b 1699 succ 1715 as Baron Baltimore d 1751. Subscriber to the articles. S and h of Benedict Leonard 4th Baron by Charlotte da of Edward Henry Lee 1st Earl of Lichfield. Governor of Maryland. M 20 July 1730 Mary da of Sir Theodore Janssen Bt of Wimbledon Surrey by Williamsa da of Sir Robert Henley of the Grange Hants.

BATTINE, William, Esq Jr. b 1723 d 1812. Elected by ballot 23rd December 1742. S of William Battine Sr by Mary neé Peacham of Little Green Compton. Lawyer.

BATTINE, William, Esq Sr of East Marden b 1684 d 1770. Subscriber to the articles. Mayor of Chichester. Agent to 2nd Earl of Tankerville and Sir Matthew Fetherstonhaugh. M Mary neé Peacham of Little Green Compton.

BEAKE, Colonel Gregory. Subscriber to the articles.

BEAUCLERK, Lord George b 1704 d 1768. Subscriber to the articles. 6th s of Charles 1st Duke of St Albans by Diana 2nd da of Aubrey de Vere 20th Earl of Oxford. Lieutenant General. M Margaret Bainbridge.

BEAUCLERK, Lord Henry b 1701 d 1761. Subscriber to the articles. 4th s of Charles 1st Duke of St Albans by Diana 2nd da of Aubrey de Vere 20th Earl of Oxford. M 1stly 21 Apr 1729 a da of Governor Philips of Stanwell Midx. M 2ndly Martha da of 4th Baron Lovelace.

BEAUCLERK, Lord William b 1698 d 1733. Likely subscriber to the Great Room. 2nd s of Charles Beauclerk 1st Duke of St Albans by Diana 2nd da of Aubrey de Vere 20th Earl of Oxford. M 13 Dec 1722 Charlotte 2nd da of Sir John Werden Bart of Holyport co Berkshire by his 1st wife Elizabeth da of Robert Breton of Norton co Northampton.

BENNET, Hon George b 1727 d 1799. Elected by ballot 10th December 1746. 2nd s of Charles 2nd Earl of Tankerville by Camilla da of Edward Colville of Whitehouse co Durham.

BERKELEY, 3rd Earl of. James Berkeley b 1678 styled 1698 Viscount Dursley succ 1710 as Earl of Berkeley d 1736. Likely subscriber to the Great Room. 2nd but 1st surviving s and h of Charles 2nd Earl by Elizabeth da of Baptist Noel 3rd Viscount Campden. M 13 Feb 1711 Louisa 1st da of Charles Lennox 1st Duke of Richmond by Anne widow of Henry 2nd Baron Belasyse da of Francis Brudenell styled Lord Brudenell s and h ap of Robert 2nd Earl of Cardigan. KG 30 April 1718.

BERKELEY, 4th Earl of. Augustus Berkeley b 1716 styled Viscount Dursley succ 1736 as Earl of Berkeley d 1755. Subscriber to the articles. S and h of James 3rd Earl by Louisa 1st da of Charles Lennox 1st Duke of Richmond. M 7 May 1744 Elizabeth 1st da of Henry Drax of Ellerton Abbey co York by Elizabeth da and h of Sir Edward Ernle Bart of Charborough Dorset.

BISHOPP, Sir Cecil, Bt of Parham co Sussex b 1700 succ 1725 as 6th Baronet d 1778. Subscriber to the articles. S and h of Cecil 5th Bart by Elizabeth da and h of Henry Dunch of Newington Oxon. M 1726 Anne 3rd da of Hugh Boscawen 1st Viscount Falmouth by Charlotte da of Charles Godfrey.

BOLTON, 2nd Duke of. Charles Powlett b 1661 styled 1689 Marquess of Winchester succ 1699 as Duke of Bolton d 1722. Likely subscriber to the Great Room. 2nd but 1st surv s and h of Charles 1st Duke being 1st s by his 2nd wife Mary widow of Henry Carey styled Lord Leppington 1st of the 3 illegit daughters of Emmanuel Le Scrope Earl of Sunderland. KG 9 Dec 1714. Lord Chamberlain. M 1stly 10 July 1679 Margaret da of George 3rd Baron Coventry by Margaret da of John Tufton Earl of Thanet. M 2ndly 8 Feb 1683 Frances da of William Ramsden of Byrom co York by Elizabeth da and h of George Palmer of Naburn. M 3rdly 15 Oct 1697 Henrietta da of James Duke of Monmouth by Eleanor Needham spinster.

BOLTON, 3rd Duke of. Charles Powlett b 1685 styled 1699 Marquess of Winchester succ 1722 as Duke of Bolton d 1754. Subscriber to the Great Room. Proprietor of Charlton hounds 1721 to 1728. S and h of Charles 2nd Duke by his 2nd wife Frances da of William Ramsden of Byrom co York. KG 13 Nov 1722. M 21 July 1713 Anne da and h of John Vaughan 3rd Earl of Carbery by his 2nd wife Anne da of George Savile Marquess of Halifax M 2ndly 20 Oct 1752 Lavinia Fenton da of Lieutenant Beswick RN.

BOSCAWEN, General Hon John b 1714 d 1767. Elected by ballot 23rd December 1742. 4th s of Hugh 1st Viscount Falmouth by Charlotte da of Charles Godfrey. M Dec 1748 Thomasine da of Robert Surman of Vanentine House co Essex.

BROOKE, 7th Baron. William Greville b 1694 succ 1711 as Baron Brooke d 1727. Likely subscriber to the Great Room. Br and h of Fulke 6th Baron being 2nd s of Francis Greville by Anne widow of Henry Baynton of Spy Park Wilts 1st da of John Wilmot Earl of Rochester. M 8 Nov 1716 Mary 2nd and yst da of Hon Henry Thynne by Grace da and h of Sir George Strode of Leweston.

BRUDENELL, G Bridges, Esq. Elected by ballot 9th February 1747.

BRUDENELL, Hon James b 1687 d 1746. Subscriber to the articles. Yr s of Francis Brudenell styled Lord Brudenell s and h ap of Robert 2nd Earl of Cardigan by Frances 1st da of Thomas Savile Earl of Sussex.

BURFORD, Earl of (see SAINT ALBANS, 2nd Duke of)

BURLINGTON, 3rd Earl of. Richard Boyle b 1694 styled Lord Clifford succ 1704 as Earl of Burlington also Earl of Cork d 1753. Architect of the Great Room and original subscriber. S and h of Charles 2nd Earl by Juliana da and h of Hon Henry Noel 2nd s of Baptist 3rd Viscount Campden. M 21 Mar 1721 Dorothy 1st da of William Savile Marquess of Halifax by Mary da of Daniel Finch Earl of Winchilsea. KG 18 June 1730.

BURY, Viscount (see ALBERMARLE, 3rd Earl of)

BUTLER, John, Esq of Ireland. Elected by ballot 23rd December 1742.

CARDIGAN, 3rd Earl of. George Brudenell b 1669 succ 1703 as Earl of Cardigan d 1732. Likely subscriber to the Great Room. Grandson and h of Robert 2nd Earl being s and h of Francis Brudenell styled Lord Brudenell s and h ap of Robert 2nd Earl of Cardigan by Frances 1st da of Thomas Savile Earl of Sussex. Master of the Buckhounds to Queen Anne and to George I. M 15 May 1707 Elizabeth 1st da of Thomas Bruce 2nd Earl of Ailesbury by Elizabeth da of Henry Seymour, styled Lord Beauchamp s and h of William, 3rd Duke of Somerset.

CARDIGAN, 4th Earl of (see MONTAGU, 1st Duke of)

CARLISLE, 3rd Earl of. Charles Howard b 1669 succ 1692 as Earl of Carlisle d 1738. Subscriber to the Great Room. S and h of Edward 2nd Earl by Elizabeth widow of Sir William Berkeley 2nd and yst da of Sir William Uvedale of Wickham Hants. M 25 July 1688 Anne da of Arthur Capell 1st Earl of Essex by Elizabeth da of Algernon Percy Earl of Northumberland. Master of the Harriers and Foxhounds.

CARPENTER, Colonel Robert. Elected by ballot 25th December 1743.

CARPENTER, Major Benjamin. Elected by ballot 18th January 1745.

CAVENDISH, Lord James b 1700 d 1741. Subscriber to the articles. Yr s of William 2nd Duke of Devonshire by Rachel sister of Wriothesley 2nd Duke of Bedford 1st da of William Russell styled Lord Russell by Rachel da of Thomas Wriothesley Earl of Southampton.

CHEALE, John, Esq of Findon. Elected by ballot 25th December 1743. Norroy King at Arms.

CHEDWORTH, 2nd Baron. Elected by ballot 24th February 1745. John Thynne Howe b 1714 succ 1722 as Baron Chedworth d 1762. 2nd but 1st surviving s and h of John 1st Baron by Dorothy 1st da of Henry Frederick Thynne of Sunbury Midx. Master of hounds in Cotswolds. M 23 Sep 1751 Martha 1st da of Sir Philip Parker-a-Morley-Long Bart by Martha da of William East.

CHOLMONDELEY, 3rd Earl of. George Cholmondeley b 1703 styled 1725 Viscount Malpas succ 1733 as Earl of Cholmondeley d 1770. Subscriber to the articles. 2nd but 1st surviving s and h of George 2nd Earl by Elizabeth da of van Ruytenburg Governor of Sas van Ghent. Chancellor of the Duchy of Lancaster. Lieutenant General. M 14 Sep 1723 Mary da of Sir Robert Walpole later 1st Earl of Orford by his 1st wife Catherine da of John Shorter.

CHURCHILL, General Charles b 1679 d 1745. Subscriber to the Great Room. S of Charles Churchill yr br of John 1st Duke of Marlborough.

CHURCHILL, Charles, Esq b 1731 d 1764. Balloted but rejected with one black ball 3rd January 1748. Elected by

ballot 24th December 1748. Satirical poet.
CLARE, Earl of (see NEWCASTLE, 1st Duke of)
CLARENDON, 1st Earl of. Thomas Villiers b 1709 cr 1756 Baron Hyde cr 1776 Earl of Clarendon d 1786. Subscriber to the articles. 2nd s of William 2nd Earl of Jersey by Judith da and h of Frederick Herne of London. Chancellor of the Duchy of Lancaster. M 30 Mar 1752 Charlotte 3rd but 1st surviving da of William Capel 3rd Earl of Essex by his 1st wife Jane da of Henry Hyde 4th and last Earl of Clarendon.
COKE, Thomas, Esq (see LEICESTER, 1st Earl of)
COLVILE, Robert, Esq. Subscriber to the Great Room.
COMPTON, General Hon Charles. 3rd s of James 3rd Earl of Northampton by his 2nd wife Mary da of Baptist Noel 3rd Viscount Campden. Subscriber to the Great Room.
CONOLLY, William Esq d 1754. Subscriber to the articles. Privy councillor.
CONWAY, Lord (see HERTFORD, 1st Marquess of)
COPE, General Sir John, Bt of Hanwell co Oxford b 1674 succ 1721 as 6th Baronet d 1749. Subscriber to the articles. S and h of John 5th Baronet by Anne da of Philip Booth. M 1696 Alice da of Sir Humphrey Monoux 2nd Bart by Alice da of Sir Thomas Cotton 3rd Bart of Connington.
CORBET, Sir William, Bt of Stoke co Salop b 1695 succ 1740 as 5th Baronet d 1748. Subscriber to the articles. S and h of Robert 4th Bart by Jane da of William Hooker s and h of Sir William Hooker Lord Mayor of London. M Harriot sister of William 1st Earl of Chatham da of Robert Pitt of Boconnock Cornwall by Harriet sister of John Villiers Earl of Grandison.
COWPER, 2nd Earl. William Cowper (afterwards Clavering-Cowper) b 1709 styled 1718 Viscount Fordwich succ 1723 as Earl Cowper d 1764. Subscriber to the articles. S and h of William 1st Earl by his 2nd wife Mary da of John Clavering of Chopwell co Durham. M 1stly 27 June 1732 Henrietta yst da of Henry Nassau de Auverquerque Earl of Grantham by Henrietta da of James Butler styled Ossory s and h ap of James 1st Duke of Ormonde. M 2ndly 1 May 1750 Georgina Caroline widow of Hon John Spencer of Wimbledon Surrey da of John Carteret Earl Granville.
CRAWFORD, 20th Earl of. John Lindsay b 1702 succ 1714 as Earl of Crawford d 1749. Elected by ballot 24th February 1745. S and h of John 19th Earl by Emilia widow of Alexander Fraser of Strichen da of James Stewart Master of Moray styled Lord Doune. Lieutenant General. M 3 Mar 1747 Jean 1st da of James Murray 2nd Duke of Atholl by his 1st wife Jean da of Thomas Frederick.
CROWLEY, Ambrose, Esq. Elected by ballot 1st January 1747. Br of Elizabeth Countess of Ashburnham being s of John Crowley Alderman of London by Theodosia da of Rev Joseph Gascoigne DD. Alderman of London.
DALKEITH, Earl of. Francis Scott b 1720 styled 1732 Earl of Dalkeith d vp 1750. Elected by ballot 24th February 1745. S and h ap of Francis 2nd Duke of Buccleuch by Jean 2nd da of James Douglas 2nd Duke of Queensberry and 1st Duke of Dover. M 2 Oct 1742 Caroline 1st da of John Campbell 2nd Duke of Argyll and 1st Duke of Greenwich.
DARCY, Sir Conyers d 1758. Subscriber to the articles. KB. M Aug 1714 Mary widow of 2nd Earl of Essex da of Hans William Bentinck 1st Duke of Portland by his 1st wife Anne da of Sir Edward Villiers.
DAYROLLES, Solomon, Esq. Elected by ballot 24th February 1741. Godson and secretary of Philip Stanhope 4th Earl of Chesterfield. Gentleman of the Privy Chamber to George II. Master of the Revels. Gentleman Usher of the Black Rod.
DELAWARR, 1st Earl. John West b 1693 succ 1723 as 16th Baron Delawarr cr 1761 Earl Delawarr d 1766. Subscriber to the Great Room. S and h of John 15th Baron by Margaret widow of Thomas Salwey da and h of John Freeman Merchant of London. Lieutenant General. Treasurer of the Household. M 1stly 25 May 1721 Charlotte da of Donogh Macarthy 4th Earl of Clancarty by Elizabeth da of Robert Spencer 2nd Earl of Sunderland. M 2ndly 15 June 1744 Anne widow of George Nevill Lord Abergavenny da of Nehamiah Walker 'a sea captain' of co Midx.
DEVONSHIRE, 3rd Duke of. William Cavendish b 1698 styled 1707 Marquess of Hartington succ 1729 as Duke of Devonshire d 1755. Subscriber to the Great Room. S and h of William 2nd Duke by Rachel sister of Wriothesley 2nd Duke of Bedford 1st da of William Russell styled Lord Russell. KG 22 Aug 1733. Lord Steward of the Household. M 27 Mar 1718 Catherine da and h of John Hoskins of Oxted Surrey by Catherine da of William Hale of Kings Walden Herts.
DEVONSHIRE, 4th Duke of. William Cavendish b 1720 styled 1729 Marquess of Hartington succ 1755 as Duke of Devonshire d 1764. Elected by ballot 18th January 1745. 1st s and h of William 3rd Duke by Catherine da and h of John Hoskins of Oxted Surrey by Catherine da of William Hale of Kings Walden Herts. Master of the Horse. First Lord of the Treasury and Prime Minister. KG 29 Mar 1757. Lord Chamberlain of the Household. M 27 Mar 1748 Charlotte Elizabeth suo jure Baroness Clifford only surviving da and h of Richard Boyle Earl of Burlington by Dorothy 1st da of William Savile Marquess of Halifax.
DIEMAR, Lord. Subscriber to the articles.
DOWNE, 3rd Viscount. Henry Pleydell Dawnay b 1727 succ 1741 as Viscount Downe d 1760. Elected by ballot

3rd January 1748. Grandson and h of Henry 2ndd Viscount being s and h of Hon John Dawnay by Charlotte Louisa da and h of Robert Pleydell of Ampney Crucis co Gloucester. Lieutenant Colonel. Mortally wounded at battle of Campden.
DURSLEY, Viscount (see BERKELEY, 4th Earl of)
EDGECUMBE, 1st Baron. Richard Edgecumbe b 1680 cr 1742 Baron Edgecumbe d 1758. Subscriber to the articles. 3rd and yst but eventually only surviving s and h of Sir Richard Edgecumbe of Mount Edgecumbe co Devon by Anne da of Edward Montagu 1st Earl of Sandwich. Chancellor of the Ducay of Lancaster. Major General. M 12 Mar 1715 Matilda da of Sir Henry Furnese 1st Bart of Waldershare co Kent Alderman of London by his 2nd wife Matilda da of Sir Thomas Vernon.
EDGECUMBE, Richard, Esq (see EDGECUMBE, 1st Baron)
EFFINGHAM, 2nd Earl of. Thomas Howard b 1714 styled 1731 Lord Howard succ 1743 as Earl of Effingham d 1763. Elected by ballot 25th December 1743. S and h of Francis 1st Earl by his 1st wife Diana da of Lieutenant General Fergus O'Farrell of Ireland. Lieutenant General. M 14 Feb 1745 Elizabeth sister of William Beckford Lord Mayor of London and da of Peter Beckford of St Catherine's Jamaica by Bathsua da of Colonel Julien Hering.
ELLIOT, Colonel W. Subscriber to the articles.
ELLISON, C, Esq. Subscriber to the articles.
FAUQUIER, William, Esq. Subscriber to the articles.
FEILDING, Hon Charles b 1705. Subscriber to the articles. 2nd s of Basil 3rd Earl of Desmond and 4th Earl of Denbigh by Hester da and h of Sir Basil Firebrace Bart. M 1737 Anne widow of Sir Brock Bridges Bart da of Sir Thomas Palmer Bart of Wingham co Kent.
FETHERSTONHAUGH, Sir Matthew, Bt of Uppark and Ladyholt Harting co Sussex b 1715 cr 1727 Baronet d 1774. Elected by ballot 27th December 1747. 1st s and h ap of Matthew Fetherstonhaugh by da and eventual h of Robert Browne. M 24 Dec 1746 Sarah da of Christopher Lethieullier of Belmont Midx.
FISHER, Brice, Esq b 1708 d 1767. Elected by ballot 24th February 1745. MP for Malmesbury.
FITZROY, Lord Charles b 1718 d 1739. Subscriber to the articles. 4th s of Charles 2nd Duke of Grafton by Henrietta sister of Henry 2nd Duke of Beaufort and yst da of Charles Somerset styled Marquess of Worcester.
FITZROY, Colonel Charles. Elected by ballot 9th February 1747.
FITZWILLIAM, Hon William b 1712. Elected by ballot 17th November 1738. 2nd s of Richard 5th Viscount FitzWilliam of Merrion by Frances da of Sir John Shelley Bart of Michael Grove co Sussex. Usher of the Black Rod. M da of Thomas Bourchier Esq.
FITZWILLIAM, General Hon John b 1714. Subscriber to the articles. 3rd s of Richard 5th Viscount FitzWilliam of Merrion by Frances da of Sir John Shelley Bart of Michael Grove co Sussex. M Oct 1751 Barbara da of Dr Chandler Bishop of Durham.
FORRESTER, 5th Baron. George Forrester b 1688 succ 1705 as Lord Forrester d 1727 Likely subscriber to the Great Room. 2nd but 1st surviving s and h of William Baillie afterwards Forrester 4th Baron by Margaret da of Sir Andrew Birnie of Saline. M 1727 Charlotte da of Anthony Rowe of Oxfordshire.
FOX, Stephen, Esq (see ILCHESTER, 1st Earl of)
GAGE, Sir William Bt of Firle co Sussex b 1695 succ 1713 as 7th Baronet d 1744. Subscriber to the Great Room. Br and h of Thomas 6th Bart being 3rd s of John 4th Bart by his 2nd wife Mary da of Sir William Stanley 1st Bart of Hooton Cheshire.
GODOLPHIN, 2nd Earl of. Francis Godolphin b 1678 styled 1706 Viscount Rialton succ 1712 as Earl of Godolphin d 1766. Subscriber to the Great Room. S and h of Sidney 1st Earl by Margaret 4th da of Colonel Thomas Blagge of Holmingsheath Suffolk. M 23 Apr 1698 Henrietta Churchill afterwards suo jure Duchess of Marlborough 1st da and coh of John Churchill 1st Duke of Marlborough by Sarah 2nd da of Richard Jennings of Sandridge Herts. Groom of the Stole. Lord Privy Seal.
GRAFTON, 2nd Duke of. Charles Fitzroy b 1683 styled Earl of Euston succ 1690 as Duke of Grafton d 1757. Subscriber to the Great Room. S and h of Henry 1st Duke by Isabella da of Henry Bennet 1st Earl of Arlington. KG 25 Apr 1721. M 30 Apr 1713 Henrietta sister of Henry 2nd Duke of Beaufort and yst da of Charles Somerset styled Marquess of Worcester by Rebecca da of Sir Joshua Child.
GRANBY, Marquess of. John Manners b 1721 styled Marquess of Granby d vp 1770. Elected by ballot 10th December 1746. 1st s and h ap of John 3rd Duke of Rutland by Bridget yr da of Robert Sutton 2nd Baron Lexington of Aram. Lieutenant General. Master General of the Ordnance. Commander in chief of land forces in Great Britain. M 3 Sep 1750 Frances 4th da of Charles Seymour 6th Duke of Somerset by his 2nd wife Charlotte 3rd da of Daniel Finch 7th Earl of Winchilsea and 2nd Earl of Nottingham.
GREY, 3rd Baron (see TANKERVILLE, 1st Earl of)
GULDEFORD, Sir Robert, Bt of Hempstead Place Benenden co Kent b 1660 cr 1686 Baronet d 1740. Subscriber to the articles. S and h of Edward Guldeford by Anne da of Sir Robert Throckmorton 1st Bart of Coughton. M

1695 Clara da of Anthony Monson of Northorpe co Lincoln by Dorothy neé Withering.
HALIFAX, 1st Earl of. George Montagu b 1685 succ 1715 as 2nd Baron Halifax cr 1715 Earl of Halifax d 1739. Subscriber to the Great Room. Nephew and h of 1st Baron Charles Montagu Earl of Halifax being s and h of Edward elder br of 1st Baron by Elizabeth da of Sir John Pelham Bart. M 1stly 8 Apr 1706 Ricarda Posthuma da and h of Richard Saltonstall of Chipping Warden Northants by Silence da of John Parker of Catesby. M 2ndly Mary 1st da of Richard Lumley 1st Earl of Scarbrough by Frances da and h of Sir Henry Jones.
HARCOURT, 1st Earl. Simon Harcourt b 1714 succ 1727 as 2nd Viscount cr 1749 Earl Harcourt d 1777. Subscriber to the articles. Grandson and h of Simon 1st Viscount being s and h of Simon 2nd but only surviving s and h ap by Elizabeth da of John Evelyn of Wotton Surrey. Lieutenant General. Ambassador to Paris. Viceroy of Ireland. M 16 Oct 1735 Rebecca da of Charles Samborne Le Bas of Pipewell Abbey Northants by Mary da of Sir Samuel Moyer Bart.
HARDENBERG, Baron. Elected by ballot 24th February 1745.
HARTINGTON, Marquess of (see DEVONSHIRE, 4th Duke of)
HAWLEY, General Henry of West Green Hartley Wintney co Southampton b 1679 d 1759. Subscriber to the articles.
HERBERT, Henry Esq (see POWIS, Earl of)
HERBERT, Lord, of Chirbury (see POWIS, Earl of)
HERNE, Rev A. Subscriber to the articles. Chaplain to the Charlton Hunt.
HERTFORD, 1st Marquess of. Francis Seymour-Conway b 1718 succ 1732 as 2nd Baron Conway cr 1750 Earl of Hertford cr 1793 Marquess of Hertford d 1794. Elected by ballot 7th December 1739. S and h of Francis Seymour Conway 1st Baron Conway by his 3rd wife Charlotte da of John Shorter of Bybrook Kent. KG 29 Mar 1757. Ambassador to Paris. Viceroy of Ireland. Master of the Horse. Lord Chamberlain of the Household. M 29 May 1741 Isabella 4th and yst da of Charles Fitzroy 2nd Duke of Grafton by Henrietta da of Charles Somerset styled Marquess of Worcester.
HOLDERNESSE, 6th Earl of. Robert Darcy b 1718 styled Lord Darcy and Conyers succ 1722 as Earl of Holdernesse d 1778. Elected by ballot 5th January 1743. 2nd but only surviving s and h of Robert 5th Earl by Fredericka suo jure Countess of Mertola da and h of Meinhardt Schomberg 3rd Duke of Schomberg. Secretary of State. M 29 Oct 1743 Mary da of Francis Doublet of Groeneveldt by Constantia Van-der-Beek.
HOME, 8th Earl of. William Home b 1715 styled Lord Dunglas succ 1720 as Earl of Home d 1761. Elected by ballot 25th December 1743. 2nd but 1st surviving s and h of Alexander 7th Earl by Anne 2nd da of William Kerr 2nd Marquess of Midlothian. Lieutenant General. Governor of Gibraltar. M 25 Dec 1742 Elizabeth widow of James Lawes and da of William Gibbons of Vere Jamaica.
HONYWOOD, General Philip. b 1710 d 1785. Subscriber to the articles.
HONYWOOD, General Sir Phillip d 1752. Subscriber to the Great Room.
HONYWOOD, Richard, Esq. Subscriber to the articles.
HOWARD, General Hon Charles b 1696 d 1765. Subscriber to the articles. 2nd s of Charles 3rd Earl of Carlisle by Anne da of Arthur Capell 1st Earl of Essex.
HOWE, 3rd Viscount. George Augustus Howe b 1724 succ 1735 as Viscount Howe d 1758. Elected by ballot 24th December 1748. 2nd but 1st surviving s and h of Emanuel Scrope 2nd Viscount by Mary Sophia Charlotte 1st da of Charlotte Sophia suo jure Countess of Darlington wife of John Adolph Baron von Kielmansegge. Brigadier General. Slain in a skirmish with the French.
HUSKE, General John b 1692 d 1761. Subscriber to the articles.
ILCHESTER, 1st Earl of. Stephen Fox (later Fox-Strangways) b 1704 cr 1741 Lord Ilchester cr 1756 Earl of Ilchester d 1776. Subscriber to the articles. 8th but 1st surviving s and h of Rt Hon Sir Stephen Fox of Farley Wilts by his 2nd wife Christian da of Rev Francis Hopes Rector of Habeby and of Aswarby co Lincoln. M Elizabeth da of Thomas Strangways-Horner of Mells Park Somerset by Susanna da of Thomas Strangways of Melbury Sampford Dorset.
IREMONGER, Josiah, Esq. Elected by ballot 10th December 1746. 2nd s of Joshua Iremonger brewer in the city of London by Sarah da of Edward Lascelles.
JENISON, Ralph, Esq. Subscriber to the articles. Knight of the Shire for Northumberland. Master of the Buckhounds to George II.
KEPPEL, General Hon William b 1727 d 1782. Elected by ballot 2nd January 1750. 3rd s of William Anne 2nd Earl of Albermarle by Anne 2nd da of Charles Lennox 1st Duke of Richmond. Commander-in-Chief in Ireland.
KEPPEL, Hon Augustus (see KEPPEL, Viscount)
KEPPEL, Viscount. Augustus Keppel b 1725 cr 1782 Viscount Keppel d 1786. Elected by ballot 24th December 1748. 2nd s of William Anne 2nd Earl of Albermarle by Anne da of Charles Lennox 1st Duke of Richmond. Admiral of the White. First Lord of the Admiralty. Master of Trinity House.
KILDARE, Earl of (see LEINSTER, Duke of)

Members of the Charlton Hunt

KINGSTON, 2nd Duke of. Evelyn Pierrepont b 1711 styled Viscount Newark styled 1713 Earl of Kingston styled 1715 Marquess of Dorchester succ 1726 as Duke of Kingston d 1773. Elected by ballot 8th November 1738. Grandson and h being s and h of William Pierrepont styled Earl of Kingston s and h ap of 1st Duke Evelyn by his 1st wife Mary da of William Feilding 3rd Earl of Denbigh. Master of the Staghounds North of Trent. KG 21 Apr 1741. General in the army. M Elizabeth da of Colonel Thomas Chudleigh Lieutenant Governor of Chelsea Hospital Midx by Henrietta his wife.

KIRKE, General P. Subscriber to the articles.

LEGGE, Hon Edward b 1712. Subscriber to the articles. Yr s of William Legge 1st Earl of Dartmouth by Anne da of Heneage Finch 1st Earl of Aylesford.

LEGGE, Hon Henry b 1708 d 1764. Elected by ballot 23rd December 1742. 4th s of William Legge 1st Earl of Dartmouth by Anne da of Heneage Finch 1st Earl of Aylesford. Chancellor of the Exchequer. M 21 Sep 1750 Mary da and h of Edward Stawell 4th Baron Stawell of Somerton.

LEICESTER, 1st Earl of. Thomas Coke b 1697 cr 1728 Baron Lovel cr 1744 Earl of Leicester d 1759. Subscriber to the Great Room. S and h of Edward Coke of Holkham Norfolk by Carey da of Sir John Newton 3rd Bart of Barrs Court. M 3 July 1718 Margaret 3rd da of Thomas Tufton 6th Earl of Thanet by Catherine suo jure Baroness Clifford da of Henry Cavendish Duke of Newcastle.

LEINSTER, 1st Duke of. James Fitzgerald b 1722 styled Lord Offaly succ 1744 as 20th Earl of Kildare cr 1761 Marquess of Kildare cr 1766 Duke of Leinster d 1773. Elected by ballot 1st January 1747. 3rd but 1st surviving s and h of Robert Earl of Kildare by Mary 1st da of William O'Brien 3rd Earl of Inchiquin. Lieutenant General. M 7 Feb 1747 Emilia Mary 2nd surviving da of Charles Lennox 2nd Duke of Richmond by Sarah da of William Cadogan 1st Earl Cadogan.

LICHFIELD, 2nd Earl of. George Henry Lee b 1690 styled 1713 Viscount Quarendon succ 1716 as Earl of Lichfield d 1743. Subscriber to the Great Room. 6th but 1st surviving s and h of Edward Henry 1st Earl by Charlotte da of Charles II by Barbara suo jure Duchess of Cleveland. M 1718 Frances da of Sir John Hales 4th Bart of Hackington Kent and titular Earl of Tenterden by his 1st wife Helen Mary Catherine da of Sir Richard Bealing afterwards Arundell.

LIDDELL, Sir Harry Bt (see RAVENSWORTH, 1st Baron)

LIFFORD, Earl of. Frederic William de Roye de la Rochefoucauld styled Count de Champagne-Mouton afterwards Count de Marthon b 1666 cr 1699 Earl of Lifford d 1749. Subscriber to the articles. 4th s of Frederic Charles de Roye de la Rochefoucauld Count de Roye by Julienne Catherine de la Tour da of Henry Duc de Bouillon.

LINCOLN, Earl of (see NEWCASTLE, 2nd Duke of)

LONSDALE, 3rd Viscount. Henry Lowther b 1694 succ 1713 as Viscount Lonsdale d 1750. Subscriber to the Great Room. Br and h of 2nd Viscount being 2nd s of John 1st Viscount by Katherine yr da of Sir Henry Frederick Thynne 1st Bart of Kempsford. Constable of the Tower of London. Lord Privy Seal.

LOUDOUN, 4th Earl of. John Campbell b 1705 styled Lord Mauchline succ 1731 as Earl of Loudoun d 1782. Elected by ballot 18th January 1745. S and h of Hugh 3rd Earl by Margaret 3rd da of John Dalrymple 1st Earl of Stair. General in the army.

LOVEL, Lord (see LEICESTER, 1st Earl of)

LOWTHER, Hon Anthony b 1698 d 1741. Subscriber to the Great Room. Yst s of John 1st Viscount Lonsdale by Katherine yr da of Sir Henry Frederick Thynne 1st Bart of Kempsford.

LUCHESI, Count. Elected by ballot 2nd January 1750. Lieutenant General.

LUMLEY, Hon John. Subscriber to the articles. 2nd but 1st surviving s and h of Richard 1st Earl by Frances da and h of Sir Henry Jones of Aston co Oxford.

MANNERS, Lord Robert. b 1722 d 1762. Elected by ballot 9th February 1747. 2nd s of John 3rd Duke of Rutland by Bridget da and h of 2nd Baron Lexinton of Aram.

MARCH, Earl of (see RICHMOND, 2nd and 3rd Dukes of)

MARLBOROUGH, 3rd Duke of. Charles Spencer b 1706 succ 1729 as 5th Earl of Sunderland succ 1733 as Duke of Marlborough d 1758. Subscriber to the articles. Nephew of Henrietta suo jure Duchess of Marlborough being 3rd but 1st surviving s and h of Charles Spencer 3rd Earl of Sunderland by his 2nd wife Anne 2nd da of John Churchill 1st Duke of Marlborough. KG 21 Apr 1741. Lord Steward of the Household. Lord Privy Seal. Master General of the Ordnance. M 23 May 1732 Elizabeth da and h of Thomas Trevor 2nd Baron Trevor of Bromham by Elizabeth da of Timothy Burrell of Cuckfield Sussex.

MARPON, M de. Subscriber to the articles.

MEADOWS, Philip, Esq. Subscriber to the articles.

MEGGOTT, Richard, Esq. Elected by ballot 8th January 1739.

MIDDLETON, Sir William, Bt of Belsay Castle co Northumberland b 1700 succ 1717 as 3rd Baronet d 1757. Subscriber to the articles. S and h of John 2nd Bart by Frances da and h of John Lambert of Carlton in Craven co York. M Anne da of William Ettricke of Silksworth co Durham by Elizabeth da of George Middleton of Silksworth afsd.

MILL, Sir Richard, Bt of Woolbeding co Sussex b 1690 succ 1706 as 5th Baronet d 1760. Subscriber to the articles. Br and h of John 4th Bart being yr s of John 3rd Bart by Margaret da and h of Thomas Grey of Woolbeding Sussex. MP for Midhurst. M 12 Mar 1712 Margaret 1st da of Robert Knollys of Grove Place Nutshelling Hants.

MILLER, Sir John, Bt of West Lavant co Sussex b 1712 succ 1733 as 4th Baronet d 1772. Subscriber to the articles. S and h of Thomas 3rd Bart by Jane da of Francis Gother. Mayor of Chichester. M 1735 Susan da of Matthew Combe MD of Winchester.

MONK, Laurence, Esq. Subscriber to the articles.

MONMOUTH, Duke of. James Fitzroy later Crofts then Scott b 1649 cr 1662 Duke of Monmouth cr 1663 Duke of Buccleuch d 1685. Proprietor of Charlton hounds 1675 to 1683. S of Charles II by Lucy da of William Walter of Roche Castle co Pembroke by Elizabeth da of John Protheroe of Hawksbrook co Carmarthen. M 20 Apr 1663 Anne suo jure Countess of Buccleuch da of Francis 2nd Earl of Buccleuch. KG 22 April 1663.

MONTAGU, 1st Duke of. George Brudenell afterwards Montagu b 1712 styled Lord Brudenell succ 1732 as 4th Earl of Cardigan cr 1766 Duke of Montagu d 1790. Subscriber to the articles. S and h of George 3rd Earl of Cardigan by Elizabeth da of Thomas Bruce 2nd Earl of Ailesbury. M 7 July 1730 Mary da of John Montagu 2nd Duke of Montagu by Mary da of John Churchill 1st Duke of Marlborough. KG 4 June 1752. Master of the Horse. Master of Confederate hunt in Leicestershire.

MONTROSE, 1st Duke of. James Graham b 1682 styled Earl of Kincardine succ 1684 as 4th Marquess of Montrose cr 1707 Duke of Montrose d 1742. Subscriber to the articles. S and h of James 3rd Marquess of Montrose by Christian 2nd da of John Leslie Duke of Rothes by Anne da of John Lindsay 19th Earl of Crawford and Lindsay. M Christian 2nd da of David Carnegie 3rd Earl of Northesk by Elizabeth da of John Lindsay Earl of Crawford and Lindsay.

MORDAUNT, Hon John b 1715 d 1767. Subscriber to the articles. 2nd s of John styled Lord Mordaunt s and h ap of Charles 3rd Earl of Peterborough by Frances da of Charles Powlett 2nd Duke of Bolton. M 1stly 1735 Mary da of Scrope 1st Viscount Howe by his 2nd wife Juliana da of William Alington 3rd Baron Alington of Killard and widow of Thomas Herbert 8th Earl of Pembroke. M 2ndly Elizabeth da of Samuel Hamilton Esq.

NASSAU, Count Maurice of. Subscriber to the Great Room. Relation of Princes of Orange.

NEWBY Charles, Esq. Subscriber to the articles.

NEWCASTLE, 1st Duke of. Thomas Pelham-Holles formerly Pelham b 1693 succ 1712 as 2nd Baron Pelham cr 1714 Earl of Clare cr 1715 Duke of Newcastle-upon-Tyne cr 1756 Duke of Newcastle-under-Lyne d 1768. Subscriber to the Great Room. S and h of Thomas Pelham 1st Baron Pelham of Laughton by his 2nd wife Grace sister of John Holles Duke of Newcastle-upon-Tyne 4th and yst da of Gilbert Holles 3rd Earl of Clare. M 2 Apr 1717 Henrietta 1st da of Francis 2nd Earl of Godolphin by Henrietta suo jure Duchess of Marlborough 1st da and coh of John Churchill 1st Duke of Marlborough by Sarah 2nd da of Richard Jennings of Sandridge Herts. KG 30 Apr 1718. Secretary of State. First Lord of the Treasury.

NEWCASTLE, 2nd Duke of. Henry Fiennes Clinton afterwards Pelham-Clinton b 1720 styled 1728 Lord Clinton succ 1730 as 9th Earl of Lincoln succ 1768 as Duke of Newcastle-under-Lyne d 1794. Elected by ballot 23rd December 1742. 2nd s of Henry 7th Earl of Lincoln by Lucy sister of Thomas Pelham Holles formerly Pelham Duke of Newcastle-upon-Tyne and Duke of Newcastle-under-Lyne and da of Thomas Pelham 1st Baron Pelham of Laughton. Cofferer of the Household. KG 4 June 1752. M 16 Oct 1744 Catherine 1st surviving da of Hon Henry Pelham by Catherine 1st da of John Manners 2nd Duke of Rutland.

NOEL, Lieutenant Colonel. Elected by ballot 10th December 1746.

NORRIS, Captain H. Elected by ballot: 2nd January 1750.

O'BRIEN, Percy Wyndham Esq (see THOMOND, Earl of)

OFFLEY, Mr. Elected by ballot 25th February 1750.

ORME Garton Esq, of Woolavington b 1696 d 1758. Proprietor of Charlton hounds with Duke of Richmond and Earl of Tankerville 1730. Subscriber to the articles. S of Robert Orme of Woolavington by Dorothea da of John Dawnay 1st Viscount Downe. M 1717 Charlotte eldest da of Jonas Hanway of Hatton garden St Andrew Holborn co Midx. M 2ndly a da of Rev Daniel Lafitte of Bordeaux Vicar of Woolavington.

OSSORIO, M le Chevalier. Subscriber to the articles.

OSSULSTONE, Lord (see TANKERVILLE, 3rd Earl of)

PAUNCEFORT, Edward, Esq of Earley Court and Witham-on-the-Hill. Subscriber to the articles.

PEACHEY, Sir James, Bt (see SELSEY, 1st Baron)

PEACHEY, Sir John, Bt of West Dean co Sussex b 1720 succ 1744 as 3rd Baronet d 1765. Elected by ballot 3rd March 1745. 1st s and h of John 2nd Bart by his 2nd wife Henrietta da of George London. MP for Midhurst. M 18 Aug 1752 Elizabeth da and h of John Meeres Fagg of Glinly by Alice da of Thomas Woodyer.

PELHAM, 2nd Baron, of Laughton (see NEWCASTLE, 1st Duke of)

PELHAM, Hon Henry b 1695 d 1754. Subscriber to the Great Room. 2nd s of Thomas Pelham 1st Baron Pelham of Laughton by his 2nd wife Grace sister of John Holles Duke of Newcastle-upon-Tyne and da of Gilbert Holles

3rd Earl of Clare. M 29 Oct 1726 Katherine da of John Manners 2nd Duke of Rutland by Catherine sister of Wriothesley 2nd Duke of Bedford and da of William Russell styled Lord Russell. First Lord of the Treasury. Chancellor of the Exchequer.
PERRY, Colonel Charles. Subscriber to the articles.
PHIPPS, Edward, Esq. Elected by ballot 18th January 1745.
POWIS, 1st Earl of. Henry Arthur Herbert b 1703 cr 1743 Baron Herbert of Chi#rbury cr 1748 Earl of Powis d 1772. Subscriber to the articles. S and h of Francis Herbert of Oakley Park co Montgomery by Dorothy da of John Oldbury of London merchant. General in the army. Treasurer of the Household. M 30 Mar 1751 Barbara posthumous da and h of Lord Edward Herbert br of William Marquess of Powis by Henrietta da of James Waldegrave 1st Earl Waldegrave.
POWLETT, Lord Nassau b 1698 d 1741. Subscriber to the articles. S of Charles 2nd Duke of Bolton by his 3rd wife Henrietta Crofts da of James Duke of Monmouth. M Isabella da of Thomas 6th Earl of Thanet by Catherine 4th da of Henry Cavendish 2nd Duke of Newcastle-upon-Tyne.
PRENDERGAST, Sir Thomas, Bt of Gort co Galway b 1700 succ 1709 as 2nd Baronet d 1760. Subscriber to the articles. S and h of Thomas 1st Bart by Penelope sister of William Cadogan 1st Earl Cadogan da of Henry Cadogan of Liscartan co Meath. MP for Chichester. M 1739 Anne da and h of Sir Roger Williams of Marle co Carnarvon.
RAVENSWORTH, 1st Baron. Henry Liddell b 1708 succ 1723 as 4th Baronet cr 1747 Lord Ravensworth d 1784. Subscriber to the articles. S and h of Sir Thomas Liddell by Jane da of Thomas Clavering of Greencroft co Durham. M 27 Apr 1735 Anne da of Sir Peter Delmé Lord Mayor of London by his 1st wife Anne da of Cornelius Macham of Southampton.
RICHMOND, 1st Duke of. Charles Lennox b 1672 cr 1675 Duke of Richmond d 1723. Likely subscriber to the Great Room. S of Charles II by Louise Renée de Penancoët de Kéroualle spinster suo jure Duchess of Portsmouth. M 8 Jan 1693 Anne widow of Henry 2nd Baron Belasyse da of Francis Brudenell styled Lord Brudenell s and h ap of Robert 2nd Earl of Cardigan by Frances da of James Savile Earl of Sussex KG 20 Apr 1681.
RICHMOND, 2nd Duke of. Charles Lennox b 1701 styled Earl of March succ 1723 as Duke of Richmond succ 1734 as Duke of Aubigny d 1750. Proprietor of Charlton hounds with Earl of Tankerville 1729 with Earl of Tankerville and Garton Orme Esq 1730 sole proprietor 1731 till his death. S and h of Charles 1st Duke by Anne widow of Henry 2nd Baron Belasyse da of Francis Brudenell styled Lord Brudenell s and h ap of Robert 2nd Earl of Cardigan by Frances da of James Savile Earl of Sussex. M 4 Dec 1719 Sarah 1st da of William Cadogan 1st Earl of Cadogan by Margaretta Cecilia da of John Munter of Holland. KG 16 June 1726. Master of the Horse.
RICHMOND, 3rd Duke of. Charles Lennox b 1735 styled Earl of March succ 1750 as Duke of Richmond d 1806. Proprietor of Charlton hounds 1756 till his death. 3rd but 1st surviving s and h of Charles 2nd Duke by Sarah 1st da of William Cadogan 1st Earl of Cadogan by Margaretta Cecilia da of John Munter of Holland. M 1 Apr 1757 Mary 3rd and yst da of Charles Bruce 3rd Earl of Ailesbury by his 3rd wife Caroline da of John Campbell 4th Duke of Argyll. KG 19 Apr 1792. Master General of the Ordnance.
ROCKINGHAM, 3rd Earl of. Thomas Watson b 1715 succ 1745 as Earl of Rockingham d 1746. Elected by ballot 8th November 1738. Br and h of Lewis 2nd Earl being 2nd s of Edward styled Viscount Sondes 1st s and h ap of Lewis 1st Earl by Catherine 4th da of Thomas Tufton 6th Earl of Thanet.
ROPER, Hon Charles. Elected by ballot 7th December 1739.
ROPER Mr, of Eltham Kent b 1639 d 1723. Huntsman of Charlton hounds from 1675 till his death. M 2nd da of James Butler of Amberley MP for Arundel.
ROTHES, 10th Earl of. John Leslie b 1698 styled 1700 Lord Leslie succ 1722 as Earl of Rothes d 1767. Subscriber to the articles. S and h of John Leslie formerly Hamilton 9th Earl by Jean 2nd da of John Hay 2nd Marquess of Tweeddale. General in the army. M 1stly 25 May 1741 Hannah da of Matthew Howard of Thorpe Norfolk and Hackney Midx by Britannia da of Thomas Cole. M 2ndly 27 June 1763 Mary da of Gresham Lloyd by Mary da of Rowland Holt of Redgrave Suffolk.
RUDDEYARD, Capt. Elected by ballot 23rd December 1742.
SAINT ALBANS, 2nd Duke of. Charles Beauclerk b 1696 styled Earl of Burford succ 1726 as Duke of Saint Albans d 1751. Subscriber to the articles. S and h of Charles Beauclerk 1st Duke by Diana 2nd da of Aubrey de Vere 20th Earl of Oxford. M 13 Dec 1722 Charlotte 2nd da of Sir John Werden Bart of Holyport co Berkshire by his 1st wife Elizabeth da of Robert Breton of Norton co Northampton.
SCARBROUGH, 2nd Earl of. Richard Lumley b 1688 styled 1710 Viscount Lumley succ 1721 as Earl of Scarbrough d 1739. Subscriber to the articles. 2nd but 1st surviving s and h of Richard 1st Earl by Frances da and h of Sir Henry Jones of Aston co Oxford. Lieutenant General. Master of the Horse.
SEBRIGHT, Capt. Elected by ballot 25th February 1750.
SEBRIGHT, Sir Thomas, Bt of Beechwood in Flamsted co Herts b 1723 succ 1736 as 5th Baronet d 1761. Elected by ballot 25th February 1750. S and h of Thomas Saunders 4th Bart by Henrietta da of Sir Thomas Dashwood

sometime Lord Mayor of London by Anne da of John Smith of Tedworth Hants.
SEDGWICK, Edward, Esq. Elected by ballot 24th February 1745. Secretary to the Charlton Hunt.
SELSEY, 1st Baron. James Peachey b 1723 succ 1765 as 4th Baronet of West Dean co Sussex cr 1794 Baron Selsey d 1808. Elected by ballot 10th December 1746. Br and h of John 3rd Bart being yr s of John 2nd Bart by his 2nd wife Henrietta da of George London. Master of the Robes. M 19 Aug 1747 Georgina Caroline 1st da of Henry Scott 1st Earl of Deloraine by his 2nd wife Mary da of Charles Howard.
SHIRLEY, Hon George b 1705 d 1787. Subscriber to the articles. 5th s of Sir Robert Shirley 1st Earl Ferrers by Elizabeth da and h of Laurence Washington of Garsden Wilts. M 28 Dec 1749 Mary da of Humphrey Sturt.
SMYTH, Sir Robert, Bt of Isfield co Sussex b 1709 succ 1717 as 2nd Baronet d 1783. Elected by ballot 24th February 1741. S and h of James 1st Bart by Mirabella da of Sir Robert Legard. M 23 Sep 1731 Louisa Caroline Isabella yst da of John Hervey 1st Earl of Bristol by his 2nd wife Elizabeth da and h of Sir Thomas Felton.
SPENCER, Hon John of Althorp co Northampton b 1708 d 1746. Subscriber to the articles. Yst s of Charles Spencer 3rd Earl of Sunderland by his 2nd wife Anne 2nd da of John Churchill 1st Duke of Marlborough. M 14 Feb 1734 Georgina Carolina 3rd da of John Carteret Earl Granville.
ST PAUL, William Frederick, Esq. Stud groom to 2nd Duke of Richmond. Subscriber to the articles.
STAFFORD, 1st Marquess of. Granville Leveson-Gower b 1721 styled 1746 Viscount Trentham succ 1754 as 2nd Earl Gower cr 1786 Marquess of Stafford d 1803. Elected by ballot 27th December 1747. 3rd but 1st surviving s and h of John 1st Earl Gower by his 1st wife Evelyn da of Evelyn Pierrepont 1st Duke of Kingston upon Hull. Lord Privy Seal. Master of the Horse. Master of the Great Wardrobe. Lord Chamberlain of the Household. Lord President of the Council. KG 25 July 1771. M 1stly 23 Dec 1744 Elizabeth da of Nicholas Fazakerly of Penwortham co Lancaster by his wife Ann Lutwyche. M 2ndly 28 Mar 1748 Louisa da of Scrope Egerton 1st Duke of Bridgewater by his 2nd wife Rachel da of Wriothesley Russell 2nd Duke of Bedford. M 3rdly 26 May 1768 3rd da of Alexander Stewart 6th Earl of Galloway by his 2nd wife Catherine da of John Cochrane 4th Earl of Dundonald.
STRICKLAND, Thomas, Esq. Subscriber to the articles.
SUSSEX, 2nd Earl of. George Augustus Yelverton b 1727 styled Viscount de Longueville succ 1731 as Earl of Sussex d 1758. Elected by ballot 2nd January 1750. 1st s and h of Talbot 1st Earl by Lucy 4th surviving da of Henry Pelham of Lewes Sussex.
TANKERVILLE, 1st Earl of. Ford Grey b 1655 succ 1674 as 3rd Baron Grey of Warke cr 1695 Earl of Tankerville d 1701. Proprietor of hounds at Charlton 1675 to 1683. S and h of Ralph 2nd Baron Grey by Catherine widow of Hon Alexander Colepeper and only surviving da and h of Sir Edward Ford of Uppark co Sussex. M Mary da of George Berkeley 1st Earl of Berkeley. First Lord of Treasury. Lord Privy Seal.
TANKERVILLE, 2nd Earl of. Charles Bennet b 1697 styled 1714 Lord Ossulstone succ 1722 as Earl of Tankerville d 1753. Proprietor of Charlton hounds with Duke of Richmond 1729 and with Duke of Richmond and Garton Orme Esq 1730. Subscriber to the articles. S and h of Charles 1st Earl by Mary da of Ford Grey Earl of Tankerville. M 1715 Camilla 6th da of Edward Colville butcher and grazier of Whitehouse co Durham by his 2nd wife Sarah. Master of the Buckhounds to George II.
TANKERVILLE, 3rd Earl of. Charles Bennet b 1716 styled 1722 Lord Ossulstone succ 1753 as Earl of Tankerville d 1767. Subscriber to the articles. S and h of Charles 2nd Earl by Camilla 6th da of Edward Colville butcher and grazier of Whitehouse co Durham. M 22 Sep 1742 Alicia da of Sir John Astley 2nd Bart of Patshull co Stafford by Mary da and h of Frances Prynce of Abbey Foregate Shrewsbury.
THOMOND, Earl of. Percy Wyndham O'Brien b 1723 cr 1756 Earl of Thomond d 1774. Elected by ballot 4th January 1747. 2nd s of Sir William Wyndham 3rd Bart by his 1st wife Katherine da of Charles Seymour 6th Duke of Somerset. Cofferer of the Household.
TOWNSHEND, Admiral Isack. Elected by ballot 18th January 1745. Rear Admiral of the Red.
TRENTHAM, Viscount (see STAFFORD, 1st Marquess of)
VANE, Henry, Esq Jr. Elected by ballot 1st January 1747.
VAREY, William, Esq. Elected by ballot 1st January 1747.
VILLIERS, Hon Thomas (see CLARENDON, 1st Earl of)
WALDEGRAVE, Hon John b 1718. Elected by ballot 10th December 1746. yr s of James 1st Earl Waldegrave by Mary 2nd da of Sir John Webbe 3rd Bart of Hatherop co Gloucester. Colonel in the army.
WATSON, Hon Thomas (see ROCKINGHAM, 3rd Earl of)
WEST, Hon John b 1721. Subscriber to the articles. S and h of John 1st Earl Delawarr by Charlotte da of Donogh Macarthy 4th Earl of Clancarty by Elizabeth da of Robert Spencer 2nd Earl of Sunderland.
WHITWORTH, Colonel Richard. Subscriber to the articles.
WILLS, General Sir Charles b 1666 d 1741. Subscriber to the Great Room.
WINCHESTER, Marquess of (see BOLTON, 3rd Duke of).

Appendix 3

Pedigree of Charlton Hounds

There were early hound lists at Charlton which unfortunately have been lost and the existing records start at the beginning of the Duke of Bolton's mastership. In this edited list, hound names appear once only in the year in which they were taken to Charlton or entered to hunt with the pack and where known, the date and reason for their disposal is also recorded. The exception is in 1731, when the Duke of Richmond became sole proprietor and a full list is included. In the original hound books, there are full lists of all the hounds in the kennel each year, except for 1721 to 1730 and 1732 to 1734. After the death of the Duke of Richmond in 1750, the pack was dispersed and the list resumes in 1757 when his son acquired new hounds to reform the pack, which included several of the old blood lines. The hounds were moved from Charlton to new kennels at Goodwood in 1790. The last list is in 1798, although the pack remained at Goodwood until 1813, when it was presented to the Prince Regent. The last remaining hounds were destroyed after an epidemic of rabies in 1821. Inevitably there are inconsistencies in the manuscript and the most likely version has been adopted. Hounds marked with + were present at the death of the bitch fox at the end of the Grand Chase of 1739.

Old Hounds - 25th November 1721 Mr Roper and the Duke of Bolton
Bell, Betty, Bluecap, Bluemaid, Curious, Diamond, Dolly, lame Dolly, Doxy, Fairmaid, Famous, Fleury, Folly, Fortune, Jolly, Lovely, Madam, Merrylass, Nancy, Phillis, Pleasant, Rockwood, Ruby, Spanker, Stately, Sweetlips, Virgin
By Sir W Goring's Emperor out of Mr Roper's Doxy: Promise
From Lord Carlisle: Ransom, Rowsey

Young Hounds - 9th December 1722 Mr Roper and the Duke of Bolton
By Mr Roper's Tipler out of Doxy'21: Favourite, Merrylass (given to Mr Bridges), Mode, Shifter
By Mr Roper's Dinger out of Fortune'21: Clouder, Conqueror, Countess, Madcap, Wanton
By Mr Roper's Jockey out of Diamond'21: Blossom, Careless, Younker
By Mr Roper's Jockey out of Promise'21: Dashwood, Lady, Singwell
From Mr Newby: Virgin
From Mr Draper: Pallas
By Mr Roper's Jockey out of Folly'21: Cryer, Folly
By Mr Roper's Tipler out of his Fury: Fury, Lofty
By Mr Roper's Jockey out of his blind Betty: Pallas
By Mr Roper's Gamboy out of Nancy'21: Ratler
By Mr Roper's Jugler out of Dolly'21: Thunder
By Mr Roper's Tipler out of Lovely'21: Capper

Young Hounds - 5th January 1723 Duke of Bolton
By Mr Roper's Dinger out of Doxy'21: Gillian, Honey, Trimmer
By Mr Roper's Tipler out of Diamond'21: Julie, Mira, Molsey, Spanker (prov'd very good, what was bred from him, given to Mr Bright 19th September 1723), Tipler, Wildman
By Mr Orlebar's Shifter out of Promise'21: Duchess, Emperor, Fubbs, Fury, Maiden, Sweetlips
By Rockwood'21 out of Mr Roper's Friendly: Flower
By Mr Roper's Emperor out of Pleasant'21: Collier, Comely, Lovesey, Sempstress

By Mr Roper's Emperor out of his Honey: Charmer, Cupid, Emperor, Toler
By Rockwood'21 out of lame Dolly'21: Snowball, Traveller
By Mr Roper's Ringwood out of Gillian'21: Gipsy, Virgin
By Mr Roper's Climbank out of Betty'21: Fanny
By Spanker'21 out of Bell'21: Ranter
From Mr Odes: Peggy

Duke of Bolton
From Mr Bright: Tuner, Dido
From Lord Burlington: Bowman, Captain, Cocker, Dido, Lemmon
From Mr May: Lemmon, Violet
From Lord Walpole: Nancy, Sally
From Mr Coke: Boxer, Tabitha
Frolic

Young Hounds - 1723/4
By Lord Brooks' Cocker out of Doxy'21: Banger (given to Mr Bright 19th September 1723), Beauty, Bluecap, Bluemaid, Blueman, Brimmer, Bumper, Pyman
By Shifter'22 out of Promise'21: Bonny, Empress, Rustler, Tomsey
By Mr Miles' dog out of Mr Roper's Jewel: Gamester
By Mr Roper's Tipler out of Diamond'21: Phoenix, Tifter, Tomboy, Warrior
By Shifter'22 out of lame Dolly'21: Carver (given to Mr Bright 19th September 1723), Fanny, Juno, Luther
By Spanker'21 out of Mr Roper's Honey: Fleury, Honey, Ruby
By Mr Odes' Rockwood out of Merrylass'21: Countess, Plunder, Smerkin
By Mr Roper's Plunder out of Bell'21: Beauty, Fairmaid
By Sir R Mill's Conqueror out of Virgin'21: Flower
By Ratler'22 out of Stately'21: Gossip, Tawny
By Mr Roper's Plunder out of Jones' Damsel: Henny, Jemmy, Melly, Royal
From Mr Godfrey: Merryman
From Mr Hutton: Bowman, Ruler

Young Hounds - 1724/5
By Duke of Grafton's Shifter (from Mr Orlebar) out of Bell'21 : Climbank, Cloudy, Driver, Lover, Ruler, Trimmer
By Ratler'22 out of Favourite'22: Charcoal, Collier, Jewel, Telltale
By Spanker'22 out of Pallas'22: Frolic, Phrenzy, Tapster
By Bowman'23 out of Lord Burlington's Lemmon'23: Cruel, Lemmon, Pleasant
By Spanker'22 out of Fury'22: Miss, Spanker, Trueman
By Snowball'22 out of Lofty'22: Gaudy, Mounter
By Duke of Grafton's Cocker out of Doxy'21: Doxy, Trueboy
By Mr Morley's Jolly out of Folly'21: Fairmaid, Leader
By Mr Odes' Rockwood out of lame Dolly'21: Dinger, Lady, Lively
By Jolly'21 out of Countess'22: Likely
By Spanker'22 out of Sweetlips'22 : Drunkard
By Clouder'22 out of Promise'21: Promise
From Mr Godfrey: Whipster
From Mr Newby: Cocker (cast 1735), Phillis
From Mr Hutton: Ranger
By Duke of Grafton's Cocker out of Wanton'24: Damsel

Young Hounds - 1725
By Mr Morley's Warrior out of Pleasant'24: Gallant (cast 1732), Mira
By Bowman'23 out of Henny'23: Chider, Clinkwood, Comfort, Darling, Folly, Lively, Tosspot
By Pyman'23 out of Violet'23: Chanter, Rockwood
By Lord Burlington's Emperor out of his Lemmon: Lovely, Madam (sent to Goodwood 1736), Peggy, Tidy
By Lord Burlington's Ranter out of Mr Roper's Music: Buxom
By Bowman'23 out of Cupid'22: Betty, Captain, Merrylass, Ratler, Violet
By Mr Morley's Warrior out of Comely'22: Famous, Topper
By Spanker'22 out of Fubbs'22: Merryman, Singwell
By Pyman'23 out of Promise'21: Capper, Dainty, Frisky, Tomboy
By Lord Brooks' Cocker out of Maiden'22: Jugler, Wildman

Pedigree of Charlton Hounds

Young Hounds - 1726
By Mr Morley's Warrior out of Favourite'22: Carver (gelt 1726, cast 1732), Gamboy, Judith
By Clouder'22 out of Mr May's Lemmon: Cruel (cast 1732), Fidler
By Emperor'22 out of Merrylass'22: Drummer
By Ranter'22 out of Nancy'23: Caesar, Molsey
By Luther'23 out of Comely'22: Gillian, Joyner
By Emperor'22 out of Maiden'22: Dancer, Pallas, Ringwood, Woodman
By Emperor'22 out of Frolic'24: Jumper, Singwell
By Ranter'22 out of Phillis'24: Careless, Thumper
By Duke of Grafton's Tipler (from Mr Orlebar) out of Henny'23: Fleury, Monkey, Music, Topper (lost 1733)
From Lord Walpole: Crimson, Cruel, Lady, Molly, Tydie

Young Hounds - 1727
By Clouder'22 out of Henny'23: Bell
By Ranter'22 out of Phillis'24: Crowner, Dolly, Lilly (cast 1732), Merrylass (cast 1732), Princess (cast 1733), Ratler
By Duke of Grafton's Tipler (from Mr Orlebar) out of Juno'23: Kitty, Nelly (cast 1732), Sukey
By Cocker'23 out of Promise'24: Tifter
By Lord Tankerville's Sober out of Favourite'22: Sober (cast 1732)
By Driver'24 out of Phrenzy'24: Caesar (cast 1732)
By Snowball'22 out of Music'26: Music

Young Hounds - 1728
By Snowball'22 out of Maiden'22: Captain, Diamond, Sweetlips (sp'd, lost 1734), Tapster, Victor (gelt, cast 1732)
By Clouder'22 out of Phillis'24: Hackwood, Lucy (cast 1732)
By Dashwood'22 out of Miss'24: Beauty, Clinkwood
By Dashwood'22 out of Cupid'22: Dashwood, Rockwood (cast 1736)
By Dashwood'22 out of Juno'23: Jockey (cast 1735), Bluecap
By Cocker'23 out of Frisky'25: Virgin
By Snowball'22 out of Phrenzy'24: Plunder
By Emperor'22 out of Nancy'23: Damsel
By Dashwood'22 out of Jewel'24: Ransom (cast 1732)
From Mr Bright: Violet, Virgin (sp'd, lost 1734)
From Lord Walpole: Cloudy, Crimson (cast 1732)

Young Hounds - 1729
By Dashwood'22 out of Cruel'24: Captain, Vulcan (cast 1732), Wildman (cast 1732), Woodman (cast 1732)
By Lord Tankerville's Sober out of Singwell'26: Doxy, Tipler, Wanton
By Duke of Grafton's Welcome out of Cupid'22: Bluemaid, Skipper
By Emperor'22 out of Nancy'23: Bluebell, Comfort (cast 1732)
By Cocker'23 out of Lilly'27: Charmer
By Clouder'22 out of Maiden'22: Careless (kept for breeding, went mad, cast 1737)
By Clouder'22 out of Princess'27: Ratler (cast 1732)

Young Hounds - 1730
By Clouder'22 out of Cloudy'28: Tifter (cast 1732), Topper (cast 1733)
By Cocker'23 out of Madam'25: Tosser (given to Duke of Bolton 1735)
By Mr Withers' Snowball out of Frisky'25: Boxer ((given to Tom Johnson 1737)

The Duke of Richmond's Hounds - 1731
Beauty from Mr Orme (died 1734)
Bell by Driver'24 out of Lucy'28 (entered 1731, given to Duke of Bolton 1736)
Biddy by Mr Morley's Bumper out of Sweetlips'28 (entered 1731, died 1738)
Bluecap by Dashwood'22 out of Juno'23 (entered 1728)
Bluemaid by Jockey'28 out of Madam'25 (entered 1731)
Bowler from Mr Orme (lost 1st December 1733)
Boxer by Mr Withers' Snowball out of Frisky'25 (entered 1730, given to Tom Johnson 1734)
Bumper by Driver'24 out of Lucy'28 (entered 1731)
Caesar by Driver'24 out of Phrenzy'24 (entered 1727)
Careless by Clouder'22 out of Maiden'22 (entered 1729, kept for breeding, mad, died 1737)
Carver by Mr Morley's Warrior out of Favorite'22 (entered 1726, gelt)

Cocker from Mr Newby (entered 1724, given to John Ware)
Cocker from Mr Orme (died 1734)
Comfort by Emperor'22 out of Nancy'23 (entered 1729, died 1735)
Crimson from Lord Walpole, Mr Bright (entered 1728, sp'd, gone)
Cruel by Clouder'22 out of Mr May's Lemmon (entered 1726)
Damsel by Lord Tankerville's Mounter out of Frisky'25 (entered 1731, given to Duke of Bolton 1736)
Daphne from Mr Orme (sp'd)
Dashwood by Lord Tankerville's Warrior out of his Sempstress (entered 1731, given to John Ware 1733)
Dido by Driver'24 out of Lucy'28 entered 1731 (sp'd, given to Tom Johnson 1736)
Dragon from Mr Orme (given to John Ware)
Driver by Duke of Grafton's Shifter out of Bell'21 (entered 1724, given to John Ware)
Driver from Mr Orme
Drummer by Mr Morley's Bumper out of Sweetlips'28 (entered 1731, given to John Ware 1733)
Drunkard by Jockey'28 out of Lovely'25 (entered 1731, given to John Ware 1733)
Duchess from Mr Orme (sp'd, gone)
Empress by Driver'24 out of Lucy'28 (entered 1731, cast 1737)
Fleury from Mr Orme (sp'd, sent to France)
Gallant by Mr Morley's Warrior out of Pleasant'24 (entered 1725)
Gamboy by Mr Roper's Jockey out of Maiden'22 (entered 1731, given to John Ware)
Goodwood by Jockey'28 out of Madam'25 (entered 1731, given to Duke of Bolton)
Jockey by Dashwood'22 out of Juno'23 (entered 1728, died 1735)
Jolly by Lord Tankerville's Mounter out of Frisky'25 (entered 1731)
Jumper by Lord Lovell's Lincoln out of his Countess (entered 1731)
Kindness by Lord Tankerville's Mounter out of Frisky'25 (entered 1731, leg broke 3rd December 1733, given to Tom Johnson 1738)
Kitty by Duke of Grafton's Tipler out of Juno'23 (entered 1727, sp'd)
Lilly by Ranter'22 out of Phillis'24 (entered 1727)
Lovely from Mr Orme (sp'd)
Lovely from Sir R Jenkinson (sent to Goodwood)
Lucy by Clouder'22 out of Phillis'24 (entered 1728)
Madam by Lord Burlington's Emperor out of his Lemmon'23 (entered 1725, sent to Goodwood, died 1736)
Madam by Jockey'28 out of Madam'25 (entered 1731, died 1737)
Madcap by Lord Tankerville's Mounter out of Frisky'25 (entered 1731, cripple, cast 1736)
Maiden by Mr Orlebar's Shifter out of Promise'21 (entered 1722)
Maiden by Mr Roper's Jockey out of Maiden'22 (entered 1731, given to John Ware)
Merrylass by Ranter'22 out of Phillis'24 (entered 1727)
Merryman by Mr Roper's Jockey out of Maiden'22 (entered 1731, cast 1736)
Music by Duke of Grafton's Tipler out of Henny'23 (entered 1726, sp'd, lost 7th January 1733)
Music from Mr Orme
Nancy from Mr Orme
Phoenix from Mr Orme
Princess by Ranter'22 out of Phillis'24 (entered 1727, died January 1733)
Ransom by Dashwood'22 out of Jewel'24 or Phrenzy'24 (entered 1728, sp'd, given to John Ware)
Ranter by Jockey'28 out of Madam'25 (entered 1731, died 1737)
Ratler by Clouder'22 out of Princess'27 (entered 1729)
Ratler from Mr Orme
Ringwood by Jockey'28 out of Madam'25 (entered 1731, given to Tom Johnson 1736)
Rockwood by Dashwood'22 out of Cupid'22 (entered 1728, died 1736)
Rockwood from Mr Orme
Sober by Lord Tankerville's Sober out of Favourite'22 (entered 1727)
Sober from Mr Orme
Spanker from Mr Orme (sent to France)
Sweetlips by Snowball'22 out of Maiden'22 (entered 1728, sp'd, lost April 1733)
Tanner by Mr Morley's Bumper out of Sweetlips'28 (entered 1731, cast 1736)
Tapster by Lord Tankerville's Mounter out of Frisky'25 (entered 1731, sheep, cast 1736)
Tifter by Clouder'22 out of Cloudy'28 (entered 1730)
Tifter from Mr Orme (given to John Ware)

Pedigree of Charlton Hounds

Toler by Mr Roper's Jockey out of Maiden'22 (entered 1731, given to John Ware)
Topper by Clouder'22 out of Cloudy'28 (entered 1730, died February 1733)
Tosser by Cocker'23 out of Madam'25 (entered 1730, given to Duke of Bolton 1731)
Trimmer by Lord Tankerville's Mounter out of Frisky'25 (entered 1731)
Victor by Snowball'22 out of Maiden'22 (entered 1728, gelt)
Virgin from Mr Bright (entered 1728, sp'd, lost 3rd December 1733)
Virgin from Mr Orme
Vulcan by Dashwood'22 out of Cruel'24 (entered 1729)
Wanton from Mr Orme
Welcome by Mr Roper's Jockey out of Maiden'22 (entered 1731, given to Tom Johnson 1735)
Wildman by Dashwood'22 out of Cruel'24 (entered 1729)
Woodman by Dashwood'22 out of Cruel'24 (entered 1729)

Bitches to be warded - 1732
Princess'27 by Tapster'31; Careless'29 by Cocker'24 (two puppys entered 1734); Kindness'31 by Lord Tankerville's Blueman; Comfort'29 by Duke of Rutland's Limner (three puppys entered 1734); Madam'31 by Duke of Rutland's Ranter (two puppys entered 1734); Dido'31 by Jumper'31 (two puppys entered 1734); Mr Orme's Virgin'31 by Jockey'28 (two puppys entered 1734); Damsel'31 by Wildman'29; Crimson'28 by Cocker'24 (four puppys entered 1734); Venus'32 by Duke of St Albans' Redcap (one puppy entered 1734)

Young Hounds - 1732
By Lord Tankerville's Mounter out of Maiden'31: Clouder (lost), Molly or Moltofts (sent to Goodwood 1736), St André (given to John Ware), Stately (given to John Ware)
From Mr Orme: Dainty (cast 1737), Cryer (given to John Ware)
From Lord Walpole: Crimson (cast 1736), Folly (given to John Ware)
By Lord Tankerville's Mounter out of Cruel'26: Truemaid (given to Tom Johnson 1736), Venus (lost 1737), +Veny (sent to Goodwood 1741)
By Driver'24 out of Frisky'25: Fairmaid (cast 1737), Trouncer (cast 1739)
From Sir T Miller: Trueboy (gone)

Bitches to be warded - 1733
Madam'25 by Wildman'29; Madam'31 by Clouder'32; Careless'29 by Luther'33; Sally'33 by Luther'33; Comfort'29 by Lord Tankerville's Clouder; Kindness'31 by Lord Tankerville's Clouder; Comely'23 by Trouncer'32 (three puppys entered 1735); Crimson'32 by Ratler'31; Blossom'33 by Ranter'31 for the Duke of Bourbon

List of puppys - 1733
By Cocker'24 out of Crimson'28: Pymont walked by George Etheredge (cast), Crowner walked by Thomas Brent (entered 1734), Curious by Farmer Savin (entered 1734), Caley and Pompey at Goodwood (entered 1734), one other at Goodwood (cast)
By Cocker'24 out of Careless'29: Sherewood walked by Richard Etheredge (entered 1734), Conqueror walked by Charles Earleys (cast), Smerkin walked by John Plot (entered 1734)
By Lord Tankerville's Blewman out of Kindness'31: Blewman walked by John Young (cast)
By Duke of St Albans' Redcap out of Venus'32: Darling walked by George Snouks (entered 1734)
By Jumper'31 out of Dido'31: Jumper walked by Ralph Street (cast), Jugler walked by Peter Dove (entered 1734), Jupiter walked by Farmer Linnington (cast), Juno walked by Farmer Linnington (entered 1734), Judith walked by Haywood Mill (cast)
By Jockey'28 out of Virgin'31: Emperor walked by Edward Wild (entered 1734), Dashwood walked by William Wings (entered 1734), Bonny walked by Peter Bailys (cast), Lovely walked by Alice Maizey (cast)
Four at Bolderwood not yet put out.

Young Hounds - 1733
By Ratler'29 out of Comfort'29: Comely, Countess (given to Duke of Bolton 1739), Dinger (given to Lord Craven), Royal (given to Duke of Bolton 1736), Trojan (given to Duke of Bolton 1737)
By Tapster'31 out of Madam'31: Gillian (cast 1739)
By Lord Tankerville's Mounter out of Maiden'31: Mimie (died 1739), Sally (died 1739)
By Tapster'31 out of Madam'25: Blossom (given to Tom Johnson), Bowman (sent to France), Charmer (sent to France), Gallant (gone), Nancy (cast 1738), Snowball (cast 1737)
By Sir R Fagg's Gallant out of Biddy'31: Biddy, Gipsy
By Lord Sunderland's Forester out of Careless'29: Forester (sent to France), Molsey (sent to France), Ruler (given to Tom Johnson 1737)
By Jumper'31 out of Princess'27: Sukey (given to Tom Johnson 1737)

By Jockey'28 out of Lovely'31: Climbank (sent to France), Gamester (given to Mr Jenison 1740), Driver
From Mr Bright by Duke of Rutland's Limner out of Mr Herbert's Rackit (sire by Lord Cardigan's Tospot out of Lot by Bloomer out of old Lot; Bloomer by Lord Byron's Bouncer; old Lot by Sir John Tyrwitt's Lifter, both out of Mr Chaworth's Comely; dam by Sir W Wyndham's Ruler by a hound of Mr Roper's [as Lord Gower says] out of Transome by Mr Roper's Tipler out of Mr Vernon's Bluebell by Mr Huddlestone's Blameless out of Mr Vernon's Bluecap; Blameless by Lord Cardigan's Sussex Gamester): Luther (cast 1735 for running at sheep)
By Lord Tankerville's Mounter out of Duke of St Albans' beagle: Mounter (sent to Goodwood 1737)
From Sir C D'Arcy by Lord Aylesford's dog hound out of Mr Thimbleby's beagle: Tapster (died August 1734)
By Lord Craven's Crowner out of his Juno: Merrylass (given to Tom Johnson 1736)

Bitches to be warded - 1734
Comfort'29 by Mr St John's Ranter (two puppys entered 1736); Careless'29 by Luther'33 (at Goodwood); Kindness'31 by Trojan'33 (whelped 3 dogs, 2 bitches, at Goodwood, three puppys entered 1736); Madam'25 by Wildman'25 (at Goodwood, one puppy entered 1736); Madam'31 by Trouncer'32 (whelped 5, three puppys entered 1736); Molly'32 by Wildman'29; Sally'33 by Luther'33 (three puppys entered 1736); Crimson'32 by Trouncer'32 (at Goodwood, one puppy entered 1736); Diamond'28 by Tapster'31; Merrylass'33 by Trouncer'32; Emily'34 by Gamester'33 (whelped 4)
Mr Spencer's bitches: Comely by Ranter'31 (one puppy entered 1736); Bridget by Lord Craven's Warrior; Lucy by Gamester'33 (sent to Sussex, one puppy entered 1736); Gaudy by Cryer'32; Busy by Lord Craven's Router; Blewett by Dashwood'34 (whelped 1 dog, 1 bitch, 1736 in Hampshire, two puppys entered 1737)

Young Hounds - 1734
Two litters bought by Colonel Hawley of Mr St John's huntsman: one litter out of Mr St John's old Pleasant of his father's old kind, got by his Spanker who was got by Bright's Dashwood; old Pleasant was out of his father's Juno by Ranter: Farmer, a spotted pyed dog (cast 1735), Spanker, a black back dog (cast 1735), Music, a spotted pyed bitch (given to Tom Johnson 1736), Pleasant, a white bitch with fallow spots (given to Tom Johnson 1736): one litter out of a bitch of Mr Bridge's called Pleasant, given him by Lord Cardigan; they were got by Mr Morley's Vulcan who was son of Mr Morley's Victor: Frolic, a black pyed bitch (cast 1735), Cleanly, a pyed bitch with a yellow side face (cast 1735)
By Cocker'24 out of Crimson'28: Caley (cast 1735), Crowner (given to Lord Cholmondeley 1735), Curious (given to Lord Cowper 1738), +Pompey (given to Colonel Hawley 1745)
By Cocker'24 out of Careless'29: Sherewood (cast 1736), Smerkin (cast 1736)
By Duke of St Albans' Redcap out of Venus'32: Darling (cast 1737)
By Jumper'31 out of Dido'31: Jugler (sent to France 1735), Juno (sent to France 1735)
By Jockey'28 out of Virgin'31: Dashwood (given to Billy Ives 1741), Emperor (given to Sir Rowland Wynne 1741)
By Duke of Rutland's Ranter out of Madam'31: Drummer (given to Mr Jenison 1740), Tantivy (given to Billy Ives 1741)
By Duke of Rutland's Limner out of Comfort'29: Diamond (cast 1740), Drunkard (blind, sent to Goodwood, given to Duke of Hamilton 1737), Emily (given to Mr Thompson 1740 but ran away to Duke of Bolton's kennel)
By Tapster'31 out of Lord Cowper's Peggy: Captain (cast 1737)
By Clouder'32 out of Lord Cowper's Lady: Warrior (given to Tom Johnson 1738)

From the Duke of St Albans - 8th January 1735
By Rockwood'28 out of his Fortune: Darling (cast 1735), Fortune (cast 1735), Jovial (cast 1737)
By Goodwood'31 out of his Music: Comely (sent to France 1735), Gamester (cast 1735), Lilly (cast 1735), Pyman (cast 1735), Snowball (cast 1735)
By his Drunkard out of his Countess: Rockwood (sent to France 1735)
By his Fidler out of his Sweetlips, sire by Mr Newby's Cocker, dam by Lord Tankerville's Sober: Dilly (sent to France 1735), Ranter (sent to France 1735), Tipler (cast 1735)

Bitches to be warded - 1735
Blossom'33 by Luther'33; Madam'31 by Tapster'31; Comfort'29 by Pompey'34 (whelped 1 dog, 4 bitches, put out by Harry Budd in Sussex 1736, one puppy entered 1737); Kindness'31 by Lord Tankerville's Bumper (whelped one bitch, in Hampshire 1736); Careless'29 by Drummer'31; Sally'33 by Ranter'31; Emily'34 by Trouncer'32 (whelped 1 dog, put out by Harry Budd in Sussex 1736, entered 1737); Molly'32 by Luther'33; Comely'34 by Ranter'31 (whelped 3 dogs, 3 bitches, 1736 in Hampshire, three puppys entered 1737); Busy'35 by Tosser'30 (whelped 4 dogs, 3 bitches, put out by Harry Budd in Sussex 1736, four puppys entered 1737); Daybell by Ranter'31 (whelped 7 dogs, 3 bitches, 1736 in Hampshire, six puppys entered 1737); Lucy'28 by Trouncer'32; Bridget'31 by Emperor'34 (whelped 1 dog, 1 bitch, 1736 in Hampshire, two puppys entered 1737); Darling'34 by Clouder'32 (whelped 1 dog, 1 bitch, 1736 in Hampshire); Promise'24 by Luther'33 (whelped 2 dogs, 2 bitches, 1736 in Hampshire); Curious'34 by Luther'33

(whelped 5 dogs, 2 bitches, put out by Harry Budd in Sussex 1736, three puppys entered 1737); Smerkin'34 by Lord Tankerville's Wildman (whelped 1 dog, put out by Harry Budd in Sussex 1736)

Young Hounds - 1735
By Trouncer'32 out of Comely '32: Princess (cast 1738), Tifter (cast 1737), Topper (shot at Binderton 2nd January 1737)
From Sir John Miller bred by Mr St John: Vulcan (cast 1738), Darling (cast 1739)
From Brigadier Hawley: Ruby (given to Lord Craven 1738)
From Mr Morley: Damsel (cast 1737)
From Lord Tankerville: Dolly (given to Duke of Bolton 1738)
From Sir John Miller: Sempstress (cast 1737), Singer (cast 1737)

Old Hounds from Mr Spencer - 1734/5
By Lord Cardigan's Royster out of Duke of Rutland's Phoenix: Conqueror (cast 1735)
Bred by Mr Morley: Driver (given to Tom Johnson 1735), Bonny (cast 1735)
By Lord Conway's Jugler out of Mr Andrews' Damsel: Gamester (cast 1735)
By Duke of Rutland's Barbary out of Mr Cocking's Dancer: Bridget (cast 1737)
By Duke of Rutland's Madcap out of Lord Gower's Jewel: Jewel (sp'd, cast 1738)
Ratler, a chance hound (given to Tom Johnson 1738)
By Sir F Skipwith's Trusty out of Mr Andrews' Merrylass: Trusty (cast 1739), Gaudy (cast 1735)
By Jockey'28 out of Mr Andrews' Phoenix: Jockey (cast 1738), Mopsy (cast 1739)
By Mr Morley's Victor out of Lord Byron's Vexer: Dashwood (cast 1735), Danger (given to Tom Johnson 1735), Vexer (cast 1735)
By Mr Andrews' Dinger out of his Juniper: Dinger (cast 1737), Darling (cast 1735)
By Lord Gower's Jowler out of Lord Griffin's Blewbell: Blewett (given to Tom Johnson 1737)
By Mr Spencer's Conqueror out of Mr Herbert's Bridget: Tanner (cast 1739)
By Mr Spencer's Conqueror out of his Gaudy: Clouder (given to Tom Johnson 1737), Cloudy (cast 1737), Curious (given to Tom Johnson 1735)
By Mr Spencer's Conqueror out of Mr Andrews' Madam: Rival (cast 1739), Roman (given to Tom Johnson 1735), Rattle (cast 1737)
By Lord Craven's Crowner out of Mr Andrews' Music: Crowner (cast 1739), Comely (cast 1738)
By Mr Noel's Captain out of his Lovely, dam out of a daughter of Sir W Wyndham's Ruler: Younker (given to Mr Fielding 1735), Gaylass (cast 1740), Busy (cast 1741)
By Captain Rider's Rockwood out of Mr Andrews' Phoenix: Rockwood (cast 1737)
By Mr Morley's Pyman out of Mr Andrews' Damsel: Placket (sp'd, given to Mr Horde 1738)
By Lord Cardigan's Carver out of Lord Cardigan's Countess: Daybell (given to Tom Johnson 1738)
By Mr Andrews' Jovial out of Mr Spencer's Strumpet: +Peggy (given to Tom Johnson 1738), Princess (given to Tom Johnson 1735), Promise (given to Tom Johnson 1737)
By Mr Noel's Ruler out of Mr Andrews' Fairmaid: Gaylass
By Lord Cardigan's Wonder out of a bitch of Mr Newby's: Lucy (sp'd by Lord Delawarr's order, cast 1739)
From Sir H Monoux: Dolphin (cast 1737)
From Duke of St Albans: Gaudy (cast 1737), Venus (given to Tom Johnson 1737), Frolic (cast 1735), Charmer (given to Tom Johnson 1737)

Bitches to be warded - 1736
Comely'33 by Emperor'34 (four puppys entered 1738); Busy'35 by Lord Tankerville's Ruler, son of his Wildman (six puppys entered 1738); Kindness'31 by Crowner'34 (five puppys entered 1738); Sally'33 by Crowner'34; Molly'32 by Crowner'34 (three puppys entered 1738); Madam'31 by Luther'33; Ruby'35 by Luther'33; Sir John Miller's Darling by Luther'33 (four puppys entered 1739); Emily'34 by Dashwood'34 (seven puppys entered 1738); Bridget'35 by Pompey'34

Old Hounds given - 12th November 1736
From Sir J Miller: Boxer (cast 1737)
By Mr Andrews' Jovial out of Mr Thompson's Frolic: Tomboy (entered 1735, cast 1737)
By Mr Andrews' Jovial out of Mr Thompson's Fortune: Tryher (entered 1735, cast 1737)
By Mr Spencer's Clouder out of Mr Andrew's Fortune: Royal (entered 1734, cast 1738)

Young Hounds - 12th November 1736
By Ranter'31 out of Comely'34: Bluemaid (cast 1737)
By Lord Craven's Warrior out of Bridget'31: Bowler (cast 1741), Bridget (cast 1737)
By Trouncer'32 out of Madam'31: Careless (cast 1742), Carver (cast 1743), Cocker (lost in New Forest 1734)

By Trojan'33 out of Kindness'31: Climbank (cast 1739), Conqueror (cast 1737), Nelly (cast 1737)
From Sir T Twisden: Cruel (cast 1741)
By Lord Griffin's Cryer out of Mr Andrew's Juniper: Dido (cast 1741)
By Trouncer'32 out of Crimson'28: Diamond (cast 1737)
By Mr Spencer's Cryer out of Gaudy'35 dam by Trusty out of Merrylass: Gipsy (cast 1737)
From Mr Noel by his Chanter, brother to Mr Herbert's Ranter: +Jenny (cast 1740)
From Kent: Jugler (cast 1737)
By Luther'33 out of Sally'33: Maiden (cast 1737), Mode (cast 1739), Tipler (cast 1739)
By Wildman'29 out of Madam'25: Nancy (cast 1740)
From Mr Noel, sire by Mr Thomson's Madcap: Phillis (cast 1740), +Taker (cast 1740)
By Gamester'33 out of Emily'34: Singwell (cast 1741)
By Gamester'33 out of Lucy'33: Truelove (cast 1737)
By Mr St John's Ranter out of Comfort'29: Victor (cast 1742), Virgin (cast 1737)
By Dolphin'34 out of Famous'25: Wanton (cast 1737), Whipster (cast 1737)
From Lord Delawarr: Bloomer, Collier, Fanny, Guider, Leader, Ruffler, Traveller (all given to Tom Johnson 1737)

Hounds given - 20th December 1737
From Mr Orlebar at Chiltom at Hampton court: Driver (given to Lord Craven 1738, later stolen)
From Mr Noel by his Captain: +Walcut (cast 1741)
From Mr Andrews by Conqueror'36 out of his Juniper: Flurry (cast 1740)
By Sir F Skipwith's Trusty out of a bitch of Lord Byron's: Trusty (cast 1739)

Old Hounds from Lord Tankerville - 20th December 1737
By Lord Tankerville's Thumper out of his Minion: Careless (cast 1740)
By Lord Tankerville's Mounter out of Sir W Twisden's Sempstress: Cruel (given back to Lord Tankerville 1741)
By Trouncer'32 out of Mr Pelham's Drinkwell: Comely (cast 1740), Daybell (given to Mr Orme 1741)
By Cocker'36 out of Lord Tankerville's Bridget: Caesar (cast 1739)
Bumper, Dolly (both given to Duke of Bolton 20th January 1738)
By Wildman'29 out of Lord Tankerville's Nelly, out of Fairmaid: Drummer (given to Mr Thompson 1740)
By Lord Tankerville's Mounter out of his Madam: +Dido (cast 1739), +Doxy (given to Duke of St Albans 1740), Princess (cast 1738)
By Lord Tankerville's Mounter out of his Nancy, sister to Mr Wither's Snowball: Finder (given back to Lord Tankerville 1742)
By Mr Withers' Finder out of Lord Tankerville's Nancy: Lilly (cast 1738)
By Duke of Hamilton's Jugler out of Mr Morley's Bonny: Madam (cast 1739)
By Wildman'25 out of Lord Tankerville's Nelly, by Mr Orlebar's Tipler: Merrylass (cast 1741), Ruler (cast 1739)
By Lord Tankerville's Ruler out of his Cruel: +Music (cast 1739), Nelly (cast 1743)
By Lord Tankerville's Tipler out of his Sempstress: Pleasant (cast 1743)
By Mr Spencer's Conqueror out of Lord Tankerville's Fairmaid: Ransom (cast 1740)
By Luther'33 out of Lord Tankerville's Betty: Ringwood (cast 1741)
By Mr Withers' Snowball out of Lord Tankerville's Pallas: Singwell (cast 1739)
By Lord Craven's Crowner out of Mr Withers' Molly: Gillian (cast 1739)
By Lord Tankerville's Clouder out of Mr Morley's Dainty: Topper (cast 1742)
By Mr Morley's Victor out of Lord Tankerville's Bridget: Thunder (cast 1744)
By Mr Withers' Snowball out of Fairmaid'32: Virgin (cast 1738)
By Tipler'34 out of Mr Morley's Dainty: Virgin (cast 1738)

Young Hounds - 20th December 1737
By Dashwood'34 out of Blewett'35: Bonny (cast 1739), Buxom (cast 1741)
By Ranter'31 out of Comely'34: +Cruel (cast 1743), +Cryer (lost at Findon 1742), Kitty (cast 1740)
By Emperor'34 out of Bridget'31: +Edmund (cast 1741), Emperor (given to Mr Kent 1741)
By Luther'33 out of Curious'34: +Lawyer (given to Mr Dodd 1743), Lewdy (given to Mr Kent 1741), Limner (given to Mr Kent 1741)
By Pompey'34 out of Comfort'29: Pompey (cast 1740)
By Ranter'31 out of Daybell'33: Racket (cast 1738), Ranter (cast 1743), +Ringwood (cast 1740), Roister (cast 1742), Rover (cast 1739), Rumsy (given to Lord Harcourt 12th January 1739)
By Tosser'30 out of Busy'35: Tattle (cast 1739), Tickler (lost at Biddydown 1742), Tipsy (cast 1742), Tosser (given to Mr Dodd 1743)
By Trouncer'32 out of Emily'34: +Traveller (cast 1740)

Young Hounds - 24th November 1738

By Dashwood'34 out of Emily'34: Drunkard (cast 1745), +Drummer (cast 1740), Driver (cast 1740), Dolly (given to Mr Sheldon), Darling (cast 1740), Dainty (cast 1743)

By Lord Tankerville's Ruler out of Busy'35: Ratler (cast 1744), Ruler (cast 1744), +Rifle (given to Mr Drax 1744), Rally (cast 1740), Rachel (given to Mr Drax 1740), +Ruby (cast 1744)

By Crowner'35 out of Kindness'31: Careless (given to Mr Orme 1741), Carver (cast 1743), Clouder, (cast 1743), Comfort (cast 1745), Kindness (cast 1740)

By Emperor'34 out of Comely'34: +Bloomer (cast 1741), Bellman (given to Mr Newby 1740), +Buxom (renamed Bouncer, given to Tom Johnson 1741), Busy (cast 1739)

By Emperor'34 out of Lord Tankerville's Princess: Pyman (given to Mr Dodd 1746)

By Crowner'35 out of Molly'32: Capper (cast 1739), +Crowner (cast 1745), +Goodwood (cast 1745)

From Mr Herbert: +Lady (cast 1739)

Hounds sent by Lady Molyneux - 24th December 1738

DOGS

Rockwood is something above two and twenty inches; he was given to Lord Molyneux by Lord Cardigan, was got by Lord Gower's Royster out of Lord Cardigan's Pegg (cast 1739)

Mendall is 22 inches, was got by Rockwood above mentioned and out of white Beauty; Beauty was got by Lord Cardigan's Captain and out of Lord Molyneux's Fleury; Fleury was got by old Mendall out of old Fortune; old Mendall was of Lord Molyneux's old kind, old Fortune of Lord Cardigan's (cast 1739)

Bumper is 21 inches, was got by Lord Cardigan's blind Rockwood and out of Countess; Countess was got by Drunkard and out of Nancy; Drunkard was got by Lord Cardigan's Trueman and out of old Fortune above named; Nancy was out of Miney of Lord Molyneux's old kind; given to the huntsman that brought him, too old

Dancer is 21 inches, was got by Lifter and out of old Beauty; Lifter was got by Lord Cardigan's Tanner and out of Fortune, daughter of old Fortune; old Beauty was got by Drunkard and out of Lord Cardigan's old Gulliver; he is kin-bred (cast 1741)

Finder is 22 inches, was got by Rockwood and out of Fortune, own sister to Lifter above mentioned; he was entered this season (cast 1741)

Trimmer is 22 inches, was got by Mendall, son of Rockwood and out of Beauty, mother of Dancer; he was entered this season (cast 1741)

Vulcan is 21½ inches, was got by Lord Molyneux's white Rockwood and out of Dido, sister to Lifter; White Rockwood was got by Lord Cardigan's blind Rockwood and out of Careless, sister to Drunkard above named; he was entered this season (cast 1741)

Ruler is something oversized, was got by Lifter and out of Gulliver; Gulliver was got by Bouncer and out of Lord Cardigan's old Gulliver; Bouncer was got by Trueman above mentioned and out of Frolic, daughter to Miney (cast 1741)

Rayman is 22 inches, was got by Lord Cardigan's blind Rockwood and out of Miney, own sister to Countess, mother of Bumper (cast 1739)

Dashwood is 20½ inches and is own brother to Bumper, but one year older (cast 1739)

BITCHES

Dido is about 20 inches, own sister to Lifter and mother of Vulcan (cast 1739)

Lofty is 20 inches, was got by the Confederate Ranter and out of old Miney, mother of Nancy, who was mother of Countess and of Miney mother of Rayman (cast 1740)

Makeless is 20 inches, was got by young Drunkard and out of young Gulliver, daughter of old Gulliver as mentioned above; Drunkard was got by old Drunkard, father of Countess and out of Fairmaid, daughter of Music, sister of Nancy; this bitch is kin-bred (cast 1739)

Duchess about 20 inches is own sister to Dancer, son of Lifter (given to Mr Kent 1742)

Phoenix is 19½ inches high, is own sister to Dashwood and Bumper (cast 1739)

Lilly is of the same height and of the same litter as Phoenix above (cast 1739)

Madam is 20 inches and own sister to Finder, son of Rockwood and of this season (cast 1739)

Lovely is 20 inches, own sister to Rayman, son of blind Rockwood, one year younger than he is (cast 1741)

Merrylass is 20½ inches, was got by Rockwood, father of Finder and Madam and out of Miney, mother of Lovely and Rayman (cast 1741)

Gipsy is 20 inches and own sister to Merrylass (cast for running at sheep 1739)

Beauty is own sister to Dancer and Duchess (cast 1743)

Young Hounds - 1st November 1739

By Walcut'37 out of Princess'37: Madam (given to Mr Kent 1743), Maiden (cast 1743), Mopsy (cast 1745), Mountain

(cast 1745), Music (given to Mr Drax 1744)
By Crowner'35 out of Nancy'36: Carver (cast 1741), Crimson (given to Mr Orme 1741), Curious (cast 1740)
By Luther'37 out of Darling'34: Lofty (given to Mr Orme 1742), Lovely (given to Duke of Newcastle 1740), Lucy (cast 1740), Luther (cast 1746)
By Luther'37 out of Cruel'36: Lifter (cast 1741), Lady (cast 1740), Looby (cast 1740)
By Drummer'37 out of Kitty'37: Dainty (cast 1743), Dido (given to Mr Drax 1744), Doxy (cast 1743)
By Luther'37 out of Lord Tankerville's Lively: Lively (cast 1747)
By Gamester'33 out of Comely'37: Gaylass (cast 1743), Gossip (cast 1747)
By Luther'37 out of Cruel'37: Looby (cast 1740)
From General Hawley by Mr St John's Ranter out of his Flurry: Clouder (cast 1740)
By Trusty'37 out of Jenny'36: Truelove (given to Mr Drax 1744), Turpin (cast 1741)

Old Hounds given - 1st November 1740
From Mr Morley by his Victor out of his Peggy: Crowner (given to David Briggs later to Billy Ives died 1743)
From Mr Newby: Fairplay (cast 1743), Trusty (cast 1742)

Young Hounds - 1st November 1740
By Bouncer'38 out of Lilly'38: Bonny (given to Mr Kent 1741)
By Lord Craven's Emperor out of Busy'38: Boxer (given to Mr Noel 1747)
By Bouncer'38 out of Ruby'38: Beauty (given to Mr Drax 1744), Brusher (given to Mr Thompson 1741)
By Cryer'37 out of Singwell'36: Captain (cast 1742), Conqueror (cast 1741), Crimson (given to Mr Drax 1744)
By Lord Tankerville's Clouder out of Molly'32: Cally (cast 1741), Capper (given to Mr Dodd 1743), Clouder (cast 1741)
By Cryer'37 out of Mode'36: Chanter (given to Lord Delawarr 1741), Countess (cast 1745)
By Finder'38 out of Tipsy'37: Fairmaid (cast 1745), Flower (cast 1745), Folly (given to Lord Eglinton 1749), Fransy (cast 1745), Fury (given to Mr Dodd 1743)
By Rockwood'38 out of Buxom'38: Racket (cast 1743), Ransom (cast 1742), Ranter (cast 1741), Rockwood (given to Mr Orme 1741)
By Rockwood'38 out of Gillian'37: Rambler (cast 1741), Ratler (cast 1749)
By Roister'37 out of Darling'34: Ravisher (cast 1744), Rector (given to Mr Dodd 1743)
By Topper'37 out of Emily'34: Tanner (cast 1741), Tapster (cast 1744), Tickle (given to Sir T Acland 1745), Topper (cast 1746), Traveller (cast 1741), Truelove (cast 1744)
By Walcut'37 out of Jenny'36: Welcome (given to Mr Orme 1741), Whimsey (cast 1741), Windsor (cast 1741)
By Walcut'37 out of Kitty'37: Wonder (cast 1743), Woodman (cast 1746)
From Mr Morley: Pyman (cast 1741)
By Render out of Rifle'38: Render (cast 1741)
From General Hawley by Duke of Bolton's Victor out of his Blossom: Valiant (cast 1743), Vulcan (cast 1747)
By Cryer'37 out of Sally'33 bred by Lord Delawarr: Maiden (given back to Lord Delawarr 1743), Music (given back to Lord Delawarr 1741)
By Mr Herbert's Walcut out of Racket'37: Racket (given to Lord Delawarr 1741)

Young Hounds - 14th November 1741
By Bloomer'38 out of Lord Tankerville's Cruel'37: Bluecap (given to Mr Kent 1742), Bridget (cast 1743), Bumper (given to Mr Kent 1742)
By Bloomer'38 out of Duchess'38: Bonny (cast 1746)
By Emperor'37 out of Crimson'39: Empress (given to Mr Drax 1744)
By Finder'39 out of Curious'39: Favourite (cast 1742), Fortune (cast 1744)
By Bouncer'38 out of Bluemaid'36: Bell (cast 1748), Bellman (given to Mr Kent 1742), Betty (given to Sir T Acland 1745)
By Finder'38 out of Tipsy'37: Fanny (cast 1749)
By Bouncer'38 out of Molly'32: Bounce (cast 1743)
By Lord Craven's Drunkard out of Ruby'38: Rebel (given to Mr Kent 1742), Ringwood (given to Mr Pelham 1746, returned 23rd March 1748), Router (given to Mr Kent 1742)
By Duke of Bolton's Swapper out of Dido'39: Swapper (cast 1747)
By Lord Craven's Blueman out of Jenny'36: Jenny (given to Mr Drax 1744)
By Lord Craven's Emperor out of Rachel'38: Rachel (given to Mr Dodd 1743)
From Sir R Fagg by Walcut'37: Thumper (cast 1747), Windsor (given to Billy Ives 1743)
From Mr Newby: Nioby (cast 1742)
From General Hawley by Duke of Bolton's Victor out of his Blossom: Venter (cast 1744)

―― *Pedigree of Charlton Hounds* ――

Young Hounds - 3rd November 1742
By Trusty'40 out of Tipsy'37: Tipsy (cast 1749), Trusty (cast 1745), Turpin (cast 1750)
By Crowner'38 out of Fairmaid'40: Careless (cast 1745), Conqueror (given to Sir T Acland 1745)
By Victor'36 out of Gossip'39: Valiant (given to Mr Dodd 1743), Venter (cast 1743), Victor (cast 1747), Vigo (given to Mr Noel 1747), Violet (given to Mr Dodd 1743)
By Victor'36 out of Comfort'38: Vander (cast 1744), Venus (cast 1747), Veny (cast 1750), Vulture (cast 1744)
By Render'40 out of Crimson'40: Rally (cast 1743)
By Tantivy'34 out of Beauty'40: Tantivy (given to Mr Dodd 1743), Truelove (cast 1747)
By Finder'37 out of Dolly'35: Frolic (cast 1747)
By Tantivy'34 out of Tickle'40: Tidings (cast 1747), Tosspot (given to Lord Dalkeith 1749), Trouncer (given to Mr Dodd 1743), Tuner (given to Mr Dodd 1743)
By Topper'40 out of Racket'40: Tipler (cast 1746)
By Carver'38 out of Sir R Fagg's Julian: Drunkard (cast 1743), Julian (given to Lord Eglinton 1749)
By Crowner'40 out of Maiden'40: Diamond (given to David Briggs 1746), Doxy (given to David Briggs 1743), Promise (given to David Briggs 1750), Tipler (given to David Briggs 1747)
By Lord Tankerville's young Banger out of Nioby'41: Nelly (cast 1747)

Old Hounds from Lord Tankerville - 13th December 1743
Bred by Sir R Fagg: Blossom, Careless, Nancy (all given to Mr Drax 1744)
Bred by Mr Gore: Mountain, Nancy (both cast 1744)
By Dashwood'34 out of Mr Morley's Folly: Banger (cast 1750), Buxom (cast 1746), Finder (given to Mr Fisher 1748), Mariner (given to Lord Dalkeith 1749)
By Lord Tankerville's Clouder out of his Monkey: Dinger (cast 1744), Plowman (cast 1744)
Bred by Sir J Miller: Phillis (given to Mr Drax 1744)
Chance hounds: Ruler (given to Mr Drax 1744), Fortune (came from Tom Johnson, cast 1744)

Young Hounds - 13th December 1743
By Lord Tankerville's Clouder out of Racket'40: Racket (cast 1745), Ranter (cast 1744), Ratler (cast 1749), Render (cast 1749), Rockwood (cast 1745), Ruby (cast 1750)
By Finder'43 out of Comfort'38: Cryer (cast 1750), Kitty (cast 1747)
By Luther'39 out of Dido'39: Lady (cast 1746)
By Lord Tankerville's Banger out of Gossip'39: Galloper (cast 1744)
By Lord Tankerville's Banger out of Fortune'41: Famous (given to Lord Dalkeith 1749), Flurry (given to Mr Drax 1744), Forrester (cast 1746), Fury (given to Lord Dalkeith 1749)
By Finder'43 out of Music'39: Fairplay (cast 1747)
By Trusty'42 out of Truelove'40: Tapster (cast 1749), Thunder (given to Mr Fisher 1749), Truemaid (given to Alderman Gascoigne 1749)
By Boxer'40 out of Maiden'40: Bouncer (cast 1746), Busy (cast 1746), Buxom (cast 1750)
By Luther'39 out of Bridget'41: Leader (given to Mr Drax 1744), Lifter (given to Mr Drax 1744), Lovely (cast 1747)
By Carver'38 out of Sir R Fagg's Julian: Chanter (cast 1746)

Young Hounds - 15th December 1744
By Turpin'42 out of Crimson'40: Tapster (cast 1745), Tattle (cast 1750), Tosser (cast 1750)
By Lord Tankerville's Vulcan out of Bell'41: Banger (given to Sir T Acland 1745), Bellman (given to Sir T Acland 1745), Betty (cast 1750), Bouncer (cast 1745), Bounder (cast 1746)
By Vulcan'40 out of Veny'42: Vulcan (cast 1750)
By Vulture'42 out of Tipsy'42: Vander (cast 1747), Virgin (cast 1750)
By Duke of Bolton's Founder out of Gossip'39: Gallant (cast 1750), Gamester (given to Sir T Acland 1745), Guider (given to Sir T Acland 1745)
By Trusty'42 out of Bridget'41: Thumper (cast 1745), Trolly (given to Sir T Acland 1745)
By Ringwood'41 out of Dido'39: Roman (cast 1745)
By Ringwood'41 out of Countess'40: Rattle (given to Sir T Acland 1745)
By Duke of Bolton's Cobbler out of Folly'40: Favourite (cast 1750), Flurry (cast 1750)
By Finder'43 out of Comfort'38: Costly (cast 1750), Curious (cast 1745)

Old Hounds from Lord Tankerville - 30th December 1745
By his Banger out of his Cloudy, dam by Mr Withers' Snowball out of Lively: Bellman (cast 1746), Fanny (given to Lord Berkeley 1747)
By his Banger out of his Blossom: Blameless (cast 1748), Bloomer (cast 1746), Bonny (cast 1746), Blossom (cast 1747), Fairmaid (cast 1746), Flurry (cast 1746), Pyman (cast 1746)

By his Trusty out of his Phillis: Bluebell (cast 1746)
By his Trusty out of his Damsel: Lady (cast 1746), Leader (cast 1749)
By his Trusty out of his Smirkin: Merrylass (cast 1750)
By his Clouder out of his Polly: Lovely (given to Mr Morley 1748)
By Cryer'37 out of Mr Morley's Polly: Ruby (cast 1750), Sweetlips (given to Sir J Miller 1746)
From Mr Newby out of Lord Tankerville's Lively: Trusty (given to Duke of Grafton 1748), Warrior (cast 1746)
By Lord Craven's Drunkard out of Duke of Bolton's Brazen: Almond (cast 1747)
By Lord Craven's Drunkard out of Duke of Bolton's Fury: Dicky (cast 1747)
From Sir John Miller: Jewel (cast 1746)
From Mr Pelham: Marplot (given back to Mr Pelham 1747)

Young Hounds - 30th December 1745

By Banger'43 out of Tipsy'42: Bluemaid (cast 1746), Bowman (cast 1746)
By Turpin'42 out of Lively'39: Lady (cast 1750), Limner (cast 1750), Lofty (cast 1750)
By Thumper'41 out of Bonny'41: Bluet (cast 1750), Bridget (cast 1747)
By Thumper'41 out of Bell'41: Tansey (cast 1747), Toler (cast 1750)
By Trusty'42 out of Comfort'38: Cloudy (cast 1750), Crimson (cast 1750)
By Boxer'40 out of Julian'42: Jenny (cast 1750), Jugler (cast 1750), Julia (cast 1750)
By Ringwood'41 out of Veny'42: Rachel (cast 1750), Ransom (cast 1746), Ranter (cast 1746), Rifle (cast 1750), Ringwood (cast 1747)
By Dinger'43 out of Kitty'43: Damsel (cast 1746), Dido (cast 1746), Doxy (cast 1750)
By Turpin'42 out of Gossip'39: Tulip (cast 1750)
By Ringwood'41 out of Duke of Bolton's Mischief: Revel (cast 1746), Ruffler (cast 1746)
By Lord Tankerville's Trusty out of his Smirkin: Silence (given to Billy Ives 1749), Singwell (cast 1750), Sober (cast 1750)
By Lord Tankerville's Trusty out of Mr Morley's Polly: Pleasant (cast 1749)

Young Hounds - 30th December 1746

By Turpin'42 out of Lively'39: Lewdy (lost in New Forest 1749), Lifter (cast 1747), Lively (given to Sir J Miller 1747), Luther (cast 1750)
By Thumper'41 out of Bonny'41: Tempest (given to Mr Fisher 1748), Tickle (given to Mr Fisher 1749), Trimmer (cast 1747), Tripsy (cast 1747)
By Marplot'45 out of Fury'43: Madcap (given to Lord Dalkeith 1749), Maiden (cast 1747), Mountain (cast 1747), Music (cast 1747)
By Marplot'45 out of Ruby'43: Merryman (cast 1750), Mopsy (given to Lord Berkeley 1749)
By Vulcan'40 out of Veny'42: Vulture (cast 1749)

Bitches to be warded - 25th December 1746 to 16th April 1747

25th December: Julian'42 by Tapster'43 (seven puppys entered 1748)
10th January: Lively'39 by Turpin'42
10th January: Music'46 by Gallant'44 (two puppys entered 1748)
13th January: Doxy'45 by Tosser'44 (two puppys entered 1748)
14th January: Bell'41 by Gallant'44
1st March: Betty'44 by Mr Noel's Pilgrim
5th March: Fury'43 by Mr Noel's Dolphin (two puppys entered 1748)
22nd March: Buxom'43 by Mr Noel's Pilgrim (four puppys entered 1748)
26th March: Rifle'45 by Mr Noel's Pilgrim (three puppys entered 1748)
27th March: Tulip'45 by Swapper'41 (one puppy entered 1748)
29th March: Folly'40 by Cryer'43 (one puppy entered 1748)
29th March: Tansy'45 by Turpin'42 (two puppys entered 1748)
11th April: Jenny'45 by Mr Noel's Dolphin
16th April: Juno by Trusty'45 (one puppy entered 1748)

Old Hounds given - 31st December 1747

From Mr Wells: Warrior (cast 1749)
From Lord Orford by his Winder out of Flacket, a hound from Kent: Ruler (given to Mr Fisher 1749)
From Lord Orford by his Calvin out of his Flurry: Capper (cast 1750)
From Lord Orford by his Fidler out of his Frisky: Doctor (cast 1750), Fidler (cast 1750), Phillis (cast 1748)
From Lord Orford by Lord Herbert's Dolphin out of Lord Orford's Wildlass: Damsel (cast 1750)
From Lord Orford by his Calvin out of his Wilfull: Wildlass (cast 1749)

Pedigree of Charlton Hounds

Young Hounds - 31st December 1747
By Lord Orford's Trojan out of his Dainty: Traffic (cast 1750), Trinket (given to Mr Fisher 1748)
By Lord Orford's Streamer out of his Whimsy: Sally (given to Lord Dalkeith 1749)
By Lord Orford's Singer out of his Diamond: Daphne (given to Mr Fisher 1748), Diamond (given to Lord Dalkeith 1749)
By Lord Orford's Streamer out of his Wilfull: Wherry (cast 1750)
From Mr Samber: Sweetlips (given to Mr Fisher 1748)
By Lord Tankerville's Rockwood out of Duke of Grafton's Dido: Careless (cast 1749), Carver (given to Lord Eglinton 1748)
By Boxer'40 out of Ruby'43: Bouncer (cast 1750), Bounty (given to Lord Berkeley 1749), Bowler (cast 1750), Brusher (cast 1750), Bumper (cast 1750)
By Boxer'40 out of Fanny'45: Billy (cast 1750), Blossom (cast 1750), Brazen (given to Mr Fisher 1748)
By Turpin'42 out of Veny'42: Trolly (cast 1750)
By Trusty'45 out of Betty'44: Bluecap (cast 1748), Bonny (given to Mr Morley 1749)
By Thumper'41 out of Rifle'45: Rebel (cast 1749), Ruler (cast 1748)
By Boxer'40 out of Julian'42: Jessemy (cast 1750), Jewel (cast 1750), Jockey (cast 1750), Jollyboy (cast 1750), Jumbler (given to Lord Dalkeith 1749), Jumper (cast 1750)
By Cryer'43 out of Folly'40: Folly (cast 1750), Fretwell (cast 1749)
By Marplot'45 out of Fury'43: Marriner (given to Mr Fisher 1748), Marvel (given to Mr Fisher 1748), Miller (given to Alderman Gascoigne 1749)
By Thumper'41 out of Lovely'43: Thumper (cast 1749), Trimmer (given to Mr Fisher 1748), Trusty (given to Alderman Gascoigne 1749)

Young Hounds - 31st December 1748
By Tapster'43 out of Julian'42: Tipsy, Trader, Trouncer, Truelass, Truelove, Trueman, Tutress (all cast 1750)
By Tosser'44 out of Doxy'45: Damsel, Dashwood (both cast 1750)
By Gallant'44 out of Music'46: Gamester (given to Lord Downe 1749), Goodwood (cast 1750)
By Swapper'41 out of Tulip'45: Smirkin (cast 1750)
By Trusty'45 out of Juno: Tifter (cast 1750)
By Mr Noel's Dolphin out of Fury'43: Darling, Dolphin (both cast 1750)
By Turpin'42 out of Tansey'45: Truelove (cast 1750), Turpin (given to Lord Dalkeith 1749)
By Mr Noel's Pilgrim out of Buxom'43: Pilgrim (given to Lord Dalkeith 1749), Plunder (cast 1750), Promise (cast 1750), Pyman (given to Lord Downe 1749)
By Mr Noel's Pilgrim out of Rifle'45: Ransom (given to Lord Talbot 1749), Rockwood (given to Lord Dalkeith 1749), Rowsey (cast 1750)
By Cryer'43 out of Folly'40: Cruel (cast 1750)
From Mr Pelham by Ringwood'41 out of his Cloudy: Crispin (cast 1750)
From Mr Pelham by Ringwood'41 out of his Famous: Tansey (cast 1750)

Old Hounds given - 31st December 1749
From Mr O'Brien by Trusty'45 out of Lord Tankerville's Lovely: Bellman, Bloomer (both cast 1750)
From Mr Bright: Charmer, Gipsy, Swallow (all cast 1750)
From Mr Bright out of his Swallow: Drunkard, Jenny (both cast 1750)
From Sir C Goring by a half bred hound out of a white stolen bitch: Diamond, Lively, Toler (all cast 1750)
From Sir C Goring by Chanter'43: Daphne, Ranter (both cast 1750)
From Kent: Lady (cast 1750)
From Sir C Goring by Vander'44: Gamester (cast 1750)
From Sir C Goring: Ringwood, Rockwood (both cast 1750)

Young Hounds - 31st December 1749
By Ratler'43 out of Doxy'45: Ranter, Ratler, Rockwood, Ruler (all cast 1750)
By Mr Morley's Tomboy out of Buxom'43: Banger, Bluet, Bridget, Buxom (all cast 1750)
By Merryman'46 out of Julian'42: Maiden, Major, Mariner, Merchant, Mischief, Miser, Mode, Modesty, Molly, Monster, Mountain (all cast 1750)
By Turpin'42 out of Pleasant'45: Trinket, Trojan, Trueboy (all cast 1750)
By Duke of Grafton's Caster out of Lewdy'46: Lively (cast 1750)

List of the fox hounds when taken to Charlton on the 16th October 1757
From Lord Chedworth: Bellman, yellow py'd dog (cast 1760), Bluebell, blue py'd bitch (died 1761), Bowler, white dog with black spot on side (given to Mr Herne 1761), Brilliant, white bitch with yellow spot on side (died 1761),

Brusher, yellow py'd dog (died 1761), Carver, yellow py'd dog (died 1761), Cocker, black py'd dog (cast 1760), Croney, black py'd bitch (sp'd cast 1760), Damsel, yellowish py'd bitch (died 1761), Danger, yellowish py'd dog (cast 1760), Dashwood, yellow py'd dog (cast 1760), Driver, blue py'd dog (cast 1760), Drummer, white dog (died 1761), Fairmaid, white bitch (sp'd cast 1760), Famous, grey py'd bitch (sp'd cast 1758), Fidler, brown py'd dog (cast 1760), Foreman, black py'd dog (cast 1760), Forrester, blue py'd dog (cast 1760), Frater, white dog (given to Mr Herne 1761), Frolic, yellow py'd bitch (died 1760), Gamester by old Bluecap, blue py'd dog (died 1762), Jenny, yellow py'd bitch (died 1761), Jovial, brownish py'd dog (cast 1761), Lively, blue py'd bitch (sp'd given to Mr Herne 1761), Lusty, blue py'd dog (died 1761), Luter, blue py'd dog (given to Mr Herne 1761), Madam, yellow py'd bitch (sp'd died 1760), Maiden, blue py'd bitch (sp'd cast 1760), Maukin, blue py'd bitch (cast 1760), Music, black py'd bitch (sp'd given to Mr Herne died 1762), Nancy, yellow py'd bitch (sp'd died 1760), Phillis, white bitch (sp'd cast 1761), Phoenix, blue py'd bitch (cast 1760), Pleadwell, yellow py'd dog (gelt given to Mr Barber 1759), Polly, yellow py'd bitch (sp'd cast 1760), Ransom, blue py'd bitch (sp'd cast 1758), Ranter, black py'd dog (died of old age 1761), Ratler, black py'd dog (died 1762), Redcap, black py'd dog (given to Mr Barber 1760), Roman, brown py'd dog (cast 1760), Ruby, black py'd bitch (died 1760), Sober, black py'd dog (died 1760), Sylvia, black py'd bitch (sp'd died 1760), Tipsy, black py'd bitch (sp'd lost 1761 died 1763), Traveller, grey py'd dog (kill'd by accident 1759), Trojan, yellowish py'd dog (died 1760), Virgin, black py'd bitch (died 1760), Windsor, yellow py'd dog (died 1760)

From Sir J Miller: Juno, yellow py'd bitch (given to Mr Barber 1760), Ramper, black py'd dog (died 1760), Tospot, black py'd dog (died 1762)

From Sir J Miller bred by Lord Granby: Brusher, black py'd dog (died 1761), Dancer, grey py'd dog (died 1761), Farmer, brown py'd dog (died of distemper 1763), Hearty, brown py'd bitch (sp'd died 1760), Jenny, blue py'd bitch (sp'd died 1762), Joyful, black py'd bitch (sp'd given to Mr Barber 1760), Lovely, yellow py'd bitch (sp'd died 1762), Phillis, black py'd bitch (in New Forest to hunt with young hounds 1762 died 1763), Prudence, black py'd bitch (sp'd died 1760), Ratler, black py'd dog (died 1762), Ruby, black py'd bitch (sp'd cast 1760), Searcher, black py'd dog (gelt died 1762), Silence, liver colour py'd bitch (sp'd given to Mr Herne died 1762), Trojan, black py'd dog (died 1762), Truelove, black py'd bitch (cast 1760)

From Sir J Miller bred by Lord Eglinton: Dido, black py'd bitch (died 1762), Maiden, grizzle bitch (died 1760), Modesty, yellowish py'd bitch out of <u>Mode</u>'49[*] in the part he bought of the late Duke of Richmond's pack (died 1763)

From Sir J Miller bred by Mr Pawlett: Mopsy, white bitch (cast 1760), Noble, yellow py'd dog (given to Mr Herne died 1762), Rifle, black py'd bitch (died 1762), Ruffler, yellow py'd dog (died 1763)

From Sir J Miller bred by Mr Taylor: Music, black py'd bitch (given to Mr Conolly 1761)

From Sir J Miller bred by Lord Newburg: Strumpet, black py'd bitch (given to Mr Butler 1760)

From Mr Gibbon bred by Lord Eglinton: Bonny, yellow py'd bitch (sp'd died 1761), Dolphin, black py'd dog (given to Lord Ilchester 1762), Jumper, black py'd dog (died 1762)

From Mr Gibbon: Merryman, black py'd dog (gelt died 1761)

From Mr Gibbon by Mr Pawlett's <u>Boxer</u> out of the late Duke of Richmond's Rowsey'48: Flurry, liver colour py'd bitch (died 1762), Frolic, liver colour py'd bitch (died 1762), Fudler, liver colour py'd dog (died 1762)

List of young fox hounds entered the 16th October 1757

From Lord Chedworth: Bonny, yellow py'd bitch (given to Mr Wilson 1760), Buxom, yellow py'd bitch (given to Mr Wilson 1760), Drunkard, black py'd dog (cast 1760), Marvel, grey py'd bitch (given to Mr Wilson 1760), Mopsy, grey py'd bitch (died 1760)

From Lord Chedworth by his Bellman: Tipler, yellow py'd dog (in New Forest died 1762), Truelove, black py'd bitch (given to Mr Barber 1759)

From Sir J Miller: Rockwood, black py'd dog (given to Mr Barber 1760)

From Sir J Miller out of his Mopsy'57: Madam, blue py'd bitch (cast 1760), Mounter, brown py'd dog (cast 1760)

From Sir J Miller by Lord Granby's Brusher'57 out of Mr Taylor's Music'57: Bowman, black py'd dog (given to Mr Barber 1760), Mermaid, black py'd bitch (sp'd died 1761)

From Sir J Miller by his Noble'57: Jewel, blue py'd bitch (given to Mr Limbry died 1764)

From Mr Gibbon by his Fudler'57 out of Mr Stuart's <u>Darling</u>: Fury, yellow py'd bitch (died 1760)

From Lord Granby: Barber, black py'd dog (died 1761), Betty, black py'd bitch (died 1760), Buxom, blue py'd bitch (died 1761), Kindness, yellow py'd bitch (died 1760), Kitty, grizzle py'd bitch (died 1760), Peggy, white bitch with yellow spot (sp'd died 1762), Pleasant, white bitch with a yellow spot (with young hounds 1764 died 1765)

Recapitulation for the year 1757

Old hounds from Lord Chedworth - 13 couple dogs, 11 couple bitches
Young hounds from Lord Chedworth - 1 couple dogs, 2½ couple bitches
Old hounds from Sir John Miller - 5 couple dogs, 8½ couple bitches

---

[*] The hounds with a line under them do not belong to the pack.

Pedigree of Charlton Hounds

Young hounds from Sir John Miller - 1½ couple dogs, 1½ couple bitches
Old hounds from Mr Gibbon - 2 couple dogs, 1½ couple bitches
Young hound from Mr Gibbon - ½ couple bitch
Young hounds from Lord Granby - ½ couple dog, 3 couple bitches   Total 51½ couple

List of young fox hounds entered the 1st October 1758
By Lord Eglinton's <u>Brimmer</u> out of Lord Granby's Truelove'57: Boxer, black py'd dog (given to Sir T Acland 1764), Bridget, brown py'd bitch (sp'd died 1761), Brimmer, black py'd dog (given to Mr Barber 1760)
By Lord Chedworth's Brusher'57 out of Mr Pawlett's Mopsy'57: Banger, blue py'd dog (in New Forest cast 1760), Blowsy, yellow py'd bitch (cast 1760), Blueman, blue py'd dog (given to Mr Conolly 1761)
From Lord Eglinton by <u>Turpin</u>'48: Crowner, yellow py'd dog (given to Mr Limbry 1764)
From Mr Pawlett: Damon, blue py'd dog (given to Mr Conolly 1761), Dinger, blue py'd dog (died of distemper 1761)
From Colonel Buck: Dashwood, black py'd dog (given to Mr Barber 1760), Dolly, black py'd bitch (given to Mr Huffle 1760), Doxy, black py'd bitch (given to General Holmes 1760), Drowsy, black py'd bitch (given to Mr Wilson 1760)
From Lord Granby out of a famous bitch: Famous, yellow tan bitch (died of distemper 1763), Fanny, white bitch with brown spot (sp'd given to Mr Conolly 1761), Faulkner, blue py'd dog (cast 1761), Filtcher, black py'd dog (in New Forest to hunt with young hounds 1762 died 1763), Founder, black py'd dog (in New Forest to hunt with young hounds 1762 died 1763), Fountain, black py'd dog (in New Forest to hunt with young hounds 1762 died 1763)
By Lord Granby's Farmer'57 out of Lord Eglinton's Modesty'57: Finder, black py'd dog (cast 1762), Fleez'em, blue py'd dog (given to Mr St Leger 1763), Merrylass, brown py'd bitch (in New Forest to hunt with young hounds 1763 died 1764), Mode, brown py'd bitch (with young hounds 1764 died 1766)
By Lord Chedworth's <u>blind Boxer</u> out of his Virgin'57: Goodlass, yellow tan (cast 1760), Granby, yellow tan (cast 1760), Grantham, brown py'd dog (in New Forest to hunt with young hounds 1763 given to Duke of Bolton 1764)
By Lord Chedworth's Fidler'57 out of Sir J Miller's Juno'57: Judy, yellow py'd bitch (given to Mr Huffle 1760)
From Lord Chedworth by his blind Boxer out of his Phoenix'57: Promise, blue py'd bitch (given to Mr Huffle 1760)
From Lord Chedworth by his blind Boxer out of his Brilliant'57: Thumper, brown py'd dog (given to Mr Barber 1760)
From Mr Pawlett out of a bitch Mr Taylor's: Tulip, black py'd bitch (lost died 1762)

Recapitulation for the year 1758
Old hounds - 23 couple dogs, 28½ couple bitches
Young hounds - 8½ couple dogs, 6½ couple bitches   66½ couple
Hounds disposed of this year - cast 1½ couple, given away 1 couple, killed by accident ½ couple   3 couple
Total of Hounds remaining   63½ couple
NB Mr Norton Pawlett's pack is now Mr Spencer's, Mr Wilson a gentleman in Norfolk

List of young fox hounds entered the 1st October 1759
By Lord Granby's Brusher'57 out of Modesty'57: Banger, black py'd dog (given to Lord Percival died 1762), Bouncer, black py'd dog (died 1764), Meddle, black py'd bitch (with young hounds 1764 given to Mr Limbry 1765), Merry, black py'd bitch (died 1761), Molly, black py'd bitch (given to Mr Limbry 1765), Myrtle, black py'd bitch (with young hounds 1766 died of old age 1768)
By Mr Pawlett's Royster out of Brilliant'57: Blewit, blue py'd bitch (given to Mr Conolly 1761), Roman, blue py'd dog (given to Mr Herne 1761), Ruler, blue py'd dog (given to General Holmes 1761)
By Fudler'57 out of Damsel'57: Dainty, black py'd bitch (lost in New Forest 1761 with young hounds 1763 died 1764), Darling, brown py'd bitch (given to General Holmes 1760), Doxy, brown py'd bitch (with beagles at Goodwood 1760), Foreman, black py'd dog (given to Duke of Bolton 1764)
By Lord Granby's Ratler'57 out of Dido'57: Daphne, blue py'd bitch (given to Mr Limbry 1764), Dolly, blue py'd bitch (died 1761), Drowsy, blue py'd bitch (sp'd given to Mr Conolly 1761), Ranger, blue py'd dog (in New Forest to hunt with young hounds 1762 given to Wild at Lyndhurst 1764), Rebel, blue py'd dog (cast 1761), Render, brown py'd dog (in New Forest to hunt with young hounds 1762 given to Duke of Bolton 1764), Roaster, blue py'd dog (given to Mr Mitchell 1764)
By Gamester'57 out of Flurry'57: Folly, black py'd bitch (cast 1761), Frisky, black py'd bitch (with beagles at Goodwood 1762), Gallant, black py'd dog (in New Forest to hunt with young hounds 1762 given to Duke of Bolton 1764), Guider, black py'd dog (with young hounds 1765 cast 1769)
By Farmer'57 out of Rifle'57: Fowler, black py'd dog (died of distemper 1763), Freeman, black py'd dog (died 1763), Rally, black py'd bitch (with beagles at Goodwood 1760)

By Mr Pawlett's Founder out of Lord Chedworth's Music'57: Fearful, black py'd dog (given to Mr Smith 1764), Gamester, liver colour py'd dog (cast 1760), Mischief, blue py'd bitch (sp'd died 1762)
By Gamester'57 out of Lord Granby's Phillis'57: Galloper, blue py'd dog (died 1761), Gameboy, black py'd dog (given to Mr Limbry 1764), Placket, black py'd bitch (given to Mr Meynell 1763), Prattle, black py'd bitch (sp'd died 1763), Princess, black py'd bitch (in New Forest to hunt with young hounds 1762 with young hounds 1764 died 1765), Purple, blue py'd bitch (with young hounds 1764 given to Mr Limbry 1765)
By Ruffler'57 out of Lord Chedworth's Jenny'57: Judy, yellow py'd bitch (with beagles at Goodwood 1760), Julian, yellow py'd bitch (with beagles at Goodwood 1760), Ringwood, yellow py'd dog (cast 1761)
By Jumper'57 out of Mr Taylor's Music'57: Jolly, blue py'd dog (given to Mr Barber 1760), Joynter, black py'd dog (given to Mr Barber 1760), Jugler, brown py'd dog (lost in New Forest died 1763), Maukin, black py'd bitch (given to Mr Bathurst 1764)
By Lusty'57 out of Lord Eglinton's Maiden'57: Leader, yellow dog (lost 1760), Limner, blue py'd dog (given to Mr Conolly 1762)

Recapitulation for the year 1759
Old hounds - 31 couple dogs, 32½ couple bitches
Young hounds - 12 couple dogs, 10½ couple bitches   86 couple
Hounds disposed of this year - cast 12½ couple, died 9 couple, given away 10 couple, with the beagles at Goodwood 2 couple, lost ½ couple   34 couple
Total of Hounds remaining this year   52 couple
NB Mr Huffle a gentleman in Holland, Mr Butler a gentleman at Rowdell in Sussex, Mr Barber at Postslade in Suffolk

List of young fox hounds entered the 1st October 1760
By Lord Granby's Brusher'57 out of Flurry'57: Bluecoat, blue py'd dog (given to Mr Bathurst died 1764), Fairmaid, black py'd bitch (sp'd sent to France 1764), Fury, black py'd bitch (with young hounds 1764 died 1765)
By Farmer'57 out of Dido'57: Decent, grizzle py'd bitch (given to Mr Limbry 1767), Duchess, grizzle py'd bitch (died 1766), Fainter, black py'd dog (in New Forest to hunt with young hounds 1762 given to Mr Limbry 1764), Fairplay, grizzle py'd dog (with young hounds 1766 given to Mr Limbry 1767)
By Farmer'57 out of Lord Chedworth's Jenny'57: Fidler, blue py'd dog (given to Mr Conolly 1762), Forrester, yellowish py'd dog (died of distemper 1763), Fox Hunter, yellowish py'd dog (given to General Holmes 1761), Jessamy, brown py'd bitch (died 1761), Juniper, black py'd bitch (died 1761)
By Founder'58 out of Rifle'57: Fearnought, black py'd dog (given to Sir J Miller 1762), Racket, black py'd bitch (sp'd sent to France 1764), Rifle, black py'd bitch (with young hounds 1764 given to Mr Limbry 1765)
By Gamester'57 out of Modesty'57: Gamester, blue py'd dog (died 1765), Gelder, yellowish py'd dog (in New Forest to hunt with young hounds 1762 died 1763), Goodwood, blue py'd dog (died 1761), Grinder, blue py'd dog (given to Mr Conolly 1765), Julian, yellowish py'd bitch (sp'd with young hounds 1766 died 1770)
By Jovial'57 out of Kindness'57: Impudence, liver colour py'd dog (cast 1761), Jollyboy, liver colour py'd dog (given to General Holmes 1761), Kindness, yellow py'd bitch (sp'd with beagles at Goodwood 1761)
By Ranter'57 out of Pleasant'57: Poppet, white bitch with a black spot (given to Mr Conolly 1762), Richmond, brown py'd dog (died of distemper 1763), Roper, black py'd dog (given to Sir T Acland 1764), Wrangler, black py'd dog (given to Mr Bathurst 1764)
By Tospot'57 out of Tulip'58: Tapster, black py'd dog (lost 1763), Tempest, yellow py'd bitch (with young hounds 1764 died 1765), Trolly, yellow py'd bitch (died 1761)

Recapitulation for the year 1760
Old hounds - 28½ couple dogs, 23½ couple bitches
Young hounds - 8½ couple dogs, 6½ couple bitches   67 couple
Hounds disposed of this year - cast 4 couple, died 11½ couple, given away 7½ couple   23 couple
Total of Hounds remaining this year   44 couple

List of young fox hounds entered the 1st October 1761
By Lord Chedworth's Brusher'57 out of Dido'57: Banter, black py'd dog (cast 1763), Bluster, black py'd dog (died of distemper 1763), Bonniface, black py'd dog (died of distemper 1763), black py'd dog (died 1762), Delicate, blue py'd bitch (died 1762), Kindness, yellow py'd bitch (sp'd to hare hounds 1762)
By Banger'58 out of Famous'58: Bender, black py'd dog (in New Forest to hunt with young hounds 1762 died 1763), Bumper, black and yellow py'd dog (given away 1763), Fancy, faint yellow py'd bitch (died 1763), Foxhound, yellow py'd bitch (with young hounds 1764 died 1765)
By Gameboy'59 out of Music'57: Granby, brown py'd dog (given to Duke of Bolton 1764), Maiden, brown py'd bitch (sp'd to hare hounds 1762)

Pedigree of Charlton Hounds

By Gameboy'59 out of Jewel'57: Jubel, blue py'd bitch (given to Mr Limbry 1765)
By Gamester'57 out of Mode'58: Matchless, yellowish grey py'd bitch (sp'd to hare hounds 1762), Minder, yellowish grey py'd bitch (with young hounds 1764 1765 and 1767 died 1770), Molecomb, yellowish grey py'd bitch (sp'd with young hounds 1767 died 1770)
By Ranter'57 out of Merrylass'58: Mopsy, black py'd bitch (given to Mr Conolly 1763)
By Mr Noel's Nimrod out of Pleasant'57: Namesake, yellow py'd dog (cast 1767), Nimrod, yellow py'd dog (with young hounds 1763 given to Mr Bathurst 1764), Pheasant, grizzle py'd bitch (to hare hounds 1762), Polly, yellow py'd bitch (sp'd with young hounds 1766 cast 1767), Positive, grizzle py'd bitch (given to Sir S Stuart 1763), Prudence, yellow py'd bitch (given to Mr Limbry 1767)
By Tospot'57 out of Princess'59: Partridge, brown py'd bitch (to hare hounds 1762), Pineapple, brown py'd bitch (sp'd to hare hounds 1762), Pretty, brown py'd bitch (died 1762), Promise, liver colour py'd bitch (died of distemper 1763)
By Lord Granby's Ratler'57 out of Modesty'57: Ratler, grey py'd dog (cast 1763), Ringwood, black py'd dog (given away 1763), Charlton, grey py'd dog (died 1763)

List of half the pack of fox hounds bought of the Dunstable Club in November 1761

From Mr Taylor: Carver, black py'd dog (cast 1762)
By Dunstable Club Victor out of a bitch of Sir P Lister: Captain, black py'd dog (cast 1762), Charmer, white bitch with a black spot (sp'd with young hounds 1763 given to Mr Bathurst 1764)
By Mr Pelham's Roller out of his Croney: Conquest, yellow py'd bitch (sp'd cast 1762)
By Dunstable Club Captain out of Mr Meynell's Damsel: Dancer, grizzle and rough coated dog (given to Mr Smith 1765), Dido, whitish bitch (with young hounds 1764 given to Mr Limbry 1765)
By Dunstable Club Newby out of their Fortune: Finder, yellow py'd dog (died 1763), Fortune, brown py'd bitch (died 1763)
By Mr Selby's Trojan out of Duke of Hamilton's Harlot: Hickman, yellow py'd dog (cast 1762)
From Duke of Hamilton: Jumper, blue py'd dog (in New Forest to hunt with young hounds 1762 died 1763), Kitty, blue py'd bitch (cast 1762)
By Mr Turner's Tipler out of Dunstable Club Mawkin who was out of Hampshire Careless: Merrylass, liver colour py'd bitch (with young hounds 1764 died 1765), Mountain, brown py'd dog (died 1763)
By Mr Meynell's Rivers out of Mr Turner's Nelly: Neptune, yellow py'd dog (given to Mr Neal 1764)
From Duke of Hamilton: Newby, yellow py'd dog (cast 1762)
By Mr Meynell's Rivers out of Mr Noel's Prudence: Painter, black py'd dog (cast 1762)
From Mr Green: Piper, grizzle py'd dog (cast 1762)
By Dunstable Club Piper out of their Pleasant: Prudence, white bitch with a black spot on her side (sp'd cast 1762)
By Duke of Hamilton's Jumper out of his Polly: Plunder, white dog with brown ears (died 1763), Rockwood, black py'd dog (in New Forest to hunt with young hounds 1762 given to Mr Conolly 1763), Ruler, black py'd dog (in New Forest to hunt with young hounds 1762 given to Mr Meynell 1763)
By Duke of Hamilton's Knightly out of Mr Pelham's Ransom: Ratler, blue py'd dog (cast 1762), Royster, yellow py'd dog (in New Forest to hunt with young hounds 1762 died 1763)
From Mr Selby: Ranter, yellow tan dog (cast 1762)
From Duke of Hamilton: Rally, black py'd bitch (sp'd cast 1762)
From Mr Calvert: Ransom, brown py'd bitch (sp'd cast 1762)
From Mr Selby: Sweetlips, grizzle py'd bitch (died 1763)
From Duke of Hamilton: Traffic, bitch (sp'd cast 1762)
From Mr Pelham: Victor, black py'd dog (died 1762)
By Dunstable Club Victor out of their Fortune: Vulcan, black py'd dog (in New Forest to hunt with young hounds 1762 given to Mr Bathurst 1764)
From Mr Turner: Violet, dark brown bitch (died 1762)
Whipster, faint yellow py'd dog (cast 1762)

Recapitulation for the year 1761
Old hounds - 24½ couple dogs, 19½ couple bitches
Old hounds from Mr Curzon - 10 couple dogs, 6 couple bitches
Young hounds - 6 couple dogs, 9 couple bitches   75 couple
Hounds disposed of this year - died 12 couple, cast 9 couple, given away 2½ couple, to the hare hounds at Goodwood 3½ couple   27 couple
Total of hounds remaining for next year   48 couple
Of which there is to compose the old pack 40 couple and to enter the young hounds with - 8 couple

List of young fox hounds entered the 1st October 1762

By Ranter'57 out of Pleasant'60: Patsy, brown py'd bitch (given to Mr Limbry 1768), Phoenix, black py'd bitch (with young hounds 1767 given to Mr Limbry 1768), Picture, grey py'd bitch (died 1765), Rebel, black py'd dog (lost 1763)

By Roper'60 out of Tempest'60: Roman, brown py'd dog (given to Mr Burrel 1765), Ruler, black py'd dog (given to Mr Bathurst 1765), Tulip, black py'd dog (died 1763)

By Fleec'em'58 out of Prattle'59: Frater, grizzle py'd dog (given away 1763)

By Guider'59 out of Lord Granby's Phillis'57: Gainer, black py'd dog (died 1766), Gambler, black py'd dog (given to Mr Smith 1764), Goodwood, black py'd dog (given to Mr Smith 1764), Patience, grey py'd bitch (died 1766)

By Lord Chedworth's Brusher'57 out of Merrylass'58: Malice, light brown py'd bitch (died 1769), Marvel, grizzle py'd bitch (to hare hounds 1763), Mendip, black py'd dog (cast 1763)

By Ranter'57 out of Myrtle'59: M, blue py'd bitch (to hare hounds 1763), Melon, brown py'd bitch (to hare hounds 1763), Ramper, black py'd dog (with young hounds 1766 given to Mr Limbry 1767)

By Banger'58 out of Music'57: Bellman, black py'd dog (given to Mr Limbry 1764), Brusher, white dog with brown spots (given to Mr Neal 1765)

By Bouncer'59 out of Dido'57: Banter, brown py'd dog (given to Duke of Bolton 1764), Bowler, brown py'd dog (cast 1763), Brimmer, brown py'd dog (cast 1763)

By Gamester'57 out of Mode'58: Grafton, grizzle py'd dog (died 1763)

By a dog of Mr Pelham's out of his Dainty, a descendant of Ringwood'41: Searcher, white dog with brown spots (died 1767), Silence, white bitch with brown spots (to hare hounds 1763), Sober, white dog with brown spots (with young hounds 1766 died 1767), Sylvia, white bitch with brown spots (to hare hounds 1763)

By Gameboy'59 out of Modesty'57: Bluecap, blue py'd dog (with young hounds 1767 given to Mr Limbry 1768), Girder, black py'd dog (to France 1765), Merry, black py'd bitch (to hare hounds 1763)

By Fleec'em'58 out of Dainty'59: Farmer, brown py'd dog (with young hounds 1767 given to Mr Limbry 1768), Faulkner, brown py'd dog (given to Lord Caulincourt 1763), Fudler, brown py'd dog (given to Lord Caulincourt 1763)

By Tospot'57 out of Purple'59: Tapster, light brown py'd dog (died 1765), Tipler, whiteish dog (given to Sir J Gresham 1763), Toper, whiteish dog (given to Sir J Gresham 1763), Tosspot, grizzle py'd dog (died 1763)

By Tapster'60 out of Molly'59: Taker, black py'd dog (died 1765)

From Sir S Stuart: Topper, yellow py'd dog (with young hounds 1767 given to Mr Limbry 1768)

List of the pack of fox hounds bought of Ashton Curzon Esq in April 1763

From Mr Biddulph: Madcap, black tan dog (with young hounds 1765 died 1769)

By Mr Curzon's Trojan out of his Romsey: Ranter, black py'd dog (entered 1759 gelt died 1764)

By Mr Curzon's Ratler out of his Truelove: Fanny, brown py'd bitch (entered 1760 sp'd given to Duke of Bolton 1764), Frater, brown py'd dog (entered 1760 gelt given to Duke of Bolton 1764)

By Mr Curzon's Cannock Whipster out of his Truelove: Nickit, black py'd bitch (entered 1761 given to Mr Meynell 1764), Noble, black py'd dog (entered 1761 gelt given to Mr Meynell 1764)

By Mr Meynell's Rivers out of Mr Curzon's Sprightly: Valiant, black py'd dog (entered 1762 with young hounds 1763 died 1765), Varlet, blue py'd bitch (entered 1762 sp'd given to Mr Bathurst 1765), Venus, brown py'd bitch (entered 1762 with young hounds 1764 given to Mr Limbry 1767), Victor, blue py'd dog (entered 1762 with young hounds 1763 died 1769)

By Mr Curzon's Redcap out of his Blossom: Capper, yellow py'd dog (entered 1762 geltdied 1764), Cloudy, yellow py'd bitch (entered 1760 with young hounds 1764 died 1765), Comfort, brown py'd bitch (entered 1760 sp'd died 1764), Conqueror, yellow py'd dog (entered 1760 died 1764)

By Mr Meynell's Gulliver out of Mr Curzon's Cloudy: Grobbler, black py'd dog (entered 1762 with young hounds 1763 given to Mr Bathurst 1765), Gulliver, brown py'd dog (entered 1762 with young hounds 1763 died 1766)

By Mr Curzon's Farmer out of his Psyche: Fairmaid, yellow py'd bitch (sp'd died of distemper 1764), Farmer, grizzle py'd dog (died 1764)

By Lord Leigh's Painter out of Mr Curzon's Betsy: Plunder, brown tan dog (gelt given to Mr Bullock 1764)

By Mr Curzon's Singwell out of his Roxey: Wanton, black py'd bitch (entered 1762 sp'd died 1764), Warbler, brown py'd bitch (entered 1762 with young hounds 1764 given to Mr Conolly 1769), Warrior, black py'd dog (entered 1762 with young hounds 1763 given to Mr Limbry 1764)

By Mr Curzon's Ratler out of Mr Fitzherbert's Riot: Traffic, brown py'd bitch (entered 1761 with young hounds 1764 given to Mr Limbry 1767)

By Mr Curzon's Ratler out of Duchess'60: Rally, black py'd bitch (entered 1762 died 1764), Ratler, black py'd dog (entered 1762 given to Mr Limbry 1768), Ruler, brown py'd dog (entered 1762 with young hounds 1763 given to Mr Meynell 1766)

Pedigree of Charlton Hounds

By Mr Meynell's Carver out of Mr Curzon's Phillis: Pleasant, brown py'd bitch (entered 1760 sp'd died 1765), Prussia, liver colour py'd dog (entered 1760 gelt died 1764)

By Mr Meynell's Conqueror out of Mr Curzon's little Lady: Blameless, reddish tan bitch (entered 1762 sp'd with young hounds 1766 died 1767), Blossom, almost white bitch (entered 1762 given to Mr Limbry 1768), Boxer, reddish tan dog (entered 1762 with young hounds 1766 cast 1767)

By Mr Meynell's Conqueror out of Mr Curzon's Brilliant: Psyche, reddish py'd bitch (entered 1762 sp'd to hare hounds 1764), Sally, grizzle py'd bitch (entered 1762 with young hounds 1764 to France 1765), Saucebox, reddish py'd dog (entered 1762 gelt with young hounds 1767 died 1768), Silence, reddish py'd bitch (entered 1762 sp'd given to Lord Caulincourt 1764)

By Mr Curzon's Cannock Whipster out of Darling'59: Trojan, yellow tan dog (entered 1762 died 1764), Trolly, bitch (entered 1762 given to Mr Limbry 1764)

By Lord Granby's Fairplay out of Mr Curzon's Dolly: Picture, yellow py'd bitch (entered 1759 sp'd with young hounds 1763 given to Mr Conolly 1764)

By Mr Meynell's Royal out of Mr Curzon's Lofty: Lofty, reddish tan bitch (entered 1762 sp'd died 1767)

By Mr Curzon's Lifter out of his Gossip: Prudence, black tan bitch (entered 1758 sp'd given to Mr Smith 1764), Lucy, grey py'd bitch (sp'd with young hounds 1763 given to Mr Limbry 1764)

By Mr Curzon's Ratler out of Mr Vernon's Dido: Racket, black py'd bitch (entered 1761 sp'd with young hounds 1765 given to Mr Bathurst 1766)

By Mr Curzon's Woodman out of Dolly'59: Tosspot, brown py'd dog (entered 1760 gelt with young hounds 1763 given to Mr Limbry 1764)

By Mr Curzon's old Madcap out of his Sprightly: Jollyboy, reddish tan dog (entered 1761 gelt died 1765)

Lilly, whiteish bitch (with young hounds 1763 given to Mr Limbry 1764)

Tickler, grey py'd dog (entered 1760 with young hounds 1767 died 1768)

Recapitulation for the year 1762

Old hounds - 27 couple dogs, 20½ bitches

Old hounds from Mr Curzon - 11 couple dogs, 12 couple bitches

Young hounds - 13½ couple dogs, 6½ couple bitches   90½ couple

Hounds disposed of this year - cast 2 couple, died 18 couple, given away 8½ couple, with hare hounds at Goodwood 3½ couple   32 couple

Total of hounds remaining for next year   58½ couple

of which there is to compose the old pack 48 couple and to enter the young hounds with 10½ couple

List of young fox hounds entered the 1st October 1763

From Mr Curzon by his Royal out of his Proxy: Acorn, black py'd dog (cast 1768), Ancaster, black py'd dog (with young hounds 1765 and 1767 given to Mr Limbry 1768), Ardent, black py'd bitch (died 1768), Arrow, black py'd bitch (given to Mr Smith 1764), April, black py'd dog (with young hounds 1765 and 1767 given to Mr Limbry 1768)

From Mr Curzon by his Singwell out of his Roxey: Arthur, almost all black dog (given to Mr Limbry 1765), Andrew, brown py'd dog (with young hounds 1765 to France 1766), Alfred, black py'd dog (given to Mr Smith 1764), Abigail, black py'd bitch (with young hounds 1765 to France 1766)

From Mr Curzon by Mr Meynell's Rivers out of Mr Curzon's Rary: Aimwell, blue py'd dog (with young hounds 1767 died 1770), Archer, dark grey py'd dog (with young hounds 1766 died 1770), Ask'em, black py'd dog (died 1764)

From Mr Curzon out of his Dido: Atom, rough coated black py'd bitch (given to Mr Limbry 1765), Ary, black py'd bitch (with young hounds 1765 sent to France 1766), Absent, black py'd bitch (to hare hounds 1764 old hound 1767 given to Mr Piggot 1769)

From Mr Curzon out of his Brilliant: Ammon, grizzle py'd white dog (sent to France 1764), Ajax, grizzle py'd white dog (sent to France 1764)

From Mr Curzon out of his Lemmon: Ambrose, black py'd dog (sent to France 1764), Abbess, light red bitch (died 1764)

From Mr Curzon: Adsdean, faint yellow py'd bitch (died 1764), Alnwick, brown py'd dog (sent to France 1764), Alsford, black py'd dog (sent to France 1764), Alton, brown py'd dog (sent to France 1764)

From Mr Meynell: Meynell, black py'd dog (sent to France 1764)

From Mr Meynell by Lord Granby's dog out of Mr Meynell's Picture: Whimsey, whiteish bitch (to hare hounds 1764 to France 1766), Whitish, whiteish bitch (sent to France 1764)

By Mr Meynell's Lawyer out of Pleasant'57: Lawyer, grizzle py'd dog (with young hounds 1766 given to Mr Limbry 1767), Leader, grizzle py'd dog (given to Mr Conolly 1766), Loyal, grizzle py'd dog (given to Mr Bathurst 1765), Lusty, grizzle py'd bitch (given to Mr Conolly 1764), Placket, grizzle py'd bitch (sent to France 1766), Prattle, grizzle py'd bitch (sp'd given to Mr Limbry 1768)

By Richmond'60 out of Sweetlips'61: Router, black mottled py'd dog (with young hounds 1766 died 1767), Royal, black mottled py'd dog (given to Mr Limbry 1767), Sempstress, black mottled py'd bitch (given to Mr Fettyplace 1769), Strumpet, black mottled py'd bitch (with young hounds 1766 given to Mr Limbry 1768), Sweetlips, black mottled py'd bitch (died 1768)

By Sir S Stuart's Bouncer out of Rifle'60: Baxter, black mottled py'd dog (with young hounds 1767 given to Mr Limbry 1768), Ready, black mottled py'd dog (died 1768)

By Dunstable Club's Captain out of Fury'60: Captain, black py'd dog (given to Mr Bathurst 1764), Colonel, black py'd dog (cast 1767)

By Richmond'60 out of Myrtle'59: Reeler, brown py'd dog (given to Mr Smith 1765)

By Lord Castlehaven's Stradler out of Positive'61: Stradler, grizzle and one ey'd py'd dog (died 1764), Striver, blue py'd dog (given to Lord Percival 1766)

By Sir S Stuart's Bowler out of Frisky'59, grizzle py'd bitch (with young hounds 1768 died 1769)

By Mountain'61 out of Purple'59: Private, black mottled py'd bitch (died 1768)

By Mr Meynell's Lawyer out of Mode'58: Limner, grizzle py'd dog (given to Mr Smith 1765), Luther, grizzle py'd dog (to hare hounds 1764)

By Guider'59 out of Prudence'57: Princess, red py'd bitch (with young hounds 1765 sent to France 1766)

By Richmond'60 out of Modesty'57: Modesty, blue py'd bitch (with young hounds 1768 cast 1769)

By Gameboy'59 out of Molly'59: Merry, red py'd bitch (to France with hare hounds 1766 old hound 1767 died 1768)

From Duke of Devonshire by his Victor: Sailor, black mottled py'd dog (with young hounds 1769 died 1770)

From Sir S Stuart by Mr Meynell's Lawyer out of Sir S Stuart's Fortune: Doxy, brown py'd bitch (with young hounds 1765 and 1768 given to Mr Conolly 1769)

From Sir S Stuart by Lord Castlehaven's dog out of Sir S Stuart's Fortune: Famous, brown py'd bitch (with young hounds 1765 to France 1766)

From Sir S Stuart by Mr Meynell's Lawyer out of Sir S Stuart's Famous: Frenzy, black py'd bitch (died 1765)

By Guider'59 out of Lord Granby's Phillis'57: Grasper, black py'd dog (given to Mr Bathurst 1765), Galloper, red py'd dog (with young hounds 1768 died 1770)

From Lord Chedworth by Richmond'60 out of Myrtle'59: Ranter, brown py'd dog (died 1764)

Recapitulation for the year 1763
Old hounds - 25 couple dogs, 5½ couple spayd bitches, 17½ couple open bitches
Young hounds - 17 couple dogs, 12 couple open bitches
Old hounds to enter the young ones with - 7 couple dogs, 1½ couple spayd bitches, 2 couple open bitches
                                                                                                                                                 87½ couple
Hounds disposed of this year - to the hare hounds 1½ couple, died 7½ couple, given away 25½ couple
                                                                                                                                                 34½ couple
Total hounds remaining this year   53 couple
There will remain to compose the old pack next year 44 couple and to enter the young hounds with 9 couple

List of young fox hounds entered the 1st October 1764

By Guider'59 out of Phoenix'62: Gauler, brown py'd dog (died 1765), Grasper, brown py'd dog (given to Mr Bathurst 1765), Growler, black py'd dog (died 1765), Promise, brown py'd bitch (died 1765), Proudly, brown py'd bitch (died 1765)

By Gamester'59 out of Patsy'62: Grinder, black py'd dog (died 1765), Pretty, black py'd bitch (with young hounds 1765 sent to France 1766), Princess, black py'd bitch (died 1765), one other dog (cast 1764)

By a dog of Duke of Devonshire out of Minden'61: Damon, liver colour dog (died 1765), Dashwood, liver colour dog (died 1765), Dolly, liver colour bitch (given to Mr Limbry 1765), Doxy, liver colour bitch (died 1766), Driver, liver colour dog (died 1765), Drowsy, liver colour bitch (died 1766)

By Roper'60 out of Purple'59: Redcap, grizzle blue py'd dog (given to Mr Bathurst 1765), Ringwood, grizzle blue py'd dog (died 1765), Royster, grizzle blue py'd dog (given to Lord Percival 1766), Rusler, grizzle blue py'd dog (given to Lord Percival 1766)

By Lawyer'63 out of Prudence'57: Lifter, liver colour py'd dog (died 1765), Lusty, liver colour py'd dog (given to Mr Conolly 1769), Luther, liver colour py'd dog (given to Lord Percival 1765)

By Fairplay'60 out of Meddle'59: Forester, grizzle py'd dog (died 1766), Fudler, brown py'd dog (died 1765), one other hound, brown py'd dog

By Lawyer'63 out of Tempest'60: Tempest, yellow py'd bitch (to France 1765), Tulip, yellow bitch (to France 1765)

By Guider'59 out of Jewel'57: Gallant, brown py'd dog (given to Mr Limbry 1767)

By Richmond'60 out of Myrtle'59: Merrylass, black py'd bitch (with young hounds 1767 and 1769 died 1770), Mode, black py'd bitch (to France with hare hounds 1765 old hound 1767 died 1770), Myrtle, black py'd bitch (died

Pedigree of Charlton Hounds

1765), Ranger, black py'd dog (given to Mr Bathurst 1765), Rebel, black py'd dog (died 1766). Redcap, black py'd dog (given to Mr Bathurst 1765)
By Rouster'59 out of Foxhound'61: Fancy, liver colour py'd bitch (died 1766), Fanny, liver colour py'd bitch (given to Mr Limbry 1767), Flurry, liver colour py'd bitch (died 1766), Foxhound, liver colour py'd bitch (died 1766), Frolic, black py'd bitch (died 1766)
By Boxer'63 out of Tempest'60: Brimmer, brown py'd dog (died 1765)
By Fairplay'60 out of Mawkin'59: Finder, grizzle py'd dog (died 1765), Founder, grizzle py'd dog (died 1765)
Out of Cloudy'63: Lindhurst, yellow py'd dog (given to Mr Bathurst 1765)
From Mr Butler: Shifter, blue mottle py'd dog (given to Sir J Miller 1765)
From Duke of Grafton: Dolphin, light grizzle whiteish dog (died 1766)
From Duke of Devonshire: Vigo, dark brown py'd dog (with young hounds 1768 given to Mr Fettyplace 1769)
By Ranter'57 out of Pleasant'61: Roper, black py'd dog (given to Mr Bathurst 1765)

Recapitulation for the year 1764
Old hounds - 25 couple dogs, 4½ spay'd bitches, 14½ open bitches
Young hounds - 15 couple dogs, 8½ open bitches
Old hounds to enter the young ones with - ½ couple dog, 8½ couple open bitches   76½ couple
Hounds disposed of this year - to the hare hounds in France 2½ couple, died 17 couple, given away 14½ couple
    34 couple
Total of hounds remaining this year   42½ couple
There will remain to compose the old pack next year 34 couple and to enter the young hounds with 8½ couple

List of young fox hounds entered the 1st October 1765

By Guider'59 out of Patsy'62: Goodness, yellow py'd dog (died 1766), Greatness, grizzle py'd dog (died 1767), Pedigree, grizzle py'd bitch (died 1766)
By Roman'59 out of Molly'59: Midnight, black py'd bitch (sent to France 1766), Roguish, brown py'd dog (died 1770)
By Conqueror'63 out of Minden'61: Crowder, grizzle py'd dog (died 1766), Cryer, yellow py'd dog (sent to France to hare hounds 1766 old hound 1767 died 1770), Mermaid, grizzle py'd bitch (died 1766), Mopsy, yellow py'd bitch (sent to France with hare hounds 1766 old hound 1767 given to Hon P King 1771)
By Tickler'63 out of Tempest'60: Tender, black py'd bitch (died 1766), Tomboy, grizzle py'd dog (with young hounds 1769 given to Mr Limbry 1770), Trouncer, grizzle py'd dog (given to Mr Limbry 1766)
By Gamester'59 out of Phoenix'62: Gimblet, blue py'd dog (died 1766)
By Madcap'63 out of Merrylass'61: Marplot, black py'd dog (sent to France 1766), Mountain, black py'd dog (sent to France to hare hounds 1766 old hound 1767 given to Mr Limbry 1768)
By Grinder'60 out of Venus'63: Gilder, yellow py'd dog (died 1766), Glazier, grizzle py'd dog (with young hounds 1766 given to Mr Limbry 1767)
By Bouncer'59 out of Cloudy'63: Baliol, black py'd dog (given to Mr Limbry 1768), Banco, brown py'd dog (given to Mr Limbry 1766), Barley, grizzle py'd dog (died 1766), Bruce, grizzle py'd dog (given to Mr Limbry 1766), Comfort, grizzle py'd bitch (died 1766)
By Bouncer'59 out of Decent'60: Bardolph, brown py'd dog (died 1766), Barefoot, brown py'd dog (died 1766), Brimmer, brown py'd dog (given to Mr Limbry 1767)
By Sober'60 out of Purple'59: Pleasure, yellow py'd bitch (sp'd given to Mr Fettyplace 1769), Plenty, brown py'd bitch (sent to France 1766), Standard, brown py'd dog (died 1766)
By Gamester'59 out of Picture'62: General, blue py'd dog (given to Mr Fettyplace 1769), Guercy, grizzle py'd dog (given to Mr Limbry 1767), Planet, blue py'd bitch (sp'd with young hounds 1769 given to Mr Limbry 1770)
By Guider'59 out of Malice'62: Gander, brown py'd dog (with young hounds 1769 died 1770), Goosecap, brown py'd dog (sent to France to hare hounds 1766 old hound 1767 given to Lord Berkeley 1768)
By Galloper'63 out of Famous'63: Feather, brown py'd bitch (sent to France 1766), Grateful, brown py'd dog (died 1766)
By Guider'59 out of Prudence'57: Geoffrey, yellow dog (given to Mr Conolly 1769), Godfrey, yellow py'd dog (died 1766), Godwin, yellow py'd dog (died 1766), Greenwich, yellow py'd dog (died 1769), Guildford, yellow py'd dog (died 1766), Percy, yellow py'd bitch (died 1770)
By Tickler'63 out of Pheasant'61: Traitor, black py'd dog (died 1766)
From Duke of Devonshire by his Pluto out of his Cherry: Pilot, whiteish grizzle py'd dog (died 1766), Plummer, black py'd dog (died 1766), Pluto, black py'd dog (died 1766)
From Duke of Devonshire by his Vigo out of his Pleasant: Peeler, black py'd dog (given to Mr Meynell 1770), Peeress, black py'd bitch (died 1766), Princess, black py'd bitch (died 1766), Principal, white py'd dog (died 1766), Prussia, white dog (given to Mr Conolly 1769)

From Duke of Devonshire by his Render out of his Duchess: Ragman, black py'd dog (died 1766), Ranter, black py'd dog (died 1766), Relish, mostly white bitch (sent to France 1766 old hound 1767 with young hounds 1769 given to Mr Limbry 1770), Rusler, black py'd dog (died 1766)

From Duke of Devonshire by his Ruler out of his Gilly: Rampter, blackish dog (died 1766), Ranger, whiteish yellow py'd dog (died 1766), Render, black py'd dog (died 1766), Rosamund, grizzle py'd bitch (died 1766), Rumbler, blackish dog (died 1766)

From Duke of Devonshire by his Rockwood out of his Garlick: Raymond, whiteish dog (died 1766), Rufler, black py'd dog (given to Mr Limbry 1767)

From Duke of Devonshire by his Striver out of his Conquest: Conqueror, grizzle py'd dog (sent to France 1766 old hound 1767 with young hounds 1768 given to Mr Conolly 1769)

From Duke of Devonshire by his Vigo out of his Dolly: Victor, black py'd dog (died 1766), Vigo, black py'd dog (died 1766)

Old hound from Mr St Leger: Stroker, black py'd dog (given to Mr Conolly 1767)

Recapitulation for the year 1765

Old hounds - 18½ couple dogs, 3½ spay'd bitches, 13 open bitches

Young hounds - 24½ couple dogs, 7½ open bitches

Old hounds to enter the young ones - 2½ couple dogs, ½ spay'd bitch, 5½ open bitches 75½ couple

Hounds disposed of this year - to the hare hounds in France 9½ couple, died 23½ couple, given away 4½ couple 37½ couple

Total hounds remaining this year 38 couple

There will remain to compose the old pack next year 29½ couple and to enter the young hounds with 8½ couple

List of young fox hounds entered 1st October 1766

By Girder'62: Girder, black py'd dog (given to Mr Fettyplace 1769)*

By Guider'59 out of Patsy'62: Gallows, brown py'd dog (given to Mr Fettyplace 1769), Groper, black py'd dog (given to Mr Limbry 1768), Pallas, black py'd bitch (cast 1771)

By Bluecap'62 out of Ardent'63: Awful, black py'd dog (given to Mr Fettyplace 1769), Banker, grizzle py'd dog (with young hounds 1770 cast 1771), Bishop, black py'd dog (given to Mr Fettyplace 1769), Burleigh, brown py'd dog (given to Lord Berkeley 1768)

By Archer'63 out of Modesty'63: Actor, black py'd dog (died 1770), Alter, grizzle py'd dog (given to Mr Fettyplace 1769), Atlas, yellowish py'd dog (died 1770), Madness, black py'd bitch (given to Duke of Grafton 1767), Milkmaid, grizzle py'd bitch (sp'd died 1769)

By Boxer'63 out of Patience'62: Painting, white bitch (sp'd with young hounds 1769 given to Lord Montagu 1770), Petworth, yellow py'd bitch (sp'd with young hounds 1769 given to Lord Montagu 1770)

By Tickler'63 out of Foxhound'61: Flutter, dark brown py'd bitch (given to Mr Conolly 1769), Townsman, brown py'd dog (given to Mr Fettyplace 1769), Trimmer, grizzle py'd dog (given to Mr Fettyplace 1769)

By Archer'63 out of Phoenix'62: Adam, black py'd dog (given to Mr Limbry 1767), Paintress, black py'd bitch (sp'd given to Mr Fettyplace 1769)

By Galloper'63 out of Malice'62: Midhurst, brown py'd bitch (with young hounds 1771 given to Mr Sturt 1772), Mistress, yellow py'd bitch (sp'd died 1771), Mopsy, grizzle py'd bitch (sp'd given to Hon P King 1771)

By Baxter'63 out of Airy'63: Boldness, black py'd dog (given to Mr Conolly 1769)

By Grinder'64 out of Warbler'63: Grumbler, black py'd dog (with young hounds 1770 cast 1771), Wishful, black py'd bitch (given to Mr Fettyplace 1769)

By Baxter'63 out of Picture'62: Blacksmith, blue py'd dog (given to Mr Fettyplace 1769), Briton, blue py'd dog (died 1769), Partridge, grizzle py'd bitch (sp'd with young hounds 1770 cast 1771), Pepper, brown py'd bitch (with young hounds 1770 cast 1771)

By Galloper'63 out of Myrtle'64: Garland, yellow py'd dog (cast 1767), Magic, yellow py'd bitch (cast 1768)

By Bluecap'62 out of Prudence'57: Brazen, grizzle py'd dog (with young hounds 1769 given to Lord Montagu 1770), Pacify, yellowish py'd bitch (cast 1767), Pineapple, grizzle py'd bitch (given to Mr Limbry 1767)

By Madcap'63 out of Pleasant'61: Pleasant, black tan bitch (died 1770)

By Tickler'63 out of Strumpet'63: Silver, grizzle py'd bitch (given to Mr Limbry 1767), Titus, grizzle py'd dog (given to Mr Limbry 1767)

By Baxter'63 out of Atom'63: Artless, blue py'd bitch (sp'd with young hounds 1770 cast 1771)

By Richmond'60 out of Fairmaid'63: Funny, blue py'd bitch (with young hounds 1768 given to Mr Conolly 1769)

Recapitulation for the year 1766

Old hounds - 18 couple dogs, 1 spay'd bitches, 10½ open bitches

Young hounds - 9 couple dogs, 10½ open bitches

---

* This hound was entered in the list later and is not counted in the total.

Old hounds to enter the young ones - 5 couple dogs, 1½ spay'd bitch, 2 open bitches   17½ couple
Hounds disposed of this year - to the hare hounds ½ couple, died 3 couple, given away 12½ couple   16 couple
Total hounds remaining this year   41½ couple
There will remain to compose the old pack next year 31½ couple and to enter the young hounds with 10 couple

Old hounds new to the pack 1st October 1767
By Fleec'em'58 out of Dainty'59: Purple, black py'd bitch entered to hare hounds 1762 (given to Mr Limbry 1768)
By Girder'62: Merryful, black bitch with white spots (sp'd with young hounds 1770 cast 1771)
From Lord G Cavendish: Dainty, grizzle py'd bitch entered 1766 (with young hounds 1772 died 1774)
From Sir J Miller: Darling, black py'd bitch (given back to Sir J Miller 1769), Frolic, black py'd bitch (given back to Sir J Miller 1768)
From Sir J Miller by Dido'61 out of Guider'59: Damsel, whiteish bitch (died 1769)

List of young hounds entered the 1st October 1767
By Archer'63 out of Modesty'63: Admiral, blue py'd dog (with young hounds 1771 given to Mr White 1773), Mermaid, brownish py'd bitch (with young hounds 1771 cast 1773), Midnight, brownish py'd bitch (lost 1771), Minsted, brownish py'd bitch (died 1770), Mourning, blue py'd bitch (died 1769)
By Tickler'63 out of Strumpet'63: Sally, brown py'd bitch (given to Lord Berkeley 1768), Trueboy, brown py'd dog (died 1770), Trueman, brown py'd dog (given to Mr Limbry 1768), Trusty, grizzle py'd dog (given to Lord Berkeley 1768)
By Tickler'63 out of Prattle'63: Pigeon, grizzle py'd bitch (lost at Findon 1768), Princess, brown py'd bitch (given to Mr Sturt 1768), Thunder, brown py'd dog (with young hounds 1771 given to Mr Sturt 1772), Tory, brown py'd dog (died 1770), Turner, grizzle py'd dog (with young hounds 1771 given to Mr Williams 1772)
By Sir S Stuart's Swapper out of Sweetlips'63: Sterling, brown py'd dog (given to Mr Conolly 1769), Streamer, brown py'd dog (died 1776)
By Peeler'65 out of Ready'63: Plowboy, blue py'd dog (with young hounds 1769 and 1771 given to Lord Berkeley 1772), Printer, blue py'd dog (given to Mr Conolly 1769)
By Girder'62 out of Absent'63: Aubigny, black py'd bitch (sp'd with young hounds 1769 given to Mr Osbaldeston 1771), Greater, dark blue py'd dog (cast 1771)
Out of Plenty'65: Painter, black py'd dog (given to Lord Berkeley 1768), Pincher, black py'd dog (given to Lord Berkeley 1768), Primrose, grizzle py'd bitch (given to Mr Sturt 1768)
By Conqueror'63 out of Fairmaid'63: Castor, grizzle py'd dog (given to Mr Conolly 1769), Cocker, grizzle py'd dog (with young hounds 1770 cast 1771)
By Conqueror'63 out of Whimsy'63: Crocker, yellow py'd dog (given to Lord Berkeley 1768), Crusty, yellow py'd dog (given to Lord Berkeley 1768)

Recapitulation for the year 1767
Old hounds - 18½ couple dogs, 3 spay'd bitches, 18½ open bitches
Young hounds - 8½ couple dogs, 5 open bitches
Old hounds to enter the young ones - 6½ couple dogs, 1 spay'd bitch, 2½ open bitches   63½ couple
Hounds disposed of this year - cast 1 couple, died 3½ couple, given away 14 couple, lost ½ couple   19 couple
Total hounds remaining this year   44½ couple
There will remain to compose the old pack next year 34½ couple and to enter the young hounds with 10 couple

Old hounds new to the pack the 1st October 1768
By Galloper'63 out of Doxy'63: Daughter, brown py'd bitch (entered 1767 died 1769), Dropsy, yellow py'd bitch (entered 1767 died 1769)

List of young fox hounds entered the 1st October 1768
By Archer'63 out of Patsy'62: Aaron, black and red py'd dog (to hare hounds 1770), Agent, blue grizzle py'd dog (given to Mr Sturt 1773), Answer, white and a few black spots dog (died 1773), Pigeon, white and a few black spots bitch (died 1777), Prattle, black py'd bitch (died 1774)
By Galloper'63 out of Absent'63: Arrow, white bitch with a few yellow spots (given to Mr Sturt 1771), Gildo, black py'd dog (given to Mr Limbry 1769), Grecian, grizzle py'd dog (given to Col Jennings 1773)
By Boxer'63 out of Purple'59: Blueskin, blue py'd dog (cast 1772), Bourbon, black py'd dog (given to Lord Berkeley 1769), Bumpkin, smutty faced brown py'd dog (given to Mr King), Panic, pale tanned bitch (given to Mr Conolly 1769), Peggy, white bitch with grizzle spots (died 1773), Pushpin, (given to Mr Gibbon 1769)
By Galloper'63 out of Ready'63: Rocket, reddish py'd bitch (given to Mr Sturt 1769), Rueful, black py'd bitch (given to Mr Limbry 1769), Ruel, black py'd bitch (given to Mr Gibbon 1769)
By Peeler'65 out of Funny'66: Findon, black py'd bitch (given to Mr Limbry 1769), Fortress, grizzle py'd bitch (cast 1775), Frigate, grizzle py'd bitch (given to Mr Conolly 1769), Piper, black py'd dog (with young hounds 1769 given

to Lord Montagu 1770), Planter, grizzle py'd dog (died 1775)
By Ratler'61 out of Frisky'59: Fuel, grizzle black py'd bitch (died 1772), River, black py'd bitch (died 1770)
By Archer'63 out of Merry'63: Anthony, reddish py'd dog (with young hounds 1770 given to Mr Williams 1772), Makeless, white bitch with reddish spots (given to Mr Sturt 1772)
By Tickler'63 out of Midhurst'66: Marvel, grizzle py'd bitch (died 1773), Mellow, red py'd bitch (sp'd given to Mr Sturt 1772), Muffin, red py'd bitch (with young hounds 1771 given to Mr Sturt 1772), Mustard, grizzle py'd bitch (sp'd cast 1772), Thumper, reddish py'd dog (cast 1771)
By Peeler'65 out of Modesty'63: Maggot, grizzle py'd bitch (died 1773), Patch'em, pale liver coloured py'd dog (given to Mr Limbry 1769), Pistol, grey py'd dog (died 1770)
By Peeler'65 out of Minden'61: Midling, blackish py'd bitch (sp'd given to Col Jennings 1775), Muddy, blackish py'd bitch (given to Mr Sturt 1769), Muslin, blackish py'd bitch (given to Mr Gibbon 1769), Pewter, blackish py'd dog (given to Mr Sturt 1769), Plasto, blackish py'd dog (given to Mr Sturt 1769)
By Guider'59 out of Warbler'63: Glorious, white dog with a few brown spots (died 1772)
By Peeler'65 out of Mopsy'65: Maukin, black py'd bitch (died 1771)
By Guider'59 out of Partridge'66: Guido, yellowish py'd dog (given to Mr Conolly 1769)
Out of Aubigny'67: Danger, black py'd dog (given to Mr Gibbon 1769), Danish, black py'd bitch (given to Lord Berkeley 1769), Dolly, black py'd bitch (given to Lord Berkeley 1769), Doubtful, black py'd bitch (given to Lord Berkeley 1769), Downly, black py'd bitch (given to Mr Gibbon 1769), Driver, grizzle py'd dog (given to Mr Limbry 1769), Droke, black py'd bitch (given to Mr Gibbon 1769), Drunkard, black py'd dog (given to Mr Sturt 1769),
By Peeler'65 out of Percy'65: Partial, reddish py'd dog (given to Mr Conolly 1769), Peevish, brown py'd bitch (given to Mr Limbry 1769), Pertness, black py'd bitch (given to Mr Sturt 1769)
By Peeler'65 out of Awful'66: Pipkin, black py'd dog (given to Mr Sturt 1769)
By Aimwell'63 out of Merryful'67: Alderman, blueish py'd dog (given to Mr Conolly 1769), Aldwick, black py'd dog (given to Capt Dyer 1769), Antient, blueish py'd dog (given to Mr Limbry 1769), Maple, black py'd dog (given to Mr Gibbon 1769), Minikin, smutty faced black py'd bitch (given to Mr Sturt 1769), Miror, black py'd bitch (died 1770), Mushroom, black py'd bitch (given to Capt Dyer 1769)

Recapitulation for the year 1768
Old hounds - 18 couple dogs, 4½ spay'd bitches, 12* open bitches
Young hounds - 13½ couple dogs, 17 bitches
Old hounds to enter the young ones - 4½ couple dogs, 1 spay'd bitches, 4½ open bitches .... 75 couple
Hounds disposed of this year - died 6 couple, given away 31 couple .... 37 couple
Total hounds remaining this year .... 38 couple
There will remain to compose the old pack next year 28 couple and to enter the young hounds with 6 couple, superannuated 4 couple

List of young fox hounds in 1769
By Madcap'63 out of Pacify'66: Madman, brown tan'd dog (to hare hounds 1770), Malster, black py'd dog (to hare hounds 1770), Manful, black tan'd dog (to hare hounds 1770), Murder, black py'd dog (to hare hounds 1770)
By Roguish'65 out of Malice'62: Mopish, smutty faced brown py'd bitch (with young hounds 1770 given to Mr Sturt 1772)
By Aimwell'63 out of Aubigny'67: Ammon, black py'd dog (given to Mr Drake 1772)
By Tomboy'65 out of Warbler'63: Watchful, black py'd bitch (died 1777)
By Peeler'65 out of Mistress'66: Plato, grizzle py'd dog (given to Lord Montagu 1770)
By Tickler'63 out of Petworth'66: Packet, white bitch with yellow ears (died 1770), Paltry, brown py'd bitch (died 1773), Precious, white bitch (died 1778), Tangmere, grizzle py'd dog (died 1775), Total, white dog (given to Mr Rowel 1775)
By Peeler'65 out of Frisky'63: Flimsy, grizzle py'd bitch (died 1770), Flora, brown py'd bitch (died 1776), Frantic, brown py'd bitch (given to Mr White 1773), Frowsy, brown py'd bitch (sp'd cast 1772), Priestcomb, brown py'd dog (died 1778)
By Roguish'65 out of Dainty'59: Daylight, brown py'd bitch (with young hounds 1771 died 1772), Dimple, brown py'd bitch (given to Mr Sturt 1772), Distance, brown py'd bitch (sp'd sent to France 1776), Dublin, brown py'd bitch (given to Mr Conolly 1770), Rider, brown py'd dog with a round spot on his side (given to Lord Montagu 1770), Rusty, brown py'd dog (died 1777)
By Peeler'65 out of Flutter'66: Fairy, brown py'd bitch (given to Mr Conolly 1770), Flatter, black py'd bitch (sp'd given to Col Jennings 1775), Flaunting, black py'd bitch (sp'd given to Mr Sturt 1771), Folly, grizzle py'd bitch (given to Lord Berkeley 1770), Plumper, black py'd dog (given to Mr Child 1770)
By Guider'59 out of Midnight'67: Mendip, grizzle py'd bitch (to hare hounds 1770)
By Sailor'63 out of Damsel'67: Dotterel, yellow py'd bitch (died 1773), Stormer, grizzle py'd dog (given to Lord

---
* This figure appears incorrectly as '13' in the hound book.

Pedigree of Charlton Hounds

Berkeley 1772)
By Peeler'65 out of Midhurst'66: Mango, brown py'd bitch (sp'd cast 1771), Minstrel, black py'd bitch (given to Mr Sturt 1770), Ponder, brown py'd dog (cast 1771), Pruner, grizzle py'd dog (given to Mr Conolly 1770)
By Streamer'67 out of Percy'65: Panting, yellow py'd bitch (given to Lord Berkeley 1770), Seymour, yellow py'd dog (given to Mr Conolly 1770), Spanker, yellow py'd dog (given to Mr Child 1770), Speaker, yellow py'd dog (given to Mr Child 1770)
By Lusty'63 out of Mopsy'65: Lifter, grey py'd dog (to hare hounds 1770), Limbo, grey py'd dog (given to Mr Child 1770), Lurcher, yellow py'd dog (given to Mr Child 1770), Mignion, yellow py'd bitch (given to Mr Conolly 1770), Monkey, grey py'd bitch (to hare hounds 1770), Mortal, yellow py'd bitch (sp'd with young hounds 1771 cast 1773), Mutual, yellow py'd bitch (given to Col Jennings 1775)
By Peeler'65 out of Mode'64: Panton, blue py'd dog (given to Mr Conolly 1770), Pedlar, liver colour py'd dog (cast 1771), Prater, blue py'd dog (cast 1773)
By Aimwell'63 out of Wishful'66: Abbot, blue py'd dog (died 1770), Action, blue py'd dog (died 1775), Witty, blue py'd bitch (cast 1774)
By Guider'59 out of Mourning'67: Garter, brown py'd dog (given to Mr Curzon 1770), Gelding, brown py'd dog (cast 1771), Gimcrack, grizzle py'd dog (given to Mr Curzon 1770), Model, black py'd bitch (given to Col Jennings 1776), Mouldy, yellow py'd bitch (given to Lord Berkeley 1770)
By Archer'63: Andover, brown py'd dog (with young hounds 1771 died 1777), Antwerp, smutty faced brown py'd dog (given to Mr Child 1770), Painful, black py'd bitch (to hare hounds 1770)
By Tomboy'65 out of Doxy'64: Danish, grey py'd bitch (died 1770), Downly, yellow py'd bitch (with young hounds 1771 given to Mr Sturt 1772), Teaser, grey py'd dog (given to Lord Montagu 1770), Toaster, yellow py'd dog (died 1771)
By Peeler'65 out of Absent'63: Anguish, black py'd bitch (died 1773), Papal, black py'd dog (given to Mr Curzon 1770), Papist, black py'd dog (given to Mr Curzon 1770), Patriot, black py'd dog (cast 1771), Payaway, black py'd dog (given to Mr Conolly 1770), Plunder, black py'd dog (given to Mr Conolly 1770)
By Peeler'65 out of Funny'66: Pilgrim, black py'd dog (given to Duke of Aremberg 1777), Pindar, dark grey py'd dog (given to Mr Child 1770), Poker, grizzle py'd dog (given to Mr Child 1770)
By Guider'59 out of Minsted'67: Gunner, brown py'd dog (given to Mr Sturt 1772)
By Grumbler'66 out of Frolic'64: Glover, black py'd dog (died 1770), Gospel, brown py'd dog (lost 1771)
By Peeler'65 out of Darling'59: Diligence, black py'd bitch (died 1770), Ditty, black py'd bitch (sp'd given to Mr Sturt 1773), Doleful, brown py'd bitch (sp'd cast 1771)
Adam, brown py'd dog (given to Mr Conolly 1770)
Devil, brown py'd bitch (given to Mr Conolly 1770)

Recapitulation for the year 1769
Old hounds - 13 couple dogs, 2½ spay'd bitches, 12½ open bitches
Young hounds - 22½ couple dogs, 18½ bitches
Old hounds to enter the young ones - 3 couple dogs, 2 spay'd bitches, 1 open bitches
Superannuated hounds - 1½ couple dogs, 1½ open bitches, 1 spay'd bitches   79 couple
Hounds disposed of this year - died 14 couple, given away 18½ couple, to the young hounds 5 couple, to the hare hounds 4½ couple   42 couple
Total hounds remaining this year   37 couple
There will remain to compose the old pack next year 32 couple and to enter the young hounds with 5 couple

List of young fox hounds in 1770
By General'65 out of Absent'63: Angry, dark blue py'd bitch (given to Mr Sturt 1773), Artful, dark blue py'd bitch (given to Mr Sturt 1778), Arundel, dark blue py'd bitch (given to Lord Berkeley 1772), Ashling, dark blue py'd bitch (given to Mr Sturt 1773), Ginger, black py'd dog (died 1772)
By Bumpkin'68 out of Midhurst'66: Boreas, brown py'd dog (given to Lord Berkeley 1772), Maiden, yellow py'd bitch (given to Mr Sturt 1773), Milkpan, brown py'd bitch (died 1776)
By Cryer'65 out of Pallas'66: Cleaver, black py'd dog (died 1773), Cringer, yellow py'd dog (died 1772), Painted, grizzle py'd bitch (died 1775), Palsy, black py'd bitch (died 1776), Papal, grizzle py'd bitch (died 1776)
By Streamer'67 out of Damsel'67: Deborah, grey py'd bitch (given to Mr Sturt 1771), Smuggler, grey py'd dog (cast 1771)
By Archer'63 out of Percy'65: Alfred, white dog (cast 1771), Arab, yellow py'd dog (given to Lord Berkeley 1772), Parable, yellow py'd bitch (cast 1771)
By Streamer'67 out of Minden'61: Malmsey, yellow py'd bitch (given to Mr Sturt 1772), Modest, yellow py'd bitch (given to Mr Sturt 1773), Scalper, brown py'd dog (cast 1771), Serjeant, yellow py'd dog (given to Mr Sturt 1773), Squander, brown py'd dog (given to Lord Berkeley 1772)

By Peeler'65 out of Pacify'66: Papist, dark blue py'd dog with tick spots (given to Mr Longman 1775), Peach'em, dark blue py'd dog (given to Col Jennings 1775), Pitiful, liver colour py'd bitch (given to Lord Berkeley 1772), Prosper, grey py'd dog (given to Col Jennings 1775)

By Grumbler'66 out of Malice'62: Gentleman, light brown py'd dog (given to Mr Drake 1772), Goring, light brown py'd dog (given to Mr Drake 1772), Governor, light brown py'd dog (cast 1772), Mushroom, grizzle py'd bitch (given to Col Jennings 1775)

By Archer'63 out of Mistress'66: Mental, yellow py'd bitch (cast 1771)

By Streamer'67 out of Dainty'59: Duchess, brown py'd bitch (died 1772)

By Peeler'65 out of Mermaid'67: Pamphlet, liver colour py'd dog (died 1772), Panther, brown py'd dog with tick spots (cast 1771), Pauncefort, black py'd dog with tick spots (given to Col Jennings 1775)

By Sailor'63 out of Minsted'67: Mulberry, dark blue py'd bitch (given to Mr Sturt 1772), Starboard, dark brown py'd dog (given to Mr Williams 1772), Subject, brown py'd dog (given to Mr Sturt 1772)

By Streamer'67 out of Midnight'65: Morning, dark brown py'd bitch (cast 1771), Soldier, brown py'd dog (died 1771), Squinter, brown py'd dog (died 1771), Stager, yellow py'd dog (given to Lord Berkeley 1772)

By Bumpkin'68 out of Midnight'67: Bacchus, brown py'd dog with a black muzzle (given to Duke of Aremberg 1777), Bumper, yellow py'd dog (given to Mr Mayner 1773), Measure, grizzle py'd bitch (cast 1771)

By Admiral'67 out of Dido'61: Anchor, brown py'd dog (cast 1771), Doubtful, blue py'd bitch (cast 1771), Dutiful, blue py'd bitch (cast 1771)

By Grumbler'66 out of Dainty'59: Glister, yellow py'd dog (to Southweek 1775), Goodwood, brown py'd dog (given to Duke of Aremberg 1777)

Lucky, brown py'd bitch came by chance (died 1772)

Recapitulation for the year 1770
Old hounds - 15½ couple dogs, 7 spay'd bitches, 14½ open bitches
Young hounds - 14½ couple dogs, 11½ bitches
Old hounds to enter the young ones - 2 couple dogs, 1½ spay'd bitches, 1½ open bitches   68 couple
Hounds disposed of this year - died 3 couple, cast 13½ couple, lost 1 couple, given away 3½ couple, to the young hounds 5½ couple   26½ couple
Total hounds remaining this year   41½ couple
There will remain to compose the old pack next year 34½ couple and to enter the young ones with 7 couple

List of young fox hounds in 1771

By Archer'63 out of Mopsy'66: August, brown py'd dog (cast 1778), Mindful, grizzle py'd bitch (given to Mr Sturt 1773), Minish, grizzle py'd bitch (dead 1775), Albion, grizzle py'd dog (given to Mr Sturt 1773), Alder, grizzle py'd dog (dead 1777), Auditor, white dog (dead 1776), Alcides, yellow py'd dog (cast 1772), Althorp, yellow py'd dog (given to Mr Longman 1775)

By Archer'63 out of Midhurst'66: Anger, brown py'd dog (given to Mr Hooper 1777), Ardour, yellow py'd dog (cast 1772), Apollo, yellow py'd dog (given to Mr Sturt 1773)

By Grater'67 out of Fuel'68: Frightful, black py'd bitch (dead 1775), Flippant, blue py'd bitch (given to Mr Sturt 1773), Flannel, blue py'd bitch (given to Mr Sturt 1775), Fulsome, grey py'd bitch (cast 1777)

By Admiral'67 out of Fortress'68: Future, brown py'd bitch (dead 1775), Austin, brown py'd dog (given to Mr Sturt 1773)

By Cryer'65 out of Pigeon'68: Pastime, brown py'd bitch (cast 1772), Primrose, dark brown py'd bitch (given to Mr Sturt 1773)

By Streamer'67 out of Pacify'66: Prateaway, brown py'd bitch (cast 1772), Smoker, yellow py'd dog (dead 1775)

By Peeler'65 out of Marvel'68: Mellet, brown py'd bitch (cast 1773), Postman, grey py'd dog (dead 1776), Madam, grizzle py'd bitch (dead 1778)

By Admiral'67 out of Middling'68: Amber, dark grey py'd dog (dead 1776), Mother, grey py'd bitch (given to Lord Berkeley 1772)

By Peeler'65 out of Dotterel'69: Panglos, dark brown py'd dog (given to Mr Sturt 1773), Pancake, grey py'd dog (dead 1776)

By Cryer'65 out of Flora'69: Ferret, blue py'd bitch (cast 1772), Candour, yellow py'd dog (given to Mr Sturt 1773), Canter, yellow py'd dog (given to Mr Sturt 1775)

By Admiral'67 out of Mellow'68: Alton, grizzle py'd dog (given to Mr Sturt 1773)

By Peeler'65 out of Makeless'68: Porter, blue py'd dog (dead 1773)

By Streamer'67 out of Mopsy'65: Milkish, dark brown py'd bitch (given to Mr Sturt 1778)

By Glorious'68 out of Midnight'67: Goldfinch, dark brown py'd dog (To Southweek 1774), Goldsmith, dark brown py'd dog (dead 1778)

By Guider'59: Grocer, dark brown py'd dog (dead 1776)

By Lord Thanet's Singer out of Lucky'70: Singer, grey py'd dog (given to Lord Berkeley 1772)
By Cryer'65 out of Arrow'68: Cromwell, yellow py'd dog (given to Lord Berkeley 1772), Airy, yellow py'd dog (given to Mr Sturt 1772)

Recapitulation for the year 1771
Old hounds - 20 couple dogs, 3 spay'd bitches, 18 open bitches
Young hounds - 12½ couple dogs, 7½ bitches
Old hounds to enter the young ones - 3 couple dogs, ½ spay'd bitches, 3½ open bitches   68 couple
Hounds disposed of this year - died 4 couple, cast ½ couple, given away 15½ couple   20 couple
Total hounds remaining this year   48 couple
There will remain to compose the old pack next year 45 couple and to enter the young ones 3 couple

List of young fox hounds entered in 1772
By Peeler'65 out of Maiden'70: Packer, yellowish py'd dog (given to Col Jennings 1775), Primer, yellowish py'd dog (given to Mr Hooper 1777), Puzzler, grey py'd dog (given to Duke of Aremberg 1777)
By Streamer'67 out of Marvel'68: Money, yellow tan'd bitch (given to Mr Jeans 1777), Moreish, brown py'd bitch (sent to France 1777), Mortgage, yellow tan'd bitch (sent to France 1777), Motion, yellow py'd bitch (sent to France 1777), Sinker, yellow py'd dog (dead 1775), Surly, yellow py'd dog (dead 1778), Swimmer, yellow py'd dog (dead 1776)
By Bumpkin'68 out of Flora'69: Banner, dark brown py'd dog (given to Duke of Aremberg 1777), Barker, grey py'd dog (given to Mr Sturt 1775), Brandy, yellow py'd dog (given to Mr Gilbert 1775)
By Mr Meynell's Boaster out of Mulberry'70: Boaster, dark brown py'd dog (given to Mr Sturt 1775)
By Peeler'65 out of Pigeon'68: Patron, brown py'd bitch (dead 1775), Purser, brown py'd dog (given to Duke of Aremberg 1777)
By Blueskin'68 out of Midhurst'66: Baker, dark brown py'd dog (given to Mr Sturt 1775)
By Streamer'67 out of Precious'69: Stranger, yellow py'd dog (given to Mr Sturt 1775), Stroler, yellow py'd dog (given to Duke of Aremberg 1777)
By Lord Castlehaven's Chanter out of Angry'70: Allum, grey py'd bitch (given to Mr Sturt 1775)
By Mr Meynell's Gallant out of Watchful'69: Gaspard, black py'd dog (cast 1780), Gifter, grey py'd dog (dead 1778), Glutton, grey py'd dog (dead 1776), Grazier, dark brown py'd dog (dead 1778), Wanton, grey py'd bitch (sent to France 1777), Wary, dark brown py'd bitch (dead 1776), Widow, grey py'd bitch (given to Mr Sturt 1778)
By Lord Castlehaven's Finder out of Fortress'68: Firkin, grizzle py'd bitch (dead 1778), Fosier, brown py'd dog (cast 1773)
By Planter'68 out of Mopsy'66: Partner, liver coloured dog (given to Mr Sturt 1776)
Out of Mermaid'65: Morsel, brown py'd bitch (dead 1776)
Out of Palsy'70: Party, grey py'd bitch (given to Mr Sturt 1775), Patty, brown py'd bitch (given to Mr Sturt 1775)

Recapitulation for the year 1772
Old hounds - 21½ couple dogs, 3 spay'd bitches, 18 open bitches
Young hounds - 10 couple dogs, 6½ bitches
Old hounds to enter the young ones - 1 couple dogs, ½ spay'd bitches, 1½ open bitches   61 couple
Hounds disposed of this year - died 5 couple, given away 11 couple   16 couple
Total hounds remaining this year   45 couple

List of young fox hounds entered in 1773
By Answer'68 out of Mustard'68: Armour, grey py'd dog (dead 1776), Mighty, yellow py'd bitch (cast 1780)
By Agent'68 out of Maggot'68: Adner, grey py'd dog (dead 1775), Arthur, yellow py'd dog, dead 1777)Miskin, grizzle py'd bitch (dead 1776)
By Blueskin'68 out of Marvel'68: Brander, yellow tan'd dog (dead 1776), Brewer, yellow tan'd dog (given to Mr Sturt 1776), Brownsey, yellow tan'd dog (given to Mr Sturt 1776), Bruiser, dark tan'd dog (given to Mr Sturt 1776), Butcher, yellow tan'd dog (given to Col Jennings 1776), one other hound
By Mr Meynell's Boaster out of Mulberry'70: Bedford, brown py'd dog (given to Mr Sturt 1774), of Mulberry'70: Sifter, grizzle py'd dog by Streamer'67 out of Witty'69 in 1774 list entered 1772 (given to Mr Longman 1775)
By Cleaver'70 out of Peggy'68: Crosser, black py'd dog (given to Mr Sturt 1778), Crowder, yellow py'd dog (dead 1776), Picksom, dark grey py'd bitch (dead 1776)
By Bumpkin'68 out of Flora'69: Female, blue py'd bitch (given to Mr White 1774), Ferry, blue py'd bitch (given to Mr White 1774)
By Lord Thanet's Tipler out of Fuel'68: Frozzel, black py'd bitch (given to Mr King 1775)
By Goodwood'70 out of Pigeon'68: Growler, brown py'd dog (given to Mr Sturt 1776), Purchase, brown py'd bitch (sent to France 1776)

By Lord Castlehaven's Bluecap out of Mutual'69: Marquee, yellow py'd bitch (given to Mr White 1774)
By Streamer'67 out of Milkpan'70: Moment, brown py'd bitch (cast 1775), Schemer, brown py'd dog (given to Mr Sturt 1778), Scourger, brown py'd dog (given to Mr Sturt 1778)
By Priestcomb'69 out of Painted'70: Pity, brown py'd bitch (dead 1778), Preface, brown py'd bitch (cast 1780), Prologue, dark brown bitch (cast 1780)
By Planter'68 out of Watchful'69: Pincher, black py'd dog (dead 1778), Prior, black py'd dog (cast 1780), Proctor, grizzle py'd dog (given to Mr Sturt 1776), Weighty, brown py'd bitch (given to Mr Sturt 1777), Winish, grizzle py'd bitch (sent to France 1776)
By Priestcomb'69 out of Prattle'68: Posey, brown py'd bitch (given to Mr Sturt 1775), Practice, brown py'd bitch (dead 1776), Prompter, liver colour'd py'd dog (given to Mr Sturt 1776)
By Streamer'67 out of Pallas'66: Piras, brown py'd bitch (given to Mr White 1774), Privy, brown py'd bitch (given to Mr White 1774), Samson, black py'd dog (given to Mr Sturt 1774), Stinter, brown py'd dog (given to Mr Sturt 1774)
By Streamer'67 out of Palsy'70: Parcel, grizzle py'd bitch (given to Mr White 1774)
By Streamer'67 out of Artful'70: Sector, brown py'd dog (given to Mr Sturt 1774), Soldier, brown py'd dog (given to Mr Sturt 1776)
By Total'69 out of Witty'69: Toter, brown py'd dog (dead 1776)

Recapitulation for the year 1773[*]
Old hounds - 25 couple dogs, 1½ spay'd bitches, 17 open bitches   59 couple
Young hounds - 9½ couple dogs, 6 bitches   7½ couple
Hounds disposed of this year - died 1½ couple, given away 6 couple
Total hounds remaining this year   51½ couple

List of young fox hounds entered 1774
By Clever'70 out of Mushroom'70: Clincher, brown py'd dog (given to Mr Sturt 1776)
By Clever'70 out of Milkpan'70: Clipper, brown py'd dog (given to Mr Sturt 1776), Motive, brown py'd bitch (given to Mr Sturt 1778), Myra, black py'd bitch (sent to France 1776)
By Glutton'72 out of Mutual'69: Gender, brown py'd dog with one wall eye (given to Mr Jeans 1777), Granter, brown py'd dog (dead 1775), Gunter, brown py'd dog (sent to France 1776), Muddy, brown py'd bitch (given to Mr Sampson 1780)
By Grasper'64 out of Peggy'68: Gimcrack, grey py'd dog (dead 1775), Graver, grey py'd, dog (given to Mr Sturt 1776), Gutler, brown py'd dog (given to Mr Sturt 1778)
By Streamer'67 out of Palsy'70: Province, brown py'd bitch (given to Mr Sturt 1778), Sceptre, yellow py'd dog (given to Farmer Osborn Jr 1778), Sharper, yellow tan'd dog (given to Mr Jeans 1777), Stamper, yellow py'd dog (dead 1778)
By Streamer'67 out of Painted'70: Pitho, brown py'd bitch (dead 1782), Proudish, brown py'd bitch (given to Mr Jeans 1777), Punctual, yellow py'd bitch (given to Mr Sturt 1777), Songster, brown py'd dog (given to Mr Sturt 1778), Spectre, brown py'd dog (cast 1780)
By Postman'71 out of Pigeon'68: Pleasing, brown py'd bitch (dead 1775), Pleasure, brown py'd bitch (cast 1780)
By Streamer'67 out of Maggot'68: Skirter, grey py'd dog (given to Mr Sturt 1776)
By Streamer'67 out of Flora'69: Slender, brown py'd dog (dead 1780), Spinner, grey py'd dog (dead 1780)
By Streamer'67 out of Watchful'69: Scalper, brown py'd dog (cast 1776), Smouser, brown py'd dog (sent to France 1777), Weasel, brown py'd bitch (sent to France 1776), Winter, brown py'd bitch (sent to France 1776), Wisdom, brown py'd bitch (sent to France 1777)

Recapitulation for the year 1774
Old hounds - 35½ couple dogs, 1½ spay'd bitches, 20½ open bitches   72½ couple
Young hounds - 9 couple dogs, 6 bitches
Hounds disposed of this year - died 7 couple, given away 12½ couple   19½ couple
Total of hounds remaining this year   53 couple

Old hound new to the pack in 1775
By August'71 out of Mighty'73: Minute, bitch (entered 1774 sent to France 1776)

List of young hounds entered in 1775
From Mr Thomas: Vengeance, brown py'd dog

---

[*] The total number of old hounds does not tally with the hound book because 5½ couple (2 dogs, 3½ bitches) listed as old hounds entered in 1772 also appear in the list of young hounds entered this year. This is obviously a mistake by the scribe and these 5½ couple have been excluded from the old hound list total. Also the number of young hounds in the list above is 21½ couple, although in the recapitulation there are only 15½ couple, a deficit presumably explained because the 6 couple given away were all young hounds which had gone before the recapitulation was written.

Pedigree of Charlton Hounds

By Tangmere'69 out of Painted'70: Temper, yellow py'd dog (cast 1780), Towzer, yellow py'd dog (dead 1780), Trembler, blue py'd dog (dead 1782)

By Priestcomb'69 out of Palsy'70: Pudding, brown py'd bitch (dead 1778), Pyecrust, brown py'd bitch (dead 1780)

By Puzzler'72 out of Widow'72: Picker, dark brown py'd dog (sent to France 1777), Pilfer, dark brown py'd dog (given to Duke of Aremberg 1777), Whisky, white bitch with a yellow spot in her rump (sent to France 1776), Willing, dark brown py'd bitch (sent to France 1777)

By Surly'72 out of Winish'73: Sounder, brown py'd bitch (dead 1780), Swapper, grizzle py'd dog (dead 1780)

By Goldsmith'71 out of Mortgage'72: Graceful, yellow py'd dog (sent to France 1777), Grandeur, brown py'd dog (cast 1780)

By Puzzler'72 out of Wanton'72: Waggish, grizzle py'd bitch (dead 1782), Wicked, grizzle py'd bitch (given to Mr Gilbert 1780)

By Rusty'69 out of Flora'69: Fancy, grizzle py'd bitch (dead 1778)

By Streamer'67 out of Mighty'73: Majesty, grizzle py'd dog (cast 1780), Mildew, black py'd dog (sent to France 1777), Seymour, brown py'd dog (given to Mr Gilbert 1780)

By Priestcomb'69 out of Milkpan'70: Magpye, brown py'd bitch (sent to France 1777), Maybe, dark brown py'd bitch (sent to France 1776), Mayflower, dark brown py'd bitch (given to Mr Sturt 1777), Mayfly, dark brown py'd bitch (sent to France 1776)

By Batchelor out of Prologue'73: Pillage, brown py'd bitch (dead 1781)

From Mr King by his Twinker out of his Charmer: Cracker, (dead 1776)

From Mr King by his Stormer out of his Jewel: Joiner, grizzle py'd dog (dead 1780)

Recapitulation for the year 1775
Old hounds - 32 couple dogs, ½ spay'd bitches, 20 open bitches
Young hounds - 6½ couple dogs, 7 bitches   66 couple
Hounds disposed of this year - died 11 couple, given away 7½ couple, went to France 5½ couple   24 couple
Total of hounds remaining this year   42 couple

Old hounds new to the pack in 1776
From Lord Egremont: Galliard, yellow py'd dog (dead 1778), Laurel, white dog with a little yellow (dead 1780), Rallywood, grey dog (sent to France 1777)

List of young fox hounds entered in October 1776
By Puzzler'72 out of Wanton'72: Peacock, blue py'd dog (dead 1781), Pillager, grey py'd dog (dead 1782), Pumpkin, grey py'd dog (dead 1782), Putnam, grey py'd dog (given to Mr Sturt 1778), Wallnut, grey py'd bitch (given to Mr Newland 1781), Woeful, grey py'd bitch (cast 1779), Wriggle, yellow bitch (given to Mr Sturt 1778), Wrinkle, grey py'd bitch (given to Mr Gilbert 1780)

By Stroller'72 out of Muddy'68: Meddling, yellow py'd bitch (given to Mr Ridge 1781), Menace, yellow py'd bitch (given to Mr Sturt 1778), Musty, brown py'd bitch (dead 1782), Sober, yellow py'd dog (given to Mr Sturt 1778)

By Lord Castlehaven's Tomboy out of Weighty'73: Tilter, brown py'd dog (dead 1777), Twitcher, brown py'd dog (given to Mr Sturt 1777), Tyrant, yellow py'd dog (given to Mr Sturt 1778), Westdean, grey py'd bitch (given to Mr Sturt 1777), Wishfort, red py'd bitch (sent to France 1777), Woodstock, grey py'd bitch (given to Mr Sturt 1778)

By Puzzler'72 out of Artful'70: Actress, grey py'd bitch (sent to France 1777), Anxious, blue py'd bitch (given to Duke of Ancaster 1779)

By Gaspard'72 out of Milkpan'70: Grabbler, black tan'd dog (given to Mr Sturt 1777), Grateful, black py'd dog (sent to France 1777), Magic, black py'd bitch (sent to France 1777), Mercy, black py'd bitch (sent to France 1777), Midway, black py'd bitch (sent to France 1777), Music, red py'd bitch (sent to France 1777)

By Galliard'76 out of Moment'73: Gaffer, yellow py'd dog (dead 1781), Glitter, brown py'd dog (given to Mr Gilbert 1780), Market, white bitch (dead 1781)

By Puzzler'72 out of Watchful'69: Wealthy, grey py'd bitch (given to Lord Stawell 1781), Whynot, grey py'd bitch (dead 1781)

By Lord Egremont's Rallywood'76 out of Miskin'73: Mexico, yellow py'd bitch (given to Mr Sturt 1778), Rouser, brown py'd dog (dead 1782)

By Lord Egremont's Guider out of Preface'73: Grandson, grey py'd dog (given to Mr Sturt 1778), Playmate, grey py'd bitch (given to Mr Sturt 1778)

By Galliard'76 out of Madam'71: Gorget, grey py'd dog (given to Mr Sturt 1778), Muscat, white bitch (given to Capt Smith 1779)

By Galliard'76 out of Punctual'74: Panting, grey py'd bitch (given to Mr Sampson 1780)

By August'71 out of Pity'73: Anchor, grey py'd dog (dead 1782), Anson, brown py'd dog (given to Mr Sturt 1778), Posset, brown py'd bitch (dead 1782)

263

By Lord Egremont's Rallywood out of Vengeance'75: Venom, grey py'd bitch (sent to France 1777)
From Mr King: Careful, black py'd bitch (sent to France 1777), Crazy, grey py'd dog (given to Mr Gilbert 1780), Tartar, blue py'd dog (dead 1782), Tulip, grey py'd bitch (dead 1782)
From Mr White: Magnet, blue py'd dog (given to Mr Sturt 1778)
From Mr Tireman: Galloper, blue py'd dog (sent to France 1777)
From Mr Tredcroft: Cockscomb, grey py'd dog (given to Lord King 1779)

Recapitulation for the year 1776

Old hounds - 26 couple dogs, 18 open bitches		
Young hounds - 11 couple dogs, 13½ bitches		68½ couple
Hounds disposed of this year - died 4 couple, given away 10 couple, went to France 11 couple		25 couple
Total of hounds remaining this year		43½ couple

List of young fox hounds on the 1st November 1777

By August'71 out of Pity'73: Allfire, brown py'd dog (dead 1782), Ambrose, brown py'd dog (sent to East Indies 1783), Arnold, yellow py'd dog (dead 1782), Partial, brown py'd dog (sent to East Indies 1783), Pitiful, brown py'd bitch (dead 1782), Princess, brown py'd bitch (dead 1781)
By Pilgrim'69 out of Majesty'75: Murmur, yellow py'd bitch (given to Mr Gilbert 1780), Muzzle, yellow py'd bitch (dead 1781), Pageant, yellow py'd dog (given to Mr Sampson 1780), Philip, grey py'd dog (given to Capt Bell 1781), Pliny, yellow py'd dog (dead 1781), Plunder, yellow py'd dog (given to Mr Newland 1781), Poland, grey py'd dog (given to Capt Smith 1779)
By Vulcan'61 out of Mighty'73: Mettle, grey py'd bitch (given to Mr Sturt 1780), Movement, grey py'd bitch (given to Mr Sturt 1780), Venter, brown py'd dog (sent to East Indies 1783), Virgil, grey py'd dog (given to Capt Smith 1779), Viscount, yellow py'd dog (dead 1782)
By Trembler'75 out of Weighty'73: Tarehim, grey py'd dog (cast 1779), Templer, brown py'd dog (given to Capt Smith 1779), Touchit, brown py'd dog (cast 1779), William, brown py'd bitch (cast 1779)
By Goldsmith'71 out of Pitho'74: Garret, black py'd dog (given to Mr Sturt 1780), Garrick, black py'd dog (given to Mr Sturt 1780), Golden, brown py'd dog (dead 1782), Pivot, yellow py'd bitch (sent to France 1779)
By Sceptre'74 out of Miskin'73: Misery, grey py'd bitch (given to Duke of Ancaster 1779), Searcher, yellow py'd dog (given to Mr Willis 1781), Smacker, yellow py'd dog (dead 1782), Smiler, yellow py'd dog (given to Duke of Ancaster 1779), Stopper, grey py'd dog (to the beagles 1778)
By Pilgrim'69 out of Muddy'68: Miserable, brown py'd bitch (given to Mr Sturt 1780), Paddock, brown py'd dog (given to Capt Smith 1779), Padlock, black py'd dog (given to Capt Smith 1779)
By Trembler'75 out of Milkish'71: Method, brown py'd bitch (to the beagles 1778), Tiger, yellow py'd dog (cast 1780), Trooper, brown py'd dog (cast 1780), Tumbler, brown py'd dog (cast 1780)
By Trembler'75 out of Artful'70: Arrant, grey py'd bitch (given to Capt Smith 1779)
By Priestcomb'69 out of Province'74: Pensive, brown py'd dog (cast 1780), Pinker, brown py'd dog (cast 1780), Portion, brown py'd bitch (to the beagles 1778), Prospero, brown py'd dog (dead 1782)
By August'71 out of Preface'73: Arbor, brown py'd dog (dead 1778), Poverty, brown py'd bitch (cast 1780)
By Goldsmith'71 out of Pillage'75: Garnish, brown motly py'd dog (sent to East Indies 1783), Pittance, brown py'd bitch (cast 1780), Prodigal, brown py'd bitch (given to Capt Smith 1779)
By Trembler'75 out of Vengeance'75: Tiburn, brown py'd dog (given to Mr Ridge 1781), Timber, brown tan'd dog (given to Duke of Ancaster 1779), Tutor, grey py'd dog (given to Capt Smith 1779)
By Goldsmith'71 out of Waggish'75: Griper, grey py'd dog (dead 1786)
From Mr Tredcroft: German, grey py'd dog (given to Duke of Ancaster 1779), Goaler, brown py'd dog (given to Mr Castleman 1781), Jangler, brown py'd dog (given to Capt Smith 1779), Lemon, brown py'd dog (dead 1782)
From Mr King: Vexer, grey py'd dog (cast 1780)

Recapitulation for the year 1777

Old hounds - 24 couple dogs, 19½ couple bitches		
Young hounds - 19½ couple dogs, 9 bitches		72 couple
Hounds disposed of this year - died 3½ couple, given away 8½ couple, to France 5½ couple		17½ couple
Total of hounds remaining this year		54½ couple

List of young fox hounds on the 1st of November 1778

By Trembler'75 out of Vengeance'75: Traitor, brown py'd dog (sent to East Indies 1783), Vainlass, yellow py'd bitch (given to Mr Castleman 1781), Veny, grey py'd bitch (given to Mr Newland 1781), Virgin, brown py'd bitch (given to Mr Newland 1781)
By Lord Egremont's Jolly out of Muddy'68: Jolly, grey py'd dog (given to Mr Sampson 1780), Jovial, grey py'd dog (given to Mr Sampson 1780), Mopsy, yellow py'd bitch (given to Mr Sturt 1780), Music, grey py'd bitch (given to Mr

Gilbert 1780)
By August'71 out of Pitho'74: Alresford, black py'd dog (given to Mr Sampson 1780), Alton, black py'd dog (given to Mr Sturt 1780), Plenty, black py'd bitch (died 1779)
By August'71 out of Province'74: Angler, black py'd dog (given to Mr Willis 1782)
By Lord Egremont's Guider out of Waggish'75: Gager, brown py'd dog (sent to East Indies 1783), Gamester, grey py'd dog (given to Mr Gilbert 1784), Guider, grey py'd dog (died 1779), of Waggish'75: Wishful, grey py'd bitch (died 1781)
By Trembler'75 out of Whynot'76: Tapster, grey py'd dog (given to Mr Sturt 1780), Triumph, blue py'd dog (sent to London 1782), Whimsy, brown py'd bitch (died 1781), Witty, grey py'd bitch (died 1779)
By Grandeur'75 out of Majesty'75: Guernsey, white dog (given to Mr Castleman 1781), Mellow, brown py'd bitch (given to Mr Gilbert 1780)
By Gifter'72 out of Mighty'73: Gelder, grey py'd dog (given to Mr Gilbert 1780), Goodness, grey py'd dog (given to Capt Bell 1781)
By Lord Egremont's Guider out of Milkish'71: Goodwill, black py'd dog (died 1779)
By August'71 out of Preface'73: Almond, brown py'd dog (died 1779)
By Andover'69 out of Mildew'75: Aimwell, brown py'd dog (given to Sir G Thomas 1782)
From Mr Thomas: Dealer, black py'd dog (died 1782), Duster, black py'd dog (given to Mr Sturt 1780)
From Mr Tredcroft: Lovely, brown py'd dog (given to Duke of Ancaster 1779), Lucy, brown py'd dog (sent to East Indies 1783), Major, brown py'd dog (died 1787)

Recapitulation for the year 1778
Old hounds - 31 couple dogs, 20 couple open bitches
Young hounds - 10 couple dogs, 6 couple bitches   67 couple
Hounds disposed of this year - died 2½ couple, given away 10 couple, went to France 1 couple   13½ couple
Total of hounds remaining this year   53½ couple

List of young fox hounds on the 1st November 1779
By Lord Egremont's Laurel'76 out of Whynot'76: Lawyer, grey py'd dog (died 1782), Lazy, grey py'd dog (given to Mr Gilbert 1780), Limber, grey py'd dog (given to Mr Castleman 1781), Luther, grey py'd dog (given to Mr Willis 1781), Whisky, grey py'd bitch (given to Mr Castleman 1781), Whisper, grey py'd bitch (given to Mr Castleman 1781), Willow, grey py'd bitch (given to Mr Castleman 1781), Wisely, grizzle py'd bitch (given to Sir G Thomas 1782)
By Lord Egremont's Laurel'76 out of Waggish'75: Ledger, grey py'd dog (given to Mr Gilbert 1780), Lightfoot, red py'd dog (given to Lord Stawell 1781), Lincoln, red py'd dog (given to Mr Gilbert 1780)
By Prior'73 out of Preface'73: Pedler, grizzle py'd dog (died 1784), Pliant, brown py'd bitch (given to Mr Newland 1781), Policy, grizzle py'd bitch (given to Mr Newland 1781)
By Prior'73 out of Mighty'73: Mercy, grey py'd dog (sent to East Indies 1783), Plymouth, red py'd dog (died 1781)
By Gaspard'72 out of Pitho'74: Gamboy, brown py'd dog (died 1789), Pallas, grey py'd bitch (died 1788), Palsy, brown py'd bitch (died 1786)
By Prior'73 out of Vengeance'75: Painter, black py'd dog (died 1781), Plowman, brown py'd dog (died 1784), Vanity, brown py'd bitch (died 1787)
By Lord Egremont's Laurel'76 out of Pillage'75: Packet, red py'd bitch (given to Mr Castleman 1781), Painful, brown py'd bitch (given to Mr Castleman 1781), Painted, black py'd bitch (given to Mr Newland 1781), Papal, brown py'd bitch (given to Mr Castleman 1781)
By Prior'73 out of Posset'76: Percy, brown py'd bitch (died 1782), Primrose, brown py'd bitch (sent to East Indies 1783), Promise, brown py'd bitch (sent to East Indies 1783)
By Spectre'74 out of Tulip'76: Truelass, brown py'd bitch (died 1788)
By Prior'73 out of Meddling'76: Panter, brown py'd dog (died 1784)

Recapitulation for the year 1779
Old hounds - 33 couple dogs, 20½ couple open bitches
Young hounds - 7 couple dogs, 8½ couple bitches   69 couple
Hounds disposed of this year - died 4 couple, given away 13½ couple   17½ couple
Total of hounds remaining this year   51½ couple

List of young fox hounds on the 1st November 1780
By Major'78 out of Muddy'74: Malster, yellow py'd dog (died 1781), Measure, brown py'd bitch (given to Sir G Thomas 1782), Mendall, brown py'd dog (died 1781), Mention, brown py'd bitch (given to Mr Tattersall 1786), Merchant, brown py'd dog (sent to France 1782), Merit, brown py'd bitch (given to Mr Willis 1781), Mystery, brown py'd bitch (given to Sir G Thomas 1782)
By Prior'73 out of Posset'76: Penman, blue py'd dog (given to Mr Gilbert 1784), Plenty, brown py'd bitch (given to

Mr Tattersall 1786), Practice, grizzle py'd bitch (given to Mr Gilbert 1784), Proudly, brown py'd bitch (died 1784), Prudence, brown py'd bitch (given to Mr Tattersall 1787), Pruner, grizzle py'd dog (given to Mr Lenox 1786)

By Rouser'76 out of Market'76: Music, yellow py'd bitch (given to Lord Berkeley 1787), Myrtle, grey py'd bitch (died 1782), Ratler, grey py'd dog (died 1787), Ringwood, yellow py'd dog (given to Col Harvey 1787)

By Major'78 out of Pityful'77: Marplot, brown py'd dog (died 1781), Merryman, brown py'd dog (given to Mr Gilbert 1780), Patient, dark grizzle py'd bitch (died 1782)

By Gaffer'76 out of Princess'77: Pittance, brown mottle py'd bitch (given to Lord Berkeley 1787), Pleasant, white bitch (died 1786)

By Major'78 out of Milkish'71: Madcap, brown py'd dog (died 1788), Miller, grey py'd dog (died 1782)

By Seymour'75 out of Pillage'75: Shifter, grizzle py'd dog (sent to France 1782)

By Spectre'74 out of a bitch of Mr Tredcroft's: Switcher, brown py'd dog (died 1784)

By Lord Egremont's Laurel'76 out of Whynot'76: Linwood, dark blue py'd dog (given to Mr Gilbert 1780), Looby, grey py'd dog (sent to France 1782), Lusty, grey py'd dog (cast 1781), Warbler, dark blue py'd bitch (died 1782)

By Lord Egremont's Glancer out of Virgin'78: Vapour, brown py'd bitch (died 1782)

Recapitulation for the year 1780
Old hounds - 23 couple dogs, 19½ couple bitches
Young hounds - 8 couple dogs, 7½ couple bitches — 58 couple
Hounds disposed of this year - died 8½ couple, given away 14 couple — 22½ couple
Total of hounds remaining this year — 35½ couple

List of young fox hounds on the 1st November 1781

By Prior'73 out of Virgin'78: Pilgrim, brown py'd dog (sent to East Indies 1783), Planter, brown py'd dog (given to Mr Tattersall 1786), Primer, grey py'd dog (given to Col Harvey 1787), Proctor, brown py'd dog (given to Lord Berkeley 1788), Venom, brown py'd bitch (given to Mr Newland 1783)

By Tartar'76 out of Meddling'76: Miskin, brown py'd bitch (given to Sir G Thomas 1782), Twister, grizzle py'd dog (given to Col Harvey 1788)

By Rouser'76 out of Pitiful'77: Picture, brown py'd bitch (died 1787), Polly, brown py'd bitch (died 1787), Ranter, brown py'd dog (died 1782)

By Lord Egremont's Glancer out of Pillage'75: Glancer, black py'd dog (died 1782), Partridge, brown py'd bitch (given to Sir G Thomas 1782), Pleasure, brown py'd bitch (sent to France 1782), Punctual, brown py'd bitch (died 1784)

By Major'78 out of Posset'76: Miser, brown py'd dog (died 1792), Mountain, brown py'd dog (died 1788), Murder, brown py'd dog (cast 1791), Pheasant, brown py'd bitch (died 1782), Pigeon, brown py'd bitch (given to Sir G Thomas 1782)

By Lord Egremont's Minor out of Musty'76: Matchless, brown py'd bitch (died 1788)

By Sounder'75 out of Pallas'79: Province, grizzle py'd bitch (died 1789), Singer, grizzle py'd dog (died 1782)

By Swapper'75 out of Percy'79: Party, grey py'd bitch (died 1782), Shiner, liver py'd dog (sent to France 1784), Stranger, yellow tan'd dog (died 1784)

By Lord Egremont's Minor out of Veny'78: Maxim, brown py'd dog (sent to East Indies 1783), Member, brown py'd dog (given to Mr Tattersall 1788), Mounter, brown py'd dog (given to Mr Tattersall 1787), Venus, yellow py'd bitch (given to Sir G Thomas 1782)

By Gamester'57 out of Vengeance'75: Gallant, brown py'd dog (sent to France 1782), Vicious, grey py'd bitch (given to Sir G Thomas 1782), Violet, grey py'd bitch (sent to East Indies 1783), Vocal, black py'd bitch (given to Sir G Thomas 1782)

By Prospero'77 out of Tulip'76: Plumber, grey py'd dog (given to Mr Banks 1782), Tipsy, grey py'd bitch (given to Sir G Thomas 1782)

By Rouser'76 out of Whynot'76: Rueful, grey py'd dog (died 1782), Rufler, grey py'd dog (died 1782), Ruler, grey py'd dog (given to Mr Banks 1782), Weazzle, grey py'd bitch (sent to East Indies 1783)

Recapitulation for the year 1781
Old hounds - 20 couple dogs, 15½ couple bitches
Young hounds - 10½ couple dogs, 9 couple bitches — 55 couple
Hounds disposed of this year - died 17 couple, given away 10½ couple — 27½ couple
Total of hounds remaining this year — 27½ couple

List of young fox hounds on the 1st of November 1782

By Lord Egremont's Gangler out of Pitho'74: Glocester, black py'd dog (died 1789), Paltry, black py'd bitch (died 1789), Pepper, yellow py'd bitch (died 1787), of Pitho'74: Princes, grey py'd bitch (died 1789)

By Gamboy'79 out of Pitiful'77: Galloper, brown py'd dog (died 1788)

By Gaspard'72 out of Proudly'80: Giant, black py'd dog (sent to France 1784), Glitter, grizzle py'd dog (given to Mr

Tattersall 1787), Glorious, black py'd dog (given to Mr Tattersall 1786)

By Lord Egremont's Minor out of Myrtle'80: Malice, brown py'd dog (given to Mr Tattersall 1786), Marquess, brown py'd dog (died 1788), Monster, smutty face brown py'd dog (died 1788), Mopsy, smutty face brown py'd bitch (died 1788)

By Pillager'75 out of Truelass'79: Pealer, brown py'd dog (given to Mr Lenox 1786), Pounder, grey py'd dog (given to Mr Tattersall 1786), Testy, grey py'd bitch (died 1789), Tipsy, grey py'd bitch (given to Mr Tattersall 1786)

By Rouser'76 out of Pallas'79: Patsy, grey py'd bitch (given to Lord King 1790), Pretty, yellow py'd bitch (died 1788)

By Lord Egremont's Gangler out of Palsy'79: Gangler, brown py'd dog (died 1789), Governor, brown py'd dog (died 1786), Painful, brown py'd bitch (died 1791)

By Griper'77 out of Posset'76: Grafton, white dog (sent to East Indies 1784), Growler, yellow py'd dog (sent to East Indies 1784), Guider, yellow py'd dog (sent to East Indies 1784)

By Pillager'75 out of Vanity'79: Plumper, grey py'd dog (sent to France 1784), Plunder, brown py'd dog (given to Mr Tattersall 1786), Vainly, brown py'd bitch (sent to East Indies 1783), Vanquish, grizzle py'd bitch (given to Mr Lenox 1786)

Recapitulation for the year 1782
Old hounds - 15 couple dogs, 12½ couple bitches
Young hounds - 8 couple dogs, 6 couple bitches   41½ couple
Hounds disposed of this year - went to the East Indies 9 couple, given away ½ couple   9½ couple
Total of hounds remaining this year   32 couple

List of young fox hounds on the 1st of November 1783
By Pillager'75 out of Polly'81: Prosper, grey py'd dog (cast 1784)

By Anchor'76 out of Vanity'79: August, brown py'd dog (given to Lord King 1789), Vainlass, grey py'd bitch (given to Mr Tattersall 1786), Vengeance, liver py'd bitch (given to Lord King 1789), Virgin, brown py'd bitch (given to Mr Tattersall 1786)

By Griper'77 out of Matchless'81: Grandeur, yellow py'd dog (died 1784), Grocer, grey py'd dog (sent to France 1784), Metal, brown py'd bitch (given to Mr Tattersall 1789), Moment, brown py'd bitch (given to Lord King 1790)

By Griper'77 out of Truelass'79: Tawny, grey py'd bitch (given to Mr Tattersall 1789), Trifle, black py'd bitch (given to subscription pack near Andover 1790)

By Ratter'80 out of Proudly'80: Pippin, grey py'd bitch (given to Mr Newland 1784), Planet, grey py'd bitch (sent to France 1784), Richmond, brown py'd dog (died 1787), Roper, brown py'd dog (died 1787), Rouser, grey py'd dog (sent to France 1784)

By Pumpkin'76 out of Violet'81: Pleader, grey py'd dog (given to Mr Tattersall 1788), Prancer, grey py'd dog (given to Mr Tattersall 1788)

By Tartar'76 out of Picture'81: Packet, grey py'd bitch (given to subscription pack near Andover 1790), Thumper, blue py'd dog (given to Mr Lenox 1786)

By Ratler'80 out of Mercy'79: Railer, brown py'd dog (died 1784)

Recapitulation for the year 1783
Old hounds - 19½ couple dogs, 14 couple bitches
Young hounds - 5½ couple dogs, 5 couple bitches   44 couple
Hounds disposed of this year - went to the East Indies 1½ couple, went to France 3 couple, given away 2 couple, died 4½ couple   11 couple
Total of hounds remaining this year   33 couple

List of young fox hounds on the 1st of November 1784
By Gager'78 out of Painful'79: Gabriel, brown py'd dog (died 1793), Poppet, white bitch with a blue spot on her rump (died 1792)

By Ratler'80 out of Province'81: Purple, white bitch with two blue spots (died 1793)

By Garnish'77 out of Pleasant'80: Gaspard, yellow py'd dog (given to Mr Tattersall 1783), Gelder, yellow py'd dog (given to Mr Tattersall 1787)

By Ratler'80 out of Pallas'79: Phoeboe, blue py'd bitch (died 1788), Phoenix, white bitch with a blue spot (died 1789), Random, blue py'd dog (died 1789)

By Twister'81 out of Palsy'79: Paris, brown py'd bitch (died 1788), Parley, brown py'd bitch (given to Mr Tattersall 1787), Tanner, brown py'd dog (given to Mr Tattersall 1786), Tapster, brown py'd dog (given to Mr Tattersall 1786)

By Gamboy'79 out of Matchless'81: Goodwood, black py'd dog (died 1786), Maiden, brown py'd bitch (given to Lord Thanet 1785), Makewell, brown py'd bitch (given to Lord King 1790), Mendit, yellow py'd bitch (given to Mr Lenox 1786)

By Twister'81 out of Picture'81: Papal, grey py'd bitch (given to Lord Thanet 1785), Pheasant, yellow py'd bitch (given to Mr Lenox 1786), Pigeon, grey py'd bitch (given to Mr Lenox 1786), Pliant, brown tan'd bitch (given to Mr Gilbert 1793)

By Gamboy'79 out of Miskin'81: Gifter, yellow py'd dog (died 1792), Guider, yellow py'd dog (given to Mr Lenox 1786)

By Ratler'80 out of Mercy'79: Ragman, white dog (given to Lord Thanet 1785), Rebel, grey py'd dog (given to Mr Tattersall 1786), Ruler, grey py'd dog (given to Mr Tattersall 1786)

By Madcap'80 out of Vanity'79: Venom, brown py'd bitch (died 1792), Vicious, yellow py'd bitch (died 1790)

Recapitulation for the year 1784

Old hounds - 16 couple dogs, 16½ couple bitches
Young hounds - 6 couple dogs, 7½ couple bitches   46 couple
Hounds disposed of this year - given away 1½ couple, died 1 couple   2½ couple
Total of hounds remaining this year   43½ couple

List of young fox hounds on the 1st November 1785

By Major'78 out of Trifle'83: Marplot, brown py'd dog (given to Col Harvey 1786), Merchant, black py'd dog (died 1792), Minor, brown py'd dog (given to Mr Tattersall 1789), Timely, black tan'd bitch (died 1793)

By Madcap'80 out of Testy'82: Monday, brown py'd dog (given to Mr Tattersall 1786), Truemaid, liver colour tan'd bitch (given to Lord King 1790)

By Ratler'80 out of Pepper'82: Ramper, grey py'd dog (given to Mr Tattersall 1789), Ranger, grey py'd dog (died 1786), Roger, grey py'd dog (given to Col Harvey 1786)

By Gamboy'79 out of Vanity'79: Garter, brown py'd dog (given to Col Harvey 1786), Vixen, yellow py'd bitch (given to subscription pack near Andover 1790)

By Major'78 out of Matchless'81: Madman, grey py'd dog (died 1793), Master, brown py'd dog (given to Mr Tattersall 1786), Muffler, brown py'd dog (died 1793)

By Ringwood'80 out of Painful'82: Prattle, brown py'd bitch (given to Mr Gilbert 1793), Raffler, brown py'd dog (given to Mr Tattersall 1786), Redcap, brown py'd dog (died 1792), Render, brown py'd dog (cast 1792)

By Miser'81 out of Province'81: Mumper, grey py'd dog (died 1788), Panting, yellow py'd bitch (given to Mr Ridge 1791)

By Major'78 out of Paltry'82: Mariner, black py'd dog (died 1789), Pity, brown py'd bitch (died 1793), Prologue, brown py'd bitch (died 1789)

By Ringwood'80 out of Punctual'81: Resten, grey py'd dog (died 1792)

By Planter'81 out of Patsy'82: Pevet, blue mottled bitch (given to Mr Tattersall 1786)

By Member'81 out of Pallas'79: Precious, grey py'd bitch (died 1794)

By Madcap'80 out of Polly'81: Micher, brown py'd dog (given to Mr Tattersall 1786)

By Major'78 out of Pretty'82: Portion, yellow py'd bitch (died 1786)

Recapitulation for the year 1785

Old hounds - 21½ couple dogs, 23 couple bitches
Young hounds - 9 couple dogs, 5 couple bitches   58½ couple
Hounds disposed of this year - given away 14 couple, died 3½ couple   17½ couple
Total of hounds remaining this season   41 couple

List of young fox hounds on the 1st November 1786

By Member'81 out of Pepper'82: Maltster, grey py'd dog (given to Lord King 1790), Miller, brown py'd dog (given to Mr Tattersall 1789), Pantry, brown py'd bitch (given to Mr Tattersall 1787)

By Ringwood'80 out of Princess'82: Pleasant, brown py'd bitch (died 1792), Rapier, brown py'd dog (died 1787), Rockwood, brown py'd dog (given to Mr Tattersall 1787)

By Madcap'80 out of Polly'81: Merryman, brown py'd dog (given to Mr Tattersall 1787), Monger, yellow py'd dog (given to Mr Tattersall 1787), Mummer, yellow py'd dog (given to Mr Tattersall 1787), Piney, brown py'd bitch (cast 1792)

By Major'78 out of Patsy'79: Manfull, yellow py'd dog (died 1793), Mender, brown py'd dog (given to Mr Tattersall 1789), Partial, brown py'd bitch (died 1794), Primrose, grizzle py'd bitch (died 1794)

By Prancer'83 out of Painful'82: Pedler, brown py'd dog (given to Mr Ridge 1793), Playmate, grey py'd bitch (given to Mr Tattersall 1789)

By Major'78 out of Pretty'82: Magnet, grey py'd dog (given to Mr Tattersall 1787), Milter, yellow py'd dog (given to Mr Tattersall 1787), Moulder, grey py'd dog (given to subscription pack near Andover 1790), Murder, grey py'd dog (died 1792), Party, brown py'd bitch (died 1787), Posey, grey py'd bitch (given to Mr Tattersall 1787)

By Primer'81 out of Truelass'79: Tulip, grey py'd bitch (given to Mr Tattersall 1787)

By Ratler'80 out of Trifle'83: Roguish, brown py'd dog (died 1787), Romsey, grey py'd dog (died 1793), Tiny, grey

py'd bitch (died 1787), Tippet, brown py'd bitch (given to Sir C Davers 1792)
By Major'78 out of Paltry'82: Marcher, brown dog (died 1787), Medler, grey py'd dog (given to Mr Tattersall 1787), Meter, brown py'd dog (cast 1789), Mighter, grey py'd dog (died 1792), Minister, grey py'd dog (died 1793), Partridge, brown py'd bitch (died 1793)
By Member'81 out of Pallas'79: Muster, brown back'd dog (given to Sir C Davers 1792)
By Prancer'83 out of Picture'81: Pleasure, grey py'd bitch (died 1787), Plowman, brown py'd dog (died 1787)
From Lord King: Vander, blue py'd dog (died 1788)

Recapitulation for the year 1786
Old hounds - 19 couple dogs, 21 couple bitches
Young hounds - 12 couple dogs, 6½ couple bitches　　　　　　　　　　　　　　　　　53½ couple
Hounds disposed of this year - given away 9½ couple, died 8 couple　　　　　　　　17½ couple
Total of hounds remaining this year　　　　　　　　　　　　　　　　　　　　　　　41 couple

List of young fox hounds on the 1st November 1787
By Monster'82 out of Testy'82: Masker, brown py'd dog (died 1796)
By Muffler'85 out of Pepper'82: Pious, grey py'd bitch (given to Mr Houndsom 1794)
By Monster'82 out of Poppet'84: Peggy, brown py'd bitch (given to subscription pack near Andover 1790), Picture, white bitch (given to subscription pack near Andover 1790), Pleasure, grey py'd bitch (given to subscription pack near Andover 1790)
By Gabriel'84 out of Venom'84: Gauger, brown py'd dog (given to Mr Houth 1793), Vision, black py'd bitch (given to Mr Gaskel 1793), Vocal, brown py'd bitch (died 1792)
By Gabriel'84 out of Vicious'84: Grammar, brown py'd dog (died 1796), Grinder, brown py'd dog (died 1793)
By Lord Egremont's Rebel out of Trifle'83: Rebel, black py'd dog (died 1790), Royston, brown py'd dog (given to Mr Murrel 1793)
By Miser'81 out of Paltry'82: Pallet, brown py'd bitch (died 1789), Pansy, brown py'd bitch (given to Mr Gaskel 1793)
By Ratler'80 out of Pity'85: Popless, grey py'd bitch (given to Mr Ridge 1794)
By Lord Egremont's Leader out of Patsy'79: Leader, yellow py'd bitch (given to Lord King 1790), Lustre, grey py'd dog (died 1795), Pigeon, grey py'd bitch (given to subscription pack near Andover 1790), Pillage, grey py'd bitch (given to Mr Tattersall 1789)
By Gamboy'79 out of Metal'83: Majesty, brown py'd bitch (given to Mr Houndsom 1791)
By Gabriel'84 out of Tawny'83: Gallant, brown py'd dog (given to Lord Berkeley 1790), Tempest, brown py'd bitch (given to subscription pack near Andover 1790), Tidings, brown py'd bitch (died 1790), Trollop, grey py'd bitch (died 1790)
By Lord Egremont's Hanibal out of Painful'82: Harpur, grey py'd dog (given to Sir C Davers 1792)
By Muffler'85 out of Pretty'82: Marker, brown py'd dog (died 1792)
By Ranger'85 out of Picture'81: Ripley, grey py'd dog (died 1791)

Recapitulation for the year 1787
Old hounds - 20½ couple dogs, 20½ couple bitches
Young hounds - 6 couple dogs, 7½ couple bitches　　　　　　　　　　　　　　　　　54½ couple
Hounds disposed of this year - given away 3 couple, died 6½ couple　　　　　　　　9½ couple
Total of hounds remaining this year　　　　　　　　　　　　　　　　　　　　　　　45 couple

List of young fox hounds on the 1st November 1788
By Gabriel'84 out of Paltry'82: Pannel, grizzle py'd bitch (cast 1792), Pardon, brown py'd bitch (given to Mr Gilbert 1792), Parent, black py'd bitch (died 1794), Preface, brown py'd bitch (cast 1791 given to Mr Gilbert 1793), Proxy, black py'd bitch (given to Mr Sykes 1794)
By Gabriel'84 out of Metal'83: Glancer, yellow py'd dog (died 1793), Midnight, grey py'd bitch (given to Mr Murrel 1793), Molly, yellow py'd bitch (cast 1792)
By Lord Egremont's Hanibal out of Panting'85: Hanibal, yellow tan'd dog (given to Mr Bolton 1795), Hector, brown py'd dog (given to Sir C Davers 1792)
By Miser'81 out of Province'81: Marygold, yellow py'd dog (died 1791), Painted, brown py'd bitch (given to Mr Newland 1790), Pensive, brown py'd bitch (given to Mr Newland 1790)
By Gabriel'84 out of Trifle'83: Glister, brown py'd dog (given to Mr Gilbert 1792), Glitter, brown py'd dog (given to Sir C Davers 1792)
By Gabriel'84 out of Vicious'84: Granby, grey py'd dog (died 1794), Gunter, brown py'd dog (given to Mr Gilbert 1792), Venus, black py'd bitch (given to Mr Beaver 1794), Veny, yellow py'd bitch (died 1794)
By Gabriel'84 out of Timely'85: Gunner, black py'd dog (given to Mr Bolton 1794)

By Muffler'85 out of Phoenix'84: Mounter, grey py'd dog (died 1789), Posset, grey py'd bitch (cast 1797)
By Gabriel'84 out of Testy'82: Guildford, brown py'd dog (given to Mr Murrel 1793), Terras, grey py'd bitch (given to Mr Sykes 1794), Trial, grey py'd bitch (died 1794)
By Lord Egremont's Rebel out of Pretty'82: Pyecrust, grey py'd bitch (cast 1797)
By Gabriel'84 out of Tawny'83: Grocer, brown py'd dog (given to Mr Bolton 1793), Tipsy, brown py'd bitch (given to Mr Newland 1790), Trophies, yellow py'd bitch (given to Mr Bolton 1793)
By Gabriel'84 out of Venom'84: Glorious, grey py'd dog (died 1789), Governor, brown py'd dog (died 1789), Groper, yellow py'd dog (sent to East Indies 1791), Vanquish, grey py'd bitch (given to subscription pack near Andover 1790), Violet, brown py'd bitch (given to Mr Houndsom 1791)
By Mariner'85 out of Moment'83: Marplot, brown py'd dog (died 1789), Merrylass, brown py'd bitch (given to Mr Beaver 1794), Monday, grey py'd dog (cast 1792), Mourner, black py'd dog (given to Mr Bolton 1793)
By Major'78 out of Phoeby'84: Milter, brown py'd dog (died 1789), Pastime, brown py'd bitch (died 1789), Posey, grey py'd bitch (died 1789), Promise, grey py'd bitch (died 1789)
By Merchant'85 out of Vixen'85: Mangler, brown py'd dog (died 1789), Montagu, brown py'd dog (given to Sir C Davers 1792), Vainlass, grey py'd bitch (cast 1789)
By Gamboy'79 out of Pity'85: Gambler, grey py'd dog (died 1789), Garret, brown py'd dog (died 1789), Giant, grizzle py'd dog (died 1789)
By Mariner'85 out of Patsy'79: Malter, grey py'd dog (died 1789), Maypole, black py'd dog (died 1791), Mercer, grey py'd dog (cast 1792), Mumbler, black py'd dog (died 1791), Parley, grey py'd bitch (given to Mr Houndsom 1791)
By Muffler'85 out of Pallas'79: Manner, brown py'd dog (died 1789), Master, grey py'd dog (died 1789), Maxim, grey py'd dog (died 1789)
By Miser'81 out of Poppet'84: Miller, brown py'd dog (died 1789), Polly, brown py'd bitch (died 1789)
By Lord Egremont's Hanibal out of Painful'82: Huckster, black py'd dog (died 1793)

Recapitulation for the year 1788
Old hounds - 20 couple dogs, 24½ couple bitches
Young hounds - 16½ couple dogs, 13 couple bitches   74 couple
Hounds disposed of this year - given away 5 couple, died 11½ couple   16½ couple
Total of hounds remaining this year   57½ couple

List of young fox hounds on the 1st of November 1789
By Grammar'87 out of Panting'85: Galloper, yellow py'd dog (given to Mr Gilbert 1792), Pencil, brown py'd bitch (given to Mr Bolton 1795), Punctual, brown py'd dog (given to Mr Gilbert 1792), Purling, yellow py'd bitch (given to Mr Gilbert 1792)
By Gabriel'84 out of Piney'86: Garnish, black py'd dog (given to Mr Bolton 1794), Garter, black py'd dog (given to Mr Bolton 1794)
By Gifter'84 out of Pansy'87: Grampus, brown py'd dog (given to Mr Beaver 1794), Granter, brown py'd dog (given to Mr Bolton 1793)
By Lord King's Minor out of Painful'82: Morgan, black py'd dog (given to Mr Gilbert 1792), Mortar, grey py'd dog (given to Mr Gilbert 1792), Parlour, grey py'd bitch (died 1795), Peeress, brown py'd bitch (died 1795), Pippin, black py'd bitch (given to Mr Gilbert 1792)
By Gabriel'84 out of Popless'87: Gleaner, grey py'd dog (given to Mr Gilbert 1792), Papist, grey py'd bitch (died 1796)
By Mariner'85 out of Moment'83: Manner, black py'd dog (given to Sir C Davers 1792), Merryman, black py'd dog (given to Mr Gilbert 1792)
By Gabriel'84 out of Vicious'84: Gabbler, grey py'd dog (died 1793), Goodwood, grey py'd dog (given to Mr Bolton 1795), Griffin, grey py'd dog (given to Mr Leach 1797), Viol, brown py'd bitch (cast 1794)
By Grammar'87 out of Princess'82: Gambler, dark grey py'd dog (died 1796)
By Grammar'87 out of Vixen'85: Varnish, yellow py'd bitch (died 1793)
By Merchant'85 out of Terras'88: Micher, brown py'd dog (died 1794)
By Grinder'87 out of Pity'85: Golden, black py'd dog (given to Sir C Davers 1792)
By Gabriel'84 out of Pious'87: Glider, grey py'd dog (died 1792)
By Gabriel'84 out of Venom'84: Virtual, grey py'd bitch (given to Sir C Davers 1792)
By Gabriel'84 out of Pliant'84: Guider, brown py'd dog (given to Sir C Davers 1792)

Recapitulation for the year 1789
Old hounds - 24½ couple dogs, 29 couple bitches
Young hounds - 9½ couple dogs, 4½ couple bitches   67½ couple
Hounds disposed of this year - given away 10 couple, died 1½ couple   11½ couple
Total of hounds remaining this year   56 couple

Pedigree of Charlton Hounds

List of young fox hounds on the 1st of November 1790

By Lord Egremont's Lacer out of Tippet'86: Laurel, yellow py'd dog (died 1795), Lawyer, brown py'd dog (given to Sir C Davers 1792), Limner, brown py'd dog (died 1797), Luter, yellow py'd dog (given to Mr Houth 1793)

By Muffler'85 out of Pleasant'86: Marcher, grey py'd dog (given to Mr Gilbert 1792), Mentor, brown py'd dog (cast 1792), Mumper, brown py'd dog (given to Sir C Davers 1792), Proudly, brown py'd bitch (died 1794)

By Rebel'87 out of Vision'87: Ratler, black py'd dog (given to Sir C Davers 1792 and to Mr Murrel 1793), Ringwood, black py'd dog (given to Mr Sykes 1794), Rouser, black py'd dog (given to Mr Murrel 1793), Vanity, black py'd bitch (cast 1793)

By Lord Egremont's Rafter out of Proxy'88: Pityless, black py'd bitch (cast 1797), Racer, black py'd dog (given to Mr Gilbert 1792), Rafter, black py'd dog (given to Mr Murrel 1793), Ravisher, black py'd dog (died 1793)

By Gabriel'84 out of Popless'87: Glasgow, grey py'd dog (died 1796)

By Gifter'84 out of Pansy'87: Gamboy, yellow py'd dog (given to Mr Sturt 1795), Garrat, brown py'd dog (given to Sir H Harper 1797), General, grey py'd dog (given to Mr Murrel died 1794), Phillis, yellow py'd bitch (given to Mr Bolton 1793), Posey, yellow py'd bitch (died 1794)

By Lord Egremont's Merryman out of Terras'88: Marplot, brown py'd dog (died 1794), Mellish, grey py'd dog (given to Mr Jordan 1793), Mercury, grey py'd dog (died 1795)

By Grinder'87 out of Trifle'83: Griper, grey py'd dog (cast 1799), Totnes, grey py'd bitch (given to Mr Leach 1797)

By Grinder'87 out of Pity'85: Gardner, brown py'd dog (died 1792), Pasty, yellow py'd bitch (given to Mr Sturt 1796), Patience, black py'd bitch (given to Sir H Harper 1797), Present, grey py'd bitch (given to Mr Newland 1796), Promise, brown py'd bitch (given to Mr Brookman 1796)

By Lord Egremont's Captain out of Partridge'86: Captain, grey py'd dog (given to Mr Bolton 1793 (1795))

By Rebel'87 out of Vixen'85: Royal, brown py'd dog (given to Mr Jordan 1793)

By Lord Egremont's Minor out of Trifle'83: Magnet, brown py'd dog (given to Mr Gilbert 1792),

By Lord Egremont's Minor out of Pardon'88: Minor, brown py'd dog (given to Mr Gilbert 1792)

By Muffler'85 out of Vicious'84: Major, grey py'd dog (given to Mr Bolton 1795), Vainlass, grey py'd bitch (cast 1794), Virgin, brown py'd bitch (given to Mr Murrel 1794)

By Gifter'84 out of Pious'87: Gallows, brown py'd dog (given to Mr Gilbert 1792)

Recapitulation for the year 1790

Old hounds - 31½ couple dogs, 24½ couple bitches
Young hounds - 14 couple dogs, 6 couple bitches 76 couple
Hounds disposed of this year - given away 2 couple, died 2½ couple, went to the East Indies ½ couple 5 couple
Total of hounds remaining this year 71 couple

Old hound new to the pack on the 1st of November 1791

From Lord King: Gaylass, grey py'd bitch (entered 1790 given to Sir C Davers 1792)

List of young fox hounds on the 1st of November 1791

By Lord Egremont's Merryman out of Proxy'88: Madcap, brown py'd dog (died 1795), Mariner, brown py'd dog (cast 1797)

By Grammar'87 out of Popless'87: Gamester, brown py'd dog (cast 1797), Garrison, grey py'd dog (died 1797), Palsy, liver colour tan'd bitch (cast 1797), Parrot, black py'd bitch (cast 1798)

By Masker'87 out of Venus'88: Messenger, brown py'd dog (died 1797), Monster, black py'd dog (given to Sir H Harper 1797), Virtue, black py'd bitch (given to Sir H Harper 1797)

By Gunner'88 out of Pious'87: Gasper, grey py'd dog (died 1793), Girder, grey py'd dog (cast 1792)

By Gifter'84 out of Pansy'87: Gaffer, yellow py'd dog (cast 1792), Playmate, yellow py'd bitch (given to Mr Jordan 1793)

By Gifter'84 out of Terras'88: Giant, grey py'd dog (given to Mr Bolton 1794), Goldsmith, grey py'd dog (died 1792), Tipsy, grey py'd bitch (given to Mr Sykes 1794)

By Morgan'89 out of Vicious'84: Maypole, brown py'd dog (given to Mr Murrel 1793), Mercer, brown py'd dog (given to Mr Murrel 1793), Mumbler, brown py'd dog (given to Mr Bolton 1793)

By Gifter'84 out of Parent'88: Genius, brown py'd dog (cast 1792)

By Masker'87 out of Midnight'88: Manager, brown py'd dog (given to Mr Murrel 1793)

By Gunter'88 out of Tippet'86: Truemaid, brown py'd bitch (given to Mr Deburgh 1793)

Recapitulation for the year 1791

Old hounds - 43 couple dogs, 28½ couple bitches
Young hounds - 8 couple dogs, 3 couple bitches 82½ couple
Hounds disposed of this year - given away 15 couple, died 7½ couple 22½ couple
Total of hounds remaining this year 60 couple

List of young fox hounds on the 1st of November 1792

By Gamboy'90 out of Venus'88: Gender, yellow py'd dog (given to Mr Bolton 1794), Glorious, yellow py'd dog (given to Mr Bolton 1794), Vapour, yellow py'd dog (given to Col Sloper 1797)

By Grammar'87 out of Pious'87: Ginger, brown py'd dog (died 1794), Pretty, grey py'd bitch (cast 1797)

By Grammar'87 out of Pyecrust'88: Gilpin, black py'd dog (cast 1799), Governor, brown py'd dog (cast 1799)

By Grinder'87 out of Tippet'86: Galloper, brown py'd dog (cast 1797), Grinder, brown py'd dog (cast 1797), Trifle, brown py'd bitch (cast 1799)

By Grammar'87 out of Popless'87: Gallant, black py'd dog (died 1794)

By Gamboy'90 out of Viol'88: Grazier, grey py'd dog (cast 1799)

By Muster'86 out of Proxy'88: Member, brown py'd dog (given to Mr Bolton 1794), Mounter, brown py'd dog (given to Mr Bolton 1794), Precious, brown py'd bitch (died 1795)

By Mariner'91 out of Tipsy'88: Merryman, brown py'd dog (cast 1799), Miner, grey py'd dog (cast 1799)

By Gamboy'90 out of Parent'88: Pleasure, brown py'd bitch (given to Mr Leach 1797)

By Pedler'86 out of Present'90: Panting, brown py'd bitch (given to Mr Houndsom 1794)

By Lord Egremont's Bluecap out of Vision'87: Violet, brown py'd bitch (cast 1798)

Recapitulation for the year 1792

Old hounds - 32 couple dogs, 26 couple bitches
Young hounds - 6½ couple dogs, 3½ couple bitches   68 couple
Hounds disposed of this year - given away 15 couple, died 9 couple   24 couple
Total of hounds remaining this year   44* couple

List of young fox hounds on the 1st of November 1793

By Gamboy'90 out of Totnes'90: Gabriel, grey py'd dog (given to Mr Gilbert 1794), Gagler, grey py'd dog (given to Mr Bolton 1794)

By Griffin'89 out of Pity'85: Glancer, yellow py'd dog (given to Mr Bolton 1796), Golden, black py'd dog (given to Mr Leach 1797), Growler, brown py'd dog (given to Mr Sykes 1794)

By Gambler'89 out of Terras'88: Gardner, grey py'd dog (died 1797), Gester, grey py'd dog (given to Mr Sykes 1794), Giddy, grey py'd dog (died 1794), Glimmer, grey py'd dog (died 1794), Trial, white bitch (cast 1799)

By Grammar'87 out of Pyecrust'88: Gauger, brown py'd dog (cast 1799), Packet, brown py'd bitch (cast 1799)

By Hanibal'88 out of Varnish'89: Hagler, black py'd dog (given to Mr Ridge 1795), Hector, black py'd dog (given to Mr Bolton 1795), Helper, grey py'd dog (given to Mr Bolton 1794), Highman, black py'd dog (cast 1799), Vengeance, brown py'd bitch (cast 1799)

By Masker'87 out of Veny'88: Miser, brown py'd dog (died 1794), Mounter, brown py'd dog (died 1794), Vicious, grey py'd bitch (cast 1798)

By Lord Egremont's Blaster out of Papist'89: Pewet, grey py'd bitch (given to Mr Eald 1794), Poppet, brown py'd bitch (died 1795), Princess, grey py'd bitch (died 1795), Provance, brown py'd bitch (cast 1799)

By Lord Egremont's Bluecap out of Viol'89: Banker, brown py'd dog (died 1796), Barfleur, brown py'd dog (cast 1799), Bouncer, black py'd dog (cast 1799), Bumpkin, yellow py'd dog (cast 1799), Vixen, black py'd bitch (cast 1799)

By Griper'90 out of Parent'88: Pigeon, grey py'd bitch (given to Sir H Harper 1797)

Recapitulation for the year 1793

Old hounds - 22 couple dogs, 20 couple bitches
Young hounds - 10 couple dogs, 4½ couple bitches   56½ couple
Hounds disposed of this year - given away 11 couple, died 7 couple   18 couple
Total of hounds remaining this year   48½ couple

List of young fox hounds on the 1st November 1794**

By Bumpkin'93 out of Tipsy'91: Brusher, brown py'd dog (cast 1799)

By Gallant'92 out of Precious'92: Pious, brown py'd bitch (given to Mr Shakespear 1797)

By Gamboy'90 out of Totnes'90: Trinket, yellow py'd bitch (given to Mr Bolton 1796)

By Griffin'89 out of Pyecrust'88: Gabriel, black py'd dog (given to Mr Thomas 1797), Gilford, black py'd dog (given to Mr Brookman 1796)

By Lord Egremont's Labourer out of Parrot'91: Leaser, brown py'd dog (given to Mr Brookman 1796), Pansy, black py'd bitch (given to Sir H Harper 1797), Labourer, brown py'd dog (died 1797)

---

* Incorrectly entered as '54' in hound book.
** The actual list and the recapitulation are missing and the hounds here are those which were in the list of old hounds the following season.

By Mariner'91 out of Vengeance'93: Molder, brown tan'd dog (cast 1797), Venham, brown py'd bitch (cast 1799)
By Masker'87 out of Totnes'90: Mendall, grey py'd dog (died 1797)
By Masker'87 out of Viol'89: Marlborough, brown py'd dog (given to Sir H Harper 1797)
By Miner'92 out of Present'90: Madcap, brown py'd dog (cast 1797), Paltry, yellow py'd bitch (cast 1798)
By Lord Egremont's Salesman out of Palsy'91: Stroler, black py'd dog (given to Sir H Harper 1797)

List of young fox hounds on the 1st of November 1795
By Bumpkin'93 out of Paltry'94: Bacchus, brown py'd dog (cast 1797), Painted, brown py'd bitch (cast 1798), Pleasant, brown py'd bitch (cast 1797)
By Lord Egremont's Bachelor out of Papist'89: Bachelor, grey py'd dog (cast 1799), Proxy, white bitch (cast 1797), Puppet, white bitch (cast 1799)
By Gamester'91 out of Pleasure'91: Gallant, brown py'd dog (given to Col Sloper 1796), py'd bitch (cast 1799)
By Griper'90 out of Vixen'93: Gangler, black py'd dog (died 1797)
From Sir W Lowther by his Masker out of his Hardmaid: Harlot, brown py'd bitch (cast 1799)
By Limner'90 out of Provance'93: Ledger, brown py'd dog (given to Col Sloper 1797), py'd bitch (cast 1799), py'd bitch (died 1797)
By Miner'92 out of Present'90: Mealman, brown py'd dog (cast 1799)
By Mariner'91 out of Pyecrust'88: Mitre, grey py'd dog (cast 1799)
By Limner'90 out of Precious'92: Painful, brown py'd bitch (cast 1799)
By Lord Egremont's Salesman out of Palsy'91: Piceley, grey py'd bitch (cast 1797), Sailor, black py'd dog (died 1796), Salesman, black py'd dog (died 1796), Specter, black py'd dog (cast 1798)
By Garrison'91 out of Pityless'90: Pallate, grey py'd bitch (cast 1797), py'd bitch (cast 1799)
By Lord Egremont's Salesman out of Parrot'91: Parley, grey py'd bitch (cast 1797)
By Bumpkin'93 out of Virgin'90: Vanity, brown py'd bitch (cast 1799), py'd bitch (cast 1799)

Recapitulation for the year 1795
Old hounds - 18½ couple dogs, 14½ couple bitches
Young hounds - 5 couple dogs, 7½ couple bitches   45½* couple
Hounds disposed of this year - given away 4 couple, died 3 couple   7 couple
Total of hounds remaining this year   33½ couple

List of young fox hounds on the 1st of November 1796
By Lord Egremont's Bachelor out of Papist'89: Bluster, yellow py'd dog (cast 1797), Paragon, white bitch with a yellow head (cast 1799), Polly, grey py'd bitch (cast 1799)
By Bumpkin'93 out of Packet'93: Baker, brown py'd dog (cast 1799), Bussler, brown py'd dog (cast 1799), Partial, dark brown bitch (cast 1799)
By Garrat'90 out of Virgin'90: Ginger, brown py'd dog (cast 1797)
By Gamester'91 out of Pyecrust'88: Guider, grizzle py'd dog (cast 1798), Pepper, grey py'd bitch (cast 1799)
By Lord Egremont's Jumper out of Vixen'93: Joiner, brown py'd dog (cast 1797), Jugler, brown py'd dog (cast 1799), Jumper, black py'd dog (cast 1797)
By Limner'90 out of Pleasure'92: Lustre, brown py'd dog (cast 1799), Pity, yellow py'd bitch (cast 1799)
By Mariner'91 out of Parrot'91: Mitre, black py'd dog (given to Col Sloper 1797), Mortar, brown py'd dog (cast 1797), Posey, brown py'd bitch (cast 1797), Purling, brown py'd bitch (cast 1799)
By Garrat'90 out of Palsy'91: Portion, black py'd bitch (cast 1799), Purple, brown py'd bitch (given to Col Sloper 1797)
By Ledger'95 out of Puppet'95: Piney, grey py'd bitch (cast 1797), Princess, brown py'd bitch (given to Mr Leach 1797)
By Griper'90 out of Peggy'95: Patty, grey py'd bitch (cast 1797)
By Mariner'91 out of Trial'93: Manful, black py'd dog (cast 1799), Tidings, brown py'd bitch (cast 1799), Trollop, grey py'd bitch (cast 1799)
By Lord Egremont's Vallet out of Totnes'90: Trinket, grey py'd bitch (cast 1798), Vexer, black py'd bitch (cast 1799)
By Lord Egremont's Salesman out of Precious'92: Pytchley, grey py'd bitch (cast 1799)

Recapitulation for the year 1796
Old hounds - 19 couple dogs, 19 couple bitches
Young hounds - 6 couple dogs, 8 couple bitches   52 couple
Hounds disposed of this year - given away 9½ couple, died 4 couple   13½ couple
Total of hounds remaining this year   39½ couple

---
* Incorrectly entered in the hound book as '45'.

Old hound new to the pack in 1797
By Lord Egremont's Giant out of Vengeance'93: Vanish, brown py'd bitch (cast 1798)

Young fox hounds in 1797
By Lord Egremont's Blaster out of Trial'93: Bluecap, grey py'd dog (cast 1799), Blueman, black py'd dog (cast 1799), Boaster, grey py'd dog (cast 1799), Tawny, black py'd bitch (cast 1799), Testy, grey py'd bitch (cast 1799), Tulip, grey py'd bitch (cast 1799)
By Bachelor'95 out of Papist'89: boxer, grey py'd dog (cast 1798), Pippin, grey py'd bitch (cast 1799), Precious, brown py'd bitch (cast 1799)
By Bumpkin'93 out of Pityless'90: Banker, black py'd dog (cast 1799)
By Gauger'93 out of Venus'95: Gallant, brown py'd dog (cast 1799)
By Lord Cranston's Knowledge out of Provance'93: Knaveish, black py'd dog (cast 1799), Knowledge, black py'd dog (cast 1799), Phillis, black py'd bitch (cast 1799), Posey, brown py'd bitch (cast 1799)
By Lord Cranston's Grecian out of Painted'95: Planet, grey py'd bitch (cast 1799), Pliant, brown py'd bitch (cast 1798)
By Bumpkin'93 out of Pyecrust'88: Pasty, black py'd bitch (cast 1799), Pudding, black py'd bitch (cast 1799)
By Bluster'96 out of Pleasant'95: Prattle, grey py'd bitch (cast 1799), Punctual, brown py'd bitch (cast 1799)
By Limner'90 out of Palsy'91: Parlour, grey py'd bitch (cast 1798)
By Barfluer'93 out of Pepper'96: Pillage, black py'd bitch (cast 1799)

Recapitulation for the year 1797
Old hounds - 11½ couple dogs, 15½ couple bitches
Young hounds - 4 couple dogs, 7½ couple bitches   38½ couple
Hounds disposed of this year - given away 2½ couple, died 1½ couple   4 couple
Total of hounds remaining this year   34½ couple

Young fox hounds in the year 1798
By Gallant'97 out of Pasty'97: Gangler, brown py'd dog (cast 1799)
By Grazier'92 out of Harlot'95: Gasper, brown py'd dog (cast 1799), Gifter, brown py'd dog (cast 1799), Handsome, black py'd bitch (cast 1799), Happy, black py'd bitch (cast 1799), Harmless, black py'd bitch (cast 1799)
By Lord Egremont's Labourer out of Trollop'96: Labourer, black py'd dog (cast 1799)
By Mitre'95 out of Puppet'95: Marker, dog (cast 1799), Mendall, grey py'd dog (cast 1799), Palace, bitch (cast 1799), Phoebe, grey py'd bitch (cast 1799)
By Merryman'92 out of Polly'96: Merchant, dog (cast 1799)
By Mariner'91 out of Primrose'95: Miser, grey py'd dog (cast 1799), Pheasant, brown py'd bitch (cast 1799), Purple, brown py'd bitch (cast 1799)
By Merryman'92 out of Trifle'92: Madcap, brown py'd dog (cast 1799), Muffler, py'd dog (cast 1799), Mumper, brown py'd dog (cast 1799)
By Mariner'91 out of Trial'93: Muster, black py'd dog (cast 1799)
By Merryman'92 out of Tipsy'91: Tipsy, greypy'd bitch (cast 1799), Trophy, grey py'd bitch (cast 1799), Tuneful, brown py'd bitch (cast 1799)
By Bachelor'95 out of Pepper'96: Pallate, py'd bitch (cast 1799), Pigeon, grey py'd bitch (cast 1799)
By Lord Egremont's Giant out of Venham'94: Vainlass, brown py'd bitch (cast 1799), Varnish, brown py'd bitch (cast 1799)
By Gamester'91 out of Pyecrust'88: Peeress, brown py'd bitch (cast 1799), Princess, yellow py'd bitch (cast 1799)

Notes and References

1. Bennett, p.74.
2. Goodwood MS 2003, pp.79-82.
3. Goodwood MS 151.
4. Watson, p.3.
5. For a full account of the circumstantial evidence on allegations that Charles II married Lucy Barlow, see Watson, pp.275-7.
6. Wood.
7. Bishop of Chichester, p.169.
8. Bishop of Chichester, pp.169-72.
9. Kenyon MS, p.143.
10. State Trials, p.127.
11. Meade-Fetherstonhaugh, p.47.
12. The paper is watermarked GOLDING AND SNELGROVE 1809.
13. Adsdean MS.
14. His christian name is not mentioned in any of the manuscript papers. There are two portraits, on one of which he is referred to as Edward, and on the other, painted when he was older, he is called Charles.
15. Archaic form of mint, meaning a vast amount of something costly.
16. Alexander Pope to Joseph Addison 19 November 1712, qu. Longrigg, p.59.
17. Add. MS 32680, f.296, qu. Cockayne and Gibbs sub Newcastle.
18. Ormonde MSS, p.107.
19. Rutland MSS, pp.58-9.
20. Times Lit. Supp.
21. Cockayne and Gibbs.
22. Ormonde MSS PP.23 & 229.
23. Macauley, vol.ii, p.271.
24. The place is now known as Dog Kennel Cottages, and lies on the road between Duncton hill and Upwaltham.
25. Andrew was Mr. Roper's whipper-in.
26. March 1910, p.103.
27. Deene Park.
28. March 1911, pp.12-13.
29. Cockayne and Gibbs.
30. Adsdean MS.
31. Goodwood MS 2003, pp.112-17.
32. Thomas Bright to Sir Henry Slingsby, 18 November 1738, qu. Longrigg, p.63.
33. Cockayne and Gibbs.
34. Portland MSS, p.476.
35. Rye.
36. Egmont, 26 April 1737.
37. Cockayne and Gibbs.
38. Goodwood MS 2003, p.106.
39. March 1911, p.46.
40. Goodwood MS 151, lines 261-5.
41. Lord Lumley was heir to the Earl of Scarbrough of Stansted and the Earl of Hertford heir to the Duke of Somerset of Petworth.
42. Berkeley, 27 February.
43. Berkeley, 31 March.
44. Montagu, 24 November 1714.
45. Montagu, 8 December 1754.
46. Cockayne and Gibbs.
47. Walpole, vol.i, pp.210-11.
48. Goodwood MS 2003.
49. Bathurst, 1938.
50. Goodwood MS 20903, p.10.
51. Scott and Seabright, ch.5. qu. Longrigg, p.63.
52. Goodwood MS 2003, pp.11-12.
53. Orlebar, p.196.
54. Bathurst, 1938, pp.5-15.
55. Longrigg, p.68.
56. Goodwood MS 2003, p.13.
57. March 1911, p.80.
58. March 1911, p.82.
59. March 1911, p.98.
60. March 1911, pp.133-4.
61. March 1911, p.152.
62. March 1910, p.109.
63. Goodwood MS 2003.
64. Cockayne and Gibbs.
65. Swift, 8 July 1728.
66. Longstaffe.
67. March 1911, p.155.
68. March 1911, p.181.
69. March 1911, p.183.
70. March 1911, p.187.
71. March 1911, pp.188-9.
72. The chantry chapel in Boxgrove priory church was built in 1532 by Thomas West, 9th Lord Delawarr, a direct descendant through the female line of Robert de la Haye, first Lord of Halnaker, who

donated the land to the monks of Lessay in Normandy in 1108 to establish the priory.
73. Goodwood MS 2003, p.21.
74. March 1911, pp.190-1.
75. This document was sold at auction at Hodson's on Wednesday 22 December 1922 to A.W.F. Fuller for 10s. Fortunately he later presented it to the West Sussex Record Office, where it still resides.
76. By present reckoning, this date would have fallen in the year 1730.
77. WSRO Add. Ms 10913/1.
78. Goodwood MS 2003, p.21.
79. Adsdean MS.
80. March 1911, pp.191-2.
81. March 1911, pp.192-3.
82. Goodwood MS 20034, p.21.
83. Goodwood MS 149 A12.
84. March 1911, p.204.
85. March 1911, pp.204-5.
86. Adsdean MS.
87. Goodwood MS 149 A11.
88. Goodwood MS 2003, pp.22-4.
89. Adsdean MS.
90. March 1910, pp.110-11.
91. March 1910, pp.111-12.
92. March 1911, pp.215-16.
93. Goodwood MS 149 A13.
94. Adsdean MS.
95. March 1910, pp.113-14.
96. March 1910, pp.132-3.
97. March 1910, pp.133-4.
98. March 1910, pp.115-17.
99. Goodwood MS 2003, p.111.
100. March 1910, pp.117-18.
101. Adsdean MS.
102. March 1910, pp.119-20.
103. Goodwood MS 2003, p.121.
104. Goodwood MS 2003, p.25.
105. March 1910, p.121.
106. March 1910, pp.122-3.
107. March 1910, p.124.
108. March 1910, pp.125-6.
109. March 1910, pp.127-8.
110. A large wood to the west of Rowland's Castle.
111. March 1910, p.130.
112. March 1910, p.129.
113. Goodwood MS 2003, p.121.
114. Goodwood MS 2003, p.26.
115. Goodwood MS 2003, pp.26, 124.
116. Goodwood MS 2003, p.115.
117. March 1910, pp.131-2.
118. Goodwood MS 2003, p.121.
119. Goodwood MS 2003, pp.27-8.
120. Cockayne, 1906.
121. Goodwood MS 2003, pp.29-30.
122. March 1911, pp.305-6.
123. Goodwood MS 2003, pp.29-30.
124. March 1910, pp.134-5.
125. Goodwood MS 1149 A29.
126. McCann, p.281.
127. Hervey.
128. Goodwood MS 152.
129. Goodwood MS 2003, pp.41-3.
130. March 1910, pp.135-6.
131. The Charlton hounds often ran through Lady Derby's coverts at Halnaker. She inherited the property from her father Sir William Morley KB. The Earl of Derby had recently died in February 1736, but Lady Derby lived to the age of 84 and was buried at Boxgrove in 1752.
132. March 1910, pp.136-7.
133. Goodwood MS 2003, p.99.
134. Goodwood MS 2003, p.99.
135. Adsdean MS.
136. Goodwood MS 2003, p.47.
137. Goodwood MS 2003, p.100.
138. Cockayne and Gibbs.
139. Jesse, iii, pp.318-49.
140. Gent. Mag., May 1734.
141. Walpole Journals, September 1773.
142. Attrib. Leigh Hunt.
143. Lord's Journal, xxxiv, p.667.
144. Goodwood MS 2003, p.100.
145. Goodwood MS 2003, p.100.
146. McCann, pp.24-5.
147. McCann, p.26.
148. Goodwood MS 2003, p.101.
149. McCann, p.26.
150. McCann, p.27.
151. Goodwood MS 2003, pp.48-9.
152. Goodwood MS 2003, p.101.
153. Cockayne and Gibbs.
154. Goodwood MS 2003, p.101.
155. March 1910, pp.140-1.
156. Goodwood MS 149 A15.
157. Goodwood MS 2003, p.83.
158. Laishley MS.
159. Goodwood MS 149 A16 and A17; Goodwood MS 153; Adsdean MS.
160. Laishley MS, Goodwood MS 149 A17, Adsdean MS.
161. Now the King's buildings to the south east of Bignor hill.
162. Goodwood MS 2003, p.102.
163. Goodwood MS 2003, p.102.
164. Goodwood MS 149 A28.
165. March 1910, p.139.
166. Bathurst, 1938, p.4.
167. Waldegrave, p.114.
168. Hervey.
169. March 1910, pp.137-8.
170. Goodwood MS 2003, p.50-4.
171. Goodwood MS 2003, p.103.
172. Goodwood MS 2003, p.103.

Notes and References

173. Goodwood MS 2003, p.84.
174. March 1910, p.140.
175. Goodwood MS 2003, p.104.
176. Goodwood MS 2003, p.104.
177. March 1910, pp.141-2.
178. Goodwood MS 149 A28.
179. Goodwood MS 2003, pp.55-60.
180. March 1910, p.78.
181. Goodwood MS 2003, p.83.
182. March 1911, pp.352-3.
183. McCann, p.50.
184. Solomon Dayrolles was elected a member in February 1741.
185. McCann, pp.50-1.
186. Sir William Gage, an original subscriber to the great Room at Charlton, was a close friend of Richmond's in another sporting sphere, cricket. See *The Duke who was Cricket* by John Marshall (Frederick Muller Ltd., London, 1961).
187. McCann, p.51.
188. McCann, pp.52-3.
189. McCann, pp.52-3.
190. McCann, p.54.
191. McCann, p.55.
192. Goodwood MS 2003, p.104.
193. Goodwood MS 2003, p.104.
194. Cockayne and Gibbs.
195. March 1911, pp.450-1.
196. Goodwood MS 149 A28.
197. Goodwood MS 2003, pp.61-4.
198. Bathurst, 1928, pp.83-4.
199. Goodwood MS 2003, p.129.
200. Goodwood MS 2003, p.105.
201. March 1911, pp.381-3.
202. McCann, p.81.
203. Goodwood MS 2003, p.85.
204. Goodwood MS 149 A28.
205. McCann, p.82.
206. March 1911, p.386.
207. Goodwood MS 2003, pp.65-8.
208. McCann, p.90.
209. McCann, p.92.
210. McCann, pp.92-3.
211. March 1910, pp.143-5.
212. Horace Walpole to Sir Horace Mann, March 1742.
213. March 1910, pp.142-3.
214. Goodwood MS 2003, p.105.
215. Goodwood MS 2003, p.106.
216. Goodwood MS 2003, p.106.
217. Goodwood MS 2003, p.86.
218. Goodwood MS 149 A28.
219. Goodwood MS 2003, pp.71-4.
220. McCann, p.130.
221. March 1910, pp.145-7.
222. Goodwood MS 2003, p.106.
223. Goodwood MS 2003, p.87.
224. March 1911, pp.431-3.
225. McCann, pp.148-9.
226. McCann, p.151.
227. McCann, p.151.
228. McCann, p.152.
229. He was elected a member at Charlton later that season.
230. The Earl of Orford, formerly Sir Robert Walpole, prime minister from 1721 to 1742, lived at Houghton in Norfolk and had his own pack of hounds.
231. Thomas Coke, Lord Lovel, lived at Holkham at Norfolk. He had been a subscriber to the Great Room at Charlton in 1720 and was later created Earl of Leicester.
232. March 1911, pp.451-2.
233. Goodwood MS 2003, p.107.
234. McCann, p.161.
235. Goodwood MS 2003, pp.75-8.
236. Goodwood MS 2003, p.78.
237. McCann, pp.162-3.
238. Goodwood MS 2003, p.107.
239. Montagu, 3 February 1748.
240. March 1911, p.536.
241. Goodwood MS 2003, p.88.
242. McCann, p.163.
243. Goodwood MS 2003, p.108.
244. McCann, p.164.
245. Goodwood MS 2003, p.108.
246. March 1911, p.450.
247. March 1910, pp.149-51.
248. Goodwood MS 2003, pp.79-82.
249. Goodwood MS 2003, p.89.
250. McCann, p.204.
251. McCann, p.204.
252. Goodwood MS 2003, p.109.
253. McCann, p.209.
254. McCann, pp.209-10.
255. McCann, p.211.
256. McCann, pp.212-13.
257. Goodwood MS 2003, p.109.
258. Walpole, *Letters*, vol.iii, pp.12-13, 1 September 1750.
259. Pitt, vol.iii, p.277.
260. *Dict. Nat. Biog.*
261. Manners, p.392.
262. Selwyn, 1782.
263. McCann, p.237.
264. Goodwood MS 2003, pp.83-6.
265. Goodwood MS 2003, p.110.
266. The Earl of Lincoln had just been appointed Cofferer of the Household.
267. McCann, p.238.
268. McCann, p.239.
269. Goodwood MS 2003, p.110.
270. Strictly speaking, Lord Lincoln at this time was not the heir to Newcastle's dukedom, but a few years later Newcastle arranged for a second dukedom, that of Newcastle-under-Lyme, to be conferred on

himself, which had a special remainder to Henry Earl of Lincoln and heirs male of his body by Catherine, his wife, niece of the grantee.
271. Goodwood MS 2003, p.90.
272. March 1910, pp.151-2.
273. McCann, pp.240-1.
274. Goodwood MS 2003, p.111.
275. McCann, p.241.
276. Goodwood MS 2003, p.117.
277. This verse was bowdlerised by the Earl of March in 1910 to read:
Some hunt after riches
    While others seek the chase,
But they who love a keener sport
    Will hunt a pretty face.
278. Goodwood MS 2003, p.111.
279. March, 1910, p.152-4.
280. Goodwood MS 149 A30.
281. March, 1911, p.621.
282. McCann, p.256.
283. McCann, p.258.
284. Goodwood MS 2003, p.112.
285. Boswell, vol.i, p.296.
286. Goodwood MS 2003, p.87-90.
287. Goodwood MS 2003, p.112.
288. Holland, p.45, 15 May 1750.
289. Chambers.
290. McCann, p.265.
291. Goodwood MS 2003, p.91.
292. *Dict. Nat. Biog.*
293. McCann, p.266.
294. McCann, p.267.
295. Goodwood MS 149 A31.
296. McCann, p.268.
297. McCann, p.268.
298. McCann, p.269.
299. McCann, pp.269-70.
300. McCann, p.271.
301. Talbot Yelverton, Earl of Sussex was married to Henry Pelham's sister. Their son George Augustus had succeeded to the title in 1731 and was later elected a Charlton member.
302. March 1910, pp.154-6.
303. Goodwood MS 2003, p.129.
304. Goodwood MS 2003, p.112.
305. Burke.
306. Goodwood MS 2003, pp.91-4.
307. Goodwood MS 2003, p.92.
308. Goodwood MS 2003, p.129.
309. March 1910, pp.158-9.
310. 'Is papa obliged to go out hunting or is it because he wants to?'—March 1911, p.698.
311. March 1910, pp.159-60.
312. March 1910, pp.160-1.
313. Goodwood MS 2003, pp.95-8.
314. Goodwood MS 2003, p.113.
315. Goodwood MS 2003, p.93.
316. Goodwood MS 2003, p.113.
317. Hunn, pp.58-9.
318. The family tree is complicated, but he was the eldest of eight sons, the youngest of whom, George, succeeded Harry Powlett, Dule of Bolton, his third cousin once removed, as Marquess of Winchester in 1794, the dukedom of Bolton at that time having become extinct.
319. Mr. Gibbon was the father of Edward Gibbon, historian and author of *The History of the Decline and Fall of the Roman Empire*.
320. Bathurst, 1938, p.23.
321. Gibbon, p.115.
322. Dallaway, qu. Hunn, p.664.
323. Shoberl, 1820, qu. Hunn, p.64.
324. The last extant hound list is in 1798, 42 seasons later, by which time 2,661 hounds had passed through the kennels at Charlton and latterly at Goodwood, since the first entry in 1721.
325. Goodwood MS 2015.
326. *Dict. Nat. Biog.* sub Frederick Augustus, Duke of York.
327. Charlemont, vol.ii, p.446.
328. *Dict. Nat. Biog.*
329. Malmesbury, vol.ii, p.446.
330. Richmond, pp.3-6.
331. *Sporting Magazine*, March 1827, vol.19 ns, no.cxiv, p.273-5.
332. Colonel George Wyndham whose kennels were at Drovers near Singleton.
333. The 5th Duke of Richmond, who succeeded 1819.
334. This is Henrietta Le Clerc who was formerly mistress to the 3rd Duke of Richmond and married Colonel Dorrien of Adsdean.
335. The 5th Duke was wounded at the battle of Orthez in 1814 when a musket ball lodged in his chest and later suffered a fall out hunting which ended his riding career.
336. It may be noted in passing that the handwriting in the hound book from this date was much less tidy than Mr. Budd and the number of mistakes, that is entries inconsistent from one season to the next, greatly increased.
337. The 11th baronet and great grandson of Sir John Cope who was an original member at Charlton in 1737; his seat was at Bramshill Park in Hampshire.
338. The Grand Chase of 1739.
339. *Sporting Magazine*, 1829 and 1830.
340. He won the Derby and the Oaks three times each.

Bibliography

Adsdean MS MF1230, West Sussex Record Office
Anon., 'The Charlton Hunt', *Chichester Observer and Recorder*, March 1888
Bathurst, Earl, *The Charlton and Raby Hunts*, 1938
Bathurst, Earl, *Supplement to Foxhound Kennel Stud Book*, 1928
Bennett, T.J., 'Charlton and the Charlton Hunt', *Sussex Arch.Coll.*, xv; 74-82, 1863
Berkeley, Lord, of Stratton, *Letters*, 1713
Boswell, James, *Life of Johnson*, Ed. Hill
Burgoyne, Mrs., *Letters*
Burke, *Complete Peerage, Baronetage and Knightage*, 1970
Burke, Edmund, *Annual Register*, 1758
Chambers, *Biographical Dictionary*
Charlemont MSS. Hist. MSS. Comm.
Chichester, Bishop of, 'Reception of Duke of Monmouth', *Sussex Arch.Coll.*, vi, 168-72, 1854
Cockayne, G.E. (ed.), *Complete Baronetage*, 1906
Cockayne, G.E. and Gibbs, V. (ed.), *Complete Peerage*, 1910-1959
Davis, R.B., 'Tom Grant', *Sporting Magazine*, XIX ns, 273-7, 1827
Deene Park, Northamptonshire, guide book
Defoe, D., *A Tour of through the whole Island of Great Britain*, 1738
Dictionary of National Biography
Drifter, 'The Old Charlton Hunt', *Horse and Hound*, 19 June, 346, 1942
Egmont, 1st Earl of, *Diaries*, Hist. MSS. Comm.
Eyre, John, 'Chronology of the History of Two Buildings at Charlton', *West Sussex History*, 51, 25-30, 1993
Gentlemen's Magazine, 1734
Gibbon, Edward, *Memoirs of my Life*, Folio, 1991
Goodwood MS 149 West Sussex Record Office. Documents relating to Charlton Hunt
Goodwood MS 151 West Sussex Record Office. Historical Account
Goodwood MS 152 West Sussex Record Office. Hunting Diaries. The diaries were written in note books and generally a new one was started each season. However there are some missing pages, some sheets are loose and a few unnumbered.
    Book i, pp.1-4, 2 Nov 1737 - 4 March 1738
    Book ii, pp.1-36, 2 Nov 1738 - 26 Feb 1739 (plus summary of season)
    Book iii, pp.1-23, 1 Nov 1739 - 17 Mar 1740 (p.17 missing)
    Book iv, pp.5-6, 12 Nov 1740 - 15 Nov 1740 (pp.1-4 & 7- missing)
    Book v, pp.1-7, 31 Jan 1741 - 24 Feb 1741
    Book vi, pp.1-10, 2 Nov 1741 - 12 Dec 1741
    Book vii, pp.1-5, 2 Jan 1742 - 16 Jan 1742 (pages not numbered)
    Book viii, pp.1-27, 1 Nov 1742 - 3 Mar 1743
    Book ix, pp.1-11, 5 Dec 1743 - 9 Feb 1744 (plus one unnumbered page)
    Book x, pp.5-17, 10 Nov 1744- 6 Mar 1745 (pp.1-4 missing; two extra unnumbered pages 10 Dec 1744)
    Book xi, pp.1-7, 27 Jan 1746- 8 Mar 1746
    Book xii, p.1, 3 Nov 1747 - 2 Feb 1748 (summary of finds and kills)
Goodwood MS 153 West Sussex Record Office. Grand Chase
Goodwood MS 1994 West Sussex Record Office. Pedigree of Charlton Hounds 1792-1798
Goodwood MS 2003 West Sussex Record Office. Pedigree of Charlton Hounds 1721-1750, including minutes, receipts and hunting songs

Goodwood MS 2015 West Sussex Record Office. Pedigree of Charlton Hounds 1757-1791
Hervey, Lord, *Memoirs*, 1735
Haslam, Charlotte, *Notes on Fox Hall*, The Landmark Trust, 1994
Holland, Lord, *Letters to Henry Fox*
Hunn, D., *Goodwood*, 1975
Jesse, *Court of England*, 1688-1760
Kenyon MS., Hist. MSS. Comm., appendix 4, 14th report
Kent, John, *Records and Reminiscences of Goodwood and the Dukes of Richmond*, 1896
Laishley MS. A full and impartial account, 1739.
Longrigg, R., *History of Foxhunting*, 1975
Longstaffe, *History of Darlington*
Lords' Journal, 1776
Macaulay, Lord, *History of England*
Malmesbury, 1st Earl of, *Letters*
Manners, *Marquess of Granby*
March, Earl of, *Records of the Old Charlton Hunt*, 1910
March, Earl of, *A Duke and his Friends*, 1911
Marshall, J., *The Duke who was Cricket*, 1961
McCann, T.J. (ed.), *Correspondence of Dukes of Richmond and Newcastle 1724-1750*, Sussex Record Society, 1984
Meade-Fetherstonhaugh, Lady, *Uppark*, National Trust, 1985
Montagu, Lady Mary, *Letters*
Orlebar, F.St J., *The Orlebar Chronicles 1553-1733*, 1930
Ormonde MSS, Hist. MSS. Comm., NS vol.vi
Pitt, William, *Correspondence*
Portland MSS, Hist. MSS. Comm., vol.v
Reese, M.M., *Goodwood's Oak*, 1987
Richmond, 5th Duke of, *Memoirs*, 1862
Rutland MSS, Hist. MSS. Comm., vol.ii
Rye, Walter, *Songs, stories and sayings of Norfolk*
Scott and Seabright, *The Druid*
Selwyn, George, *Memoirs*
Sporting Magazine
State Trials, vol.ix
Swift, Dean, *Letters*
Times Literary Supplement, 1681
Waldegrave, James, 2nd Earl, *Historical Memoirs*, 1754-8
Walpole, Horace, *Journals*
Walpole, Horace, *Letters*
Walpole, Horace, *Memoirs of the reign of George II*
Watson, J.N.P., *Captain General and Rebel Chief*, 1979
West Sussex Record Office, Add. MS 10913/1 Treaty of Peace Union and Friendship
Wood, *Athenae Oxoniensis*

Index

Notes: **Bold** page numbers refer to illustrations (the colour plates as **128/9**). Only Appendix 1 (Fox Hall) is indexed. The references to local place names which appear frequently in the hunt diaries are indexed only as 'hunting days'.

Abraham walls, hunting days, 142, 145, 155
Adsdean, hunting days, 101, 103, 108, 131, 152, 157, 159
Adsdean earth, hunting at, 157
Adsdean wood, hunting days, 108, 144
Albemarle, George Keppel, 3rd Earl of (as Lord Bury), **151**, 171, 172, 179–80, 183; Hunt Club dinners, 176, 184
Albemarle, William Keppel, 2nd Earl of, 22, 47, 115, 169–70, **179**; at Culloden, 179; Hunt Club dinners, 130, 147, 172, 176
Alcock, Rev., 203
Aldingbourne: hunting days, 124, 169; last hunt (1895), 221
Aldsworth common, hunting at, 157
Almanza, battle of, 14
Ambersham, Grand Chase (1739), 114, 118
Andrew, whipper-in, 37, 80
Andrews, Mr., hound breeder, 77, 86
Anne, Queen, 16, 23
Anstis, John, Garter King of Arms, 33
Applesham, hunting at, 147
Arber, Mr., Petworth huntsman, 217
Arundel, Earls of (Fitzalan family), 6
Arundel, hunting at, 104
Arundel park, hunting days, 109, 124, 154
Arundel river, Grand Chase (1739), 120
Ascot Races, 16
Ashburnham, John, 2nd Earl of, 182, **182**, 184, 185
Ashlee, hunting at, 145
Ashling, hunting days, 101, 125
Ashling woods, hunting days, 131, 143, 144, 152, 154, 157, 159, 160
Aukers furze, Grand Chase (1739), 114
Austrian Succession, War of, 156

Baltimore, Charles Calvert, 5th Lord, 48, 73, **75**, 130, 184
Barlavington, hunting at, 134
Barlavington common, hunting at, 144
Barlavington coppice, hunting at, 169
Barlavington hanger, hunting days, 109, 142, 144, 145, 158, 166, 169
Barlavington hill, hunting days, 124, 135, 145
Barlow, John, of Barlow Hall, 7
Barratt, Harry, whipper-in, 36
Battine, William (junior), 152–3, **152**, 158, 175; Hunt Club meetings, 181, 194
Battine, William (senior), 87, 89, 153, 158, 175; Hunt Club meetings, 181, 194
Bay comb, hunting days, 140, 144, 154
Beacon hill, hunting at, 158
beagles, 35, 69
Beake, Colonel Gregory, 89, 115, 147, 159
Bear Forest (Rowland's Castle), 79; hunting days, 107, 131
Beauclerk, Lord George, 30, 60, 115; Hunt Club dinners, 130, 147, 172, 176
Beauclerk, Lord Henry, 30, 60, 103, 108, 125; at Grand Chase (1739), 116, 119; Hunt Club meetings, 2, 99
Beauclerk, Lord William, probable subscriber to Great Room, 20, **29**, 30
Beckford, [?], *Thoughts on Hunting*, 90
Bedford, Duke of, 50
Bedford Head Tavern: Hunt Club dinners (1739-40), 115–16, 130, 137; Hunt Club dinners (1744-9), 159, 172, 176, 190, 195; Hunt Club general meeting (1738), 1–2, 98
Bellegarde, Marquis de, 187
Belvoir, Vale of, 181
Benges, the, hunting days, 106, 144, 158, 177
Bennet, Hon. George, 181, 184
Bennett, T.J., 223
Bentinck, Hon. Charles, 130, 132
Bepton, Grand Chase (1739), 118
Berkeley, Augustus, 4th Earl of, **62**, 115, 158, 185; Hunt Club dinners, 130, 147, 155, 176
Berkeley, George, Earl of, 11
Berkeley, Henrietta, 11–12
Berkeley, James, 3rd Earl of, probable subscriber to Great Room, 20, **22**
Berkeley, Mary, 11
Bickley bushes, Grand Chase (1739), 114, 119
Biddulph, Charles, 145, 165; at Grand Chase (1739), 117
Biddulph, Richard, 145, 165; at Grand Chase (1739), 117
Bignor hanger, hunting at, 131
Bignor hill, hunting days, 144, 145
Bignor park: earthstopping, 187; hunting days, 142, 145, 155, 158
Bilsom, hunting at, 169
Bilsom, Mr., stabling, 191

Binderton, hunting days, 107, 166
Binderton down, 106; Grand Chase (1739), 114, 116, 119
Binderton farm, Grand Chase (1739), 114, 115
Binderton orchard, 143
Binsted, hunting at, 169
Bisshop, Sir Cecil, 72, 73, 97, 103, 108, 140; deer at Parham, 177
Black bushes, hunting days, 144, 152, 154, 157, 159, 160
Black patch, hunting at, 146
Blendworth, hunting at, 131
Bolderwood (New Forest), 50, 52, 70, 135; hounds from, 85; Richmond at (1747), 187
Bolton, 2nd Duke of, probable subscriber to Great Room, 20, 33, 35. 89
Bolton, Charles, 3rd Duke of, and 2nd Duke of Richmond, 40, 45, 79, 97, 135–6; hound breeding, 89, 129, 176; Hunt Club dinners, 115, 130, 159; joint master with Roper (1721/2), 30; and Lavinia Fenton, 42–4, **43**, **44**; marriage to Lady Anne Vaughan, 31, **32**, 35, 42, 44; resignation, 44, 46, 47; as sole proprietor, 37, 43; subscriber to Great Room, 2, 18
Bolton, Henrietta, Duchess of, 11, 25, 27, **27**, 33
Booker, Abram, huntsman, 216
Boscawen, Hon. John, 1–3, 179; Hunt Club dinners, 155, 159, 176, 184
Bosham, hunting days, 144, 160
Bourbon, Duke of, hounds from, 79
Bourne, hunting at, 108
Bourne common, hunting days, 108, 157
Bourne wood, hunting at, 159
Bow hill, 5; hunting days, 101, 107, 132, 143, 152, 154, 157, 159, 160, 178
Bowen, Mr., 50
Boxgrove: hunting at, 144; last hunt (1895), 221
Boxgrove common, hunting at, 169
Boxgrove street, hunting at, 124
Bradleys bushes, hunting days, 107, 157
Briggs, David, whipper-in, 99, 108–9, 128, 130, 133, 142; 1744/5 season, 166, 173; at Grand Chase (1739), 111, 117; horse, 156
Bright, Thomas, breeder of foxhounds, 35, 77, 79, **80**, 196

Broad Halfpenny, hunting at, 131
Broadham, hunting days, 134, 166, 168
Brooke, 7th Lord, of Warwick Castle, probable subscriber to Great Room, 20, 29–30, **30**
Broughton, Michael, 56
Browne, Sir Anthony, 109
Broyle copse, hunting days, 125, 137, 140, 144, 154, 159, 173
Broyle house, hunting at, 143
Brudenell, Francis, Lord, 21
Brudenell, George Bridges, 185, 187, 191
Brudenell, Hon. James, 39, 102, 108, 163
Bubholts, the, hunting days, 114, 124, 134, 155, 168, 169
Buccleuch, Anne, Countess of, 11
Buckleys, Grand Chase (1739), 111, 114
Bucknall, Thomas, map, 223, **224**
Budd, Harry, gamekeeper at Charlton, 12, 24
Budd, Joe, hunt servant, 93, 128, **128/9**; at Grand Chase, 111
Budd, John, 57, 77, 191; song, 186
Budd, Mr., Charlton huntsman, 203, 216
Bull, Captain, 178
Bunbury, Louisa, 203
Burford, Earl of, 30
Burke, Edmund, 205, 214
Burlington, Richard Boyle, Earl of, 19; design of Great Room, 18, **19**, 223, 225
Burnt Oak, hunting at, 145
Burton, hunting days, 59, 106
Burton hanger, hunting at, 81
Burton hill, hunting at, 145
Burton mill pond, hunting at, 129
Burton park, hunting days, 109, 124, 142, 144, 145, 153, 169
Burton pond tail, hunting days, 145, 155, 169, 178
Bury, Lord *see* Albemarle, 3rd Earl
Bury chalk pit, hunting at, 109
Bury course, hunting at, 155
Bury hill, hunting days, 81, 109, 145
Bushy field, hunting at, 141
Butler, James, of Amberley, 10, 13
Butler, John, 145, 153; Hunt Club dinners, 155, 159, 176
Butt hill earth, hunting at, 154
Byron, Lord, hounds from, 79, 86

Cadogan, Lady Sarah *see* Richmond, Sarah, Duchess of
Cardigan, George, 4th Earl *see* Montagu, Duke of
Cardigan, George Brudenell, 3rd Earl of, **20**, 21–2, 79, 181; probable subscriber to Great Room, 20; support for Duke of Richmond (nephew), 39–41
Carlisle, Charles Howard, 3rd Earl of, subscriber to Great Room, 19, 28, **28**
Carlton, Guy, Bishop of Chichester, 9
Carpenter, Benjamin, 170, 187, 194; Hunt Club dinners, 172, 176
Carpenter, Colonel Robert, 102, 105, 158, 191, 192; Hunt Club dinners, 159, 172
Castle hanger (Arundel), hunting at, 124
Castle Howard, 28
Castlehaven, Lord, 216
cattle, quarantine regulations, 188
Cavendish, Lord James, 60, 103, 106, 115, 130

Chambers, William, designed stables at Goodwood, 202
Champion, George, Southdown huntsman, 219
Chanctonbury hill, 1741/2 season, 147
Chantilly, France, 13
Charles II, King, 7
Charlton, 5–6, 51; Great Room at, 18, 24, **128/9**, 223–5, **224**; hunting boxes, 18, 51, 53–5, 59, 73, **128/9**, 191; kennels, 52, **58**
Charlton, Andrew, 4, 14, 59–60, 73, 76
Charlton copse, hunting days, 106, 108, 114, 124, 153, 156, 158
Charlton country, 48, 127; annexed by Leconfield, 218, 221
Charlton down, hunting at, 158
Charlton forest, 6, 99; Grand Chase (1739), 111, 114, 115, 116; hunting days, 101, 109, 124, 125, 132, 133–4, 152, 157, 166, 167, 168, 173, 176, 178
Charlton Hunt: 1738/9 season (best), 99–110, 124–6; 1739/40 season, 127, 128–9, 130–6; 1740/1 season, 137–42; 1741/2 season, 142–8; 1742/3 season, 149–56; 1743/4 season, 156–60; 1744/5 season, 165–70, 172–3, 175; 1745/6 season, 176–8; 1746/7 season, 186–7; 1747/8 season, 188–94; 1748/9 season, 195; annual dinners, 115–16, 130, 137, 147, 155, 159, 172, 176, 184–5, 190, 196–7; Club formed (1738), 1–2, **3**, 98; and death of Duke of Richmond, 199; decline, 202–3; establishment by Roper, 15–18; expenses, 57, 63, **64**, 126, 136, 142, 147, 155; flag commissioned, 55–6; the Grand Chase (26 Jan. 1739), 111–21, **128/9**; livery, 89, 219; restarted by 3rd Duke, 199–203; rules and bye-laws, 1–2, 98, 125, 127, 197; verse history of, 2, 4; weighing scales installed (1731), 56, *see also* Goodwood Hunt; horses; hounds; hunt servants
Chaworth, Mr., hounds from, 79
Cheale, John, Norroy King of Arms, 145–6, 153, 169–70, 175, 183; Hunt Club dinner (1745), 172
Chedworth, Lord, 174, 175; and restarting Charlton pack (1757), 199
Chesterfield, Philip Stanhope, Earl of, 141–2
Chichester, 9, 125
Chichester, Lord, 203
Chiddingfold, Leconfield and Cowdray Hunt, 222
Chilgrove, hunting days, 132, 143, 152, 178
Chilgrove hanger, hunting at, 154
Chitty, Mr., lodgings and stables, 191
Cholmondeley, George, Earl of, 60, 115
Chudleigh, Elizabeth, marriage to Duke of Kingston, 100–1, **100**
Churchill, Charles, 189–90, 194
Churchill, Colonel Charles, subscriber to Great Room, 19, 41–2, **42**
Churchill, Henrietta, married to Earl of Godolphin, 41
Clarendon, Thomas Villiers, Earl of, **61**, 62, 159
Clifford, Elizabeth, Lady, married 4th Duke of Devonshire, 170–1
Coates, hunting at, 109

Cobden farm, hunting at, 147
Cobden, Mr., Drought farm, 117, 165
Cockaine, Sir Thomas, breeder of foxhounds, 35
Cocking, hunting days, 81, 109
Cocking causeway, Grand Chase (1739), 114, 115, 118–19
Cocking chalk pit, hunting at, 134
Cocking coney copse, hunting at, 178
Cocking course, hunting days, 124, 135, 169
Cocking highway, hunting days, 121, 125, 158, 166
Cocking hilltop, hunting at, 133–4
Cocking warren, hunting days, 102, 143, 144, 166, 178
Coke, Thomas (later Earl of Leicester): breeder of foxhounds, 29, 35, 70, **165**; subscriber to Great Room, 19
College of Arms, 33, 146
Colvile, Robert, subscriber to Great Room, 19
Colville, Camilla, married 3rd Lord Tankerville, 45, 93
Colworth, Grand Chase (1739), 111, 118
Colworth down, hunting days, 134, 143, 166
Compton, General Hon. Charles, subscriber to Great Room, 14, 19
Compton, hunting at, 107
Compton down, hunting at, 131, 157
Coney copse: Grand Chase (1739), 111, 117, 118; hunting days, 125, 134, 135, 143, 166
Coney copse (West Dean), hunting at, 109
Coneygates, hunting at, 145
Coneygates earth, hunting at, 155
Confederate Hunt (Cottesmore), 106, 181, 182
Conolly, Rt. Hon. William, 47, **49**, 115, 185; Hunt Club dinners, 147, 159, 172, 176, 184; Hunt Club meetings, 2, 183
Conway, Francis Seymour-Conway, Lord, 129–30, **131**, 132; Hunt Club dinners, 147, 155, 172, 176
Cope, Sir John, 47, 172, 216
Corbet, Sir William, 47, 89, 115, 186–7, 191; Hunt Club dinners, 130, 147, 155, 159, 172, 176, 184, 190
Court hill, hunting at, 124
Cowdray, Lord, 222
Cowdray Park, 109, 219; hunt formed (1921), 222
Cowper, Earl, 47, 83, **84**, 115, 159; Hunt Club dinners, 147, 155, 159
Craven, Lord, hounds from, 86, 97, 129
Crawford, John Lindsay, 20th Earl, 174–5, **174**, 179
Crocker hill, hunting days, 124, 169
Crowley, Ambrose, 184, 187, 191
Crows Hall, hunting days, 101–2, 107, 125, 157, 166
Croxton Park, Confederate hounds at, 181
cubhunting, 68
Cuckolds lee, hunting days, 107, 125
Culloden, battle of, 179
Cumberland, Duke of, and Jacobite Rebellion, 176, 177
Curzon, Ashton, hounds from, 201

Index

Dalkeith, Francis, Earl of, 173–4, **173**, 178–9, 195; Hunt Club dinner (1747), 184; Hunt Club meetings, 183, 194; hunting days, 186, 197
Darcy, Sir Conyers, **60**, 62, 115
Davis, R.B., interview with Tom Grant (1827), 215–18
Davis, Sir John, 203
Dawtrey's hooks, hunting days, 106, 114, 121, 124, 142, 145, 158, 178
Dayrolles, Solomon, 139, 141–2, 191; Hunt Club dinners, 155, 159, 184; Hunt Club meetings, 152, 158, 181; hunting days, 165, 166; visit to Euston, 164
Deans, the, hunting days, 144, 145, 154, 169
Dearling, Mr., lodgings, stables and fodder, 191
Defoe, Daniel, 225
Delawarr, John West, 16th Lord, 40, **65**, 102–3, 180, 187; advice to Richmond, 129; annotation to hound lists, 93; chairman of Hunt Club general meeting (1738), 1; correspondence with Richmond, 192–3; as deputy master (from 1731), 63, 66, 69–73, 76–7; horse for Richmond, 78–9; Hunt Club dinners, 130, 147, 155, 195, 196; Hunt Club meetings, 98, 99; hunting box and stables, 40, 73, 191; imported foxes, 77; joint proprietor, 48–51; and war with Spain (1740), 135; weight, 56, 66
Dell bottom (comb), hunting days, 134, 141
Dell Quay, hunting at, 144
Derby, Lady: estate at Halnaker, 97–8, 105, 169; rook wood, 114, 115
Dettingen, battle of, 156, 174
Devonshire, William, 3rd Duke of, 14; Hunt Club dinners, 115, 147, 155, 172, 176, 184; hunting box, 73; subscriber to Great Room, 19, **74**
Devonshire, William, 4th Duke of (as Hartington), 170–1, **170**, 178, 181, 186; Hunt Club dinners, 172, 176, 184
Diana, **128/9**
Didling hanger, hunting at, 158
Diemar, Lord, 89
Ditcham park, hunting at, 134
Dorchester, Catherine Sedley, Countess of, 23
Dormer, Lord, 14
Dorrien, Mrs. (Henrietta Le Clerc), 203, 215
Down farm, hunting days, 143, 152, 154
Down farm (Frame) copse, hunting days, 154, 157
Downe, Henry, 3rd Viscount, 189, **189**, 191, 197
Downley farm, hunting at, 160
Downley (near Singleton), 76, 114
Downley ruins, Grand Chase (1739), 114, 115
Draper, Mr., of Beswick (Yorks), hound from, 35
Droke hanger, hunting at, 178
Droke house, hunting days, 125, 134
Drought common, hunting at, 133–4
Drought house: Grand Chase (1739), 111, 114, 116, 117, 119; kennels, 214

Duncton, 109
Duncton chalk pit, hunting days, 125, 135, 145, 153, 166, 169
Duncton common, hunting days, 145, 155
Duncton hanger, hunting at, 144
Duncton highway, hunting days, 131, 135
Duncton hill, hunting days, 124, 145
Dunford farm, Grand Chase (1739), 114
Durden, Tom, hunt servant, 93
Dursley, Lord (son of Earl of Berkeley), 60

Eagly copse, hunting at, 155
Eartham bushes, hunting days, 114, 144, 169
Eartham Common, 97; Grand Chase (1739), 114, 115; hunting days, 109, 121, 140
Easebourne Priory, nuns of, 109
East Dare copse, hunting at, 145
East Dean, 5, 97
East Dean common, hunting at, 121
East Dean park: hunting at, 177; hunting days, 106, 108, 114, 124, 134, 137, 140, 152, 153, 155, 156, 158, 166, 169
East Dean wood: earthstopping, 187; Grand Chase (1739), 111, 114, 115, 117; hunting days, 59, 81, 101, 108, 109, 124, 125, 133–4, 135, 141, 145, 155, 157, 166, 167, 168, 169, 173, 176, 178
East Hampnett, last hunt (1895), 221
East Marden, hunting at, 102
Eastergate, hunting at, 169
Eastergate common, hunting days, 140, 144
Eastom, John, Molyneux's huntsman, 106
Edgecumbe, Richard, 47, **49**
Effingham, Lord, 186, 191; Hunt Club dinners, 159, 172, 184
Eglinton, Lord, 195, 196; hounds for new pack, 199
Egmont, Lord, at Cowdray, 219
Egremont, Lord, **205**, 216; Petworth pack, 203, 205
Elliot, Major William, 62, 115, 172
Ellison, Charles, 89, 176, 184
Elmer copses, hunting at, 169
Elmes, William, bricklayer, 223
Emsworth Common, hunting at, 107
Euston, Suffolk, 20

Fagg, Sir Robert, 72, 73
Fair mile: Grand Chase (1739), 114, 115; hunting days, 124, 134, 154, 166
Fair mile bottom, hunting at, 169
Farm wood: earthstopping, 187; hunting days, 59, 106, 131, 134, 135, 142, 145, 153, 158, 166, 169, 178, 187
Fauquier, Francis, 98, 125
Fauquier, William, 60, 103, 110, **120**, 132, 138; at Grand Chase (1739), 115, 117, 118; Hunt Club dinners, 130, 147, 155, 159, 172, 176, 184, 190; Hunt Club meetings, 2, 98, 99, 132, 141; sketch of Doxy, **96**, 97
Feilders furze: Grand Chase (1739), 118; hunting at, 178
Feilding, Hon. Charles, 62, 99, 179; Hunt Club dinners, 130, 172
Feilkens's hole, hunting days, 124, 144

Fenton, Lavinia, mistress of 3rd Duke of Bolton, 42–4, **43**, **44**
Fetherstonhaugh, Sir Harry, 203
Fetherstonhaugh, Sir Matthew, 93, 183, 188–9, **189**; Hunt Club meetings, 194; lodgings and stabling (1748), 191
Fielder's hop garden, Grand Chase (1739), 114
Findon: hunting country, 72–3, 79, 218; kennels and stables at, 18, 52, 71, 72, 156, 215
Fisher, Brice, 171, **171**, 172, 175, 178, 187; Hunt Club dinner (1747), 184; Hunt Club meetings, 181; lodgings and stabling (1748), 191
Fittleworth bridge, hunting at, 109
Fittleworth common, hunting at, 155
Fitzroy, Colonel Charles, 135
Fitzroy, Lord Charles, 60
Fitzroy, Lady Charlotte, 20
FitzWilliam, Hon. John, 89, 99, 115, 179; Hunt Club dinners, 172, 176, 190
FitzWilliam, Hon. William, 99, 101
Fletcher, Mr., 166
Ford, Sir Edward, 8
Forrester, 5th Lord, probable subscriber to Great Room, 20, 37–8, **38**
Forrester, Lady, 25, 37–8, **38**
Foster, Thomas, 225
Fountain Tavern, Hunt's 4th annual meeting, 247
Fountains copse, hunting at, 153
Fox, Henry, father of Charles James, 56, 195
Fox, Stephen (later Earl of Ilchester), 47, **48**, 115
Fox Hall (Great Room), 13, 24, **128/9**, 223–5, **224**; subscribers (1718), 18–20
Fox Inn (Charlton), account of Grand Chase, 116–21
fox(es): bag, 159; earth-stopping, 72, 187; Grafton beaten by gallant, 186; hunted into sea, 144, 147; imported, 77; pet vixen, 160–2, 168–9; shortage, 135; taken live 103, 135
Foxley copse, hunting days, 109, 168
France: hounds banished to, 84; hunting in, 46, 47
Freeman, Luke, Petworth huntsman, 203, 205, 216

Gage, Sir William, 102, 105; Hunt Club dinners, 147, 159; subscriber to Great Room, 19
Gainsborough, Lord, 18?, 132
Gardiner, Jemy, hunt servant, 128, **128/9**
Gardner, William *see* Yeakell, Thomas
Garroway, Mr., 10
Gascoigne, Sir Thomas, 203, 216
George I, King, 23–4
George IV, King (as Prince Regent), 214
Germanleith, hunting days, 132, 134, 135
Gibbon, Edward, and restarting Charlton pack (1757), 199
Gibbons, Elizabeth, married Earl of Home, 253
Glanville corner, hunting at, 131
Glatting beacon, hunting days, 81, 124, 134, 144, 145, 166, 169
Glatting hanger, hunting days, 106, 131, 134, 144, 145, 156, 166, 169, 178

283

Glatting hill, hunting at, 156
Glover, Mr., stabling, 191
Godolphin, Francis, 2nd Earl of, 2; subscriber to Great Room,a 19, 41, **42**
Goldings copse, hunting days, 134, 140, 178
Goodwine, Mr., horse doctor, 57
Goodwood, 51, 86; bought by 1st Duke of Richmond (1697), 21; kennels, 202, **203**, 205, 219; racing at, 219; stables, 202, **202**
Goodwood Hunt (1883-95), 218-20; last meet, 220-1
Goodwood park: Grand Chase (1739), 114, 115, 116; hunting days, 106, 108, 124, 140, 178
Goodwood warren, hunting days, 134, 144, 156, 158, 166
Gordon, Adam Lindsay, poem, 222
Gore, Arthur, 110, 125
Goring, Sir Charles, 140, 196
Goring, Sir William, 14, 16-17, 200
Gough, John, whipper-in, 36
Gower, Earl, 86, 181, *see also* Stafford
Graffham: Grand Chase (1739), 111, 118; hunting days, 106, 125, 167, 176
Graffham common, hunting at, 168
Graffham hanger, hunting at, 158
Grafton, Charles Fitzroy, 2nd Duke of, 40, 87, 127, **128**; and Dayrolles, 164; hounds from, 50; Hunt Club dinners, 115, 147, 155, 159, 172, 176, 184, 190, 196; Hunt Club general meeting (1738), 2; hunting days, 166-7, 178, 185-6, 192; lodgings and stabling, 40, 73, 191; subscriber to Great Room, 18, 20
Granby, John Manners, Marquess of, 181-2, **182**, 184; and restarting Charlton pack (1757), 199
Grant, Tom, last Charlton huntsman, 215-18, **215**, 223
Grayling well, hunting at, 143
Great Oldwick, hunting at, 157
Great Room (Fox Hall), 18, 24, **128/9**, 223-5, **224**; subscribers (1718), 18-20
Greatham bridge, hunting at, 153
Green, Mr., of Findon, 137, 139
Green Ribbon Club, 8, 10
Green, Will, hunt servant, 128
Gregory, Dixie, 50
Grey, 1st Lord, 8
Grey, Ford, Lord *see* Tankerville, Earl of
Grey, Mary, married Lord Ossulstone (later Earl of Tankerville), 18, 45
Grey, Ralph, 2nd Lord, 8
greyhound, catches fox, 154
Griffin, Lord, hounds from, 86
Guldeford, Sir Robert, 14, 98, 108; loan of picture, 130
Gumber, the, hunting at, 166
Gumworth, hunting days, 134, 140, 142, 145, 155
Gumworth warren, Grand Chase (1739), 120

Hacking place, the: Grand Chase (1739), 111; hunting days, 125, 135, 158, 166
Halfpenny wood, Grand Chase (1739), 114
Halifax, 1st Earl of, 40, **74**; hunting box and stables, 40, 73, 103, 191; subscriber to Great Room, 19
Halifax, Mary, Countess of, 103

Halnaker, hunting days, 108-9, 144
Halnaker hill, hunting at, 114
Halnaker park: Grand Chase (1739), 119; hunting days, 106, 124, 140, 141, 155
Halnaker windmill, 97, 98; Grand Chase (1739), 114, 115; hunting at, 140
Halsteds down, hunting days, 106, 124, 141, 155
Hambrook common, hunting days, 157, 160
Hamilton, William, 203
Hammer pond, hunting at, 129
Hampden-Smith, Mrs., 225
Hampnett, hunting at, 144
Hanbury Williams, Sir Charles, sonnet, 41-2
Hanway, Charlotte, wife of Garton Orme, 53, **54**
Harcourt, Simon, Viscount, 73, 87, 97, 103, 132, **138**; at Grand Chase (1739), 115, 116, 117, 118; Hunt Club dinners, 130, 147, 155, 159, 172, 176, 184, 190; Hunt Club meetings, 2, 98, 132, 141, 152, 158, 181; hunting days, 137-8, 139, 146, 150, 152, 157, 158, 165, 166, 186, 197; lodgings and stabling, 191
Hardenberg, Baron, 164-5, 174, 175
harriers, 90, 201
Harroways, the, hunting days, 107-8, 114, 124, 155, 158
Harting beacon, hunting days, 132, 134, 135
Harting hill, hunting at, 132
Harting windmill, hunting at, 134
Hartington, Marquess of *see* Devonshire, 4th Duke
Haslecomb, hunting at, 145
Haslett hanger, hunting at, 157
Hasletts, the: earthstopping, 187; hunting days, 102, 103-4, 107, 132, 143, 152, 157, 159
Hat hill, hunting days, 108, 158, 166
Havant, hunting at, 107
Hawley, Brigadier Henry, 60, 80, 83, 97, 103, 108, 125; at Grand Chase (1739), 116, 117, 119, **119**, 120; Hunt Club meetings, 98, 99, 129, 132; hunting box, 191; and Jacobite Rebellion, 177, 179, 180
Haye's bushes, 106; Grand Chase (1739), 114, 115, 119
Hayley, Mrs., stabling, 191
Heberden copse, hunting days, 109, 144, 145, 154, 156, 169
Heberden farm, hunting days, 140, 144
Heberden's fields, hunting days, 105, 106
Henley copse, Grand Chase (1739), 114
Henshaw, Elizabeth, 84
Herbert of Chirbury, Lord *see* Powis, Earl of
Herbert, Henry, Lord *see* Pembroke, 9th Earl
Herne, Rev., 89, 99
Herons wood, hunting at, 131
Herringdean: Grand Chase (1739), 111, 117, 118; hunting days, 81, 109, 121, 125, 133, 134, 135, 168, 178
Herringdean barn: Grand Chase (1739), 114, 119; hunting at, 124
Hessiod down, hunting at, 124
Heydon barn, Grand Chase (1739), 114, 115

Heyshott hanger, hunting at, 109
High down, hunting at, 146
Hill Lands, hunting at, 132
Hill, Thomas, 47, 165, 166, 178
Hobbs, Mr., 57
Holdernesse, Robert Darcy, Earl of, 154, **154**, 155, 184
Home, William, Earl of, 153, 158, 172, 173, 179
Honywood, Philip, 47, 110, **121**, 125, 187; at Grand Chase (1739), 116, 117, 120; Hunt Club dinners, 130, 147, 159, 172, 184; Hunt Club meetings, 141; and Jacobite Rebellion, 179; lodgings and stabling (1748), 191
Honywood, General Sir Phillip, 4, 38, **39**, 103; Hunt Club dinners, 115, 147, 172; subscriber to Great Room, 19
Honywood, Richard, 38, 103, 108, 115; Hunt Club dinners, 130, 147, 159; Hunt Club meetings, 2, 98, 141
Hooksway, 99
horses, 93, 128; 1738/9 season, 99; 1740/1 season, 137, 142; 1742/3 season, 149; 1743/4 season, 156; 1744/5 season, 165; 1745/6 season, 176; acquisition of, 40-1, 77, 78, 79; at Petworth, 217-18; Bay Bolton, 46, 60, **128/9**; Cheat, 93, 99, 137; Fidler, 99, 128; Gin, 93, 99, 129, 149; Grey Cardigan, **128/9**; Grey Carey, 80, 82, 93, 99, **128/9**, 137; health and treatment, 41, 46, 76-7, 110; Looby, 93, 99, 142; Red Robin, **128/9**; Saucy Face, 93, 99, 119, 128; Sheldon, **128/9**, 156, 165; Slug, 93, 99, 129, 156, 176; Sturdy Lump, 93, 99, 107, 156, 176; Sultan, **128/9**, 137, 156, *see also* stables
Houghton, hunting days, 81, 82, 146
Houghton bridge, hunting at, 190
Houghton forest: Grand Chase (1739), 114, 115, 116, 120; hunting days, 124, 155, 166, 169
Houghton hangers, hunting days, 109, 124
Houghton pound, hunting at, 158
Houghton steeps, hunting days, 131, 144
hounds: 3rd Duke's lists, 201, 202-3, **204**; 1733/4 season, 78, 79; 1738/9 season, 99; 1740/1 season, 142; 1743/4 season, 156; 1745/6 season, 176; 1746/7 season, 183, 187, 189; 1748/9 season, 195; advice on breeding (in verse), 63-8; advice from Delawarr, 128-9; at Grand Chase (1739), 121; Bolton's pack, 42-3; conformation of ideal, 35, 63-4; on death of 2nd Duke, 199; descendants acquired by 3rd Duke, 200-1; Doxy, **96**, 97, 128-9, 200; Emperor, 26, 84-5, 200; first list, 33, **34**, 35; food (oatmeal and oats), 126, 136; from Confederate Hunt, 181; from Lady Molyneux, 106; from Lord Brooke, 30; given to Prince Regent (1813), 214; health and medication, 69-70, 76, 77-8; improvements in breeding, 93, **94-6**, 97; lists from Richmond's time, 93, **94-6**, 97; Lord Carlisle's, 28; Luther (pedigree), 79, **80**, 84, 85; painted by Stubbs, 201; Petworth pack, 217; Promise (descendants of), **34**, 35, 200-1; replacements (1735), 85-6;

Index

Ringwood'41 (pedigree), 142; scenting days, 66, 108, 155; sheep killing incident, 84–5, 181; Tankerville's rival pack, 45, 52–3, 56; Tapster'31, 77, 84, **128/9**; to other packs, 89, 195–6; training, 67–8; united pack (1730/1), **58**
Howard, Hon. Charles, 47, **48**, 179, 184
Howe, George, 3rd Viscount, 181, **193**, 194
Hucks wood, hunting at, 131
Huddlestone, Mr., hounds from, 79
Hunston farm, hunting at, 155
hunt servants, 89, 93, 126, 203; drunk, 70–1; livery, 89, 219; Tankerville's Instructions to, 90–1
Hurlands, Grand Chase (1739), 118
Huske, General John, 2, 41, 85, 115; at Culloden, 179; Hunt Club dinners, 130, 147

Idsworth park, hunting at, 131
Inholmes, the, hunting days, 103, 132
Iremonger, Josiah, 183, 187, 191, 194
Ives, Billy, hunt servant, 93, 99, 106, 107, 128, **128/9**, 142; at Grand Chase, 111, 115, 117, 119, 120
Ives, Nim, whipper-in, 99, 103, 128, 132, 142; at Grand Chase (1739), 111, 116, 117, 120

Jackson, Mrs., affair with Tankerville, 92–3
Jackson, William, smuggler, 92
Jacobite Rebellion (1745), 174–5, 176, 177, 179–80
James II, King, as Duke of York, 8, 9, 11
Jenison, Ralph, 38, 73, 80, 177, 178; at Grand Chase (1739), 116, 117; Hunt Club dinners, 130, 147, 155, 159, 172, 184; Hunt Club meetings, 2, 98, 141, 152, 158, 181; hunting days, 165, 166, 187, 197; Master of Royal Buckhounds, 90, 101
Jenkinson, Sir Robert, 56
Jennings, Sir Philip, 216
Jess, servant, 50
Johnson, Mr. (of Chichester), at Grand Chase (1739), 117
Johnson, Tom, huntsman, 85–6, 89, 93, 106, 124–5, **128/9**, 181; 1739/40 season, 132, 134, 135, 136; at Grand Chase (1739), 111, 116, 117, 120; death and memorial, 167, **168**; gout, 130, 149, 160; horses, 83, 99, 128; last days, 160, 166
Johnson, Yarrall, 157, 165, 178
Juniper bottom, hunting days, 101, 131, 152, 157, 159
Juniper bushes, hunting at, 147

Kelsom pond, hunting at, 129
Kemp's high wood: Grand Chase (1739), 116, 120; hunting days, 114, 121, 124
Kemp's rough piece: Grand Chase (1739), 120; hunting at, 145
kennels: Charlton, 52, **58**; Cowdray, 222; Goodwood, 202, **203**, 205, 219; Petworth House, 205, 214, 222; Singleton, 214, 218; Twines, 17, 203; Uppark, 18, 45, 52, see also Findon

Kent, John, racing trainer, 219
Keppel, Hon. Augustus, 194, **194**
Keppel, Captain Hon. William, 196, **197**
Keroualle, Louise de (Duchess of Portsmouth), 21, 22–4, **24**
Kildare, James, Earl of (later Duke of Leinster), 183–4, **183**, 184
King, Lord, 203
Kingley bottom, hunting days, 157, 159, 160
Kingley Vale (yew forest), 5–6
Kings Arms Tavern, Hunt Club dinner (1749), 196
King's buildings (Mr. Butler's), hunting at, 124
Kingston, Duchess of, 100–1, **100**
Kingston, Evelyn Pierrepont, Duke of, 99–101; Hunt Club dinners, 130, 147, 184; and Jacobite Rebellion, 179, 180
Kirke, General, 2, 38, 115, 130, 140
Kirke, Moll, 11
Konigsmarck, Count, 16

Labbé, Mr., secretary, 47, 223
Lady Derby's decoy, hunting at, 169
Lady Holt park, hunting days, 131, 134
Ladyholt (near Emsworth), 106, 107
Laffite, Rev. Daniel, 53
Lancing windmill, hunting at, 147
Landmark Trust, 225
Lardner, Mr., horse doctor, 57
Lavant, hunting at, 105
Lavant fields, hunting at, 156
Lavant river, Grand Chase (1739), 114
Le Clerc, Henrietta (Mrs. Dorrien), 203, 215
Leaver, Tom, hunt servant, 93; at Grand Chase, 111
Lebeck's Head (Chandos Street), Hunt Club annual dinner (1743), 155
Leconfield, Charles Wyndham, 3rd Lord, 221–2
Leconfield, Henry Wyndham, 2nd Lord, 218, 221; and dispute over Stansted coverts, 218, 220
Leethorn, hunting at, 155
Leeves, Mr. and Mrs., 203
Legge, Hon. Edward, **88**, 89; Hunt Club dinners, 130, 155; Hunt Club meetings, 132, 152
Legge, Hon. Henry, 153; Hunt Club dinners, 155, 159, 172, 176
Leggit, Will, 50
Leigh, Lord, 195–6
Lennox, Lady Anne, married Earl of Albemarle, 21, 22, **23**, 24
Lennox, Lady Caroline, married Henry Fox, 56, 195
Lennox, Lady Emily, later Duchess of Leinster, 86, **87**, 175, 183–4
Lennox, Lady George (Louisa), 203
Lennox, Lord George, **128/9**, **161**, 203, 205; pet vixen, 161–2, 168–9
Lennox, Lady Louisa, married Earl of Berkeley, 22, **22**
Lennox, Lady Louisa, married Thomas Connolly, **128/9**
Lennox, Lady Margaret, death of, 139–40
Lennox, Mary, 203
Lennox, Lady Sarah, 195
Lethieullier, Sarah, married Sir Matthew Fetherstonhaugh, 189

Levin down, 5, 14; hunting at, 166
Lewknor's copse, hunting days, 102, 125, 132–3, 135, 143, 152, 154, 158, 159, 166
Lichfield, 2nd Earl of, subscriber to Great Room, 19, 20–1, **21**
Liddell, Sir Henry, Bt. (later Lord Ravensworth), 60, 103, 141, 191; at Grand Chase (1739), 115–16, 117, 119; Hunt Club dinners, 130, 147, 155, 159, 172, 184, 190; Hunt Club general meeting (1738), 2, 98
Lidsey, hunting at, 124
Lifford, Frederic, Earl of, 2, 47; Hunt Club dinners, 130, 155, 159, 172, 176
Lincoln, Henry Fiennes Clinton, 9th Earl of, 102, 103, 104–5, **104**, 146; election, 151, 152–3; Hunt Club dinners, 155, 159, 172, 176, 184; Hunt Club meetings, 158, 183, 194; hunting days, 178, 180, 186, 192, 197; invitations to Goodwood, 163, 193; lodgings and stabling (1748), 191
Little Oldwick, hunting at, 157
Littleton, hunting days, 101, 121
Littleton bottom, hunting days, 121, 124, 144, 177, 178
Littleton farm, hunting days, 144, 145
Long, Walter, master of Hambledon Hunt, 218, 220
Long down: Grand Chase (1739), 114, 115, 120; hunting days, 114, 140, 169
Long hill, hunting at, 132
Lonsdale, Henry Lowther, 3rd Viscount, subscriber to Great Room, 19, 29, **29**, 182–3
Lord Derby's lavender garden, hunting at, 155
Lord Montagu's copse, hunting at, 81
Lordington, hunting at, 160
Lordington wood, hunting at, 108
Loudoun, John Campbell, Earl of, 171, **179**; Hunt Club dinners, 172, 190; and Jacobite Rebellion, 179, 190
Lowther, Hon. Anthony, subscriber to Great Room, 19, 29
Lowther, Sir William, 183
Luchesi, Lieutenant General Count, 196
Lumley, Hon. John, 47
Lumley, Lord, 12
Lymington, Lord, 79
Lyons bank, hunting at, 147

Macey, Will, hunt servant, 93, 128, **128/9**
Madehurst: Grand Chase (1739), 114, 115, 116, 120; hunting days, 134, 145
Madehurst common, hunting at, 166
Madehurst fields, hunting at, 166
Mallards Berry, hunting at, 155
Manhood, the, hunting at, 144
Manners, Lord Robert, 185–6, **197**
March, Lord see Richmond, 2nd and 3rd Dukes of
Markwells, the, hunting at, 107
Marlborough, Charles Spencer, 3rd Duke of, **85**, 86, 130
Marlows, the: earthstopping, 187; Grand Chase (1739), 111, 117, 118; hunting days, 102, 121, 125, 134, 135, 152, 158, 166, 178
Marpon, M. de, 2, 93, 98

Martin, Colonel Edmund, 176
Master of Foxhounds Association, 218, 220
Matt, coachman, 50
Mawdelin, hunting at, 147
Mays bottom, hunting at, 134
Mays copse, hunting at, 107
Mays farm, hunting days, 142, 145
Meadows, Philip, 47, **49**
Meads, Dr., receipt for rabies, 72
medication: for horses, 76–7, 110; for hounds, 69–70, 76, 77–8
Meggott, Richard, 101, 104, 108, 115, 176, 179
Mellish, Mr., 165
Melton Mowbray Hunt, 201
Merryfields, hunting days, 129, 144, 145, 155, 158, 178
Meynell, Hugo, Quorn Hunt, 201
Middleton, John, 140
Middleton, Sir William, 48, 158, **159**; Hunt Club dinners, 147, 184
Midhurst river, hunting at, 109
Midlavant, hunting days, 107, 143
Mill, Sir Richard, 47, 159
Miller, Sir John, 60, 108, 138–9, 148, 163; and bag fox, 159; cattle quarantined with, 188; hounds from, 176; Hunt Club meetings, 99, 129, 132, 141, 152, 181; hunting days, 165, 175, 178, 187, 192, 197; restarting Charlton pack (1757), 199, 200, 201, 216
Miller, Sir Thomas, 77
Mitchell grove, hunting days, 146, 190
Molecomb, hunting days, 156, 166
Molecomb furze, hunting days, 144, 158, 177
Molyneux, Mary, Lady, hounds from, 106, **107**, 129, 155, 181
Molyneux, Richard, Viscount, 106
Monk, Laurence, 89, 147
Monkton furzes (near Treyford), 37, 102
Monkton park, hunting days, 102, 132, 134, 135, 144, 154, 158, 178
Monmouth, James, Duke of, 7, **7**, 8–9, 27; at Chichester, 9–10; Rebellion, 12, 13; and Rye House Plot, 11
Montagu, Anthony Browne, Viscount, 109, **110**
Montagu, George Brudenell, 1st Duke of, 86, 87, **88**, 185, 190
Montagu, John, 2nd Duke of, 160–2, **160**
Montagu, Lady Mary, 171
Montrose, James Graham, 1st Duke of, **37**, 37–8
Mordaunt, Hon. John, 89, 150, 179; Hunt Club dinners, 155, 159, 172
Morley, Mr., hounds from, 86
Morris, Roger, assistant to Burlington, 225
Moutenes, the, hunting days, 154, 159
Mulgrave, Lord, 11
Mundean, hunting at, 157
Muntam, hunting at, 146–7

Nassau, Count Maurice of, subscriber to Great Room, 2, 19, 159
Needham, Eleanor, 11, 27
New Forest, 77, 90, 135; hunt expenses (1730s), 63; hunting rights in, 78, 196, *see also* Bolderwood

Newburg, Lord, hounds from, 199
Newby, Charles, hound breeder, **88**, 89, 176
Newcastle, 2nd Duke *see* Lincoln, Earl of
Newcastle, Thomas Pelham-Holles, 1st Duke of, subscriber to Great Room, 18, 28–9, **104**, 147; correspondence with Richmond, 102–5, 138–9, 146, 102–5, 138–9, 149–50, 163–4, 178, 185; Hunt Club dinners, 147, 155, 159, 172
Newmans copse, hunting at, 144
Newmans down, hunting at, 157
Nightingale bottom: Grand Chase (1739), 111, 114, 115, 117, 119; hunting at, 133
Noel, Colonel Thomas, breeder of foxhounds, 35, 86, 182–3
Noman's land, hunting days, 121, 124, 144, 156, 177
Nore hill, hunting days, 140, 144, 145, 156
Norfolk, 15th Duke of, 221
Norfolk, Duke of (1731), 59
Norris, Captain Henry, 196
North Combe: earthstopping, 187; hunting days, 59, 106, 131, 133–4, 142, 144, 145, 166, 169
North down, hunting days, 153, 167
North hanger, hunting days, 106, 114, 124, 125, 134, 141, 144, 158, 169, 178
North Marden, hunting at, 158
North Marden fields, hunting days, 132, 143
North wood, hunting days, 108–9, 125, 141, 142, 144, 156
Northwood farm, Grand Chase (1739), 111, 114
Norton, Alderman, 178
Norton, hunting at, 124

Oars, the, earthstopping, 187
O'Brien, Percy Wyndham (later Earl of Thomond), 184, **185**, 187, 191, 196
Offham down: Grand Chase (1739), 120; hunting at, 131
Offley, Mr., 197
Ogle, Henry Cavendish, Earl of, 16
Old Lodge, hunting at, 108
Old Park, hunting days, 59, 109
Old Warren, hunting days, 106, 125
Old Warren (West Dean), hunting at, 166
Oldbury farm, last hunt (1895), 221
Oldfield, Anne, 41
Oldwick, hunting days, 101, 125, 173
Oldwick, Great and Little, hunting at, 157
Orlebar, Richard, of Hinwick Hall, hounds from, 35
Orme family, 53
Orme, Garton, **54**, 149; joint master (1730/1), 53, 54, 56, 59
Ossorio, M. le chevalier, 89, 172
Ossulstone, Lord *see* Tankerville, 3rd Earl

Paddock wood, Grand Chase (1739), 114
Parham common, hunting at, 146
Pauncefort, Edward, 60, 103, 108, 125, 148; at Grand Chase (1739), 116, 117, 120; Hunt Club dinner (1745), 130, 147, 159, 172; Hunt Club meetings, 2, 98, 99, 129; hunting days, 138, 139, 165, 166, 185, 187; lodgings and stabling, 75–6, 190, 191

Pawlett, Norton, hounds from, 199, 201, 214, 216
Peachey, Sir James, 183, **183**, 184
Peachey, Sir John, 89–90, 175, 183; Hunt Club dinners, 176, 184
Pearson, Hon. Clive, 222
Pearson, Hon. Harold, 222
Peckham, Mr., 203
Peckham, Rev. Mr., 178
Pedigree of Charlton Hounds, 33
Peerman, Mr., at Grand Chase (1739), 117
Pelham, Charles, hound breeder, 142, **143**, 176
Pelham, Hon. Henry (prime minister), **92**, 92–3, 102, 103, 147, 163; Hunt Club dinners, 155, 159, 172, 176, 184; subscriber to Great Room, 19, 29
Pelham, Lord *see* Newcastle, 1st Duke of
Pembroke, Henry Herbert, 9th Earl of, 37, **37**, 87, 148
Percy family, earls of Northumberland, 15–16
Percy, Lady Elizabeth, marriage to Duke of Somerset, 15–16
Perry, Colonel Charles, 62, 89, 115, 135; Hunt Club dinners, 147, 159, 172, 176; and Jacobite Rebellion, 179
Petworth House, 15, 16; Egremont's hounds at, 203, 205, 214–15; hunting at, 218; kennels, 203, 205, 214, 222
Phillis wood, hunting days, 102, 132, 135, 143, 152, 154, 158
Pierson, Sir Matthew, horse breeder, 46, **128/9**
Pine pit hanger: Grand Chase (1739), 111, 114, 117; hunting days, 114, 158, 166
Pinnell, Rev. Mr., 165
Pitlands, 103, 132, 159
Pitt, William, on Granby, 181–2
Popish Plot, 8–9
Portland, Hans William, Earl of, 130
Portsmouth, Louise de Keroualle, Duchess of, 21, 22–4, **24**
Powis, Henry Herbert, 1st Earl of, **61**, 62, 99, 115, 179; Hunt Club dinners, 130, 172, 184
Powlett family, 31, 44, *see also* Bolton, Dukes of
Powlett, Lord Nassau, 2, 27
Prendergast, Sir Thomas, 47, 147, 184
Preston corner, hunting at, 152
Preston farm, hunting days, 143, 166
Priestcomb: earthstopping, 187; hunting days, 81, 82, 106, 109, 124, 131, 144, 155, 158
Punters copse: Grand Chase (1739), 111, 114, 115, 117, 118; hunting days, 121, 125, 152, 157, 173, 178
puppy walkers, 67
Puttocks copse, Grand Chase (1739), 111, 118, 119

quarantine: for cattle, 188; for puppies, 67
Quorn Hunt, 201

rabies, 69–70, 72, 128
Racton farm, hunting at, 108
Racton park, hunting days, 157, 160

Index

Radnor, Lord, hounds from, 219
Randall's bottom, hunting days, 133, 157, 158
Raughmere, hunting days, 143, 144
Ravensworth, Lord *see* Liddell, Sir Henry
Read, old, Grand Chase (1739), 111
Red copse, 97, 98; hunting days, 106, 108, 114, 124, 153, 169, 177
Red hill, hunting days, 109, 145, 153, 169
Redvins, the, hunting days, 105, 106, 124, 134, 140, 141, 155, 177
Rewell chalk pit, hunting at, 144
Rewell hanger, hunting at, 166
Rewell, the: Grand Chase (1739), 120; hunting days, 109, 124, 140, 144, 145, 154, 156, 169
Rewell wood, 97–8; hunting at, 59
Ribblesdale, Lord, on Lord Leconfield, 218
Richmond, 1st Duke of, probable subscriber to Great Room, 20, **20**, 21, 39
Richmond, 6th Duke of, attempt to re-establish pack at Goodwood, 218–21
Richmond, 7th Duke of (as Lord March), 218, 219
Richmond, Anne, Duchess of, 21, **21**, 30
Richmond, Charles, 2nd Duke of, 56, **128/9**, 148, 163, 186; account of Grand Chase, 111, **112–13**, 114, 115–21; ambassador in Paris (1749), 195; appointed Master of Horse, 83; broken leg, 62, 63, 72; campaign against smuggling, 92; continental tour (1728), 46–7; correspondence with Newcastle, 102–5, 138–9, 146, 149–50, 175, 178; death (1750), 198, 199; ends agreement with Tankerville, 56, **57**, **58**; hound lists, 93, **94–6**, 97; Hunt Club dinner (1750), 130, 147, 155, 159, 172, 184, 190, 196; Hunt Club general meeting (1738), 2, 98; Hunt Club meetings, 99, 132, 142, 141, 158, 181; hunting diaries (from 1737), 93, 126, 127, 165, 181; and Jacobite Rebellion, 176, 177, 179–80; joint proprietor of Charlton Hunt, 47–51; lodgings and stabling (1748), 191, 225; as Lord March, 21–3, **23**; marriage, 24, **25**; peace treaty with Tankerville, 51–3; reluctance to go to London, 149–50, 188, 190, 191–2; succeeds father (1723), 39–41
Richmond, Charles, 3rd Duke of, **128/9**, **200**; as Lord March, 83, 98, 161, 177; restarts Charlton Hunt, 199–203
Richmond, Charles, 4th Duke of, 205, 214, **214**
Richmond, Charles Stuart, Duke of (d.1672), 20–1
Richmond, Charlotte, Duchess of, ball before Waterloo, 214
Richmond, Mary, Duchess of, **128/9**, 203
Richmond, Sarah, Duchess of, 24, **25**, 83, 110, 175; at Grand Chase (1739), 116; visit to Claremont, 169–70
Rifles, the, hunting days, 125, 144, 154, 160, 172
rook wood, Lady Derby's, Grand Chase (1739), 114, 115
Rooks, the, hunting days, 109, 124, 169

Roper, Hon. Charles, 129, 132, 158, 159
Roper, Mr. (Edward), huntsman, 9, **10**, 11, 12, 27, **36**, 84, 200; death, 36–7; exile with Monmouth, 13; hound breeding, 66; as joint master (1721/2), 30, 35–6; quarrel with Duke of Somerset, 15–17; toast to (1747), 184
Roper's Chair, 30, 158, 181
Rothes, Earl of, 47–8, 179, **180**; Hunt Club dinners, 172, 176, 184
Row copse, hunting days, 101, 125, 143, 144, 159, 160, 173
Row, Jack, whipper-in, 142, 166, 178, 195
Rowdel, hunting at, 146
Rowell, John, kennelman, 69, 76, 78
Rowlands Castle, hunting days, 108, 131
Royal Buckhounds, 78
Rudd, Moll, lodgings, 191
Ruddeyard, Captain, 153, 179
Rupert, Prince, receipt for rabies, 72
Russell, John, Clerk of the Cheque (Woolwich), 55
Rutland, 3rd Duke of, 86, 181
Rye House Plot, 11–12

Sadlers furze, hunting days, 102, 134, 158, 178
St Albans, Duke of, 73, 83, 97–8, 103, **117**, 125; at Grand Chase (1739), 116, 118, 119, 120; Hunt Club dinners, 130, 147, 155, 159, 172, 176, 184; Hunt Club general meeting (1738), 2, 98; Hunt Club meetings, 99, 129, 132, 141, 152, 158; hunting days, 115, 137, 178
St John, Rev. Ellis, hound breeder, 83, 129
St Mary wood, hunting days, 124, 144, 156, 177
St Paul, William Frederick, Richmond's stud groom, 93, 99, 128, 152; at Grand Chase (1739), 117; Hunt Club dinners, 176, 184, 190
St Roche's hill *see* Trundle
St Roche's windmill, hunting days, 107, 156
St Victor, French huntsman, 13
Scarbrough, Earl of, 47, 51, 103, **105**
Seabeach, hunting at, 141
Seabeach farm: Grand Chase (1739), 114, 115, 116, 119; hunting at, 140
Sebright, Captain, 197
Sebright, Sir Thomas, 197, **198**
Sedgwick, Edward: agent at Goodwood, 172, 175, 223; Hunt Club dinners, 176, 184
Seeley copse: Grand Chase (1739), 114, 115, 116, 119; hunting days, 108, 178
Selby, Mr., Whaddon Chase hunt, 195–6
Selham furze, Grand Chase (1739), 114, 118
Selhurst park, hunting days, 106, 137, 140, 141, 144, 169, 177
Seymour, Charles *see* Somerset, Duke of
Seymour, Francis, 15
Seymour, Lady Frances, married Marquess of Granby, 181
Shaftesbury, Earl of, Lord Chancellor, 8
Shaw, John, whipper-in, 80, 83
Shearman, Will, Cowdray huntsman, 222
Sheepwash earth: earthstopping, 187; hunting days, 155, 166
Shepherd, Mr., Petworth huntsman, 218, 221

Sherwood: Grand Chase (1739), 120; hunting days, 109, 144
Shirley, Hon. George, **61**, 62, 115
Shopham bridge, hunting at, 145
Shopwyke, hunting at, 155
Sidney, Henry, 16
Singleton, 5, 51; hunting at, 114; Petworth hounds kennelled at, 214, 218
Singleton forest: Grand Chase (1739), 111, 118; hunting days, 125, 166
Skipwith, Sir Francis, hounds from, 86
Slindon common, 97; hunting days, 144, 156
Slindon down, hunting days, 134, 144, 145
Slindon in-down, Grand Chase (1739), 114, 115
Slindon park, hunting days, 121, 140, 145
Slindon windmill, hunting days, 144, 156
smallpox, 140
Smith, John, huntsman, 173, 195
Smith, Mr., of Ashling, 203
smugglers, 92–3
Smyth, Sir Robert, 132, **133**, 141, 182
Somerset, Charles Seymour, 6th Duke of, 15–17, **15**, 110, 203
Somerset, Duchess of, 110
songs: December 1733 point, 80, 81–2; John Budd's, 186; Sussex Garland, 26–7
South Lancing, hunting at, 147
South Stoke, Grand Chase (1739), 111, 115, 120
South wood: Grand Chase (1739), 114, 115, 120; hunting days, 109, 124, 131, 144
Sovereigns, the, hunting days, 125, 135
Spencer, Hon John, **85**, 86, 87
Squires, Mr., Petworth huntsman, 218
stables, 40, 73, 128, 149, 190–1; Fincon, 18, 52, 71, 72, 137–8, 215; Goodwood, 202, **202**; hacking, 156; huntsmans, 12, 93, 99, 128, 149
Stafford, Granville Leveson-Gower, 1st Marquess of, 188, 191, 194
Stansted forest, hunting days, 108, 131, 152
Stansted park: disputed coverts, 218–19, 220; hunting days, 103, 107, 108, 131
Stedham (near Midhurst), hunting at, 106
Steele, Messrs., 203
Steyning holt, hunting at, 147
Stoke, hunting at, 101
Stoke coney copse, hunting days, 144, 159, 160
Stoke copse (Stoke Clump), 106–7, 108; hunting days, 103, 108, 143, 144, 154, 159
Stoke down, hunting at, 157
Stoke lithe, earthstopping, 187
Stony Deans, hunting at, 147
Stony house, hunting days, 134, 143
Stopham, hunting at, 109
Stopham Common, hunting at, 109
Stoughton, 101
Stoughton down, hunting days, 145, 160
Strettington road, Grand Chase (1739), 114, 119
Strickland, Thomas, 47, 97, 152, 141
Strickland's furze, 97, 106; hunting days, 106, 108, 124, 134, 155

Stubb copse, hunting at, 125
Suncombe, Grand Chase (1739), 114
Sussex, Earl of, 196
Sussex Garland song, 26–7
Sutton, hunting days, 134, 142
Swift, Theophilus, 214
Syndals, the, hunting at, 108

Taaf, Mr., visitor, 177
Tangmere, last hunt (1895), 221
Tankerville, Charles, 2nd Earl of, 18, 45, 56, 93; affair with Mrs Jackson, 92–3; hounds from, 50, 56, 79, 93, 129, 176, 183; Hunt Club dinner (1747), 184; Instructions to hunt servants, 90–1; joint master (1729/30), 50; Master of Royal Buckhounds in New Forest, 78–9, 90; retires to Northumberland, 93; rival pack, 45–51, 78–9, 101–2; treaty of amalgamation with Charlton Hunt, 51–3, 56, **57**
Tankerville, Charles, 3rd Earl of (as Lord Ossulstone), 2, 45, 60, 93, **118**, 141, 181; at Grand Chase (1739), 115, 117; Hunt Club dinners, 147, 184
Tankerville, Ford Grey, 1st Earl of, 2, **8**, 9, 10–11; death (1701), 18; and Rye House Plot, 11–12
Tattersalls, sale of Goodwood pack, 221
Taylor, Mr., hounds from, 199
Teen wood, hunting at, 169
Teesdale, Colonel, 203
Tegleaze: Grand Chase (1739), 111, 114, 118; hunting days, 59, 81, 101–2, 106, 108, 121, 124, 131, 134, 142, 145, 153, 155, 157, 158, 166, 173, 176, 178
terriers, 69, 89
Thomson, Mr., at Grand Chase (1739), 117
Thynne, Thomas, of Longleat, 16
Tinniswood, Mr., 225
Todham furzes, Grand Chase (1739), 111, 118
Toghill, Rev. Moses, 203
Tortington common, hunting at, 154
Tortington woods, hunting at, 156
Townsend, Admiral Isaac, 171, 172, **172**, 184
Tredcroft, Messrs, 203
Treges, Daniel, earth stopper, 153
Trentham, Lord *see* Stafford
Treyford, hunting at, 158
Treyford earth, hunting days, 134, 135
Trotrow, hunting at, 134
Trumley copse, hunting days, 107, 108, 125, 157
Trundle (St Roche's hill), 5, 97, 98; hunting days, 106, 134, 152, 177
Twines, 17, 203; hunting days, 144, 145, 155, 157
Tyrwhitt, Sir John, hounds from, 79

Up Marden, hunting at, 135

Uppark, 8, 12, **128/9**; hunting days, 131, 134, 158; kennels at, 18, 45, 52; sold to Fetherstonhaugh, 93, 189
Upwaltham, hunting days, 101, 133

Valdoe, the: Grand Chase (1739), 114, 115, 119; hunting days, 99, 102, 103, 105, 106, 107–8, 124, 134, 137, 140, 144, 156, 157, 166, 177, 178; last hunt (1895), 221
Vanbrugh, John, 28
Vane, Henry, 184, 191, 194
Varey, William, 184, 187, 191
Vaughan, Lady Anne, married 3rd Duke of Bolton, 31, **33**, 42
Venus copse, hunting days, 125, 135
Venus wood, Grand Chase (1739), 111
Vernon, Mr., hounds from, 79
Villiers, Thomas *see* Clarendon, Earl of
Vincent, huntsman, 53

Walberton, hunting at, 140
Walberton copse, hunting days, 145, 156
Waldegrave, Colonel Hon. John, 182, 183, 184, 187, 191
Walderton hill, hunting at, 131
Walpole, Horace, on 3rd Duke of Bolton, 31
Walpole, Robert, Lord, 40, **74**, 130; breeder of foxhounds, 35; hunting box and stables, 40, 73
Walpole, Sir Robert, 20, 41, 60, 62, 93, 147
Walter, Lucy, 7
Waltham, hunting days, 141, 155, 157
Waltham bottom, hunting days, 142, 157
Waltham common, hunting at, 158
Waltham down, hunting days, 156, 157
Waltham hanger, hunting days, 155, 156
Waltham park, hunting days, 109, 158
Ware hill hanger, hunting at, 166
Ware, John, huntsman, 37, 53, 59, 70, 80; dismissed, 83–4; poor reputation of, 43, 54–5, 69, 71, 77–8, 79
Warren house, Cocking, fox down chimney, 135
Warren house, West Dean, hunting at, 143
Waterbeach gate, hunting at, 178
Watergate, hunting at, 131
Watergate hanger, hunting days, 107, 108
Waterloo, battle of, 214
Watersfield warren, hunting at, 153
Watson, Hon. Thomas (later Earl of Rockingham), 99, 101, **101**, 103, 115
Watson's piece, hunting at, 144
Webster, Sir Godfrey, 203
Well copse, hunting at, 131
Wells, Henry, 165
Wentworth, Henrietta, 11
West, Hon. John, subscriber to Great Room, 2, 19
West Burton hanger, hunting days, 109, 131
West Burton hill, hunting at, 124

West Dean, 5, 97, 98; hunting at, 109
West Dean down, hunting at, 166
West Dean forest, Grand Chase (1739), 118
West Dean warren: Grand Chase (1739), 114, 115, 117, 119; hunting days, 107, 143, 166
West Lavant, hunting at, 157
West Marden, hunting at, 107
West wood bottom, hunting days, 156, 157
Westbourne, hunting at, 107
Westerton, hunting days, 108, 144
Whistling Alley copse, Grand Chase (1739), 114, 115
Whitburn, Mr., 178
White, Charles, Petworth huntsman, 221
White, Fred, whipper-in, 221
Whitworth, Colonel Richard, 62, 115, 130, 159
Wildbrook, hunting at, 146
Wildham, the: earthstopping, 187; hunting days, 101–2, 103–4, 107, 132, 157, 159
Wildham wood, hunting days, 143, 152
William III, King, and Mary II, Queen, 12, 23
Williams, water man, 50
Williams, Roger, groom, 77
Wills, Sir Charles, subscriber to Great Room, 19, **19**
Winchester, Marquess of *see* Bolton, 3rd Duke of
Winden, the, hunting days, 132, 134, 135, 142–3
Wing, Moses, whipper-in, 166
Winkins, the, hunting days, 106, 124, 141, 144, 177, 178
Wiston malthouse, hunting at, 147
Woodcote, last hunt (1895), 221
Woodmancote, hunting at, 157
Woods, Harry, 71–2
Woods, Jack, acting huntsman, 166
Woolavington: Grand Chase (1739), 111, 118; hunting at, 125
Woolavington down, hunting days, 109, 124, 131, 145
Woolavington hanger, hunting days, 124, 135, 173, 178
Woolavington park: Grand Chase (1739), 111, 114, 118; hunting days, 124, 155
Wyndham, Colonel George (later Lord Leconfield), Petworth hounds, 214–15, 217, 218
Wyndham, Henry, 215, 218
Wyndham, Sir William, hounds from, 79
Wynne, Sir Rowland, 84

Yapton, hunting at, 169
Yeakell, Thomas, and William Gardner, maps, **206–13**, **224**, 225
Yewtree bottom, hunting at, 158
York, Duke of, 205

E Marden
Compton Down
Westmarden
OF W BOURNE
AND
SINGLETON
Northwood
Lodg
Burston
Watergate
Stainstead Park
Walderton Place
Stoughton
Lordington
Walderton Street
Pound house
Racton
Racton P
Adsden
Two Stone gate
Aylsworth
W Bourne Common
Woodmancote
Parsonage
W Bourne
Emsworth
Hermitage bridg
Inland
Prinstead
Nutbourn
Hamlrook Common
Funtington
W Ashling
E Ashling
Deansworth
W Stoke
W Stoke place
HUNDRED
OF
BOSHAM
Napp
Ham
Broadbr
Prebend
Bosham
Chidham
THORNEY
W Thorney
ISLE
Hayley Island
Fishbourn
Saltwater Mill
Fishbourne
CHICHESTER
BOX
Saltfox
Chilgrove
Warren Lodg
W Dean
Charlton
Singleton
Preston
Cromhol
Binderto
Rooks W.
St Rooks hill
Goodwood Park
Midlavant
W Lavant
E Lavant
Halnecker Street
OF
Streetington
W Hamptnet
Peastree
Hampnet Place
Tangmere
Shopwick
AND
Oveing
Rumbaldweek
Kingstone
STOCKBRIDGE
Apledrum
Donnington
Leethorn
Merston
Hunston Com
N Mundham
Hunston
Boars bridg
North Be
Lagnersh
ALDW
Sefter
Bowley
Bognets
Nentimber Green
Grove
Pagham
Old Park
Cowdry
Birdham
Birdham Wind
Birdham Common
W Itchenor
Lavenders
Chichurst
Elinot
W Wittering
Whitestone
Sidlesham
Sidlesham Mills
W Wittering Windm.
Cockbush
Cackham
Summerly Green
E Wittering
HUNDRED
D E A N R Y
R A P
OF
BOX
P A G H A M
G R O V E
OF
Brackelsom
Earnley
MANHOOD
Chichester Shoals
Chichester Harbour Mouth
Called Hormouth
Thorney
Selsey
Parsonage
Park
Wood
SELSEY
PENINSULA
Medmery
Brackelsome
Bay
Fishing houses
Selsey Bill
Pagham Sa
Gravel dry at Ebb
The Park Good Anchoring Ground
Meridian
Malt Owers a hard Black Rock
Semi and Seminot open with Culver Cliffs
The Looe Stream